Evaluating the geography curriculum

W. E. Marsden
Senior Lecturer in Education, University of Liverpool

Oliver & Boyd
Edinburgh & New York

Oliver & Boyd
Croythorn House
23 Ravelston Terrace
Edinburgh EH4 3TJ
A Division of Longman Group Limited

Published in the United States of America
By Longman Inc., New York

© W. E. Marsden 1976. All rights reserved. No part of this publication may be reproduced, stored in a retrieval system, or transmitted in any form or by any means, electronic, mechanical, photocopying, recording or otherwise, without the prior permission of the copyright owner or publisher. All enquiries should be sent to the publisher in the first instance.

First published 1976

Library of Congress Cataloging in Publication Data

Evaluating the geography curriculum.

(Geography for teachers)
Includes bibliographical references and index.
1. Geography—Study and teaching. 2. Curriculum planning. I. Title.
G73.M33   375'.09'1   76-103

ISBN 0-05-002900-2
ISBN 0-05-002791-3 pbk.

Contents

Preface vii

Acknowledgements viii

1 Introduction 1
Theory and practice; meanings of evaluation and models of the curriculum process; the plan of this book

Section 1 Aims and Objectives

2 Aims 9
The development of 'personal autonomy' as an educational aim; aims and the subject context; guidelines

3 Objectives 22
Operational or behavioural objectives; objections to the objectives approach; counter-arguments; types of objectives; guidelines

Section 2 Geography in the School Curriculum

4 The structure of knowledge 47
A basis for curriculum planning; the forms and fields of knowledge; the position of geography

5 The changing nature of geography 57
Academic geography in mid-century; geography 'revived'; characteristic features of the 'new geography'; the systems approach; models; quantification; the behavioural aspects of geography; geography and social issues; a 'paradigm for modern geography'

6 Geography in school 73
Antecedents; an historical perspective; implications of the 'new geography' for school geography

7 Curriculum integration and geography 105
Integration in practice; theoretical distinctions; problems and resolutions; conclusions

8 Pupils and teachers — 131
Relationship to aims and objectives; meaningful learning in geography; developmental theories of learning; forming concepts in geography; individual differences; the influence of the teacher; summary of guidelines

Section 3 Assessment

9 Purposes and techniques of assessment — 165
The purposes of summative assessment; the purposes of formative assessment; an historical perspective on external examinations; gearing examinations to educational aims and objectives; techniques of assessment

10 Essays — 175
The disadvantages of essays as means of assessment

11 Multiple choice — 189
Objective forms of assessment; types of objective test; advantages of multiple choice tests; disadvantages; types of multiple choice items; principles of writing multiple choice items; test specifications; assessing different 'abilities' through multiple choice tests; item analysis; item banking

12 Structured questions — 228
Their nature; the advantages of structured questions; principles of writing structured questions; examples of structured questions

13 Other types of assessment — 239
The assessment of course work; advantages of assessing course work; problems of assessing course work: principles of organising and assessing project work; the assessment of attitudes; dimensions; means of assessing attitudes

Section 4 Synthesis: The Geography Curriculum

14 Frameworks — 255
The concentric approach; an alternative procedure

15 Units — 265
Guidelines; first curriculum unit: an aboriginal group in Malaya; second curriculum unit: the changing accessibility of Southport

16 Conclusion — 305

Index — 308

Preface

The intention of this book is to relate curriculum theory to geography; to illustrate the need to evaluate what goes into as well as what comes out of the geography curriculum, and to show, by means of examples from this particular subject area, how closely theory and practice are bound together. While much of the content is of a practical nature, there is no attempt to deal with many important, everyday problems of geography teaching—how to draw maps on the blackboard, find source materials, use visual aids, plan field trips, design and equip geography rooms and so forth—on which excellent advice is available in a number of readily accessible texts. The strictly practical offerings of this text relate rather to assessment procedures, syllabus construction and the planning of course units.

The book is aimed at several groups of readers. As a contribution to teacher education, the first group are obviously 'geographers in training', whether engaged in pre- or in-service education courses. Secondly, it is hoped the book will be of interest and help to practising teachers, including those sceptical of the value of educational theory, who are increasingly undertaking syllabus reconstruction, often associated with curriculum integration. It is a basic contention here that the geographical dimension should not be lost from the school curriculum, even if the label 'geography' no longer appears on the timetable. The third group are specialists in curriculum work in general, and perhaps those who are advocates of integration in particular, in the hope that they may be stimulated by the experience of seeing broad, familiar ideas applied in detail to a particular subject area about which they might have stereotyped views. Curriculum theorists, perhaps too easily, tend to assume that good general ideas can be applied sweepingly across the board.

My thanks are due to the following colleagues who made expert and constructive observations on various sections of the text: Ray Derricott, Gordon Elliott, Gerry Hones, Derek Meakin and Ron Stewart.

April, 1975

Acknowledgements

The author and publishers wish to thank the following for permission to reprint material in this book:

Addison–Wesley Publishing Company for the quotations from *Microteaching* (1969) by D. Allen & K. Ryan; American Educational Research Association for quotation from Elliot W. Eisner, 'Instructional and expressive educational objectives' in W. James Popham (ed.) *Instructional Objectives*, AERA Monograph Series on Curriculum Evaluation, No. 3, 1969; Edward Arnold (Publishers) Ltd. for quotations from H. C. Prince, 'Real, imagined and abstract worlds of the past', in Board, Chorley, Haggett & Stoddart (eds.) *Progress in Geography* 3, 1971, and from *Locational Analysis in Regional Geography* (1965) by P. Haggett; The Association of American Geographers for a quotation from D. Lowenthal, 'Geography, experience and imagination: towards a geographical epistemology' in *Annals of the Association of American Geographers*, **51**, 1961, and for quotations from two High School Geography Project Publications – *The Local Community: A Handbook for Teachers* and 'Habitat and resources', Unit 5 of *Geography in an Urban Age*; the Librarian, the University of Birmingham for quotations from the unpublished M.Ed. dissertation by A. J. Lunnon, 'The understanding of certain geographical concepts by primary school children' (1969); R. J. Cootes for the use of material from his London University unpublished M.A. dissertation, 'Integrated humanities in the secondary school curriculum' (1972); Fearon Publishers, Inc., for quotations from Carswell, 'Evaluation of affective learning in geographical education' in Kurfman (ed.) *Evaluation in Geographic Education* (1970); the Geographical Association and W. Kirk for Table 5.1; the Geographical Association and G. Woodward for Fig. 12.2; the Geographical Association and M. Pacione for Fig. 12.3 and Tables 12.1–12.5; the Geographical Association and M. Pearce for a quotation from 'An individual method for the teaching of geography', *Geography*, **15**, 298–302; Dr. Ruth Hannam for the use of short quotations from her Leeds University Ph.D. thesis (1969) and for Table 8.1 (p. 125 of her thesis); A. M. Heath & Company Ltd. and John Slimming for quotation from *Temiar Jungle: a Malayan Journey* (1958); Heinemann Educational Books Ltd. for the quotation from *The New Social Studies* (1973) by D. Lawton and B. Dufour; Hodder & Stoughton Educational for Figs. 1.2 and 1.3, and the use of material based upon ideas in *Introducing Transportation Networks* (1972) by Ken Briggs; *Journal of Engineering Education* and Professor J. Chesley Posey, Jr. for Fig. 10.1 (Copyright 1932 by the American Society of Engineering Education); Longman Group Ltd. for Fig. A and Table B reproduced in the First Curriculum Unit; John Marshall for Plate 5; Methuen & Co. Ltd. for quotations from *Asia: a Regional and Economic Geography* (revised edition, 1952) by L. D. Stamp and P. R. Gould's 'The open geographic curriculum' in R. J. Chorley (ed.), *Directions in Geography* (1973); National Council for Geographic Education (U.S.A.) and Professor Gary Manson for Fig. 8.2 and the quotation from 'Classroom questioning for geography teachers,' *Journal of Geography*, **72**, 1973, No. 4, 24, 27; OECD, Paris for Fig. 1.4; Regional Science Association (U.S.A.) for quotations from J. D. Nystuen, 'A graph theory interpretation of nodal regions,' *Papers RSA*, **7**, 1962, 29–42; Pergamon Press Ltd. for quotation from *Secondary School Examination: Facts and Commentary* (1969) by G. Bruce and, with C. Harrison, R. V. Cook and J. H. Johnson, for Fig. 6.1; the South Western Examinations Board for the quotation from their CSE regulations in geography; Marion Ward for the use of material from *Malaya and Singapore* (How People Live Series, 1963) by Marion Ward; the Editors, *Educational Review*, for the quotation from W. Rhys 'Geography and the Adolescent' (*Educational Review*, **24**, No. 3).

Although every effort has been made to trace copyright owners, in some cases this has not been possible, and we apologise for any omission in the above list.

1 Introduction

Theory and practice

'In other words, theory is practice become conscious of itself, and practice is realised theory', concluded James Welton, Professor of Education in the University of Leeds, in the early years of this century. Without such theory, the 'mechanical teacher does as he was done by; with him progress implies change, and change is unwelcome, for he cannot adapt himself to it.' At the same time, the theory should not be 'an unsubstantial vision spun out of the clouds of an untrammelled imagination . . . a theory of teaching which deserves the name is in the closest possible touch with school work.'[1]

In the years which followed, this maxim seemed to be forgotten. Perhaps in consequence, generations of teachers have continued to be suspicious of educational theory. They are not alone in this. A number of educational theorists have also registered their doubts. Pring, for example, has branded it as 'a systematic mislabelling of what teachers are doing.'[2] Ausubel has similarly referred to 'much disillusionment . . . regarding the relevance and usefulness of learning theory for educational practice.'[3]

One of the tensions that must be faced is that theory does not make life easier for the teacher by providing a set of recipes. Far from ensuring successful practice, it 'draws attention to the complexity of educational issues'.[4] It can only present generalisations, and the practitioner must exercise skilled judgement as to how to apply them in particular situations.[5]

There are very many generalisations applicable to practice, however, and some are more directly relevant than others. A distinction needs to be made between 'basic' and 'applied' theory. Other things being equal, research based on classroom experience is more likely to be seen as relevant to practice than, for example, extrapolation from laboratory experiments into the behaviour of animals. The gap between theory and practice, illustrated in Fig. 1.1, has, fortunately, been narrowed in recent years by the emergence of a body of curriculum theory grounded on the school and the classroom.

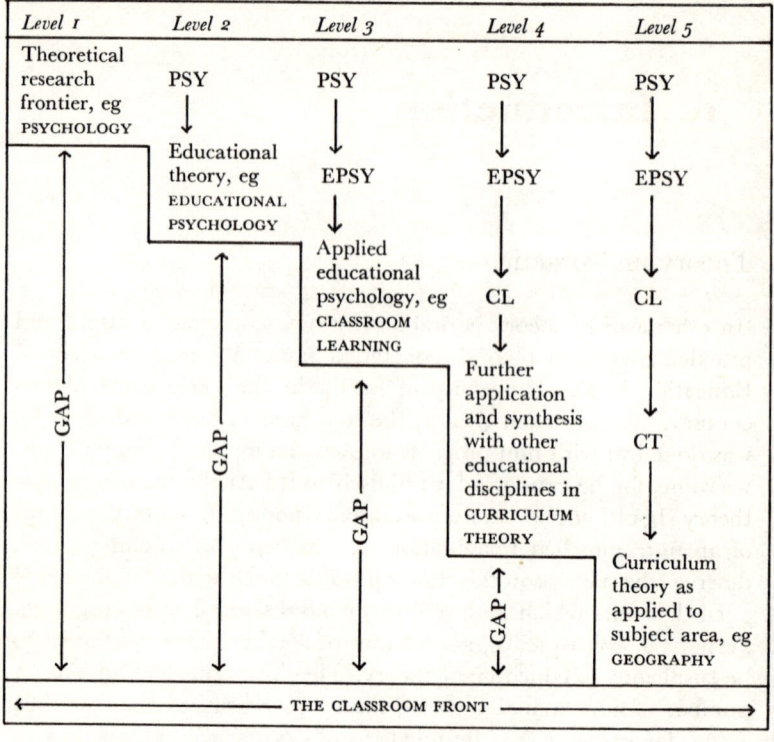

Fig. 1.1 The narrowing gap between theory and practice

A considerable gap is shown between the 'pure' discipline, with its research frontiers, and the classroom. But the understandings provided by such research might well have educational implications, some of which might be transmitted under the umbrella of 'educational psychology'. This, too, with its erstwhile stress on Pavlov and Freud, has often seemed remote from the classroom, though courses in recent years have tended to concentrate rather on figures such as Piaget, whose work has undoubted and direct implications for practice. Yet the hard-pressed teacher-trainee might well still complain that he has not the time to read Piaget 'in the raw'.

Thus bridge-building even beyond the stage of classroom learning theory and general curriculum theory is now advocated:

> ... the early part of the education course ... must also acknowledge, at least for graduates, their pre-occupation with *their* subject. Further, the course must acknowledge from the start the psychological inability of the student to incorporate in his personalized and narrowly specific

schema of education any broad generalized concepts such as the psychology of learning, the sociology of the school or theories of teaching until his concerns begin to broaden out. This does not mean that groundwork for the later study of educational psychology, sociology and philosophy cannot be laid down. It can, but only if its subject matter is highly concrete and of practical relevance to the classroom.[6]

A major function of this text is to meet the need for providing concrete exemplars which it is hoped will assist in the development of the ability to apply general theoretical concepts in varied classroom situations. Thus, while much of it is related to level 5 on Fig. 1.1, considerable attention is also paid to levels 3 and 4, and some to level 2, in attempting to establish the prerequisite connections.

The psychological component is, of course, only one of the variables to be considered in providing an adequate theoretical base for curriculum planning. In narrowing the gap between theory and practice, curriculum study draws on other elements of educational theory, notably the sociology and philosophy of education, while the historical perspective, also, must not be neglected. Educational theory is, therefore, seen here as a co-ordinated set of principles drawn from the disciplines of education which are intended to guide educational practice.

Meanings of evaluation and models of the curriculum process

'Evaluation' is now a widely used word in educational circles, and some elucidation of the various meanings attached to it is necessary. Though defined broadly as 'to determine the value of', 'evaluation' has increasingly been applied in education as a euphemism for assessment. Rowntree refers to this as an area of 'tortured educational semantics' and offers fairly complex criteria for logically distinguishing the two.[7] His distinction is not taken up here, however, and all that is contended in this text is that evaluation of what goes in is equally important as evaluation of what comes out of the curriculum. The term 'assessment' is reserved for 'evaluation of outputs'.

Evaluation is, therefore, regarded in what follows as the making of qualitative and quantitative judgements about the value of the various curriculum processes. Criteria for making the judgements are derived from various branches of educational theory, from the subject area itself and also from common sense and experience.

Evaluation of outputs is often seen as the end-component in simple models of the curriculum process as depicted, for example, in the 'preliminary' models of Kerr (Fig. 1.2)[8] and Wheeler (Fig. 1.3).[9] While it is the function of models to eliminate inessential 'noise', such examples make the curriculum process appear *too* simple, with 'evaluation' usually presented as a piece of terminal evidence making possible a redefinition of aims, objectives, content and learning experiences. This is particularly the case with the Wheeler model, where it is placed as the end product of a simple, cyclical process. These and other oversimplified models have often been reproduced in the curriculum literature, almost as the final word, even though both Kerr and Wheeler in their texts have out-

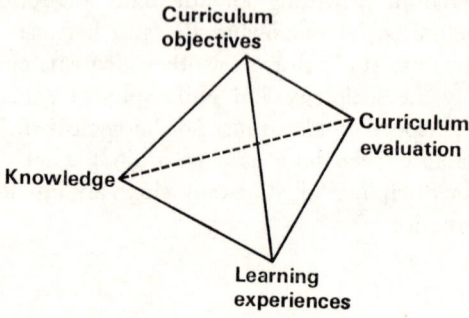

Fig. 1.2 Kerr's 'Simple model of the curriculum'

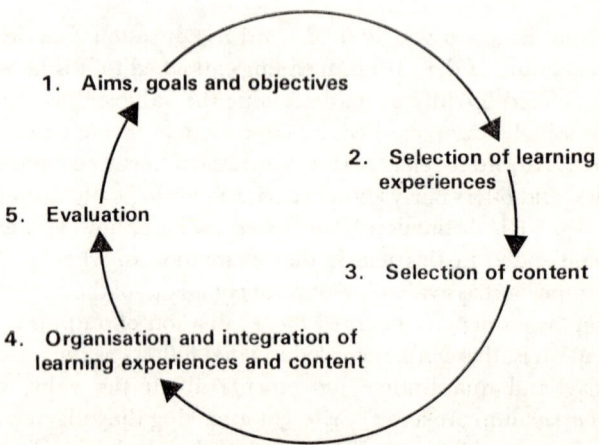

Fig. 1.3 Wheeler's 'Simple curriculum process'

lined more sophisticated models stressing rather the complex nature of the interaction of the variables.

The idea that evaluation performs an absolutely central role in the curriculum process is made clear in a model (Fig. 1.4) provided by OECD's *Centre for Educational Research and Innovation* (CERI).[10]

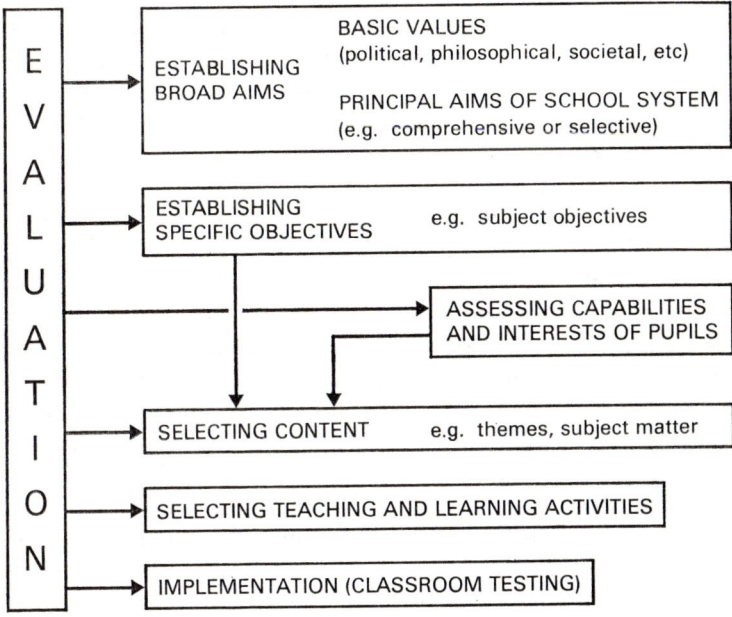

NOTE: The arrows from the evaluation block indicate the different levels at which evaluation can take place.

Fig. 1.4 An example of evaluation in curriculum development

Evaluation is thus envisaged as critical *at each stage of* the curriculum process, from the first stage of evaluation of the broad aims of a course, to the late stage of evaluating which instruments of assessment to use and the final one of making judgements anew on the basis of the evidence which these instruments provide. Decisions made at a particular stage will affect and even prescribe those at subsequent stages, while these in turn will feed back to previous ones.

It is this type of model which lies behind the thinking which has gone into this book, for it picks out more realistically than 'evaluation as end-product' models something of the inevitably complex interaction of the curriculum process. The variables identified and discussed in the following chapters do not, however, exactly match those of the OECD model.

The plan of this book

In general, each chapter contains an introductory discussion of principles involved in the topic under consideration. The second part, wherever appropriate, consists of an analysis of the application of these general principles in the geographical context. This may take the form of the presentation of relevant research findings, as in the field of the formation of geographical concepts, or may merely illustrate the operation of a particular aspect through a series of geographical examples, as in the section on assessment.

Each chapter is followed by a series of questions for investigation and discussion, together with suggestions for an order of priorities for supplementary reading. The numbered references in the text refer not to these priority readings, however, but to the detailed lists of references. While the assignments are designed primarily for students in pre- and in-service training, it is hoped that practising teachers will also find them of interest. Understanding of the text does not, however, depend on their completion. The detailed references will, it is hoped, provide useful bibliographical information for tutors. In total, these references are clearly beyond the scope of students—a reason for providing a more limited list of 'priority readings'.

Following this introduction, Chapters 2 and 3 provide a discussion of the role of aims and objectives, and complete the opening section of the book. Chapter 4 serves as an introduction to the second section, and consists of a brief survey of the literature on the structure of knowledge and its relation to the curriculum. Chapters 5 and 6 cover in some detail the context of a single discipline, the first reflecting on the nature of geography, its changing emphases and distinctive offerings to the curriculum; while the second pursues the implications of these for geography in the classroom. Chapter 7 debates the vexed question of curriculum integration, and the function of geography in such integrated schemes. Chapter 8 summarises and applies relevant research in the area of children's learning, stressing the teacher's role.

Section Three focuses on assessment, Chapter 9 including a discussion of the purposes and a brief outline of the main forms of assessment, introducing more detailed coverage in the following chapters: Chapter 10 on essays, 11 on multiple choice items, 12 on structured questions and 13 on other forms of assessment—here the assessment of course work, and of attitudes. In the final section an attempt is made to bring together the variables previously discussed through the presentation of examples of geographical curriculum frameworks (Chapter 14) and units (Chapter 15), to demonstrate theory merging into practice.

Priority readings

1. KERR, J. F. (ed.) *Changing the Curriculum* (University of London Press, Unibooks), Paper 1, pp. 13–38.
2. WHEELER, D. K. *Curriculum Process* (University of London Press, Unibooks), Chapters 1 and 2, pp. 11–54.
3. ENTWISTLE, H. 'The relationship between theory and practice' in TIBBLE, J. W. (ed.) *An Introduction to the Study of Education: an Outline for the Student* (Routledge & Kegan Paul), pp. 95–113.
4. EATON, J. *An ABC of the Curriculum* (Oliver & Boyd). A useful reference to much of the technical language used in this text.
5. JENKINS, D. & SHIPMAN, M. D., *Curriculum: an Introduction* (Open Books, London), Chapter 5, pp. 82–125, for a counter-view to Kerr & Wheeler, and the 'rational curriculum planning' movement in general.

Questions for investigation and discussion

1. Certain terms and statements in educational texts are sometimes stigmatised as 'jargon'.
    (a) With the help of a dictionary, make clear what is meant by 'jargon'.
    (b) In the light of such definition refer to the following:
        A 'Evaluation'; 'models of the curriculum process'.
        B 'Premonitory indications harbingering a near-epidemic of measles are so apparent as to give cause for anxiety.'[11]
        C 'The fourth division comprises all that is left—consisting mainly of sedimentary rocks of Palaeozoic and Mesozoic ages; folded by pre-Tertiary and especially by the Caledonian movements, which took place at the close of the Silurian and in the Devonian periods, and the Armorican or Hercynian movements of late Carboniferous and Permian times, as well as by movements in the Mesozoic period, and more

characteristic of Asia than of Europe. These older fold ranges have often cores of old rocks; they are often separated by minor stable blocks of varying character. Some of the latter are of great size—notably that of Southern China.'[12]

  (i) Which of the above statements would you regard as 'jargon'? Explain why.
  (ii) For any you do so regard, try to provide in your own words clearer and/or more compact definitions or explanations than those given.
2. Refer to the more complex curriculum models of Kerr and Wheeler, on pages 20 and 52 respectively of the texts given under 'Priority readings' (page 7). Indicate similarities and differences between (a) these two models, (b) the two models (Figs. 1.2 & 1.3) and the OECD model (Fig. 1.4) which helps to provide the framework for this book.

References

1. WELTON, J. (1906) *Principles and Methods of Teaching* (University Tutorial Press, London), 17–18.
2. PRING, R. (1971) 'Bloom's taxonomy: a philosophic critique (2)' *Cambridge Journal of Education*, **2**, 85.
3. AUSUBEL, D. P. (1967) 'A cognitive-structure theory of school learning' in SIEGEL, L. (ed.) *Instruction: Some Contemporary Viewpoints* (Chandler Publishing Co., Scranton, Pennsylvania), 257.
4. NAISH, M. & HARTNETT, A. (1975) 'What theory cannot do for teachers' *Education for Teaching*, **96**, 17.
5. See ENTWISTLE, H. (1971) 'The relationship between theory and practice' in TIBBLE, J. W. (ed.) (1971) *An Introduction to the Study of Education: an Outline for the Student* (Routledge & Kegan Paul, London), 101.
6. TAYLOR, P. H. (1975) 'A study of the concerns of students on a postgraduate certificate in education course' *British Journal of Teacher Education*, **1**, 158.
7. ROWNTREE, D. (1974) *Educational Technology in Curriculum Development* (Harper & Row, London), 131–3.
8. KERR, J. F. (1968) 'The problem of curriculum reform' in KERR, J. F. (ed.) *Changing the Curriculum* (University of London Press), 17.
9. WHEELER, D. K. (1967) *Curriculum Process* (University of London Press), 31.
10. CERI (1972) *The Nature of the Curriculum for the Eighties and Onwards* (Report on a Workshop held at Kassel, Germany (1970), OECD, Paris), 61.
11. Extract from a nineteenth-century elementary school log book.
12. STAMP, L. D. (1929) *Asia: A Regional and Economic Geography* (Methuen, London, 1952 edition), 11.

Section 1: Aims and Objectives

2 Aims

'Aims' are here taken to refer to the wider ends towards which a school is working. The term 'objectives' is reserved for more specific goals: of classroom teaching, for example. These are, of course, convenience definitions. Both words are used more freely and even interchangeably in ordinary speech.

Statements of aims serve an orientation function providing, among other things, guidelines for the planning of curricula. They involve making value judgements and, as such, will be influenced by external factors, cultural, social, political and economic, which operate differentially from place to place and from time to time. They represent, therefore, relative and not absolute statements.

Statements of aims are statements of aspiration, and are at a stage removed from making detailed decisions. The terms in which they are specified are frequently vague and ambiguous, and may even be in the nature of window dressing. For all their lack of precision, the process of thinking about aims should never be omitted from curriculum planning. Our aims in education are closely associated with the values we hold, and decisions about them are necessarily judgements about what ends we believe to be worthwhile.[1]

The development of 'personal autonomy' as an educational aim

Harris has argued that the development of personal autonomy is *the* overarching educational aim.[2] This is a view adopted by the writer as a basis of justification for many of the judgements made in this text. Of course it is only one of a number of possible standpoints, and would presumably not be acceptable in an ideological system which did not place a high regard on independent thought and choice.

In singling out autonomy as the key, Harris makes four overlapping points, here paraphrased and adapted to lines of argument used later.

1. Autonomy implies *knowledge*, without which responsible choice, a hallmark of an autonomous person, is meaningless. Knowledge in this instance means far more than specific facts, and includes such frequently stated intellectual aims as 'promoting the acquisition of thinking skills'; 'forming concepts and principles'; 'fostering scientific methods of enquiry'; 'cultivating discriminatory, critical and imaginative thinking.' These should not be seen as narrow academic attributes, but as contributing to personal development in a wider sense.

2. Autonomy implies the *availability of interests* which an individual wishes to pursue. A person should have an inclination to engage in some valued activity, and a school should aim to provide opportunities for this to develop.

3. Autonomy is also related to the *satisfaction of needs*. Leaving aside basic physiological requirements, these include the need to achieve; the need to have interests (a cognitive drive); the need to belong to or affiliate with (a parent, teacher, friend or peer group). A dilemma is presented, however, in that satisfaction of personal needs can be held to imply self-regarding ends, which it hardly seems the job of education to promote.

4. The achievement of autonomy must, therefore, presuppose the development of an awareness of the experiences and feelings of others, or *empathy*. The pursuit of autonomy aim is inevitably linked with *moral education*. Harris sees a person lacking in autonomy if he cannot make moral judgements, which by definition are (a) prescriptive in so far as the individual is concerned: ie a person making such a judgement in principle must allow it to guide his actions, and (b) universal, in the sense that they must also apply to other people in relevantly similar situations. An aim of the school must, therefore, be to help to develop the skills required in making moral judgements. Such judgements allow the reconciliation of the satisfaction of personal needs aim, and the development of the child as a social being aim.

Clearly there is a strong 'moral element' in the area of social and environmental education, with which this book is much concerned. Teachers of geography and history have traditionally tended to neutralise or avoid moral questions, and some have argued that direct exposure of children to what are often tendentious issues carries the danger of indoctrination. This anxiety can be countered by insisting that consideration of such issues should be related to (though not necessarily determined by) standards of rational judgement. These 'standards' mean ensuring that the facts supporting the judgement are true, relevant, comprehensive and balanced. The value principles implied by the judgement must be acceptable to the person making the judgement, and not be inculcated.[3] They must also be capable of justification by that person.

Aims and the subject context

The aims of teaching geography

If Harris's analysis is accepted, it is incumbent upon curriculum planners to see that the curriculum as a whole strives to contribute to the development of the various skills required in the achievement of personal autonomy. It is clearly unnecessary for each individual area of study to try to cover all the skills. Subjects other than geography may have more to contribute to the fostering of such skills as literacy, numeracy, creativity, aesthetic awareness and moral judgement, for example. On the other hand, geographers would claim for their subject a distinctive function in the pursuit of certain social and intellectual aims. Personal autonomy implies integration of the individual with his environment, and geographers feel they have something very direct to contribute to the understanding of 'environment', which their definition broadens out from the 'action space' of the individual to encompass the world as a whole, covering not only its places but the peoples in these places (page 58).

Statements of aims in the subject context, however, usually constitute the claims that subject makes for a place in the curriculum. The nature of the claims which geography has advanced in its successful quest for a place in the curriculum is a fascinating and pertinent study. The claims can be considered under two headings: social utility, and the development of intellectual skills and interests.

1. *Social utility*

Utility can be defined in instrumental terms—'merely useful'—in which context it is more often used. Here, its meaning is extended to include the development of empathy, which has a social utility of a more estimable order than the 'merely useful' type. Hence two dimensions are considered: the idea that the study of geography has something useful to contribute to the narrower national interest; and the idea that it contributes to the wider international interest, in promoting a sympathetic understanding and an imaginative awareness of the feelings and experiences of other peoples, as well as of fellow nationals.

(a) *Geography in the national interest* In the nineteenth century, geography was viewed uninhibitedly as the subject *par excellence* suited

> to children of a race like ours, which of all others may in a certain sense be said to be the most geographical; a race of boundless and ever-expanding energies which, pent up within its island limits has at all times felt so powerfully the attraction of perpetual ocean contact; a race 'born to create empires', and which has spread itself, its laws, its manners, its language in all continents of the globe. . . . It is furthermore a patriotic study, for it makes our children alive to the position of their country in the world, and this leads me to express the wish that a map were hung up in every school showing the portions of the globe where the English tongue is spoken.[4]

To this 'ideological utility' was added a more mundane usefulness. Geography was seen as a subject helpful to promoters of emigration, the progress of which bound the country 'by ties of blood relationship to so many distant communities'.[5] The lower classes thus needed geography, for it would not be in the national interest if the more intelligent of the population emigrated, but the more ignorant did not.[6] Geography was also helpful in commerce and state affairs, as the knowledge 'which it yields is as profitable to the man of business, who seeks new outlets for his merchandise, as it is to the statesman, who directs the destinies of a nation'.[7] To the military man as well, geographical knowledge could be made 'to serve the highest purposes of strategy. In the campaign of the late war the superior knowledge of the Germans in geography gave them an overwhelming advantage over the French.'[8] In a period when the dark corners of the earth were being explored and annexed, geography was a subject of compelling interest.

The instrumental and controlling role it was given emerges quite blatantly in a textbook written for pupil teachers, in which the most neutral-seeming content is infused with jingoism. The following statements are abstracted from an introductory section on the British Isles.[9]

Headings	Selected textbook comment
THE BRITISH ISLES	The most important and famous group of islands in the world....
Position	... the most convenient and desirable on the globe.
Climate	... humid, but genial and healthy weather.
Industries:	
agriculture:	The United Kingdom is famed for the skill of its farmers, the excellence of the buildings, implements and cattle on its farms, and the yield of its crops and livestock.
mining:	... the most productive mining country in the world
manufactures:	Thanks to the native energy and ingenuity of her inhabitants, and to the wealth of her minerals, the United Kingdom is the chief manufacturing nation of the world.
commerce:	... that trading spirit which has made the foreign commerce of the United Kingdom the greatest in the world.
External communication:	Fine ships steam daily from the ports of the kingdom.... For size, convenience, regularity, speed, and safety these ocean steamers are unequalled.
National defence:	The Royal Navy ... is the most famous and formidable navy in the world.
Education:	Education at some recognised school is compulsory. There is much room for improvement in both Elementary and Secondary schools.

The character of the English people was described as 'industrious, liberty-loving, independent, enterprising, wealth-respecting, law-abiding, steadfast, illogical and rather solemn'. The national vices mentioned were 'drunkenness and gambling'. The subtle infusion of negative comments on the state of education, to the promotion of which the recipients of the text would later be devoting their energies, will not be missed.

Today we would be at pains to avoid chauvinism, though as late as the 1920s Fairgrieve was arguing, though not as 'a point to be pressed', and not as a main point for including the subject in the curriculum, that 'geography pays'.[10]

The aims met with so far clearly do not meet the criteria previously advanced, not only because they are 'self-regarding' when looked at from the global point of view, but also because they are blatantly instrumental. This is not to say that aims related to the national interest are necessarily illegitimate. They may well equate with the wider interest. Hence geography might aim to instil a respect for the environment, to promote its constructive use and conservation. This is of particular help in the national interest, but is also of general help in the interests of mankind. It remains an instrumental view, however, unless the focus is on promoting the ability to make responsible choices.

(b) *Views of other peoples: fighting stereotypes* Two television producers were reported (1974) combing Stockholm to find a suitably 'sleazy' neighbourhood in which to film drop-outs and drug addicts in a 'type' environmental setting. Spying some condemned buildings, they headed straight for the basement, where they encountered some 'cheery squatters'. ' "You won't find any drug addicts here," they said, "they're all across the way in that big block of expensive flats —that's where all the junkies hang out these days!" ' [11]

Nearly two hundred years prior to the above incident, an American textbook writer, Nathaniel Dwight, was claiming that geography 'will teach us that mankind are one great family', and that it 'promotes social intercourse and mutual happiness.'[12] If the phenomenon of the stereotype was not invented by the writers of eighteenth- and nineteenth-century school geography texts, it reached a zenith in some of their perpetrations. Notwithstanding his aims, Dwight was able to categorise the Germans as 'grave, able and fond of parade', and the Turks as 'indolent, superstitious, morose, treacherous, passionate and unfriendly.'[13] Similarly, Vaughan quotes the Rev. J. Goldsmith's account of Africa as 'the country of monsters. . . . Even man, in this quarter of the world, exists in a state of lowest barbarism.'[14]

This type of content persisted throughout the nineteenth century, though not all promoters of geography were prepared to accept such 'fiercely uncharitable' stereotypes. A reviewer of an English geography text of the 1870s, for example, took the lady writer to task for portraying the English as 'a happy people because they are well treated by the Queen and the great lords', in stark contrast to those of other lands. The reviewer's disapproval was excited by such epitomes as: in Sicily 'the rich people think only of pleasure. They ride in their carriages by the seaside during the day, and at night they play at cards . . . ', while in Italy, 'once a year the people meet together to kiss the Pope's great toe. Do you laugh? It would be better to cry.'[15]

By the end of the century, advocates of geography were concerned to advance more consciously its purported power to heighten sympathy towards other peoples. Hence Trotter was writing in the 1898 edition of the American *Journal of School Geography*:

> The *end* in view of the study is to develop a *social intelligence* and consequently, a *social disposition*; to break down *local prejudice* and to produce a broader spirit of sympathy and a tendency towards more efficient cooperation.[16]

Yet in the same journal the following year, the editor recommended as 'deserving of consideration' a 'model lesson' on Russia. In this, a series of first-hand descriptive passages were provided as resources upon which a series of exercises were set. In response to extracts which showed Russian peasants variously as wife-beaters, vodka drinkers to excess, superstitious, servile and poverty-stricken, the questions culminated in: 'How do you think the civilisation of the Russian people compares with that of the United States?'[17]

Twentieth-century statements, in intention at least, show jingoism in retreat. In his influential *Geography in School* (1926), Fairgrieve strives to integrate the 'brotherhood of man' ideal with the purposes of geographical education, stressing that geography's aims should not be divorced from the broader ends of education as a whole. He saw knowledge of geographical content as crucial to a training in citizenship:

> ... one may go so far as to say that setting aside original sin, or whatever is its modern equivalent, and present day weakness in the teaching of history, there is not one single thing which stands so much in the way of social and international advance as a lack of knowledge of geography. Better than most subjects, because it has a warmth of sympathy tempered by dispassionate accuracy, it is fitted for the promotion of goodwill throughout the world.[18]

To meet this ideal, Fairgrieve adopts a concentric strategy, moving out from the home region to the homeland and then the world. 'How people live' is an important facet of the first two years of the course. Yet, despite the laudable intention, stereotyping is implicit. 'One should begin with the simpler types—Eskimoes, negroes and pygmies; later in the year lessons may be given on Greeks, Japanese, Swiss and Norwegians, in which cases human response to geographical control is more complicated.'[19]

Similarly, in an advanced text on North America, written in

1924, Bryan carefully pointed out, in a section on the impact of the boll-weevil on the Cotton Belt, the need for intelligent application of an insecticide spray, if it was to be effective in controlling the pest. But the labour supply was negro and Bryan is at pains to suggest that it was not even negro labour 'of the best type, since the more intelligent type of negro moves out of the Belt to the northern industrial regions. . . .'[20]

In his amusing caricature of school stereotypes ('gum-chewing Americans'; 'fickle French' with 'unmentionable plumbing'), Haddon highlights their continuing presence.[21] A subject with a long-standing aim to inhibit stereotyping still seems more successful at reinforcing it.[22] Perhaps this is because too much is expected of school geography. Hence Carnie's investigations suggest that 'much of what children learn and remember in their junior and secondary years is affected by previous experiences and prevailing attitudes well beyond the influence of traditional teaching methods,' and that 'children's ideas of other lands and peoples are at least as much determined by attitudes towards them as by knowledge of them.'[23]

Writers of recent methodological texts have been wise to make more modest claims than those advanced by Fairgrieve and his predecessors.[24] Yet while a degree of scepticism is appropriate, subjects such as geography must make the attempt to grapple with entrenched attitudes. Perhaps one of its failings has been its reluctance to engage in controversial issues (see pages 10, 68, 92-3 and 286-7). We need to provide not only information about other peoples, but also consciously to ask questions that require an exploration of other people's feelings as well as our own (see pages 90-1).

Attention so far has been drawn to stereotyping of other peoples. It must clearly be a complementary aim of geography teaching to guard against the stereotyping of landscapes and geographical processes, of which 'hot dry summers and warm wet winters' is symptomatic. Haddon's exposures of distorted images of foreign lands remain too close for comfort.[25]

2. *The development of intellectual skills and interests*

This section is shorter than that on social aims because a consideration of intellectual aims leads us quickly into more detailed specifications which are more appropriately covered in the next chapter. If the occupational hazard of the geography teacher in social terms is the presentation of stereotypes, in the intellectual field it is the purveying of a descriptive wash of facts about the earth.

The close association of nineteenth-century school geography with the 'capes and bays' tradition made it intellectually suspect as a subject for the higher reaches of education (page 76). In one of the early methodological texts, Geikie was careful to point out that there was more to geography than a training of the memory. He placed geography at the heart of the scientific tradition, in fact, with the potential of 'a discipline of a high order in education'. In justifying this claim, he sought to use geography to exercise the observing faculty; to stimulate the reasoning powers, by teaching the value of the classification and co-ordination of facts and the methods of scientific induction; to afford ample exercise of the memory, but not in the manner of rote learning; and to supply information and excite interest in various aspects of nature. Although Geikie's social aims had an undeniably nineteenth-century intonation of patriotism and character-strengthening, they also had an intellectual underpinning. The conception of the fatherland was to be a 'just' one; and the character development included 'habits of reflection'.[26]

This dissociation of geographical information from rote learning and its association with fostering interest remains a significant distinction. Geography teachers have long seen their role to stimulate interest and appreciated their good fortune in possessing subject matter of such rich potential. As early as 1789 Dr Morse, an American textbook writer, was writing of no science being more able than geography to captivate the attention of youth.[27] Even those public school headmasters of the nineteenth century who suspected the intellectual respectability of the subject, respected its potential for stimulating interest if taught by an expert.[28] At a time when the misuse of geographical facts has given them a degree of disrepute, it is well to reaffirm that the world and its environments are part of each child's cultural heritage, and one of geography's functions must be the transmission of information about that heritage.

Guidelines

As we have seen, the purpose of outlining aims is to provide broad guidelines for statements of objectives, for selecting curriculum content and thus for planning learning experiences. The current aims of geography must be aligned with the wider ends of education, namely the balancing of the pursuit of critical thinking and other cognitive skills with the development of social awareness and empathy. In practice, the two cannot legitimately be divorced.

For the geography teacher, the needs are clear in general terms: to substitute meaningful for uncritical learning; to pay more than lip service to the promotion of social aims, which involves the infusion of a wide range of problem issues—social and political as well as economic and environmental—into the syllabus.

It is appropriate that pupils should be encouraged to make value judgements, about world problems for example. The fact that these judgements should be *defensible* implies the development of skills necessary in making rational decisions, and also a disposition to make such decisions. Thus Harris's requirement for introducing moral education into the curriculum should not be regarded as something quite divorced from geography's concerns.

The basic skills, though not the final judgements, are mainly cognitive. Development of social awareness must have a cognitive base, although at the same time cognitive skills are being devoted to lesser ends if socially relevant content is not introduced. There are no short cuts to social awareness, and behind this type of aim, as Hirst and Peters have asserted, 'there must necessarily be the achievements of objective experience, knowledge and understanding. If this be so, it suggests that the logically most fundamental objectives of all are those of a cognitive kind.'[29]

Priority readings

1. WHEELER, D. K. *Curriculum Process* (University of London Press Unibooks), Chapter 4, pp. 74–98.
2. LONG, M. & ROBERSON, B. S. *Teaching Geography* (Heinemann), Chapter 1, pp. 1–14.
3. GRAVES, N. J. *Geography in Secondary Education* (Geographical Association), Chapter 1, pp. 1–3.
4. CARNIE, J. 'Children's attitudes to other nationalities' in GRAVES, N. J. (ed.) *New Movements in the Study and Teaching of Geography* (Temple Smith), Chapter 10, pp. 121–34.
5. CARNIE, J. 'The development of national concepts in junior school children' in BALE, J., *et al.* (eds.) *Perspectives in Geographical Education* (Oliver & Boyd), pp. 101–18.
6. HADDON, J. 'A view of foreign lands' *Geography*, vol. 45, pp. 286–9.

Questions for investigation and discussion

1. Discuss a possible practical outcome of the 'personal autonomy' aim: that pupils might demonstrate their autonomy by opting out of schooling.
2. (a) Try to identify the 'fact' and 'value' statements in the following extract from a nineteenth-century primary school textbook.
   (b) See if you can find analogues in contemporary textbooks.

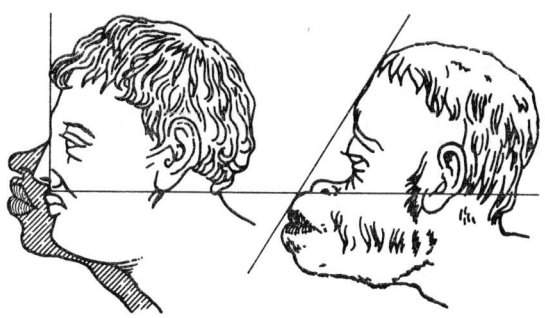

Faces of the Negro, European, and Orang-o-tang

'I. **Caucasians**, such as Europeans and Arabs. Their fair blushing skin, high forehead, thin nose, long and soft hair, and great variety of expression, mark this most favoured kind. These white men have settled in every quarter of the globe, and have usually become rulers.

II. **Mongolians**, who dwell in China, Japan, and the Arctic regions. An olive or yellow skin, strong hair, slanting eyelids, and high cheek bones are their main features.

III. **American Natives**, whom a red skin, long skull, and aquiline nose easily distinguish. Their many tribes are quickly dying out; their greatest enemies being spirituous liquors, which they call "fire-water", and diseases brought in by Europeans.

IV. **Ethiopians**, are at once known by a black skin, woolly hair, projecting jaws, a broad nose, long heels, and flat feet. These points do not give any reason why we should not love the negro as a brother, and among the next, are more lowly groups of mankind.

V. **Australia**, and the islands near it, are peopled by Malays and a kind of Negro, nearly as black as that from Africa. The latter have narrow foreheads, flat noses, wide mouths, low stature, and weak legs. It is harder to awaken the belief in God among them than among any other nation on the earth.'[30]

3. Stereotyping has been referred to as 'inferior judgemental processing . . . a short-circuiting or blocking of potentially higher mental processes in favour of a well-worn, catch-all reaction. . . .'[31] Discuss this definition in the light of the examples given earlier in this chapter, and in Haddon's article (see Priority reading 6).
4. 'When attention is concentrated on the school subjects, there is always a danger that a narrow concern for intellectuality will lead to the neglect of social functions and individual development.'[32]

    Outline the points you would make, as a subject specialist, in response to a head teacher using an argument such as this in a proposal to exclude geography from the timetable.
5. Make and justify a personal checklist of aims for (a) schooling in general; (b) the school curriculum; (c) your particular subject (or an integrated group of subjects in which it would figure).

References

1. See PRING, R. (1972) 'Aims and objectives' in Unit 7: *Curriculum Philosophy and Design* (Open University Press), 84–5.
2. HARRIS, A. (1972) 'Autonomy' in Unit 8: *ibid*, 119–48.
3. See COOMBS, J. R. (1971) 'Objectives of value analysis' in METCALF, L. E. (ed.) *Values Education: Rationale, Strategies and Procedures* (National Council for Social Studies, Washington, Forty-first Yearbook), 27.
4. *Reports of the Committee of Council on Education* (1878–9) 'Report of H. W. G. Markheim, HMI, on the Northallerton District' (HMSO, London), 643.
5. RGS (1871) 'Extract from a letter sent to the Vice-Chancellors of the Universities of Oxford and Cambridge' in *Report of the Proceedings of the Society in Reference to the Improvement of Geographical Education* (Murray, London, 1886), 80.
6. RGS (1886) *ibid*, from a reference in a discussion following a lecture by E. G. Ravenstein, 180.
7. RGS (1886) *ibid*, lecture by E. G. Ravenstein on 'The aims and methods of geographical education', 165–6.
8. ANONYMOUS (1871) 'The neglect of geography in our higher schools and the remedy', *School Board Chronicle*, **3**, 51–2.
9. YOXALL, J. H. (1891) *The Pupil Teacher's Geography* (Jarrold & Sons, London, 2nd edition), 17–32.
10. FAIRGRIEVE, J. (1926) *Geography in School* (University of London Press, 1937 edition), 7.
11. *Radio Times*, 30 November–6 December 1974, 4.
12. BRIGHAM, A. P. & DODGE, R. E. (1933) 'Nineteenth-century textbooks of geography' in WHIPPLE, G. M. (ed.) *The Teaching of Geography*, Thirty-second Yearbook of the National Society for the Study of Education (University of Chicago Press), 7.
13. *Ibid*, 8.
14. VAUGHAN, J. E. (1972) 'Aspects of teaching geography in England in the early nineteenth century' *Paedagogica Historica*, **12**, 140.
15. Extract from an anonymous review of a textbook *Geography for Children* (author also anonymous) *School Board Chronicle* (1871) **1**, 26.
16. TROTTER, Dr (1898) Statement discussed in an article by DODGE, R. E. 'The social function of geography' *Journal of School Geography*, **2**, 329.

17. PLACE, C. L. (1899) 'A lesson on Russia' *Journal of School Geography*, **3**, 24–8.
18. FAIRGRIEVE, J. (1926) *op. cit.*, 8–10.
19. *Ibid*, 137.
20. JONES, L. R. & BRYAN, P. W. (1924) *North America: An Historical, Economic and Regional Geography* (Methuen, London), 179.
21. HADDON, J. (1960) 'A view of foreign lands' *Geography*, **45**, 286–9.
22. See SHORTLE, D. (1971) 'Citizenship and geographical education' in BIDDLE, D. S. & DEER, C. E. (eds.) (1973) *Readings in Geographical Education: Selections from Australian and New Zealand Sources*, Vol. 2, 1966–1972 (Whitcombe & Tombs, Sydney, for the Australian Geography Teachers' Association), 37.
23. CARNIE, J. (1972) 'Children's attitudes to other nationalities' in GRAVES, N. J. (ed.) *New Movements in the Study and Teaching of Geography* (Temple Smith, London), 121.
24. See, for example, LONG, M. & ROBERSON, B. S. (1966) *Teaching Geography* (Heinemann, London), 7–13; and also GOPSILL, G. H. (1956) *The Teaching of Geography* (Macmillan, London, 4th edition, 1973), 12.
25. See HADDON, J. (1960), *op. cit.*, 286, for an Australian landscape stereotype, for example.
26. GEIKIE, A. (1887) *The Teaching of Geography* (Macmillan, London, 1908 edition), 4.
27. BRIGHAM, A. P. & DODGE, R. E. (1933), *op. cit.*, 7.
28. RGS (1886) 'Opinions of headmasters of English public schools as to the value of geography and the place it ought to have in schools and universities', *op. cit.*, 90–6.
29. HIRST, P. H. & PETERS, R. S. (1970) *The Logic of Education* (Routledge & Kegan Paul, London), 62–3.
30. MAPOTHER, E. D. (1870) *The Body and its Health* (John Falconer, Dublin), 9–11.
31. FISHMAN, J. A. (1956) 'An examination of the process and function of social stereotyping' *The Journal of Social Psychology*, **43**, 31–5.
32. WHEELER, D. K. (1967) *Curriculum Process* (University of London Press), 94.

3 Objectives

Objectives are seen as more limited in their scope than aims, requiring more precise statement. They serve in part to translate the broad guidelines provided by statements of aims into what it is possible to achieve. The purposes for which the objectives are formulated will help to determine how specific they need to be. They can, for example, be related to three levels of educational provision: overall curriculum planning for the school; overall syllabus planning within an area of study; and planning at the level of short course or lesson units.

The first two cover long-term planning, and similar objectives should be specified for the wider, extra-curricular provision by the school. Objectives might equally be viewed in terms of what the learner is expected to have achieved by the time he leaves school, by the end of a particular stage of schooling or by the end of a course unit. This chapter is chiefly concerned with the specification of short-term, course or lesson unit objectives.

Operational or behavioural objectives

The most precise statements of objectives are those termed 'operational' or 'behavioural'. These refer to pre-specified observable changes in pupil behaviour. The word 'behaviour' is not, of course, being used in this case in the sense of 'conduct' but refers rather to cognitive behaviour.

Precise statements of objectives are regarded by some curriculum developers as indispensable in the preliminary stages of planning teaching programmes. Among the first of such curriculum developers were those responsible for the educational codes which followed the institution of the 'payment by results' system in this country in the 1860s. Their objectives were impressively 'operational'. Thus, to be deemed successful at Standard I level, according to the code of 1872, a child had to be able to: 'read one of the narratives next in order after monosyllables in an elementary reading book used in the school'; 'copy in manuscript character a line of print and write from dictation a few common words'; and 'do simple addition and subtraction of number of not more than four figures, and the multiplication table, to multiplication of six.'[1]

Teachers were held accountable for the results, on which the government grant in part depended. The rigidities and humiliations associated with this system, now enshrined as one of the 'folk-memories' of the teaching profession, provoked a backlash. It is difficult even today to dissociate objectives approaches from illiberal approaches. Such an association has been pinpointed in recent years in the United States, where educational funding agencies and state legislatures have increasingly been attempting to make teachers accountable for the success of their pupils by assessing whether pre-specified behavioural objectives are achieved.

In the United States, the desire to clarify objectives was in evidence when the National Society for the Study of Education devoted its Thirty-second Yearbook (1933) to *The Teaching of Geography*. One of the papers in it was by Marguerite Uttley, who formulated in considerable detail specific attainments in geography for the elementary school in a way which seemed to presage later developments. She first pointed out that 'such objectives as "appreciation of the interdependence of nations" and "development of sympathy for, and understanding of, peoples in distant lands" are rather far-reaching and relatively intangible.'[2] This was followed by a series of guideline statements precise enough to be described as 'objectives'. Thus one of a set of four objectives related to 'the ability to use pictures in landscape reading' read: 'Ability to read into pictures probable relationships. Example: Picture of persons in loosely flowing clothes taking down tents and packing possessions on camels. Inference: this is a picture of nomadic grazers. It is a dry region, there is not enough pasturage in one place for long. Herds must be moved frequently. Tents are the most convenient kind of house for this type of life.'[3] Ability to make such inferences would mean the pupil had achieved this objective.

In recent years, the quest for highly specific and even measurable objectives has at times been stretched to extremes. It is exemplified in such targets as 'State the behaviour in a way that somebody else could count it.'[4] Perhaps the clearest exposition of the unashamed behavioural objectives approach is provided by Mager. He insists that statements of objectives should conform to the following criteria.

(a) They should be stated in performance terms that describe what the learner will be DOING when demonstrating his achievement of the objective.

(b) The language in which the statement is expressed should communicate the same thing to different people, and not be open to a wide variety of interpretations. In any statement of objectives, infinitives such as 'to identify' are more satisfactory than those such as 'to understand'.

(c) The conditions under which the behaviour is to occur should be stated. The materials to be used, and even the time allowed for the task, should be specified.

(d) The lowest level of acceptable performance should be stated.

(e) A separate statement should be associated with each objective, as the more statements made, the more likely they are to be clear in their intent.[5]

The implications of the Mager approach can be examined briefly through a geographical illustration provided by Clegg.

> Given data from the 1960 and 1970 censuses, the students will be able to construct a bar graph showing the change in population for the following cities: New York, Chicago, Detroit, Cleveland, St Louis, and Seattle. Data will be correct to the nearest ten thousand.[6]

Objections to the objectives approach

The many objections which have been made to the use of objectives approaches in education have focused particularly, though not entirely, on more extreme examples, such as Mager's. Among the most forceful dissenters are those affronted by the apparent inhumanity of the approach as, for example, Charity James:

> This is the language of assembly-line processing of products. . . . The underlying image is of the factory rather than the consulting room or the school . . . the whole exercise of thinking in terms of block objectives . . . is a system for disregarding individual needs, a system for creating conformity.[7]

The implication is that instruction is pre-empted and will tend to emerge as didactic, authoritarian and instrumental. Referring back to the 'payment by results' experience, with all the procedures previously laid down, the teacher is regarded as likely to 'stick to the rule book' and close up opportunities for creative and spontaneous work.

The objectives approach is held also to be based on an oversimplified view of the relationship between knowledge and behaviour. Knowledge is expressed in language, yet language is not just 'verbal behaviour'. Sockett points out that if a child makes a statement which has meaning, it is thereby satisfying a particular behavioural objective. But the teacher has still to ask:
(a) Does the child know what the statement means?
(b) Does he mean by the statement what the teacher means?[8]

The phenomenon of dealing in words rather than meanings is well-known in schooling and surfaces too frequently in school geography. As in the 'payment by results' system, the verbal response to the prespecified objective may be impressively precise, but may not reflect understanding.

Another criticism is that behavioural objectives are too much associated with easily measurable and relatively trivial content. It is easy to specify, for example, that at the end of a unit of work on South America the pupil will be able to list the main exports of each country. It is more difficult, however, to identify higher level outcomes with such lack of ambiguity. These would include what Eisner has termed 'expressive objectives'.[9]

In addition, the highly specific objectives of educational activity as a whole are too numerous for them all to be stated conveniently, a point again explored by Eisner.

> Let's assume that a teacher has one unit of content to be learned by a group of thirty children for each of seven subject areas a day. Let's assume that she has her class divided in thirds in order to differentiate content for students with differing abilities. This would mean that the teacher would have to formulate objectives for seven units of content, times five days a week, times three groups of students, times four weeks a month, times ten months a school year. She would therefore have to have 4,200 behaviourally defined objectives for a school year. A six-year school employing such a rationale would have to have 25,200 behaviourally defined educational objectives.[10]

The level of detail and its potential for proliferation, illustrated previously in Clegg's statement of a geographical objective, can easily result in a treadmill. The supply of teacher time and energy is scarce, in relation to the demands made upon them. The prior identification of every probable outcome at this level of precision is surely not the teacher's most important task!

Counter-arguments

Supporters of the operational objectives approach would counter by saying that these objections are based on misunderstandings, or on the tendency to regard extreme manifestations of an approach as the norm. It has been stressed, for example, that far from leading to trivialisation of content, the identification of objectives clarifies which particular objectives are trivial and which are not.[11] In this way trivia are brought into the open and can be kept under scrutiny. It is possible to specify beforehand that only a small proportion of the marks for a particular unit of work will be allotted for copying or recall of facts. In contrast, such laudable general aims as 'producing better citizens', or ambitious sounding essay titles (pages 180–3), can conceal superficial content under a grandiose heading.

Prespecification of outcomes does not necessarily imply that the means to achieve them should *all* be outlined. There are many routes to the same destination. There is no need to stifle the spontaneous use of unexpected opportunities for open-ended discussion which may crop up during a lesson. The authentic behaviourist would say, however, that expert help is needed to guide these opportunities towards the end in view. In addition, the unanticipated outcomes of instruction can be assessed as well as those prespecified. The latter would tend to form the essential core of what all children would need for later progress. Over and above this, it would not be necessary to tie work to pre-ordained objectives.

The use of a wide range of assessment techniques (page 171) makes possible the testing of the whole spectrum of intellectual skills. One of the necessary refinements of the assessment procedure is the use of a test specification (pages 209–10) to control any tendency to over-emphasise less important educational activities, such as the recall of superficial content.

In meeting the criticism that the pure behaviourist approach entails an unacceptable proliferation of objectives, Tyler has asserted that clarity is a more important criterion than extracting the last ounce of specificity. He regards 'knowledge of the meaning of the most common 2,500 French words' as being too specific; but 'ability to read French' as too vague. 'Ability to identify the subjunctive' would be about the right level of generality.[12] Two important suggestions emerge:

(a) that concepts (such as the subjunctive) and principles of particular disciplines form a more manageable check-list for the specification of objectives than descriptive content;

(b) that the level of generality at which objectives are expressed is a crucial factor in determining whether they can provide a useful structuring principle, without the participant becoming bogged down in a multiplicity of highly specific content statements.

The Tyler analysis is just one example of a useful compromise. Other authorities also subscribe to a tempered objectives approach. Kratwohl, for example, regards Gagné's distinction between mastery objectives and transfer objectives as significant. The former are those objectives which must be mastered as keys to later learning. The latter cover those in which it is impossible to predict all the situations which a student will encounter.[13] Nearly all complex intellectual skills take the form of transfer objectives. Mastery skills are more applicable in industrial and vocational training and less so in general education, though there are, of course, school contexts in which they are important. But transfer objectives will be met with more frequently there, especially in subjects in the humanities and social sciences. While the specification of transfer objectives will necessarily be more inexact, this does not mean that the criteria cannot be made explicit. While it may be impracticable to prespecify individual responses to a work of art, for example, there are canons or criteria for judging the appropriateness of the response, and these can be made explicit.[14]

Though fiercely critical of doctrinaire behaviourist approaches, in which the achievement of outward visible signs appears more important than the state of mind desired, Hirst nevertheless regards the specification of objectives as essential in curriculum planning.

> With no clear statement of objectives set out to guide them, teachers only too easily take the statement of the mere content of the curriculum or syllabus as a statement of the objectives to be pursued.[15]

Hirst regards as central those objectives which contribute to the development of a rational mind, though he qualifies this by stating that he is not merely concerned with intellect to the neglect of emotional development. A rational mind cannot be developed without the acquisition of knowledge which involves, among other things, the learning of many different concepts, the mastery of many logical operations and principles and applying the criteria of different types of judgements. All intelligibility is seen as depending on the achievement of an array of concepts, which build up to form distinctive networks or relationships. These distinctive sets of relationships provide the basis of the different forms of knowledge (pages 49–52).[16]

A critical distinction is thus made between those objectives which contribute to the development of rational understanding, and those which merely pay lip service to knowledge. It is important to perceive that 'memorisation of facts' is not true acquisition of knowledge. The former process is associated with a lack of reasoning. The latter is not.

The practical assistance which a moderate objectives approach can provide is conveniently summarised by Skilbeck.[17]

1. A wide range of content and materials present themselves to the teacher. A clear specification of worthwhile objectives provides *criteria of choice*. Significant content can be given precedence over trivial.
2. Important *variables relating to the pupil* are made explicit, including an assessment of his state of readiness, an examination of the possibilities of sequencing material according to principles derived from learning theory and a recognition of the need to individualise learning to meet the needs of particular pupils.
3. *Detailed feedback*, of use to teachers and pupils, is made possible (see pages 192 and 229).
4. In so far as the teacher is concerned, the approach (a) presupposes the sort of *critical thinking from the teacher* that he in turn expects from his pupils, and (b) helps to *make explicit the success or otherwise of his teaching*. This information must, of course, be viewed with caution, bearing in mind the variable nature of the objectives adopted and the situations in which different teachers find themselves. Trivial objectives are relatively easy to achieve, and some children are easier to teach than others.

Types of objectives

Undoubtedly the most influential work on educational objectives in the last twenty years has been that of Bloom and his co-workers, as realised in the *Taxonomy of Educational Objectives*. This taxonomy is split into three 'domains', the cognitive (1956), affective (1964), and psycho-motor. The functions of the taxonomy are rather different from Mager-type specifications, though they have in common the desire (a) to facilitate communications between workers in the field of education by defining terms more precisely; and (b) to specify the intended behaviour of students.

Cognitive objectives

Bloom's cognitive domain

The detailed categories and sub-categories of Bloom's 'cognitive domain' are readily accessible[18] and are not repeated here, though and example of the application of its main ideas in a geographical context is given below. The cognitive domain covers a range of intellectual skills, including 'knowledge'. The scheme follows a hierarchical principle by which each of the higher level categories comprises more complex abilities than the lower ones. Hence category 4.00 (analysis), is seen as subsuming the lower categories of application (3.00), comprehension (2.00) and knowledge (1.00).

Applying the cognitive domain to geography

Attempts to apply the categories of the Bloom scheme to geography have been made by Cox,[19] Gunn,[20] Monk,[21] and Senathirajah and Weiss,[22] mostly in the context of test construction. Here the taxonomy is adapted for a possible course unit on the English Lake District, to illustrate its potential for the structuring of content.

Bloom categories   *A geographical application*

1.00 KNOWLEDGE: (*largely recall of specific facts or their recognition on maps and photographs*)

To *recall* in words and/or to *recognise* on photographs or in the field specified features which make up the Lake District environment eg bad drainage, interfluve, corrie, drainage, fell, crag, bracken, rough pasture, quarrying, etc; to *name* and *locate* places of local importance, eg Scafell, Helvellyn, Thirlmere, Windermere, Keswick, Langdale, etc.

2.00 COMPREHENSION

2.10 *Translation*

To *translate* the diagnostic characteristics of features such as corries from one mode of representation to another, eg from a photographic representation to an annotated sketch; a contoured map to a labelled relief section.

2.20 *Interpretation*

To *explain* the impact of physical, economic and social factors on such activities as farming and tourism.

To *elucidate* the interdependence of man and environment with the help of detailed illustration from a case study of a particular farm.

2.30 *Extrapolation*

To *predict* the weather conditions likely during the day after consulting an early morning weather chart.

To *infer* the consequences of (a) increased 'second house' buying and (b) trunk road construction on lakeland communities.

3.00 APPLICATION *The use of abstractions in particular and concrete situations*

To *apply* the concepts derived from a particular farm study in a Lake District valley more generally (a) to other Lake District valleys; (b) to mountain areas elsewhere; (c) to a hypothetical mountain area.

4.00 ANALYSIS *Breakdown of a communication into its constituent elements*

To *abstract* from a complex of previously unseen information, including verbal-descriptive, numerical, cartographic and visual materials, *essential or key elements* of the lakeland scene and its economic base.

5.00 SYNTHESIS *The putting together of elements to form a whole*

To *produce a short report*, based on first hand investigation, on the changing economy and ways of life of a particular area of the Lake District.

6.00 EVALUATION *Making judgements about the value of something in quantitative or qualitative terms*

To *appraise* the visual elements in the Lake District landscape which are said by some to make it especially attractive.

To *judge* what it is like to live in a relatively unspoilt mountain region as compared, for example, with an industrialised conurbation; to *justify* the values manifested in taking sides in various environmental issues related to the Lake District.

This is clearly a selective breakdown both in terms of available geographical content and of the Bloom taxonomy itself. The outline is not as precise as in a Mager-type scheme, though each statement could be made into an operational objective with the preface: 'Having completed the course unit on the Lake District, the pupil will be able to . . . in response to appropriately framed tasks.' Of far more significance, however, is whether the scheme provides a particularly cogent way of structuring content. It will be argued later that there are educationally more valid ways than this of undertaking a curriculum planning exercise. Nevertheless, as Hirst has emphasised,[23] the taxonomy is invaluable in highlighting the range of abilities which should be considered in both curriculum planning and assessment.

Arguments against the cognitive domain

The relatively uncritical acceptance of the Bloom taxonomy by many curriculum designers justifies some discussion of its disadvantages, a number of which were recognised by the Bloom team from the start.[24]

First, considerable difficulties are posed by the subsumption element in the scheme, that is the idea that the higher category abilities form an umbrella for the lower ones. This raises the question of where to place behavioural objectives which are present in more than one of the categories. Bloom is quite clear on this: 'a particular behaviour is placed in the most complex class that is appropriate and relevant.'[25] In practice, however, while there may be agreement over the meaning of each of the categories, it is less easy to establish a consensus as to which category a particular behaviour belongs.

This difficulty is made worse by the fact that different pupils come to a piece of assessment through different experiences. What for one pupil may be a 'knowledge' (recall) question, for another may demand 'application'.

There is an additional questionable assumption that 'knowledge' questions are to be regarded as more straightforward than those in higher level categories. Yet the recall of things can be very difficult if:

(a) there is a lot to be remembered;
(b) the way in which the knowledge has been structured is loose;
(c) the recall of facts does not appeal to the pupil as a fruitful way of using his mind.

It may further be asked whether 'absence of recall' means that the facts were never stored in the first place, because the topic had never been covered in class, for example, or that the facts were stored and for some reason the pupil could not recall them from storage. Which of these does the static category of knowledge refer to?[26] This is, of course, an argument against too much weight being placed on assessing recall of facts than on the Bloom scheme as such.

The crucial point at issue is how the term 'knowledge' should be interpreted. Unlike the other categories, it is not a mental process. Sanders has in consequence redesignated it as 'memory'.[27] The process of 'remembering' is widely referred to by Bloom himself, in defining the knowledge objective as that which 'emphasizes most the psychological process of remembering'. But, in apparent contradiction, he goes on to stress that (my italics): '*Knowledge may also involve the more complex processes of relating and judging.*'[28]

There does indeed seem to be a basic distinction between the sub-category 1.10 in the scheme, 'Knowledge of specifics' and others, such as 'Knowledge of principles and generalizations' (1.31). How can the latter exist without understanding? But it is hard to evade the usual interpretation placed on the 'knowledge' category, that it means factual recall *with or without understanding*. The fact that an objective may be achieved without understanding is, in educational terms, subversive, a point that has been seized upon by critics such as Hirst,[29] Sockett[30] and Pring.[31] Can ability to parrot the words 'Paris is the capital of France' be regarded as 'knowledge' in any educationally valid sense? Hirst emphasises that 'it is quite impossible to learn facts, to know them as facts, without acquiring the basic concepts and criteria for truth involved . . . a fact is not a logically primitive objective. . . . One might, of course, teach "words", but that is not the point.'[32]

Hirst's view is thus that acquisition of knowledge is not just a worthwhile educational objective, it is the *fundamental* educational objective. To equate knowledge with memorisation is to devalue something which ought to be valued.

Other cognitive schemes as a basis for educational objectives

The successful diffusion of the Bloom taxonomy has tended to obscure the presence of other schemes. Some of these are also based on hierarchical principles but, in the two cases to be considered here, were born in a different context. The Ausubel and Gagné schemes are both associated with developmental learning theories, which would seem an appropriate start for planning cognitive objectives.[33]

1. *Ausubel*[34] Ausubel's scheme can, in fact, be matched quite closely with Bloom's cognitive domain.

(a) *Rote learning* is the lowest level category, which Ausubel equates with Bloom's 'knowledge' category. It would seem to relate much more specifically, however, to the sub-category 1.10, 'knowledge of specifics'. In contrast to Bloom's taxonomy, where 'knowledge' looms large as a category, Ausubel does not regard rote learning, in itself, as a worthwhile educational objective. It is seen in the long term as an extremely inefficient method of learning.

(b) The next level is *meaningful learning*, which presupposes the learning of concepts and principles, and covers the Bloom 'comprehension' category.

(c) *Application* is common to both schemes, defined by Ausubel as applying a principle in new circumstances in a fairly direct way. He sees it as difficult to distinguish from the category below.

(d) *Problem solving*, which Ausubel uses in preference to 'analysis' describes a more complex process than 'application', and involves the student in identifying and transforming relevant principles to achieve a desired result, namely, the solving of an intellectual problem.

(e) Ausubel's highest category is *creativity*, which demands the use of relationships in the student's mind to achieve a unique end product. Here the principles, concepts and strategies which are brought to bear by the student have not been taught as specifically relevant to the task in hand. Ausubel equates this category with Bloom's 'synthesis'. 'Evaluation' is not mentioned.

2. *Gagné*[35] Gagné's hierarchy is made up of eight 'types of learning': (a) signal learning; (b) stimulus response learning; (c) chaining; (d) verbal association; (e) multiple discrimination; (f) concept learning; (g) principle learning; (h) problem solving. The first three cover pre-school stages of learning and are not considered here.

(d) *Verbal association* and (e) *multiple discrimination* are roughly equatable with rote learning, though this admittedly is an oversimplification of Gagné's definitions.

In (f) *concept learning*, the learner shows the ability to make common responses to classes of stimuli (for example, flowers) which differ widely from each other in physical appearance. The acquisition of concepts presupposes the ability to discriminate, to allot objects to particular classes, to distinguish exemplars from non-exemplars. Verbal definition is not enough. Concept formation is thus a vital early stage in the discovery of meaning.

(g) *Principle learning* involves the linking of two or more concepts, a process referred to by Ausubel as 'proposition learning'.[36] Gagné's final category, (h) *problem-solving*, demands the ability to combine concepts and principles and apply them in new situations.

Gagné's 'concept learning' and 'principle learning', therefore, seem to cover Ausubel's 'meaningful learning' and Bloom's 'comprehension' categories, while his 'problem solving' covers 'application' and 'problem solving' in Ausubel's scheme and 'application' and 'analysis' in Bloom's. The higher level activities are valued by Ausubel and Gagné as cognitively efficient. 'A "higher-order" principle resulting from an act of thinking appears to be remarkably resistant to forgetting.'[37]

Affective objectives

Kratwohl/Bloom's affective domain

Although the discussion of educational aims (page 18) resulted in accepting the view that the fundamental objectives of education are cognitive, this acceptance was conditional on regarding cognitive objectives as means rather than ends. If they are not so regarded, the individual emerging at the end of the educational process may be one-sided, autonomous in terms of reasoning power but emotionally or expressively inhibited.[38] Values, attitudes and beliefs must, therefore, take priority as ends, though the school's prime task is still to develop a rational basis for them.

Values and attitudes must, therefore, be covered by the affective domain in the Kratwohl/Bloom scheme.[39] Few attempts have been made to apply this scheme to a geographical context, one exception being that of Carswell.[40] As the source is relatively inaccessible to British readers, this interpretation is quoted *in extenso*.

1.0 RECEIVING

    1.1 *Awareness*

    Awareness of geography as a discipline (In what subject would you learn most about maps?)

    1.2 *Willingness to receive*

    Acceptance of the importance of geography (Do you think geography is an important subject to study?)

    1.3 *Controlled or selected attention*

    Sensitivity to news about geography (Do you like to hear about and discuss goegraphical matters?)

2.0 RESPONDING

    2.1 *Acquiescence in responding*

    Willingness to read the assigned literature on geography (Do you read about geography only when required?)

    2.2 *Willingness to respond*

    Voluntary acquaintance with the current geographical literature (Without a specific assignment, do you read about geography frequently?)

    2.3 *Satisfaction in response*

    Enjoyment of arguing current issues in geography (Do you get satisfaction from arguing about the merits of different approaches to geography?)

3.0 VALUING
- 3.1 *Acceptance of a value*
  Feeling himself to be a geographer (Do you think of yourself as a geographer?)
- 3.2 *Preference for a value*
  Assumption of an active role in geography (Do you volunteer your services to a geography club?)
- 3.3 *Commitment*
  Loyalty to geography (Do you attend meetings and other activities connected with geography?)

4.0 ORGANISATION
- 4.1 *Conceptualisation of a value*
  Development of a rationale about the role of geography (Do you agree that the role of geography is to help man better understand the world in which he lives?)
- 4.2 *Organisation of a value system*
  Formation of judgements reflecting beliefs that geography provides a system of enquiry that helps to understand and solve world problems (Do you agree that consciousness of world problems acquired through study of geography contributes to intelligent decision-making?)

5.0 CHARACTERISATION BY A VALUE OR A VALUE COMPLEX
- 5.1 *Generalised set (learner ordering things around him in stable frame of reference)*
  Viewing of problems primarily from a geographic point of view (Would you classify pollution as primarily an aesthetic, political, geographic, economic or educational problem?)
- 5.2 *Characterisation (Formulation of personal code of conduct or philosophy)*
  Development of a philosophy of life consistent with geographic theory and practices (Write a lengthy statement in which you express and justify your personal philosophy of life.)

There seems an uneasy juxtaposition here of attitudes towards geography as an academic discipline and towards its social content, as well as a rather grandiose association of geography theory and practice with a personal philosophy of life. Nevertheless, this spelling out in subject terms of the range of attitudes and values that together make up the affective domain is to be welcomed. The fact that these categories are less tangible and more difficult to interpret than those of the cognitive domain does not mean they should be ignored. Attitudes and values are so much more difficult to assess (but see pages 246–50) than cognitive objectives which are covered by external examinations. The latter provide clearcut measures of success, but easily represent also the total commitment a student is willing to give to the area of study which has been covered. Even Mager's almost cynical statement of the minimum acceptable objective for the affective domain—'. . . to send the students away from instruction with at least as favourable an attitude toward the subjects taught as when they first arrived'[41]—is easily unachieved.

The inevitably close association between cognitive and affective components is illustrated by two attempts to draw up schemes of affective objectives, in which there is at least implicit recognition that the attitudes and values to be encountered therein cannot be divorced from the content with its cognitive associations.

Thus Marguerite Uttley (see page 23), in specifying 'habits and attitudes to be developed' through various geography units, joined each affective objective to a specific content. The 'habits to be developed' included a series of intellectual skills and procedures, such as checking relationships discerned in a picture by reference to textual material. Her final five in a group of objectives for a fourth grade geography unit were as follows:[42]

8. Realisation of the importance of pictures and actual landscapes as a source of information about people in different regions.
9. Interest in reading landscapes when travelling, in reading pictures in geographic magazines and travel books.
10. Appreciation of maps and globes as necessary tools for finding the location of places.
11. Sympathy and understanding for peoples who are out of contact with the rest of the world or whose environments are not so rich as those in the greater part of our country.
12. Readiness to give primitive peoples credit for what they have been able to accomplish in overcoming handicaps and in taking advantage of the resources that nature provided in their home region.

More recently, an 'Interim Statement' of the Schools Council Project *History, Geography and Social Science, 8–13* has identified pieces of evidence which reveal whether changes in 'attitudes, values and interests' have been changes in the right direction.[43] In terms of *interests*, for example, distinction is made between the child 'who shows a passive interest in people and physical features of an environment' but no more, the one 'who considers, willingly, questions asked by others about the environment'; and the one who spontaneously collects materials, or has a strong desire to find out things for himself about the environment, and so on.

In terms of *attitudes and values* an analogous group of qualities is looked for, as with the child 'who is wary of over-commitment to one framework of explanation and is alert to the possible distortion of facts and omission of evidence', or the one 'who is willing to identify with particular attitudes and values about the environment and relates these to other peoples.'

Guidelines

Two basic dimensions emerge from this discussion of objectives (1) *abilities*; (2) the *principles, concepts and exemplars* which make up subject content and furnish particular *levels of generality* at which statements of objectives can conveniently be made. Both provide initial guidelines for the structuring of curriculum units.

1. *Abilities*

Common elements have already been noted in the schemes of Bloom, Ausubel and Gagné. It is suggested that for broad structuring purposes a *four-fold division* of the abilities dimension is sufficient. To clarify again the terminology:

(a) *Recall* refers to the process of remembering, so that assessment of this ability involves asking questions that require recall of memorised material. The answers alone will not provide evidence of whether the memorising has been with or without understanding. In the latter case, the process assessed will have been rote learning.

(b) *Comprehension* is used to cover the three sub-categories of translation, interpretation and extrapolation in Bloom's scheme, the various skills associated with Ausubel's meaningful learning and Gagné's concept and principle learning.

(c) *Problem solving* is extended to include Bloom's application, analysis and, to some extent, evaluation categories.

(d) *Creativity* covers Bloom's synthesis category. The ability to 'synthesise' is peculiarly appropriate to the traditions of geography. For the curriculum as a whole, however, a wider definition of creativity than 'synthesis' is required.

2. *Principles, concepts and exemplars*

This second dimension is clearly bound up with the first, for principles, concepts and exemplars form the raw materials of the intellectual processes grouped under the heading of 'abilities'. Principles, concepts and exemplars can all furnish educational objectives. The contention here is that it is the principles and concepts representing the higher levels of generality that provide the most convenient and cogent structures for curriculum planning. This is because (a) they derive from the structure of knowledge itself (Chapter 4), and (b) they provide a selecting mechanism for the choice of content, thus avoiding proliferation.

Three levels of generality are identified, and the function of each is illustrated by reference to the topic of water supply.

Level A: Principles

As previously noted, these are formed by the linking of concepts. In Peters' definition, they are higher level assumptions or rules 'that can be appealed to in order to substantiate and give unity to lower order ones. . . . Evidence that the principle has been grasped is provided if a person knows how to go on and deal with new situations in the light of it.'[44]

The following principles[45] could be chosen as a basis for a unit on water supply.

1. The supply of water is associated with the natural hydrological cycle.
2. Essential to life, water supply has from time immemorial been a critical factor in the siting of settlements.
3. Water supplies do not necessarily occur where they are most needed.
4. The growth of population and large urban complexes has increased the need for extra-local water resources.
5. Technological and economic factors strongly influence the provision of water supplies in a situation of growing industrial and domestic demand.
6. Various hazards may constrain the provision of a reliable water supply, including environmental (drought), economic (cost escalation) and political (border disputes).
7. While on the face of it water supply is an inexhaustible resource, in practice cost factors make it a scarce resource.
8. Water supplies are prone to pollution, and polluted supplies constitute a health hazard.

9. Water supply can be viewed as an extractive industry, affecting amenity, particularly in rural areas.
10. In some areas water supply is one of a number of competing land uses, with consequent conflicts of interest.

While at first sight these generalisations may seem to state the obvious, they do provide a check-list of worthwhile objectives which helps select significant content, and inhibits the choice of the trivial or peripheral.

Level B: Concepts

In each of the above statements concepts can be identified. In the last statement, for example, apart from 'water supply' itself, 'competing land uses' and 'conflicts of interest' are manifestly important concepts. Yet these are highly abstract. How do they relate to such terms as 'river' or 'reservoir' which must also be classified as concepts? A breakdown of the general term 'concept' is needed, if only to draw attention to some entrenched differences of usage.[46]

Two dimensions are explored: the abstract-concrete and the technical-vernacular, to give a four-fold classification (Table 3.1).

Table 3.1

Dimension 1	*Dimension 2*	
	Technical	Vernacular
Abstract	B1	B2
Concrete	B3	B4

The *abstract-concrete* dimension has important connotations in relation to the development of children's thinking (pages 136–40), but is introduced here to distinguish those phenomena which belong to the world of reasoning from those which belong to the world of direct experience. The *technical-vernacular* can be regarded as synonymous with the *non-spontaneous—spontaneous* concepts distinction of Piaget, and the *scientific-everyday (or vernacular)* concepts of Vygotsky.[47] The first group (technical/scientific) covers those concepts decisively influenced by instruction; the second (vernacular/spontaneous) those concepts likely to be developed without systematic instruction. The distinction is not a black and white one; the term 'market', for example, can rank as a concrete concept in the vernacular sense, whereas its technical use in economics is abstract.

Pursuing the water supply illustration, the following is one possible exemplification of the four types of concepts:

Level B1: Abstract technical concepts
    Physical concepts
    eg the hydrological cycle (and its breakdown)
    Change through time
    sequent occupance, technological change
    Distribution and access
    friction of distance, cost distance
    Economic concepts
    eg demand/supply, competition (for land)
    Resource
    eg resource management (link with decision making)
    Amenity
    pollution and conservation
    Hazards
    environmental, economic, political.

The connection between abstract technical concepts (B1) and principles (A) is close. Abstract technical concepts combine with each other and with more concrete concepts to form principles. These abstract technical concepts and/or principles provide about the right level of generality at which to state objectives, for at this level the objectives do not over-proliferate; nor, on the other hand, are they too vague.

Level B2: Abstract vernacular concepts Levels A and B1 provide some but not all the checks needed to ensure that the objectives selected are worthwhile. Abstract vernacular concepts have been referred to as *key concepts* on both sides of the Atlantic.[48] Examples of them can be found in the Schools Council Project *History, Geography and Social Science, 8–13* as shown below. Their relevance to the water supply topic is indicated in brackets.

SCHOOLS COUNCIL PROJECT
Key Concepts
1. *Communication* (Questions of distance and access)
2. *Power* (Who is the arbiter of choice of dam sites, for example?)
3. *Values and beliefs* (Attitudes of people affected by such choice)
4. *Conflict/consensus* (Between groups engaged in the issue of site choice)
5. *Continuity/change* (Growth in demand for water, technological change)
6. *Similarity/difference* (Contrasts in time and space)
7. *Causes and consequences* (Demand for water supply, environmental factors in choice of supply area).[49]

These concepts are less directly helpful in the detailed structuring process, as they overlap considerably.[50] They are essentially transdisciplinary, and will figure in virtually all social science schemes. The extent to which the geography teacher will take them into account will reflect how strongly he frames his own subject area. Some might argue that they are 'not really geography'. It is this kind of viewpoint, however, that has led to the blandness and dehumanised nature of so many geography syllabuses. Without such criteria of choice, the selection of content may become too narrowly subject-centred. They bring into focus the notion that geography is part of the social science complex (though it is not contended that the subject belongs to this alone), and should be issue-based and problem-orientated. They are, therefore, arbiters of 'worthwhileness', and can be seen as some of the 'uniting concepts' of human experience, with a universality which gives them a 'central importance' in social education.[51]

Level B3: Concrete technical concepts In the water supply example, the following would represent concepts of this type:

Spring/well/dam/reservoir
Porous rock/aquifer/ground water
Pipeline/aqueduct/purification plant
Gradient/'head' of water/regulation of flow.

It is probable that many children will pick up some of these concepts without systematic instruction which would, by definition, put them in the 'vernacular' category. It would, however, be advisable for the teacher not to make such assumptions, but to include them formally in the course unit. Even then, care must be taken to see that these concepts are not acquired purely at the level of verbal definition; indeed, this cannot be counted as concept acquisition.

Level B4: Concrete vernacular concepts These would include, for example, rain, cloud, river, lake, hill, upland, rock, soil, sea, town, sewage, health, sanitation and so on. We would probably, though perhaps perilously, assume that children, by the secondary stage at least, had acquired such concepts in the normal course of events.

The concrete concepts have a distinctive role to fulfil in structuring the curriculum. They are the raw material for the more composite concepts and principles at levels A and B1/2. In return, these more general levels help to make explicit the relationships between the concrete concepts, as in the case of the hydrological cycle.

Level C: Exemplars

The term 'exemplar' is chosen in preference to 'fact' (a) because facts have a strongly verbal connotation, and we should be thinking in terms of more than just verbal data, (b) because 'fact' can be taken to include 'concrete concept'; and (c) because the term 'fact' has in geography acquired a rather soured image. This is a pity, for geographical facts should be seen as fascinating. Properly selected, they are components of each child's cultural heritage. It is *they* which add the reality, flavour, interest and vigour to lessons, at the same time as the concepts and principles are providing, it is hoped, skeletal structure and the prospect of intellectual rigour.

The exemplars should, therefore, be treated as resources—presented not only as verbal data, but also in photographic, cartographic, diagrammatic, tabular and numerical forms.

Each 'level of generality' has thus a distinctive role to play in the 'orchestration of the curriculum'.[52] They provide for the teacher a conceptual framework which, together with a consideration of the different ability levels to be assessed, gives a firm foundation for the selection of the content, materials and learning activities which make up the curriculum unit (see pages 265 and 267–8).

As has already been mentioned (page 37), the use of the two dimensions of 'abilities' and 'principles, concepts and exemplars' provides guidelines for the initial structuring of content. Consideration of these dimensions alone, however, could lead to an intellectualising of the curriculum which does not match up to our previously accepted aims. It is vital, in addition, to regard the development of attitudes and values as an objective of fundamental importance. This 'third dimension' will obviously have further consequences for the selection of content.

Geography as a subject stands squarely at a bridging point between these intellectual and social dimensions, not only as all subjects do, but also because so much of its substance derives from the social and environmental contexts in which man is placed.

Priority readings

1. WHEELER, D. K. *Curriculum Process* (University of London Press Unibooks), Chapter 2, pp. 31–4, and Chapter 5, pp. 99–128.
2. AUSUBEL, D. P. & ROBINSON, F. G. *School Learning* (Holt, Rinehart and Winston), Chapter 3, pp. 50–75.

3. GAGNÉ, R. M. *The Conditions of Learning* (Holt, Rinehart and Winston), Chapter 2, pp. 31–61.
4. BENNETTS, T. 'Objectives for the teacher' in GRAVES, N. J. (ed.) *New Movements in the Study and Teaching of Geography* (Temple Smith,) pp. 42–54.
5. BENNETTS, T. 'Objectives' in WALFORD, R. (ed.) *New Directions in Geography Teaching* (Longman), pp. 152–74.
6. SOCKETT, H. *Designing the Curriculum* (Open Books, London), Chapter 3, pp. 37–59.

Questions for investigation and discussion

1. Refer to the following two statements:
   A. 'Measurability implies accountability'. Teachers should 'be judged on their ability to bring about desirable changes in learners'.[53]
   B. 'I am committed to the point of view that those who discourage educators from precisely explicating their instructional objectives are often permitting, if not promoting, the same kind of unclear thinking that has led in part to the generally abysmal quality of instruction in this country' [USA][54]
   (a) Discuss the implications of these statements in the British context, bearing in mind previous experience of making teachers accountable for their results.
   (b) If you agree with the above critique, how would you argue that the objectives approach might lead to improvement?
2. Refer to the following two quotations, and quotation B above:
   A 'What I am trying to suggest here is that, when you are formulating your objectives, it is very important that you have clearly in your mind your conception of the learning process and the process of education . . . this conception [includes] the notion that the learner is active, that he is looking at the world, and is trying to make something out of it. We are trying to guide him in his continued activity rather than trying to close the world for him by giving him all the answers.'[55]
   B 'To isolate the facts from the theoretical framework within which these are to be identified *as facts* is to make of them a set of noises, which might be repeated upon a given signal but which are removed from the possibility of intelligent grasp or comprehension. Such "logical atomism" misses the important point that for something to be recognised as a fact requires some comprehension of the concepts employed and thus of the conceptual framework within which the concepts operate.'[56]

Identify in each case the quotation which reflects (i) an unfavourable, (ii) a favourable, (iii) a qualified view of the stating of objectives in operational terms. Discuss the pros and cons of the arguments.

3. The following are questions paraphrased from 'O' level geography papers.

   A 'Study the 1″ OS map extract and in your answer book draw a sketch map on half the scale of the map extract to show the main features of the relief and drainage of the area.'

   B '(i) Name five major coalfields in Britain
   (ii) Using these as examples, explain what is meant by an exposed coalfield, open-cast mining, submarine mining.
   (iii) Explain the influence two of the coalfields mentioned in (i) have had on industrial development in their particular areas.'

   C 'The two main problems facing the people of the Indian sub-continent are the unreliability of the monsoon rains and soaring population growth.' Discuss.

   (a) Analyse carefully the content of these questions and identify those which are stated in terms consistent with an operational objectives approach. For those which are not, point out the words and phrases which exclude them from being so considered.

   (b) Try also to identify the main category or sub-category of Bloom's scheme into which each of the questions or sub-questions fits. What evidence would you be looking for in the answers to these questions to suggest they were genuinely in particular ability categories?

4. Refer to the section of the chapter (pages 37–42) which illustrates through the example of water supply the use of principles, concepts and exemplars for structuring curriculum units.

   (a) With the help of this section, and the Bennetts articles (Priority readings nos. 4 and 5) choose a different topic from water supply and work out a similar structure.

   (b) Compare notes with your colleagues.

   (c) Outline any limitations you see in this method.

References

1. *Report of the Committee of Council on Education* (1871–2) 'New Code' (1872) (HMSO, London), lxxxiii.
2. UTTLEY, M. (1933) 'A provisional formulation of attainments in geography for the elementary school' in WHIPPLE, G. M. (ed.) *The Teaching of Geography* Thirty-second Yearbook of the National Society for the Study of Education (University of Chicago Press), 247.
3. *Ibid*, 253.
4. NEISWORTH, P., et al. (1969) *Student Motivation and Classroom Management: a Behavioristic Approach* (Behavior Technics, Inc., Lemont, Pennsylvania), 5.
5. MAGER, R. F. (1962) *Preparing Instructional Objectives* (Fearon Publishers, Belmont, California), 10–12.

6. CLEGG, A. A. (1970) 'Developing and using behavioural objectives' in BACON, P. (ed.) (1970) *Focus on Geography: Key Concepts and Teaching Strategies* (National Council for Social Studies, Washington), 292 and 294.
7. JAMES, C. (1968) *Young Lives at Stake* (Collins, London), 88.
8. SOCKETT, H. (1973) 'Behavioural objectives' *London Educational Review*, **2**, 43.
9. EISNER, E. W. (1969) 'Instructional and expressive objectives' in POPHAM, W. J. et al. (eds.) *Instructional Objectives* (AERA Monograph Series on Curriculum Evaluation, Rand McNally & Co., Chicago), 1–31. See also ORMELL, C. P. (1974) 'Bloom's taxonomy and the objectives of education' *Educational Research*, **17**, 3 and 6.
10. EISNER, E. W. (1969) *op. cit.*, 13–14.
11. POPHAM, W. J. (1968) 'Probing the validity of arguments against behavioural goals' in STONES, E. & ANDERSON, D. (1972) *Educational Objectives and the Teaching of Educational Psychology* (Methuen, London), 229–30.
12. TYLER, R. W. (1964) 'Some persistent questions in the defining of objectives' *Ibid*, 118.
13. KRATWOHL, D. R. (1965) 'Stating objectives appropriately for program, for curriculum, and for instructional materials development' in KAPFER, M. B. (ed.) (1971) *Behavioral Objectives in Curriculum Development* (Educational Technology Publications, Englewood Cliffs, N.J.), 42–5.
14. See WHITFIELD, R. (1972) 'Curriculum objectives, examinations and curriculum change' *Cambridge Journal of Education*, **2**, 80.
15. HIRST, P. H. (1974) *Knowledge and the Curriculum* (Routledge & Kegan Paul, London), 4.
16. *Ibid*, 28.
17. See SKILBECK, M. (1971) 'Preparing curriculum objectives' *The Vocational Aspect of Education*, 2–3.
18. BLOOM, B. S. (ed.) (1956) *Taxonomy of Educational Objectives: Handbook 1: Cognitive Domain* (Longman, London, 1972 edition), 201–7.
19. COX, B. (1966) 'Test items in geography for a taxonomy of educational objectives' in BIDDLE, D. S. (ed.) *Readings in Geographical Education* (Australian Geography Teachers' Association, Whitcombe & Tombs, Sydney), 249–64.
20. GUNN, A. M. (1970) 'Evaluation of geographic learning in secondary schools' in KURFMAN, D. G. (ed.) *Evaluation in Geographic Education* (Fearon Publishers, Belmont, California), 41–52.
21. MONK, J. J. (1971) 'Preparing tests to measure course objectives' *Journal of Geography*, **70**, 157–61.
22. SENATHIRAJAH, N. & WEISS, J. (1971) *Evaluation in Geography* (Curriculum Studies/10, Ontario Institute for Studies in Education, Toronto), 13–17.
23. HIRST, P. H. (1974), *op. cit.*, 18.
24. BLOOM, B. S. (ed.) (1956), *op. cit.*, 15–16.
25. *Ibid*, 16.
26. KROPP, R. P. et al. (1966) *The Construction and Validation of Tests of the Cognitive Processes as Described in the Taxonomy of Educational Objectives* (Department of Educational Research and Testing and Institute of Human Learning, Florida State University, Tallahassee), 16.
27. SANDERS, N. M. (1968) *Classroom Questions: What Kinds?* (Harper & Row, New York), 3.
28. BLOOM, B. S. (ed.) (1956), *op. cit.*, 29.
29. HIRST, P. H. (1968) 'The contribution of philosophy to the study of the curriculum' in KERR, J. F. (ed.) *Changing the Curriculum* (University of London Press), 44–9.
30. SOCKETT, H. (1971) 'Bloom's Taxonomy: a philosophic critique' (1) *Cambridge Journal of Education*, **1**, 16–25.

31. PRING, R. (1971) 'Bloom's Taxonomy: a philosophic critique' (2) *Cambridge Journal of Education*, **2**, 83–91.
32. HIRST, P. H. (1968), *op. cit.*, 45–6.
33. See BLOOM, B. S. (ed.) (1956), *op. cit.*, 27.
34. AUSUBEL, D. P. & ROBINSON, F. G. (1969) *School Learning: an Introduction to Educational Psychology* (Holt, Rinehart & Winston, New York), 72–4.
35. GAGNÉ, R. M. (1965) *The Conditions of Learning* (Holt, Rinehart & Winston, New York), 31–61.
36. AUSUBEL, D. P. & ROBINSON, F. G. (1969), *op. cit.*, 64.
37. GAGNÉ, R. M. (1965), *op. cit.*, 57.
38. See WHITE, J. P. (1973) *Towards a Compulsory Curriculum* (Routledge & Kegan Paul, London), 83.
39. KRATWOHL, D. R., *et al.* (1964) *Taxonomy of Educational Objectives: Handbook II: Affective Domain* (Longman, London, 1971 edition), 176–85.
40. CARSWELL, R. J. B. (1970), 'Evaluation of affective learning in geographical education' in KURFMAN, D. G. (ed.) *op. cit.*, 113–15. See also SENATHIRAJAH, N. & WEISS, J. (1971), *op. cit.*, 17–19; and STYLES, E. (1972) 'Measurement of affective educational objectives in geography' in BIDDLE, D. S. & DEER, C. E. (1973) *Readings in Geographical Education*, Vol. 2, 1966–1972. (Australian Geography Teachers' Association, Whitcombe and Tombs, Sydney), 412–17.
41. Quoted by CARSWELL, R. J. B. (1970), *op. cit.*, 107.
42. UTTLEY, M. (1933), *op. cit.*, 253–4.
43. BLYTH, W. A. L., *et al.* (1972) *History, Geography and Social Science*, 8–13: *An Interim Statement* (Schools Council Publications, London), 5–6.
44. PETERS, R. S. (1967) 'What is an educational process?' in PETERS, R. S. (ed.) *The Concept of Education* (Routledge & Kegan Paul, London), 18–19.
45. See also BENNETTS, T. (1972) 'Objectives for the teacher' in GRAVES, N. J. (ed.) *New Movements in the Study and Teaching of Geography* (Temple Smith, London), 52–3.
46. See HUDMAN, L. E. (1972) 'Geographic concepts: a need to be explicit' *Journal of Geography*, **71**, 525.
47. See VYGOTSKY, L. S. (1934) *Thought and Language* (MIT Press, Cambridge, Mass., 1962), 84–5.
48. See TABA, H., DURKIN, M., FRAENKEL, J. R. & McNAUGHTON, A. (1971) *A Teacher's Handbook to Elementary Social Studies* (Addison-Wesley, Reading, Mass.), 12 and MORRISSETT, I. (1967) 'The new social science curricula' in MORRISSETT, I. (ed.) *Concepts and Structure in the New Social Science Curricula* (Holt, Rinehart & Winston, New York), 3.
49. BLYTH, W. A. L. *et al.* (1976) *Curriculum Planning in History, Geography and Social Science* (W. Collins, Glasgow, for the Schools Council) 94.
50. KINGDOM, E. F. (1975) *Key Concepts and Curriculum Content* (Schools Council Project 'History, Geography and Social Sciences 8–13' Occasional Paper No. 5), 29 pp. This contains an incisive critique of the 'key concepts' notion.
51. See BRIDGES, D. (1975) 'Understanding others' societies' in ELLIOTT, J. & PRING, R. (eds.) (1975) *Social Education and Social Understanding* (University of London Press), 69.
52. See SENESH, L. (1967) 'Organizing a curriculum around social science concepts' in MORRISSETT, I. (ed.), *op. cit.*, 24.
53. POPHAM, W. J. (1968), *op. cit.*, 234.
54. *Ibid*, 229.
55. TYLER, R. W. (1964), *op. cit.*, 186.
56. PRING, R. (1971), *op. cit.*, 89–90.

Section 2 Geography in the School Curriculum

4 The Structure of Knowledge

A basis for curriculum planning

The standard combination of subjects in the secondary school timetable seems part of an established order of things. Few of the basic subjects in the curriculum have been introduced recently. Most date back to the considerable widening of the curriculum base which took place in the second half of the nineteenth century. The subjects represent selections from the spectrum of knowledge which, if shown to be rationally based and well balanced, would be justifiably regarded in general, though not in detail, as valid. Whether to select physics or biochemistry might be negotiable, but no argument could be brooked over the status of the natural science component in general.

This kind of standpoint has been radically challenged in recent years. The idea that the nature of knowledge is absolute has been brought into question. It is argued that it is a relative, socially determined phenomenon.[1,2] Different types of knowledge are given a different prestige. Translated to the school situation, this means that some school subjects have traditionally had a higher status than others, such as Latin than geography and geography than woodwork. School-type knowledge is similarly seen as of higher status than common-sense knowledge. Beethoven is regarded as better than, rather than different from, the Beatles. The selection of what goes into the traditional curriculum derives largely from a high-culture view of knowledge, that held by the decision-makers who control what is made accessible to different types of children through the curriculum. During the nineteenth century, for example, different curricula were in operation in elementary and secondary schools, the two systems at the time being almost completely separate. Equally today, different curricula are regarded as necessary for high ability and low ability children.

The sociologists of knowledge[3] who have advanced these ideas contend that the arbiters of what counts as knowledge should be the recipients rather than the providers. Curricula should be much more individually determined. Countering this view, Pring agrees that 'the way we come to organise, select, value and transmit our knowledge is *to some extent* explicable by reference to those who do the organising, selecting, valuing and transmitting.[4] While it is right that the relationship should be kept under surveillance, it is essential to keep separate two sets of questions. The first set comprises those questions about the rationale of the introduction and the way in which various components of knowledge are used in the curriculum, which do require this type of scrutiny. The second comprises those questions about what counts as knowledge, what constitute valid judgements and criteria for truth. These are more fundamental questions.

The position taken here is that the structure of knowledge *should* be regarded as a key variable in curriculum planning. This is important in both cross-disciplinary terms (in that there is need in the overall curriculum for a balanced selection from the domain of knowledge) and in intra-disciplinary terms, in that the use of the underlying conceptual frameworks of disciplines is equally needed in detailed course planning within subjects. While the balance of the selection, the details, the uses to which the choice is put, must to some extent be arbitrary and relative the underlying principle is inviolate.

This stipulation may be justified from two broad points of view.

1. *The philosophical*

In pursuit of the aim of autonomy, guidance can be obtained from the classical concept of a 'liberal education'. This means, to use Hirst's description, 'freeing the mind to function according to its true nature, freeing reason from error and illusion and freeing man's conduct from wrong'.[5] This type of freedom can only ensue from the development of understanding which in turn requires the acquisition of knowledge; knowledge, of course, being defined not as a collection of facts, but as the complex ways of understanding experience through the development of various skills. The curriculum thus needs to be founded on the structure of knowledge as a prerequisite for achieving its primary aim, the development of autonomy.

2. *The psychological*

A strong advocate of the need to pursue 'structure' as a curricular objective[6] is Bruner. Apart from the pleasure it may give, he sees as a central goal of learning the promotion of transfer of training. Various skills, principles and attitudes are acquired in school but, to be worthwhile, must later be applicable and of service in life situations. The training must therefore be transferable. In essence, this 'consists of learning initially . . . a general idea, which can then be used as a basis for recognising subsequent problems as special cases of the idea originally mastered.'[7] Such continuity of learning thus requires mastery of the structure or fundamental ideas behind the subject matter. These fundamental ideas relate to the generalisations, principles and concepts, and their interconnections, of the disciplines. Teaching for structure is seen as having advantages for motivation, in that a subject cannot be exciting if its principles are not grasped, and particularly for cognition, since grasp of the structure makes the detail more easily remembered, a point reinforcing those of Ausubel and Gagné (page 33). Unconnected facts alone have 'a pitiably short half-life in memory.'[8]

The forms and fields of knowledge

The knowledge domain has been broken down into what have been claimed as distinctive, non-arbitrary 'forms'[9], 'realms of meaning'[10] or disciplines. Hirst's distinction between 'forms' and 'fields' of knowledge has been a particularly strong influence on curriculum thinking since it appeared in 1965. Hirst stressed that the disciplines are not 'collections of information', but 'the complex ways of understanding experience which man has achieved which are publicly specifiable and which are gained through learning'.[11]

The disciplines were regarded as *forms of knowledge*, each having distinctive. (a) *central concepts* peculiar to the form, such as gravity in physics, number in mathematics, and sin in religion; (b) *logical structures*, involving a meaningful relationship between the elements; (c) expressions or statements testable against experience according to *criteria of truth* particular to the form; (d) *techniques and skills* for exploring and testing experience. Sub-divisible, the forms of knowledge according to this scheme were *mathematics*; *physical sciences*; *human sciences*; *history*; *religion*; *literature/fine arts*; and *philosophy*.[12]

In contrast, the *fields of knowledge* were seen as lacking such tight structures but held together by their subject matter. They relied not on indigenous but on derived concepts, logical structures and methodologies, taken from the forms of knowledge. Such 'fields' could be constructed *ad hoc* to serve particular theoretical or practical interests. Geography, for example, described in an over-simplified way by Hirst as 'a study of man in relation to his environment', was seen as a theoretical 'field', and engineering as a practical one.[13]

Hirst's thesis occasioned great interest and also provoked criticism. The scheme was taken to task for implicitly justifying traditional subject divisions in the timetable, an interpretation which Hirst had openly repudiated. 'School subjects in the disciplines as we at present have them are in no way sacrosanct either on logical or psychological grounds.'[14] At the same time, a curriculum scheme based on the 'forms' was preferred by Hirst to one based on the 'fields'. Though the latter could be 'valuable and useful in many ways, and perhaps essential', it would be unlikely to lead to a liberal education unless every attempt was made to achieve a fuller grasp of the disciplines. It also demanded the highest degree of skill from the teacher.[15]

Whether Hirst intended it or not, a value-laden distinction *was* read into the scheme, the 'forms' being regarded as somehow more pure and true than the 'fields'. The primacy Hirst attached to the forms was later made quite explicit. The need for the study of inter-form relations (ie 'fields') was granted important but secondary status.[16]

Further reservations have been expressed about the over-neat compartmentalisation of the forms of knowledge and the concepts they embody. While Hirst accepted that the criteria for recognising forms of knowledge were 'neither clear enough nor sufficient for demarcating the whole world of modern knowledge as we know it',[17] it can still be argued, for example, that the distinction between different types of concepts was not sufficiently stressed in the forms of knowledge thesis.[18] While it is relatively easy not to confuse, say, 'sin' and 'neutron', belonging to religious knowledge and physics respectively, the problem is infinitely greater with more general concepts. Concepts which embody the substance of a tightly knit and highly structured discipline, such as 'neutron' in physics, are more likely to find a natural home in a particular discipline area. Others, such as 'cause' and 'effect' are essentially transdisciplinary. There is a clear distinction between 'technical' and 'vernacular' concepts (see page 39) in this context.

Particular confusion is apparent in the area of history and social sciences. History, for example, was classified in Hirst's 1965 scheme as a distinctive 'form' of knowledge. Yet it is, in fact, as difficult in history to identify discrete concepts which are not reducible to the human sciences, such as economics, psychology, sociology or political science, as it is in geography, classified at that time as a 'field' and thus set apart from history.

Since 1965, Hirst has reformulated his thesis more than once. The 'forms' of knowledge were categorised in a 1970 statement as *formal logic and mathematics, physical sciences, 'our awareness and understanding of our own and other people's minds', moral judgement and awareness, aesthetic experience, religious experience* and *philosophical experience.*[19]

In a further exposition of 1974, 'revisiting' the forms of knowledge, there is a distinct shift from equating the 'forms of knowledge' with 'disciplines'. All that are now seen as fundamentally distinctive and irreducible are the forms of knowledge themselves. University disciplines and school subjects, though still related to the forms of knowledge, serve different functions. The term 'discipline' is described as 'rather emotive'. While disciplines might well have tight conceptual structures characteristic of forms or sub-sections of forms of knowledge, the term can be used to cover a broader meaning, their concerns being more wide-ranging and extending into the practical world. School subjects can be viewed as curriculum units constructed purely for educational purposes, embodying no ultimate truth outside themselves, in the way claimed for the forms of knowledge. Most disciplines and even more school subjects are here regarded as being concerned with concepts and truths of different kinds, thus giving them an inter-form character.[20]

Nothing is said of the 'fields of knowledge', though in a separate paper of this period Hirst refers to subjects such as English, geography and religious knowledge as having a 'multi-form' character.[21] More specifically, he has for some time regarded it as inadmissable to consider history and the social sciences as forms of knowledge as such, in that they are both concerned with two contrasted groups of truths: those of the physical world, as in their interest in empirical observation and experiment; and those of a personal kind, exemplified by their concern for explanations of human behaviour in terms of intention, will, hopes and beliefs. Each of these sets of truths is different from and not reducible to the other.[22]

Hirst accepts that the forms of knowledge share broad concepts such as 'space' and 'time', but does not regard this as contradicting his basic thesis, because such concepts, when applied to a particular form of knowledge, are given a character as it were *idiomatic* of that form.[23] And while each form will share concepts with other forms, it will also have its own unique concepts. The network of structural relationships will also in major respects differ between forms, being tighter in those related to mathematical or scientific knowledge than in those concerned with states of mind and moral judgements. Neither is the presence of 'common-sense' or 'vernacular' knowledge seen as countermanding the general thesis, for it is 'simply that collection of elementary knowledge, or what is claimed to be such, from the different forms, which is largely taken for granted in a given society.'[24] It is not therefore regarded as logically distinct from more advanced areas of knowledge.

While effectively dissociating the forms of knowledge from the permutation of such forms in school subjects, Hirst still regards the disciplines as of major importance, prerequisite to a liberal education. But liberal education is qualified as not a total education, for it explicitly excludes objectives that the school should also subscribe to, such as matters of social concern.[25]

The position of geography

As the nature of geography itself is a major factor in deciding what goes into the geography curriculum, a separate chapter is reserved for discussion of the topic. Attention is here restricted to responses from geographers provoked by Hirst's 1965 categorisation of geography as a 'field of knowledge'.

Thus Graves and Simons agreed that geography, depending as it does on a wide variety of concepts, language and methodology from other disciplines, fell at all of Hirst's fences. They were 'happy to view' the subject as a 'field' rather than a 'form' of knowledge.[26] Initiation into many, if not all, forms of knowledge was regarded as essential to the geographer. Implications for the curriculum were noted in the need to broaden the subject's already wide bounds, for instance into the field of the social sciences.[27]

In a later discussion, Graves and Moore confirmed that geographical concepts such as 'moraine' and 'conurbation' are not peculiar to the subject. Neither are geographical tests for truth different from those of the social sciences or physical sciences.[28] The fact that geography falls within at least three forms of knowledge would suggest that in the school curriculum different parts of the subject need different patterns of learning from others. Hence physical geography would gain from a more scientific approach, the human aspects would benefit from the introduction of a social science methodology, and so on.[29]

In contrast, Blachford claimed that geography *is* a form of knowledge, arguing that it has discrete concepts (such as 'location', 'region' and 'spatial interaction'), a distinctive logical structure in its 'spatial framework', distinctive tests for truth or significance (the geographer 'viewing experience as if through maps'); and a distinctive 'mode of enquiry' (in this case seemingly general scientific enquiry applied in a particular way).[30] Blachford denied Hirst's contention that geography is distinguished rather by its subject matter, and took the view that the man/environment theme is common to many other disciplines.[31]

In a theoretical sense, Hirst's more recent expositions of the forms of knowledge thesis make these responses outmoded. But in practice geography *can* only claim a place in the curriculum if it has something distinctive to offer. And the fact is that the geographer, historian and social scientist *do* produce differing course units even on a similar topic (see pages 97–9 and 122–3).

The distinctiveness of geography does not lie in its concepts, as Graves, Simons and Moore have shown. Most of the concepts stressed in geography are important elsewhere. A number of disciplines are interested in 'space', for example, with geometry representing the fundamental science of spatial patterns. The argument for the distinctiveness of geography is a composite one. The first truly discrete element is the *manner* in which concepts are used (see page 51, reference 23).[32] This is linked with the *scale* at which spatial patterns are studied, what Harvey has called the 'resolution level'.[33] Geography's spatial resolution level is essentially a regional one, though varying in its scope between the local and the global. It is in the middle of an extreme range covering the study of atoms on the one hand, and of the universe on the other. Another distinctive quality is the unique interest geography takes in space as *man's place*, connected with its focus on the inter-relationships between *physical and social* environments.[34] Finally, the criterion of *mappability* (pages 57 and 79–80) is one that is central to the subject.[35]

Distinctiveness accrues, therefore, from a whole *assemblage* of criteria. The significance and vitality of geography have been attributed to its 'vital regard for the aggregate',[36] and its failure to fit neatly into conventional classifications of knowledge has been presented as a positive quality.[37] It would indeed be surprising if the separate criteria of distinctiveness worked neatly parallel to each other, the concepts, structures, criteria for truth and methodologies not only having barriers between disciplines, but barriers at the same points. The complex nature of geography is oversimplified in such tidy definitions as 'the study of man in relationship to his environment', for each represents only one of geography's traditions.

Priority readings

1. HIRST, P. H. 'Liberal education and the nature of knowledge' in PETERS, R. S. (ed.) *The Philosophy of Education* (Oxford University Press), pp. 87–111.
2. HIRST, P. H. *Knowledge and the Curriculum* (Routledge & Kegan Paul), pp. 84–100.
3. BRUNER, J. S. *The Process of Education* (Vintage Books, Random House, New York), Chapters 1 and 2, pp. 1–32.
4. WHITE, J. P. *Towards a Compulsory Curriculum* (Routledge & Kegan Paul), pp. 73–87.
5. GRAVES, N. J. & SIMONS, M. 'Geography and philosophy' in BALE, J., GRAVES, N. J. & WALFORD, R. (eds.) *Perspectives in Geographical Education*, (Oliver & Boyd), pp. 27–34.
6. GRAVES, N. J. & MOORE, T. 'The nature of geographical knowledge' in GRAVES, N. J. (ed.) *New Movements in the Study and Teaching of Geography* (Temple Smith), pp. 17–28.
7. PRING, R. *Knowledge and Schooling* (Open Books, London), Chapter 2, pp. 25–46.

Questions for investigation and discussion

1. Refer to the following quotations:
    A 'The world presents to us an undifferentiated mass of data which only the mind can organise into manageable proportions through a series of models and conventions which make thinking possible, let alone fruitful. Subject areas are made up of these models and conventions. . . .'[38]
    B 'The most impressive claim the academic disciplines have upon the educator is that they are the outcome of learning that has actually been successful. A discipline is a field of enquiry in which learning has been achieved in an unusually productive way. . . . Each discipline has distinctive concepts which set it off from other

disciplines. In each case these characteristic ways of enquiry have proved their power to increase knowledge and to economise learning effort. . . .'[39]

c. 'If the content fields are viewed not as treasures of knowledge to be transferred but as understanding a limited number of basic ideas, the problem of scope [ie coverage of content] acquires different meaning. . . . Only after the basic ideas are determined does the question emerge as to what specific facts are necessary to accomplish this task more effectively. . . . By reducing the load of obscuring detail, attention can be devoted to developing a clear and precise understanding of ideas.'[40]

   (a) Discuss the extent to which the views contained in the above quotations reinforce those of Hirst.
   (b) Examine their significance for teaching, and the extent to which they constitute forceful arguments for retaining the subject disciplines in the curriculum.

2. Having read the two Hirst references (Priority readings 1 and 2), and the section from White quoted in Priority reading 4:
   (a) discuss the validity of White's critique of the first of the Hirst statements, and the extent to which it has been met in the second;
   (b) see if you can identify a different ethos in the writing of Hirst and White and, if so, indicate which you find the more congenial, and why.

3. On the basis of your reading of the text and Priority readings Nos. 5 and 6, and of your own knowledge and interest in the subject, illustrate by detailed geographical examples the extent to which the subject, if at all, fails to meet Hirst's four criteria for distinctiveness. To what extent are these important in school terms?

References

1. See, for example, YOUNG, M. F. D. (1971) 'An approach to the study of curricula as socially organized knowledge' in YOUNG, M. F. D. (ed.) *Knowledge and Control: New Directions for the Sociology of Education* (Collier-Macmillan, London), 19–46.
2. For a geographical application, see HUCKLE, J. (1975) 'Geography—a vested interest in education' *Classroom Geographer*, February 1975, 6–10.
3. See YOUNG, M. F. D. (1971), *op. cit.*, 1–17; and GORBUTT, D. (1972) 'The new sociology of education' *Education for Teaching*, **89**, 3–11.
4. PRING, R. (1972) 'Knowledge out of control' *Education for Teaching*, **89**, 28.
5. HIRST, P. H. (1965) 'Liberal education and the nature of knowledge' in PETERS, R. S. (ed.) (1973) *The philosophy of education* (Oxford University Press), 96.
6. See HIRST, P. H. (1968) 'The contribution of philosophy to the study of the curriculum' in KERR, J. F. (ed.) (1968) *Changing the Curriculum* (University of London Press), 60–1.

7. BRUNER, J. S. (1960) *The Process of Education* (Vintage Books, Random House, New York), 17.
8. *Ibid*, 31.
9. HIRST, P. H. (1965), *op. cit.*, 87–111.
10. PHENIX, P. (1964) *Realms of Meaning* (McGraw Hill, New York).
11. HIRST, P. H. (1965), *op. cit.*, 95–6.
12. *Ibid*, 102–5.
13. *Ibid*, 104–5.
14. *Ibid*, 109.
15. *Ibid*, 110.
16. HIRST, P. H. (1974) 'Curriculum integration' in HIRST, P. H. (1974) *Knowledge and the Curriculum* (Routledge & Kegan Paul, London), 151.
17. HIRST, P. H. (1965), *op. cit.*, 103.
18. WHITE, J. P. (1973) *Towards a Compulsory Curriculum* (Routledge & Kegan Paul, London), 74.
19. HIRST, P. H. & PETERS, R. S. (1970) *The Logic of Education* (Routledge & Kegan Paul, London), 63–4.
20. HIRST, P. H. (1974) 'The forms of knowledge revisited' in HIRST, P. H. (1974), *op. cit.*, 97.
21. HIRST, P. H. (1974) 'Curriculum integration', *ibid*, 144.
22. HIRST, P. H. (1974) 'The forms of knowledge revisited', *ibid*, 86.
23. *Ibid*, 89–90,
24. *Ibid*, 90.
25. *Ibid*, 96–9.
26. GRAVES, N. J. & SIMONS, M. (1966) 'Geography and philosophy' in BALE, J., *et al.* (eds.) (1973) *Perspectives in Geographical Education* (Oliver & Boyd, Edinburgh), 27–34.
27. *Ibid*, 32.
28. GRAVES, N. J. & MOORE, T. (1972) 'The nature of geographical knowledge' in GRAVES, N. J. (1972) *New Movements in the Study and Teaching of Geography* (Temple Smith, London), 24.
29. *Ibid*, 27–8.
30. BLACHFORD, K. R. (1971) 'Why is geography in the curriculum?' in BIDDLE, D. S. & DEER, C. E. (1973) *Readings in Geographical Education*, Selections from Australian and New Zealand Sources, Vol. 2, 1966–1972. (Whitcombe & Tombs, Sydney, for the Australian Geography Teachers' Association), 19–23.
31. *Ibid*, 21 and 24.
32. See SIMONS, M. (1971) 'Geographical concepts and education' *Geographical Education*, **1**, 201.
33. See HARVEY, D. (1969) *Explanation in Geography* (Edward Arnold, London), 485.
34. See Australian Geography Teachers' Association (1973) 'Geography in Education' *Geographical Education*, **2**, 7.
35. See, for example, SIMONS, M. (1969) 'What are geographers doing' in BALE, J. *et al.* (eds.) (1973), *op. cit.*, 47–59; and KIRK, W. (1963) 'Problems of geography' *Geography*, **48**, 363.
36. Australian Geography Teachers' Association (1973), *op. cit.*, 8.
37. See BLACHFORD, K. R. (1973) 'Myths in geographical education' *Geographical Education*, **2**, 19.
38. BANTOCK, G. H. (1968) *Culture, Industrialisation and Education* (Routledge & Kegan Paul, London), 37.
39. PHENIX, P. (1964), *op. cit.*, 315.
40. TABA, H. (1962) *Curriculum Development: Theory and Practice* (Harcourt, Brace & World, New York), 10–11.

5 The Changing Nature of Geography

Academic geography in mid-century

A cross-section of the state of academic geography in mid-century is provided in Griffith Taylor's well-known survey.[1] The ambitious spread of interest revealed in this and other geographical publications of its time was among the factors which led David in 1956 to question the subject's pretensions as an honours degree discipline.[2] The writings and sayings of well-known geographers were reviewed in a search for distinctiveness and found wanting. David concluded that virtually all geography's substance would find a place in other university disciplines. He suggested that geography should be relegated to a subordinate 'means to an end' role in the university, subsidiary to social science and history courses, but that it should be strengthened and extended in school, where it was potentially 'stimulating and exacting and useful.'[3]

David exposed in his critique two basic definitions of geography: the man-environment definition, which he dismissed as grandiose and not distinctive of geography in particular;[4] and Hartshorne's 'areal differentiation' definition, which he regarded with more respect, but pointed out that it was not one accepted by influential members of the academic community of geographers.[5]

The demand for a neat, monistic definition, which in a sense anticipated Hirst's more penetrating overall analysis ten years later, was implicitly rejected by Pattison, who interpreted the nature of geography in terms of four continuing, complementary, but overlapping traditions.[6] These were

1. the *spatial tradition*, which reflects the geographer's concern with spatial patterns, with geometry and movement, and the special attachment to the use of maps as tools;

2. the *area studies tradition*, which reinforces the idea that the geographer is concerned with the unique character of places, embodied in the regional approach;

3. the *man-land tradition*, which is concerned with the interrelationship between man and his environment, a tradition somewhat discredited in the past because of its deterministic overtones;

4. the *earth science tradition*, which emphasises the description and explanation of the physical features of the earth's surface.

Pattison's distinctions thus highlight the diverse nature of geography. Furthermore, at any particular time they are in a state of transition and of differential emphasis. But what holds the traditions together? As has just been suggested (page 53), in part it is the *assemblage as a whole* that is distinctive. Pattison's interpretation is clearly in the nature of a redefinition rather than a radical reappraisal. During the late 1950s and early 1960s, however, a far more serious attack on established geography than David's was brewing from within.

Geography 'revived'

A number of factors led to disillusion among younger geography teachers in the university departments over this period. Edge has identified several circumstances as fostering change.[7] The first, echoing David, was discontent with the apparently low repute in which academic geography stood, and its isolation from the mainstream of scientific thought. Its links were seen as more with nineteenth-century historical than twentieth-century scientific approaches. Secondly, the long and appropriately held opposition to the deterministic environmentalism of the late nineteenth and early twentieth centuries had petered out, leaving the way open for the introduction of new scientific approaches. Thirdly, the spread of quantification provided a handy tool for new and more precise methodologies.

The term 'revolution' has been applied to the events of the 1960s, so rapid was the pace of change. It may be, however, that 'revitalisation' is more appropriate. The idea that the difference between the 'old' and the 'new' is one of degree rather than kind is now accepted by some of the 'revolutionaries'.

> During the 1960s there was a skirmish between those geographers anxious to innovate with mathematical methods and those sceptical of their utility in solving orthodox problems. Today the general acceptance of such techniques, the more complete mathematical training of a new generation, and the widespread availability of standard computers on

campus make the conflict of a decade ago seem unreal. The first few years of over-enthusiastic pressing of quantitative methods on a reluctant profession have given way to the present phase in which mathematical methods are just one of many tools for approaching geographic problems.[8]

Characteristic features of the 'new geography'

Bearing in mind that there has been a switch of emphasis rather than a change of face, the most obvious shift has perhaps been the move away from the area studies towards the spatial tradition, with a contingent stress on scientific approaches.

Idiographic and nomothetic approaches

Distinction can be made between idiographic and nomothetic approaches to the study of geographical phenomena.[9] *Idiographic* refers to the empirical study of unique, non-recurrent events, perhaps best exemplified in the area studies tradition. This is devoted to the 'real world' and accounts of different places and regions. It is concerned with the examination of a wide range of variables in single areas, as can be found in regional and case studies approaches.

The *nomothetic* approach is more scientific, engaged in the search for patterns and processes, for generalisations and laws. It is concerned with repeatable events, and involves the study of a single variable or small number of variables over a wide range of areas. It thus relates more to systematic than regional methods.

While the 'new geographers' commend the empiricist idiographic tradition for providing a 'solid backlog of knowledge to aid our interpretation of the geographical patterns of the world', they are more concerned to emphasise its dangers. 'Research can easily degenerate into a mere collection of uncodified and trivial facts, and the discipline may become fascinated by a concern for the particulars, rather than the generalities dealt with by science.'[10]

Scientific methods of explanation

These are particularly associated with the nomothetic approach. The object of explanation in science is to establish general laws explaining the behaviour of events. Two basic approaches are available: the *inductive*, starting with particular cases and moving towards universal statements; and the *deductive*, starting with a universal statement and then making statements about sets of events. The inductive approach is regarded as the weaker route to explanation.[11] In the social sciences, no more than 'empirical laws' or 'theories of the middle range',[12] which relate only to particular circumstances and which are, therefore, less 'universal' than the basic laws of the physical sciences, can be achieved.

Harvey usefully categorises six *explanatory forms* available to the geographer.[13]

1. *Cognitive description* refers to the collection, ordering and *classification* of phenomena, the last of which makes possible generalisation. A contingent question would be 'How many of the phenomena being studied can be ordered and grouped?'

2. *Morphometric analysis* is associated with the frameworks by which the geographer examines shapes and forms in space, such as patterns of settlement and the structure of networks. An accompanying question might be 'How are the phenomena organised in terms of their spatial structure and form?'

3. *Cause and effect analysis* involves the search for factors influencing simple geographical distributions. This has in the past, unfortunately, acquired the taint of determinism. The simple accompanying question is 'How were the phenomena caused?'

4. *Temporal modes* of explanation are concerned with a 'causal chain'. They are symptomatic of the fact that cause and effect involve events following each other in time. The weakest form of temporal explanation is

(a) *narrative*, of the type 'Lancashire had a damp climate and so the cotton industry developed', which wrongly implies an underlying law.

Intermediate temporal modes are

(b) the *evolutionary* or

(c) the *cyclical*, as in the case of Davisian types of explanation in geomorphology. These two forms are closely linked.

(d) The most powerful temporal mode is that based on *process*, which can be variously applied in explanation—for example, of drainage and transport networks.

In temporal modes of explanation, therefore, the question is asked 'How did the phenomena originate and develop?'

5. *Functional/ecological analysis* describes attempts to analyse phenomena in terms of the role they play within a particular organisation

(eg towns in the national economy, leading to a 'functional classification' of towns). Ecological explanation involves a study of inter-relationships, a biological concept much applied in geography which has been seen by some as a study of 'human ecology'[14] and which lies at the heart of Pattison's 'man-land tradition'. The question to be asked here is 'How do particular phenomena relate to and interact with phenomena in general?'

6. *Systems analysis* entails a step beyond functional/ecological analysis, and involves a study of the structure of the organisation within which the phenomena to be studied are placed, as a system of interlocking parts and processes. This is particularly appropriate in such a subject as geography, which normally deals with complex multivariate situations. The question to be asked is 'How are phenomena organised as a coherent system?'

A useful distinction can be made between systems analysis and *locational analysis*, which is closely associated with morphometric analysis (2). Whereas systems approaches are in essence a form of synthesis, an attempt to come to grips with the complexities of reality, locational analysis seeks to simplify reality by abstracting from its complexity a limited set of relationships.

The systems approach

A system has been defined as a set of objects, plus their attributes, *plus inter-relationships*. The 'set' is in some way organised by the inter-relationships of the units. In a systems approach the stress is on *functioning*, on process rather than on form, on dynamic rather than static aspects of reality.[15] Consequently, anything which affects the working of the system must be regarded as relevant. Closed definitions of what is and what is not geography are not compatible with the pursuit of a systems approach.

In the case of social systems, there is a further need to link *real* and *perceived* environments. We have to consider 'things' (linked by flows of matter and energy) and 'images of things' (linked by flows of information).[16] Acceptance of a systems approach thus makes it obligatory to enter the field of behavioural geography (pages 65–8).

A basic distinction between 'open systems' and 'closed systems' is made in Fig. 5.1 (page 62).

The total consists of

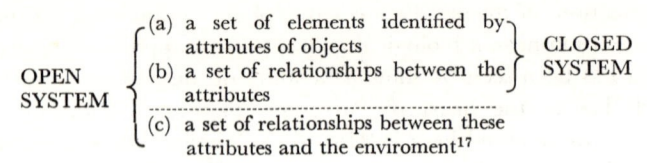

OPEN SYSTEM	(a) a set of elements identified by attributes of objects (b) a set of relationships between the attributes	CLOSED SYSTEM
	‐‐	
	(c) a set of relationships between these attributes and the enviroment[17]	

Fig. 5.1

'The environment' is therefore seen as a higher order system of which a lower order system is a part. An example of a lower order system is a farm, which, of course, is part of the higher order—environment—from the point of view of (a) the biosphere and (b) the economy.

Stoddart views the 'ecosystem' concept as bringing together 'environment, man and the plant and animal worlds within a single framework, within which the interaction between the components can be analysed.'[18] The problem in geography is that a system such as 'Britain' is too complex to be handled and, therefore, has to be broken down into simpler systems at the level of, for example, a settlement pattern or even a farm. Primitive societies are much easier to study in systems terms than 'developed' economies. Stoddart regards an ecosystems approach as one linking geography with the mainstream of scientific thought, providing a basis for interdisciplinary study, and a means of applying theory to real problems.

In this advocacy of a systems approach, Haggett stresses that '... Geographers are concerned with the structure and interaction of two major systems: the ecological system that links man and his environment, and the spatial system that links one region with another in a complex interchange of flows' [19] (Fig. 5.2).

Man-environment ecological systems { The human response (2) ← → Inter-regional stresses (4) } Region-inter-region spatial systems
↑   ↑
The environmental challenge (1) → The regional mosaic (3)

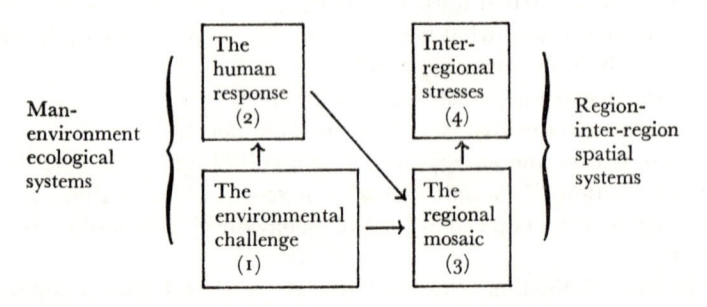

Fig. 5.2

1. The *environmental challenge* refers to the uncertain planetary environment on which human population has evolved and now lives at ever increasing densities.

2. The *human response* to environment is seen in terms of adaptation *of* and *to* the environment.

3. The *regional mosaic* represents the spatial structure of man's organisations on the earth's surface, and makes explicit how geographers divide the earth's surface into significant regional units, defined rather on an administrative basis (for which data are available) than a 'mystical' one.

4. *Inter-regional stresses* reflect the interactions between regional structure and the problems to which they give rise, providing for the 'new geography' a strong 'applied' tinge.

It is not difficult to see why many geographers who find many of the abstractions of locational analysis uncongenial, look to systems approaches and discover the more familiar territory of synthesis. Yet they should not be equated with the conventional regional synthesis, in which the stress was so often on the artefacts of the landscape. The accent of the systems approach is on physical and socio-economic environments as functioning organisms.

Models

Models provide means of dealing with the complexities of the real world by simulation, substituting for reality similar but simpler forms, eliminating inessential 'noise'. Their construction involves 'a highly *selective* attitude to information.'[20] Haggett's categorisation of models is given in Fig. 5.3.[21]

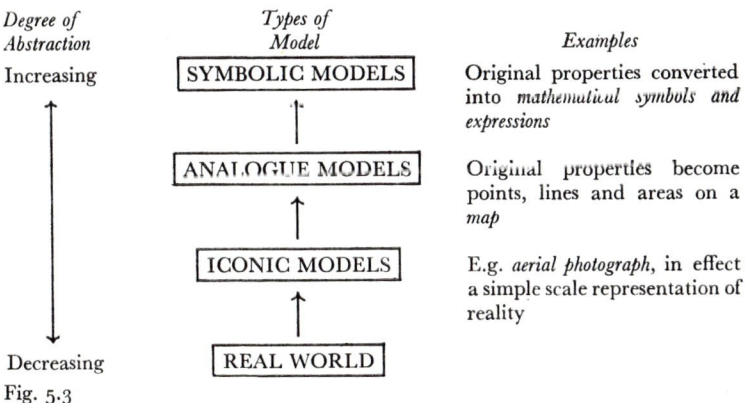

Degree of Abstraction	*Types of Model*	*Examples*
Increasing ↑	SYMBOLIC MODELS ↑	Original properties converted into *mathematical symbols and expressions*
	ANALOGUE MODELS ↑	Original properties become points, lines and areas on a map
	ICONIC MODELS ↑	E.g. *aerial photograph*, in effect a simple scale representation of reality
Decreasing ↓	REAL WORLD	

Fig. 5.3

Thus the map is of great help in functioning as a type of model selecting and simplifying significant aspects of reality, as a convenient storage device, a general description of what reality looks like, a basis for generating expectations of what will happen if we go into a certain area, and a basis for thinking about complicated relationships in patterns which may suggest generalisations.[22]

A further distinction can be made between *working models* and *abstract models*. The latter are based on theoretical assumptions being aimed primarily at the formulation of generally applicable theory, transcending reality. The former are empirical, taking reality as the point of departure (by drawing on reality for elements of the model) and as a point of destination (by comparing results with the actual state of affairs).[23]

Quantification

Another way of coping with the complexities of reality is to turn to the computer. This alone is capable of processing quickly the masses of data which many current investigations of social phenomena generate. Computer language is, of course, part of the language of mathematics and this, plus the wide variety of statistical techniques now being used by geographers, has resulted in a major shift towards quantification. It is, however, a distorted belief that the so-called 'new geography' is synonymous with quantification.

Cole has pointed out an important distinction between *mathematics* (based on inviolate laws) and *statistics* (based on mathematics but catering for exceptions).[24] Both are useful tools for the geographer. Examples of such tools include the use of sampling techniques in the collection of data, of matrices, Venn diagrams and graphs in the preparation and storage of data, and of calculating machines and computers in the processing and output of data.[25]

The basic language of spatial form is of course *geometry*. At its simplest this functions as a means of providing absolute locations for objects and events through the use of co-ordinates (eg latitude and longitude, or a grid system). But the traditional Euclidean system is not the only geometrical system that is applicable to geographical phenomena.[26]

The branch of geometry known as *topology*, sometimes referred to as 'rubber-sheet' geometry, is of great utility to geographers. Like Euclidean geometry, it is concerned with *points*, *lines* and *areas*, and with their relationships or *connectedness*; but, unlike it, NOT with distances between points, the straightness of lines or the size of areas. It is particularly useful in the study of transport networks, and is thoroughly familiar to those who have used maps of the London underground and other transport systems. On such maps, relationships and the connectedness of points are clearly revealed by excluding, at the expense of distorting shape and distance, those elements not essential for the function of the map.

Statistical techniques are inextricably linked with probability theory. Probability is seen as a particularly useful concept in geography for it is a means both of avoiding determinism of and catering for uncertainty.

> Instead of saying that actions are absolutely predictable in the sense of being dictated by pre-ordained inflexible conditions stemming from climate, terrain, heredity, or functions of the brain, we may now relax the rules and state that there are everywhere a large number of possibilities (shades of Vidal de la Blache!), uncertainties and latent opportunities. By examining large numbers of individual examples, we may seek to reduce the area of doubt surrounding the processes most likely to have been necessary and sufficient to cause the recorded outcomes. And we may evaluate the likelihood or probable frequency of particular exceptional events occurring or being repeated.[27]

Implicit in probability theory is the assumption that there is a relationship between the number of times a particular outcome of an event is recorded, and the total number of events.[28] Instead of investigating a totality, therefore, it is possible to take a sample, which must be carefully selected to be representative of the population as a whole. The results of such sampling are expressed in probabilistic terminology, namely that the relationships between the variables investigated through the sample are *significant*. The term significant refers to the degree of probability that a given difference could have arisen by chance.

The behavioural aspects of geography

In the last decade or so, innovation with some far-reaching implications has been taking place in a field apparently remote from quantification, namely the behavioural. Thus Lowenthal writes:

> The universe of geographical study may be divided into three realms: the nature of the environment; what we think and feel about the environment;

and how we behave in, and alter the environment. These realms are everywhere related. None can be understood in isolation. Until recently, geographers have been content to explore the first of these realms—that is, what they consider the real world. Yet in daily practice, we all subordinate reality to the world we perceive, experience and act in. We respond to and affect the environment not directly, but through the medium of a personally apprehended milieu.[29]

Of British geographers, Kirk drew attention to the relevance of the behavioural environment in the early 1950s.[30] In a later and more accessible article,[31] he divided the 'geographical environment into two major sub-sections, the 'behavioural' and the 'phenomenal'.[32] (Table 5.1).

Table 5.1

Geographical Environment	BEHAVIOURAL ENVIRONMENT	Development of geographical ideas and values	Cultural environs of geographical ideas Socio-economic processes and changing environmental values
		Awareness of environment	Changing knowledge of man's natural environment
	PHENOMENAL ENVIRONMENT	Physical relics of human action	Sequent occupance of environments Man as an agent of environmental change
		Natural phenomena	Organic processes and products (including human populations) Inorganic processes and products

The concept of the 'phenomenal environment' includes not only the natural environment, but also the environment altered and in some cases made by man, in other words, the cultural environment. The concept of the 'behavioural environment' is shown to be much less familiar to geographers, and the relationship is exemplified:

> The Coal Measures of the concealed coalfields of Britain have existed for millions of years in the Phenomenal Environment but did not become geographically significant until geological discovery, improvements of mining techniques, and demand for power brought them into the Behavioural Environment of British entrepreneurs.[33]

Thus the concealed coalfields were part of the phenomenal environment of megalithic times, but did not enter into the problems of the geographical environment of the peoples of that period.

An important component in behavioural geography is the process of decision making. Decision making responds to personal perceptions of the environment, for the decisions are influenced not so much by the environment as it is, but by how it is perceived.[34] These perceptions are associated with 'mental'[35] or 'cognitive maps'.[36] Downs and Stea have explained the process as follows:

> Cognitive mapping is a construct which encompasses those cognitive processes which enable people to acquire, code, store, recall and manipulate information about the nature of their spatial environment. This information refers to the attributes and relative locations of people and objects in the environment, and is an essential component in the adaptive process of spatial decision making.[37]
>
> It is a coping mechanism through which the individual answers two basic questions quickly and efficiently: (1) Where certain valued things are; (2) How to get where they are from where he is.[38]

Thus on a familiar journey to work cognitive maps are used, however subconsciously, as a basis for making the many decisions involved on such a journey. As part of the cognitive map, a series of *attitudes, preferences* and *traits* are present. An unfortunate past incident, for example, may colour one's attitude towards a certain route and so another route is preferred. This preference may harden and become a trait, which is longer lasting than a preference.[39] Cognitive maps are frequently value-laden, and prone to incompleteness, inaccuracy and distortion. Ambrose identifies cultural background, level of education, tastes, value systems and age as significant factors in influencing cognitive or mental maps.[40]

The scope of behavioural geography thus includes (a) environmental perception, (b) attitudes and responses towards the environment, (c) environmental space preferences (for residence, holidays, etc.) and (d) environmental perception as it affects decision-making behaviour,[41] such as man's perceptions of natural hazards.[42, 43]

Lowenthal sees our personal maps as complex and impressionistic, and his much quoted summary constitutes a powerful antidote to any prescription of the 'new geography' as cold, rational and objective.

> Every image and idea about the world is compounded, then, of personal experience, learning, imagination and memory. The places that we live in, those we visit and travel through, the worlds we read about and see

in works of art, and the realms of imagination and fantasy each contribute to our images of nature and man. All types of experience, from those most closely linked with our everyday world to those which seem furthest removed, come together to make up our individual picture of reality. The surface of the earth is shaped for each person by refraction through cultural and personal lenses of custom and fancy. We are all artists and landscape architects, creating order and organising space, time and causality in accordance with our apperceptions and predilections. . . . As Raleigh wrote, 'It is not truth but opinion that can travel the world without a passport.'[44]

Geography and social issues

Interest in systems thinking and behavioural aspects of geography has widened the scope of the subject beyond even its previous broad bounds, so that the attention recently paid to social welfare issues seems almost a natural extension of an existing trend. Smith has noted 'a shift away from the mechanistic approaches of the quantitative and model-building "revolution" towards more involvement in contemporary social issues along with a renewed interest in applied geography and public policy.' Human geography is regarded as having a definite 'axe to grind', and an applied purpose in helping to understand and improve the human condition.[45, 46]

The characteristic geographic contribution is to judge spatial distributions from the point of view of social justice. The derived concept is 'spatial injustice', seen as becoming 'one of the major themes of the new socially activist geography'. The idea of territorial discrimination finds its most intense expression in the metropolitan area, with urbanism a prime topic for study, in response to the composite question—who gets what *where*, and how effectively?[47]

The most important manifestation of this trend to date is perhaps Harvey's *Social Justice and the City*,[48] in which its philosophic rationale is outlined. The dualistic thinking which artificially distinguishes 'pure' and 'applied', 'thought' and 'action' and, more specifically, 'spatial form' and 'social process', is rejected. 'Space', 'social justice' and 'urbanism' are not abstract concepts, things in themselves, but relate to and stem from human concern and human practice.[49] An important concept, 'created space', is introduced, a construct of modern industrial society, reflecting 'the prevailing ideology of the ruling groups and institutions in society'. As a result of 'the dynamics of market forces which can easily produce results which nobody in particular wants',[50] antipathy and alienation towards the urban environment is created.

A 'paradigm for modern geography'

Smith's conclusion is that the 'challenge to contemporary geography would appear to be how to design an education which combines the technical strengths of the quantitative and model-building era with a passionate concern for the condition of mankind.'[51] Similarly, Berry looks for a grand synthesis, what he terms 'a paradigm for modern geography', through an ecosystems approach covering inter-acting natural and cultural processes. In a model of 'behaviour and process in ecosystems', the presence of personal perceptions, cognitive maps and beliefs looms large, reflecting Berry's view that 'beliefs and perceptions may be among the most critical elements because what men believe determines what they do.'[52] The ecological, urban orientation of Berry's model also testifies to the convergence of what is 'scientifically fruitful' and 'socially relevant.'[53]

The current trend in academic geography would seem, therefore, to reinforce the view that its central role lies in the field of the social sciences, in which the spatial, area studies and man-land traditions converge; in which numeracy is as necessary a skill as literacy and graphicacy; in which inter-disciplinary thinking is prerequisite; and in which 'meaning' has a social as well as an intellectual relevance.

Priority readings

1. PATTISON, W. D. 'The four traditions of geography' in BALE, J. et al. (eds.) *Perspectives in Geographical Education* (Oliver & Boyd), pp. 2–11.
2. DAVID, T. 'Against geography', *ibid*, pp. 12–26.
3. SIMONS, M. 'What are geographers doing?' *ibid*, pp. 47–59.
4. GOULD, P. R. 'The new geography', *ibid*, pp. 35–46.
5. AMBROSE, P. J. 'New developments in geography' in WALFORD, R. (ed.) *New Directions in Geography Teaching* (Longman), pp. 69–84.
6. HARVEY, D. 'The role of theory' in GRAVES, N. J. (ed.) *New Movements in the Study and Teaching of Geography* (Temple Smith), pp. 29–41.
7. COLE, J. P. 'Mathematics and geography' in BALE, J. et al. (eds.) *op. cit.*, pp. 222–38.
8. COLE, J. P. 'Perception in geography' *ibid*, pp. 239–48.

9. STODDART, D. R. 'Geography and the ecological approach: the ecosystem as a geographic principle and method', *Geography* (1965), **50**, pp. 242–51.
10. KIRK, W. 'Problems of geography', *Geography* (1963), **48**, pp. 357–71.
11. GOULD, P. & WHITE, R. *Mental Maps* (Penguin Books).

Questions for investigation and discussion

1. (a) Indicate how, if at all, the attack by David on academic geography can be related to Hirst's view of geography as a 'field' of knowledge (page 50).
   (b) To what extent do you feel that the articles by Pattison and Simons (Priority readings 1 and 3) would constitute an adequate rejoinder to the idea that geography is not a distinctive discipline?
2. (a) How far is it fair to suggest that 'preoccupation with the region as the organising framework for much of our teaching' tends 'to lead to the compilation of inventories rather than the solution of problems or the development of concepts and theories.'[54]
   (b) What are the similarities and differences between traditional regional and systems approaches?
3. Relate back to the main elements in the geography courses you followed at school and university or college. Place these elements within the four traditions of Pattison, analysing the weight given to each at different stages.
4. What opportunities and dangers do you see in the trend of geography applying itself to questions of social justice in particular, and of forming closer alliances in the field of the social sciences in general?

References

1. TAYLOR, G. (1951) *Geography in the Twentieth Century* (Methuen, London).
2. DAVID, T. (1956) 'Against geography' in BALE, J., *et al.* (eds.) (1973) *Perspectives in Geographical Education* (Oliver & Boyd, Edinburgh), 12–26.
3. *Ibid*, 25.
4. *Ibid*, 14.
5. *Ibid*, 15–16.
6. PATTISON, W. D. (1963) 'The four traditions of geography' in BALE, J. *et al.* (eds.) (1973), *op. cit.*, 2–11.
7. EDGE, G. (1971) 'Why has geography changed?' Part 3 of *Evolution or Revolution in Geography?* (Open University Press), 57–72.
8. HAGGETT, P. (1972) *Geography: A Modern Synthesis* (Harper & Row, New York), 460.
9. See HARVEY, D. (1969) *Explanation in Geography* (Edward Arnold, London). 50–4.

10. DAVIES, W. K. D. (ed.) (1972) *The Conceptual Revolution in Geography* (University of London Press), 10.
11. See HARVEY, D. (1969), *op. cit.*, 32–6.
12. See MUSGRAVE, P. W. (ed.) (1970) *Sociology, History and Education* (Methuen, London), 3.
13. HARVEY, D. (1969), *op. cit.*, 78–83.
14. See CHORLEY, R. J. (1973) 'Geography as human ecology' in CHORLEY, R. J. (ed.) (1973) *Directions in Geography* (Methuen, London), 155–69.
15. LANGTON, J. (1972) 'Potentialities and problems of adopting a systems approach to the study of change in human geography' in BOARD, C., *et al.* (eds.) (1972) *Progress in Geography* Vol. 4. (Edward Arnold, London), 128–131.
16. *Ibid*, 132.
17. HARVEY, D. (1969), *op. cit.*, 451.
18. STODDART, D. R. (1965) 'Geography and the ecological approach: the ecosystem as a geographic principle and method' *Geography*, **50**, 243.
19. HAGGETT, P. (1972), *op. cit.*, xiv–xv.
20. CHORLEY, R. J. & HAGGETT, P. (1967) 'Models, paradigms and the new geography' in CHORLEY, R. J. & HAGGETT, P. (eds.) *Models in Geography* (Methuen, London), 23.
21. HAGGETT, P. (1972), *op. cit.*, 15.
22. HARVEY, D. (1972) 'The role of theory' in GRAVES, N. J. (ed.) *New Movements in the Study and Teaching of Geography* (Temple Smith, London), 32.
23. LANGTON, J. (1972), *op. cit.*, 132.
24. COLE, J. P. (1969) 'Mathematics and geography' in BALE, J. *et al.* (eds.) (1973), *op. cit.*, 223.
25. See COLE, J. P. & KING, C. A. M. (1968) *Quantitative Geography* (Wiley & Sons, London), Chapter 2.
26. HARVEY, D. (1969), *op. cit.*, 205.
27. PRINCE, H. C. (1971) 'Real, imagined and abstract worlds of the past' in BOARD, C., *et al.* (eds.) (1971) *Progress in Geography* Vol. 3. (Edward Arnold, London), 55.
28. HARVEY, D. (1969), *op. cit.*, 235.
29. LOWENTHAL, D. (ed.) (1967) *Environmental Perception and Behaviour* (University of Chicago Department of Geography Research Paper No. 109), 1.
30. See KIRK, W. (1951) 'Historical geography and the concept of the behavioural environment' *Indian Geographical Journal*, Silver Jubilee Vol., 152–60.
31. KIRK, W. (1963) 'Problems of geography' *Geography*, **48**, 357–71.
32. *Ibid*, 364.
33. *Ibid*, 367.
34. See COLE, J. P. (1968) 'Perception in geography' in BALE, J. *et al.* (eds.) (1973), *op. cit.*, 241.
35. See GOULD, P. & WHITE, R. (1974) *Mental Maps* (Penguin Books, Harmondsworth, Middlesex).
36. See DOWNS, R. M. & STEA, D. (1973) 'Cognitive maps and spatial behaviour: process and products' in DOWNS, R. M. & STEA, D. (eds.) (1973) *Image and Environment* (Edward Arnold, London), 8–26.
37. *Ibid*, xiv.
38. *Ibid*, 10.
39. *Ibid*, 14–15.
40. AMBROSE, P. J. (1969) 'Perceptions of space, distance and the environment' in AMBROSE, P. J. (ed.) (1969) *Analytical Human Geography* (Longman, London), 172–4.
41. WOOD, L. J. (1970) 'Perception studies in geography' *Transactions of the Institute of British Geographers*, **50**, 131.

42. See SAARINEN, T. F. (1966) 'Perception of the drought hazard' in AMBROSE, P. J. (ed.) (1969), *op. cit.*, 180–96.
43. See WHITE, G. F. (1973) 'Natural hazards research' in CHORLEY, R. J. (1973) *op. cit.*, 193–216.
44. LOWENTHAL, D. (1961) 'Geography, experience, and imagination: towards a geographical epistemology' *Annals of the Association of American Geographers*, **51**, 260.
45. SMITH, D. M. (1974) 'Who gets what *where*, and how: a welfare focus for human geography' *Geography*, **59**, 289.
46. See also STEEL, R. W. (1974) 'The third world: geography in practice' *Geography*, **59**, 206–7.
47. SMITH, D. M. (1974) *op. cit.*, 295–6.
48. HARVEY, D. (1973) *Social Justice and the City* (Edward Arnold, London).
49. *Ibid*, 10–17.
50. *Ibid*, 309–10.
51. SMITH, D. M. (1974), *op. cit.*, 297.
52. BERRY, B. J. L. (1973) 'A paradigm for modern geography' in CHORLEY, R. J (ed.) (1973), 14–15.
53. BARTELS, D. (1970) 'Between theory and metatheory', *ibid*, 36.
54. McCASKILL, M. (1967) 'Concepts in sixth form geography' in BIDDLE, D. S. & COLLINS, K. J. (eds.) (1967) *Geography in the Senior Forms* (F. W. Cheshire, Melbourne, for the Victoria and N.S.W. Geography Teachers' Association), 1.

6 Geography in School

Antecedents

No curriculum planning exercise in a subject area can afford to neglect the historical perspective. A subject's traditions, both at the frontiers of knowledge and at school level, are variables to be considered. The study of the continuing traditions of geography, however, is not necessary because they are deserving of exaggerated respect nor because we merely wish to learn from the mistakes of the past, but rather because we need (a) to 'know our place' both in terms of the particular segment of the cultural heritage with which we are concerned and also of the curricula of the past; and (b) to own that, as Charlton has put it 'exemplars live on . . . in the present, and they live on because in the past they have been considered by some teachers as acceptable, even authoritative. No new generation of teachers thinks out afresh an independent set of aims, though individuals may claim this is what they have done. . . .'[1]

This concern with the past is not only needful in principle. It is also expedient. So many teachers, not necessarily reactionary, have been alienated from change because the innovators have made presumptuous claims for the 'new' and poured scorn on the 'old'; because the term 'traditional' has often been used negatively.

It may be useful, therefore, to distinguish in school geography not so much traditions as types of 'traditionalism'—two in this case.

(a) The first, which may be called *'hard-core' traditionalism*, derives largely from the 'capes and bays' approach. This can be interpreted as having a narrow *area studies* emphasis, distinguishable by its heavy stress on rote learning and factual recall, its use of geographical facts and factors as ends in themselves, its reliance on deterministic explanations, its pursuit of world coverage often attained by superficial consideration of a descriptive wash of material, its heavy reliance on external examinations as the main motivating force and, in terms of values, its glorification of the work ethic and the competitive spirit.

In Bernstein's terminology (see page 111), it is associated with 'strong classification' and 'strong framing'.[2] There is a clear-cut demarcation between teacher and taught, with lessons dominated by chalk, talk and note-taking, and use of a very limited range of materials, consisting of blackboard, atlases, textbooks of pre-war vintage or derivation and, perhaps, mapograph outlines.

It will be obvious that this portrait contains an element of caricature, but few would pretend that this type of traditionalism is in imminent danger of extinction. It is unfortunate that the most reactionary methods of teaching are also the least demanding.

(b) The second type, *'enlightened' traditionalism* (the word 'enlightened' being used in a relative and not absolute sense), refers to an approach that is still strongly and even narrowly subject-orientated and which is not dissimilar to 'hard-core' traditionalism in its *area studies* mould, with world coverage and landscape description often well to the fore. But it is defined as more enlightened in having greater reference to intrinsic values, and in perceiving that the interests of the child should be appealed to rather more than competitive success.

It is also possible to identify a concern that content should be regarded as a means to an end, a search for relevance through reality, linked with field work and case studies, a use of a variety of materials in addition to the printed page, a greater attention to the improvement of attitudes as a means of raising standards and thus a less single-minded pursuit of examination success. Thus the first three years of the secondary school curriculum are not necessarily regarded as directly geared to the content of the external examinations syllabus.

It may not be unfair, however, to suspect that many 'enlightened traditionalists' are content to maintain a comfortable *status quo* and are distrustful of many of the recent changes in geography. They may also be reluctant to give sufficient weight to variables in curriculum planning which are not derived from the subject itself. To this extent 'enlightened' traditionalism functions as a force constraining change in the geography curriculum.

An historical perspective[3]

The two types of traditionalism have always coexisted; it would be quite wrong to suggest that 'enlightened' traditionalism succeeded 'hard-core'. The forces of progress and reaction have been present at all periods in the history of geography in school.

(a) *Geographical information*

Geographical information is today in some degree of disrepute, a situation which can in part be traced back to revulsion against the 'capes and bays' image of the subject. It is thus important to realise that the essence of the 'capes and bays' approach lay not so much with geographical facts as such, though these were undoubtedly given a heavy emphasis, but with the *rote learning* of these facts. To reveal the true nature of 'capes and bays' geography, the Rev. Goldsmith's introduction to a geographical textbook of 1823 is quoted:

> The proper mode of using this little book to advantage, will, it is apprehended, be to direct the pupil to commit the whole of the facts to memory, at the rate of one, two, or three a day, according to his age and capacity, taking care, at the end of each section, to make him repeat the whole of what he has before learned.[4]

The spirit of the exercise was faithfully reflected in examination questions such as:

> State all you know about the following: Machacha, Pilmo, Schebulos, Crivoscia, Basecs, Mancikert, Tatheu, Citeaux, Meloria, Zutphen.
>
> Name the highest peak of the Karakoram range.
>
> What is the number of universities in Prussia?
>
> Name the length and breadth of the stream of lava which issued from the Skaptar Jokul in the eruption of 1783.[5]

The deficiencies of the approach were well realised at the time, by Her Majesty's Inspectorate, for example. Similarly, in his celebrated report to the Royal Geographical Society in the 1880s, Scott Keltie quotes a contemporary's view that: 'No drearier task can be set for the worst of criminals than that of studying a set of geographical text books such as the children in our schools are doomed to use . . . they are handbooks of mnemonics, but they are in no sense handbooks of geography.'[6]

The 'capes and bays' approach was concordant with the nineteenth-century elementary school ethos, though it was also practised in those secondary schools in which the subject was studied. Apart from the three Rs, geography became the most popular elementary subject, its compendious nature fitting in well with a system in which facts were useful because they were easily measurable.

The political consequences of geography's association with popular education were damaging to the subject's status at secondary and still more at tertiary levels. The Royal Geographical Society publications of the late nineteenth century made clear the difficulty experienced in getting geography established in the great public schools and ancient universities. The Society solicited the views of headmasters on the value of geography as a subject in schools, and many were dismissive, drawing attention to its lack of intellectual rigour as it was then practised.

> The subject is merely an effort of memory. We cannot make a discipline of it, nor set problems in it. . . . As a compulsory subject in public schools, and taught—as it must be under those conditions—by a number of assistants who have no special interest in the work, and cannot clothe the dry bones, it must fail. As an *optional* subject, with a competent teacher, good results might be obtained; but a great portion of time would have to be deducted from other work.[7]

The intellectual respectability of geography has never, in fact, been accepted by some of the major boys' public schools and grammar schools, in which it remains a 'soft option' to be taken by the lower streams. There has long been a desire by geographers in such schools (and indeed also at university level) to cast off the old stigma. This need to demonstrate 'rigour' has been one of the reasons for the grammar school disposition to regard interest-based approaches with suspicion. As late as 1964 Marchant was admitting that in the lower streams 'the stress is on reality', while 'in the upper streams there is a determination that geography shall prove its worth as a mental discipline . . . in some schools there has been an undiluted dose of principles in the first year—or even two years—in order, as with the older teaching of Latin, that grammatical foundations shall be firmly laid at the outset, and in order also that rigorous habits of hard thinking should be early established.'[8]

It is worth noting too that one of the planks in the case for the 'new geography', shortly to be considered, is this need to make the subject respectable. Hence Fitzgerald suggests in his preface to *Science in Geography*, that the disappearance of geography from the timetable would be highly undesirable educationally, 'but quite deserved while geography continues to provide little intellectual rigour.'[9]

Yet geography, like education as a whole, must serve all pupils. There is an unfortunate assumption that elementary schools and less able children cannot take 'principles', or the higher processes of thought. Yet there is little intellectual justification for education if the bare facts are all that is thought appropriate. Much of the evidence from the time Marchant was writing would suggest that what was then offered as geography to less able pupils was not so much interest-based as watered down factual content, with an avoidance of anything that would provoke thought. In a pessimistic summary to a study of the kind of geography taught in secondary modern schools, Roberson stated:

> There are grounds for thinking that the teachers believed the children's ability to reason was low. There was an abundance of factual material required, and a paucity of thought.[10]

(b) *An earlier 'new geography'*

Writers such as Geikie, Mackinder and Herbertson are linked with earlier attempts to systematise geography and rescue it from its encyclopaedic image. Herbertson and Fairgrieve deplored the nineteenth-century tendency to divide geography into distinct compartments, particularly physical and political. In many schools the concentration on political geography placed a burden on the child's memory through the use of a multitude of divisions, such as countries and counties, as units of study.

Herbertson evolved a new and more sophisticated 'model', based on the so-called 'higher units'. In place of a framework of numerous political divisions, he proposed the use of fourteen 'natural regions'. In pursuit of his duty to be 'not merely descriptive but scientific', the geographer needed to study 'distributions of various forms and forces on the Earth's surface and their inter-relation.'[11] As Jay has documented, Herbertson lost no time in diffusing his ideas into the schools.[12] His *Senior Geography*, first published in 1907 and remaining in print until 1952, opened with a chapter on the natural regions of the world.

Later textbook writers such as Newbigin, Unstead, Stamp, Stembridge and Pickles were all influenced by Herbertson. Hence in Pickles *The World* (1939) it is claimed that

> it is possible by ignoring minor differences to divide the world into a dozen or so climatic regions. . . . By this means a survey of the world is

made relatively easy since when we have learnt the geography of one region we can easily learn the geography of another region of the same type.[13]

The possibilities for generalisation provided by this scheme appear an important step forward. At the time they undoubtedly were. Unfortunately,

(i) the scheme was based on 'a semi-scientific content with notions of causality on the nineteenth-century determinist model';[14]

(ii) the theoretical attractions of the scheme seemed never to have been firmly translated in any widespread way into good educational practice. By the post 1945 period 'natural regions' geography was barely distinguishable from the 'capes and bays' geography which had gone before. It merely provided a more effective framework for the rote learning of facts.

Jay points to some of the specific deficiencies of Herbertson's scheme:

(i) For each natural region or sub-division of one, stress came to be laid on 'the short sentence or phrase which summarises the climatic conditions over a wide area of the earth's surface, at the expense of the more detailed description which gives a region its character.'[15] Eyre's critique is complementary. 'The really insidious educational danger of broad climatic-vegetation correlations is that, in a very general way, they correspond with reality; . . . generic relationships between climates, vegetation and soil are extremely subtle. . . . "Climatic classifications" make them appear simple, exact and direct.'[16]

(ii) Linked with this are the over-simplified, static, deterministic generalisations about the relationship between man and his environment, which have brought upon this tradition almost as much criticism as the areal studies tradition and its 'capes and bays' representation in school. Hence the Pickles-type text outlines the following general truths about the world's wheat growing and the conditions favouring it: '10 to 15 inches of rain, most of which should fall in the growing season; warm, sunny dry weather for ripening; at least 100 days growing season between the last frost of spring and the first frost of autumn; fertile soil, preferably a heavy loam; level or undulating land to facilitate farming operations; easy transport to a good market.' This attempt at 'generalisation' could apply to almost any place, and contains no information characteristic of a particular identifiable region, even though it is supposedly referring to the Canadian Prairies. The vague and inert nature of the adjectives used becomes almost a caricature of itself. One wonders whether the children would respond any differently to 'warm soils and a fertile climate'; 'good transport to easy markets'; or 'a skilled supply of land and undulating labour'!

(iii) Another characteristic of the framework is the division of natural regions first into major territorial units and then into subdivisions such as position and extent; structure, relief and drainage, climate, vegetation and soil; agriculture, trade and industry; settlement and communications, and the like. This has proved an effective pedagogic device and, had the stress been on the links rather than on static attributes, we might have had something analogous to a working systems framework (see pages 62–3). Unfortunately, this again has been used merely as a frame for superficially generalised content, susceptible to rote learning. Though it was no intention of Herbertson's, determinism has remained.

The 'factors', to be considered truly geographical, have had to be largely physical factors, or to some extent economic. Social variables have been lost, or perhaps never found.[17] Thus the first major conceptional revolution in school geography, however unintentionally, blended too easily with the pre-existing rote learning mode of operation in schools. Geographical facts continued in very many cases to be ends in themselves, effectively devalued as material of legitimate concern in a progressive education.

(c) *Maps*

As Vaughan has noted, 'even the Rev. J. Goldsmith claimed that to teach geography without maps was absurd and that "a proper mode of familiarising very young pupils with an idea of the meaning and intention of Maps, is to lay before them a Plan or Map of the District in which they reside" '.[18] Hence even an arch-advocate of rote learning processes in geography was well aware of the central role that maps should play in the subject.

The nineteenth century was a great age of exploration, in which knowledge of the unexplored interiors of continents steadily accumulated. It was also a great age of surveying and mapping, both abroad and at home. The maps of the Ordnance Survey, on a variety of different scales, appeared during the century and their quality and utility were quickly appreciated, not least by methodologists of education. While in the schools the most ubiquitous maps were small-scale wall maps of the world in which the imperial possessions were highlighted, the potential of Ordnance Survey maps did not go unnoticed. Jelinger Symons enthused, 'there is nothing which so keenly enlivens and excites as maps. They are the salt of schools; and the teacher is dull indeed if they do not savour the other food,'[19] and proposed the availability in schools of $\frac{1}{3}''$:1 mile scale county maps, reduced from Ordnance Survey maps. At the turn of the century one preparatory school head, in his guidelines for teaching geography in such schools, was no less warm: 'Of making maps there should be no end.'[20]

It is curious, however, that the use of sketch maps, that is diagrammatic rather than true cartographical exercises designed to exclude the 'noise' of an atlas and to focus on features particular to a topic, did not appear until quite late in the history of the subject in school. Jay suggests that the 'realisation that the sketch-map was capable of illustrating causal relationships and of stimulating new trains of thought'[21] was the work of Mackinder, whose school texts appeared from 1906.

The rote remembering and reproduction of sketch-maps, however, became as much part of the 'system' as the learning of verbal facts. The employment of maps rather as a means of storing and processing data has become rapidly more sophisticated in recent times, and this potential is gradually being applied in school geography. 'Correlative thinking by maps' is thus a desired intellectual skill to be sought and something more, 'a useful criterion for determining the external relations of our subject'.[22]

In the school context, Balchin and Coleman have gone so far as to advance the view that *graphicacy* should be the 'fourth ace' in the educational pack, already made up of literacy, numeracy and articulacy. Graphicacy is defined as 'the communication of relationships, that cannot be successfully communicated by words or mathematical notation alone,'[23] its expression being chiefly through maps and graphs. The cognitive and affective dimensions of graphicacy are ranked as critical components of education. Balchin suggests that if graphicacy is accepted as a hallmark of a well educated person as much as the other three 'aces' and geography is the only subject geared to a rigorous teaching and training in this skill, then it emerges as a foundation subject of education along with English and mathematics.[24] There appears, however, to have been no rush to support this claim by the educational world in general.

(d) *'Reality' in geography teaching*

Apart from its association with maps, the most characteristic offerings geography has made to the school curriculum have probably lain in its advocacy of field study and case study techniques. The value of these three aspects in 'bringing the world into the classroom' have made them diagnostic features of 'enlightened traditionalism.'

(i) *Field work*

> L'importance de l'observation directe en geographie n'est pas une decouverte de la pedagogie contemporaire.[25]

Field work as we know it is often taken to derive from the nineteenth-century *heimatskunde* (locality studies) practice in Germany. Before this time references to field work could be found, but sporadically. By the nineteenth century, the process of using the environment for educational purposes had a broad backing of educational thought behind it. A graphic account of the *heimatskunde* approach is provided in a letter from a 'young gentleman' travelling in Germany to the well-known nineteenth-century scholar, George Combe:

> During the summer months, pedestrian excursions are undertaken. . . . Everything worthy of attention is pointed out to the boys as they go along; and deviations are made on all sides, for the purpose of inspecting every manufactory, old castle and other remarkable object in the neighbourhood. . . . If they happen to be travelling in the mountainous districts of the Harz, they descend into the mines, and see the methods of excavating the ore. . . . In this way, I may say without exaggeration, they acquire in the course of a single forenoon, a greater amount of useful, practical and entertaining knowledge than they could obtain in six months at a grammar school. . . . How different were my feelings, when thus employed, from those which tormented me in that place of misery, the High School at Edinburgh.[26]

Watts identifies three main strands in the evolution of the environmental idea: the epistemological, philosophical and naturalist.[27] He ascribes its establishment in Britain chiefly to the naturalist tradition, whose image was national rather than foreign, and which gave to environmentalism enthusiasm and popular appeal. Wordsworth is seen as a powerful voice.[28]

The impetus to field work was, therefore, through nature study, rural life and grand scenery. A delightful example of an anticipation of ventures to come is provided by a Hampshire teacher, John Dawes, who saw the purpose of education 'to make the children observant and reflective; to make them think and reason about the objects around them.' They were therefore encouraged to look and think. 'They watched the animals in the fields and collected statistics as to how they moved. They followed the progress of the seasons by observing the sun. . . . Geography was taught in relation to the locality and to the observations of the sky and the weather made by children in their scientific work, and even history, normally presented as a mere exercise of memory, was made an instrument of reasoning:

> John of Gaunt used to live where this school stands. Do you think he had tea and coffee with sugar for breakfast? Give your reasons for thinking he had or had not.

Similarly, he once asked some boys whether the same body would weigh more at the equator or at the pole:

> I observed the eyes of one of them glistening with delight, thinking he had it, who answered "At the pole, sir—at the pole" twice repeated. "Why?" "Because sir, at the equator one sweats so much." Now this, though not exactly the answer I expected, was that of a reasoning mind. This boy would not have sent a cargo of skates to Buenos Ayres, as . . . a Sheffield cutler did, in 1806.[29]

A conscious attempt was therefore made to use the field stimulus to promote reasoning powers. This potentiality for infusing realism and therefore an element of meaning was appreciated by members of the inspectorate, such as HMI for the Preston district, who wrote in 1876:

> I have seen Preston boys receive quite a new sensation on being told that when they walked up the river and saw the Darwen join the Ribble, they had before them what the geography books describe in mystic terms as a 'tributary' and a 'confluence'.[30]

The migration of famous physical geographers and geologists into the educational sphere gave to field work a stronger scientific thrust. W. M. Davis, for example, stressed that there was more to field work than mere observation.

> It should be quite clearly understood that work of this kind (ie field work) is not limited merely to matters of observation and record. These are truly the first steps, but they must be followed by abundant thinking; indeed, the soul of the work is gained only when the thinking that is inspired by the observations is logical, searching, critical.[31]

The notion of the field as the 'laboratory' of the geographer was put forward.[32] But in the time preceding the 1930s this laboratory was widely comprehended as almost exclusively a rural one. The town was seen as an obstacle to the 'true method of teaching geography' by Laurie in 1888, and a particular problem for London children, so far from the countryside:

> ... but what a happy chance is afforded to a paternal Board of giving the children a day in the country at the expense of the rates, on the plea that the excursion is a geography lesson! ... Much may be done also by proper apparatus to counteract the misfortune of living in a large town.[33]

This view continued to prevail. The expense of transporting children into the country was seen as inhibiting the spread of field work. As a Cardiff geography mistress complained:

> ... money for tram or bus fare is almost a necessity in order to get into the country. ... Distance from the country involves not only money, but also time and worry. That great question of our towns comes to the front so often when we attempt educational reforms.[34]

Blyth suggests that the real turning point came when Cons and Fletcher in 1938 showed that what was possible in the countryside was equally applicable to the inner suburbs.[35] Almost contemporary with this was a Cadbury publication entitled *Our Birmingham* which contained a useful example of local urban social geography, in which 'groups of scholars visited not only their own districts but congested areas and Municipal estates' in the Aston area of the city.[36]

Though the advocacy of field work was of long standing, diffusion of the idea through the school system was slow to come. Why did teachers prevaricate for such a time in the face of so powerfully argued and seemingly irrefutable a case? Apart from the matter of expenditure of time and money, one reason may have been lack of confidence. Davis, for example, found 'a great diffidence among teachers as to outdoor observation', even among those well versed in theory.[37] He ascribed this hesitancy to lack of liberal guidance in the previous experiences of the teacher.

But not all teachers have been agreed on the desirability or effectiveness of field work. Lyde opposed it in 1901 as a basis for geography teaching on the grounds that teachers could not afford the time, the boys 'regarded it as a picnic', while 'the road to knowledge' must not 'appear too easy'.[38] At the conference at which Lyde expounded these views, it was said that for field work to become extablished it would have to obtain much larger recognition in public examinations. The thought was prophetic, for just over sixty years later, in the face of considerable teacher opposition, insistence on a field work component in the newly formed CSE examination system triggered off a considerable leap forward.

(ii) *Bringing the world into the classroom*

Despite the need to stress firsthand experience, the nature of the content of geography makes it inevitable that much of its world must be seen at second hand. The better nineteenth-century textbook writers strove to impart this sense of the real into school or, indeed, home lessons. Hence Miss Willard starts her *Geography for Beginners* (1826) with an 'Introductory Conversation', associated with an illustration of a 'Country Store, exhibiting the Productions of Various Countries', which runs thus:

> *Mother* Have you been interested, my son, in viewing those animals which your father took you to see?
> *Frank* O very much. But, my dear Mother, when will you fulfil your promise of teaching me geography? My father told me that the elephant was brought from India, the lion from Africa, and the monkeys from South America. I wish to know where these places are, and what kind of countries those must be, which produce such wonderful animals. The other day my good papa told me from what places some of the articles in our store (frontispiece) were brought. The oranges are from Havanna, the raisins from Spain, and the tea from China. The cloth for my new coat, my father says, was made by people who live in England.[39]

A widespread feature of elementary school work in late nineteenth-century England was the use of 'object lessons', a device to introduce a greater sense of reality into teaching. Fitch (1884) describes vividly the operation of the technique:

> A teacher takes a piece of Coal in his hand and asks the children what it is. He asks them to look at it, and tell him what they can see, that it is black and shiny; to handle it, and to find out that it is hard, that parts of it are easily rubbed off, and that it is of a certain weight. He asks what would happen if he put it in to the fire, and he finds that they can tell him not only that it burns, but that there is a gaseous flame at first, afterwards a duller burning, and finally nothing left but cinders. He makes them tell its familiar uses.[40]

This led on to a consideration of coal mining, the fossil character of coal, helped by pictures of the primaeval forest.

> ... at the end his black board presents a summary of the lesson, shewing in succession the qualities, the uses, and the history of coal, and the mode of procuring it.

Fitch saw object lesson techniques as useful in the hands of a good teacher, but made clear that many object lessons degenerated into rote activity, which he well knew as a school inspector.

> ... one is doomed to hear one object after another treated in exactly the same way, and to see it solemnly recorded on a board that a cow is graminiverous, or that an orange is opaque.[41]

The elementary school inspectors were ready to publicise in their reports examples, isolated though they might be, of progressive approaches, as in the case of the inspector for the Northallerton district of Yorkshire in the late 1870s.

> At one of the Whitby schools the geographical teaching is a model of intelligence and ingenuity. The subject is the geography of Yorkshire, and a sand map of the county, with all the important physical features, has been carefully modelled on a terrace adjoining the school room. The sand has been brought by the children from the beach, and has been moulded by them, with the assistance of the teachers, into mountains, hills, valleys and rivers. ... The proportions are observed with wonderful accuracy ... everything speaks to the eye.[42]

The concept of moving out from the local area to the wider world was appreciated at the time, and advocated by Fitch: 'we should begin with what is known and what is near, and let our knowledge radiate from that as a centre until it comprehends what is larger and more remote.'[43] The prediction of a concentric approach is obvious.

Case studies (sample studies)

> How can the geographer 'cover the world' yet not over-simplify to the point of dull triviality or even untruth?[44]

Long and Roberson date the conscious study of *sample* human societies from around the turn of this century, though the basic idea can be traced back at least to 1877, when T. H. Huxley was writing in connection with his text *Physiography* of the need:

to illustrate my method by a concrete case; and, as a Londoner addressing Londoners, I selected the Thames, and its basin, for my text. But any intelligent teacher will have no difficulty in making use of the river and river basin of the district, in which his school is situated, for the same purpose.[45]

Many examples are present in the literature of the twentieth century, with offerings from such writers as Fairgrieve, Cons and Scarfe. Formal discussion of the sample study method dates from articles by Hickman in 1950[46] and Roberson and Long in 1956.[47] Since then a flood of such materials has been unleashed on the schools, and their use is now widespread. The term 'sample study' has tended to be replaced by 'case study' because the term 'sample' may be confused with its more technical use in statistics.

Case studies have the potential advantage of providing vivid, thorough and accurate detail, in a sense simulating field work in the classroom. Their use is flexible, and their wide availability now makes them a viable prospect for almost any syllabus at any level. Yet, if improperly used, they can lapse into an analogue of the descriptive world coverage approach, full of trivial facts, signifying little or nothing. Bloomfield has insisted that they should be carefully associated with a series of cognitive and social objectives which require the pupil to engage in problem-solving operations.[48]

Like any other method, case studies must contribute to the attainment of wider aims and objectives. More specifically, they constitute a creative response to Mackinder's plea to abandon 'natural regions, except for the initial home region, and substitute focal points, from which the visualising and rationalising eye can sweep over gradually widening areas.'[49] Fitting well into both concentric and concept-based schemes, they can be a very effective teaching device.

Implications of the 'new geography' for school geography

The view is firmly taken here that much of the 'new geography' is entirely compatible with good educational practice, proper adaptation having been made. Much of the 'new geography' is not, of course, new. Good traditional teaching has always been concerned with explanation as well as description, with meaningful rather than rote methods of learning, and has been quite ready to incorporate conceptual models such as the Davisian cycle and the Herbertsonian natural regions. Of Harvey's explanatory forms (pages 60-1) cognitive description, cause and effect analysis, certain temporal modes of explanation and some functional/ecological analysis have all been present in different degrees, some admittedly rudimentary.

Among the changes in the new approaches are a switch from inductive to deductive methods of reasoning, from data collection to data manipulation using appropriate quantitative techniques, from unique events to general patterns, from static to dynamic framings of content, from the phenomenal to the behavioural environmental and from neutrality to commitment in the consideration of problem issues. The field is much wider than that of quantification though this has received most publicity to date.

Some of these trends, such as the use of deductive reasoning and an abstract methodology of generalisation and theorisation, seem on the face of it contrary to the approved pedagogic practice of moving from the real to the abstract, the familiar to the unfamiliar, the particular to the general (pages 134-5). Scarfe has asserted that 'All conclusions must be based on exact down-to-earth evidence. That is why the present emphasis on abstract models is pedagogically quite unsound in school.'[50] Thomas similarly considers that 'school geography cannot be expected to commit itself to the search for universally valid generalisations, unless it is to abandon its traditional function of introducing the child to the significant variations between the several parts of the earth.'[51]

If what was being advocated was a mere dilution of more advanced techniques for school use, such arguments might be justified. They were in fact put forward at a time of reaction to some of the more extreme claims being made for the 'new geography'. The spectrum of new thinking is now wider and more balanced, however, and potentially there seems to be a fruitful blend for school geography in the infusion not only of mathematical and scientific thinking, but also of concepts from the social/behavioural sciences. The stress on conceptual thinking and on problem orientation represents a convergence of ideas from the subject frontiers and from curriculum theory.

The impact of quantification

The quantitative aspects of the new geography remain the bugbear for many teachers, however. It is useful here to reiterate the distinction between mathematics and statistics. 'Mathematical geography' has long been a feature of geography syllabuses, which have included studies of the earth and the solar system, latitude and longitude, time, navigation and map projections. As long ago as 1912, elementary geometry was being presented, admittedly by a mathematician, as the true basis of 'Scientific Geography'.[52]

In part, the quantitative revival reaffirms this connection between geography and mathematics, and the moving together of the 'new geography' and the 'new mathematics', a world of co-ordinates, sets, Venn diagrams and matrices, is of special interest.[53] In the geometrical connection emphasis has shifted from Euclidean geometry to topology, which is of pedagogic interest in that topological thinking, in terms of the child's mental development, predates understanding of Euclidean geometry (see page 135), and of geographical importance in that map transformations provide an exciting means of exploring various geographical phenomena, such as transport networks (see pages 301–3).

The introduction of statistical techniques into school poses different questions. Some of the simpler techniques, such as measures of central tendency and spread, scatter graphs and more straightforward correlation techniques, might well come early in the secondary stage. Others may be more appropriate at sixth form level. One of the problems, in the absence of calculating machines and even computer links, is the need for repetitive calculation in many of the techniques, though a division of class labour to reduce the burden is often possible.

Fitzgerald makes a necessary proviso to the effect that 'in any teaching situation, although it is important to emphasise a need for precision, it is important to choose statistical techniques that both suit the task in hand and the level of attainment of the pupil concerned.'[54] Once such provisos are met, there seems a strong case for taking advantage of the wide range of opportunities which the new techniques offer to schools. Apart from anything else, the techniques of social analysis are not entirely *terra incognita* to young people who live in a world of questionnaires, random samples and statistical tables and graphs. It is well that they should be better acquainted with quantifiable social data, and become cognisant of the modest claims made by statisticians (if not by the newspapers) on the basis of carefully collected and processed information. The misapplication of such data is a subject worthy of study in school geography, and worthwhile study requires an understanding of the processes used.

The use of systems and models

At first sight, the use of systems and models seems yet another way of diverting geography teaching from reality. Again it is argued that this is only a difficulty where the techniques are introduced in an inappropriate way. At what stage the children should formally be presented with systems and models will depend on the complexity of those systems and models, but this type of thinking is useful to the teacher in helping in the choice of significant 'connectable' content at any stage.

On the physical side of geography, the ecosystems approach, proselytised by Eyre,[55] Stoddart[56] and Renner,[57] is increasingly being viewed as the central structuring mechanism. A simple example is shown in Fig. 6.1 of the dynamics of a woodland ecosystem,[58] in which the worlds of biology and geography overlap in the ecological notion of the adaptation of organisms to their environment in an interacting system.

The systems approach may conceivably be the most significant 'discovery' of all for geography in school, providing at last a technology that makes it possible to put in practice the intentions long made by those who have seen geography as the key inter-relating subject:

> ... for the subject of Geography, of all school subjects, if rightly taught, may enable a child to realise that the world in which he lives is not a mere sum of facts, but an inter-related system, a cosmos, in which fact is related to fact and conditions and is conditioned by the nature of the whole.[59]

Objections against the use of models have been made on the grounds of complexity, use of jargon and abstractness.[60] In fact their whole purpose is to simplify, to eliminate some of the 'noise' of reality. Slater advances a number of arguments in favour of the use of models in school, in the opportunities they provide for evaluating general ideas and theories against real world data, the frameworks they provide for placing unique facts in more general patterns and the insights they give into the inter-relatedness of phenomena.[61]

One possible way of introducing models in schools is for the teacher himself to produce a detailed case study, say of a farm, on the framework of a systems approach *prior* to introducing the model itself. Subsequently he may ask the pupils to test the model against other sets of real data.[62]

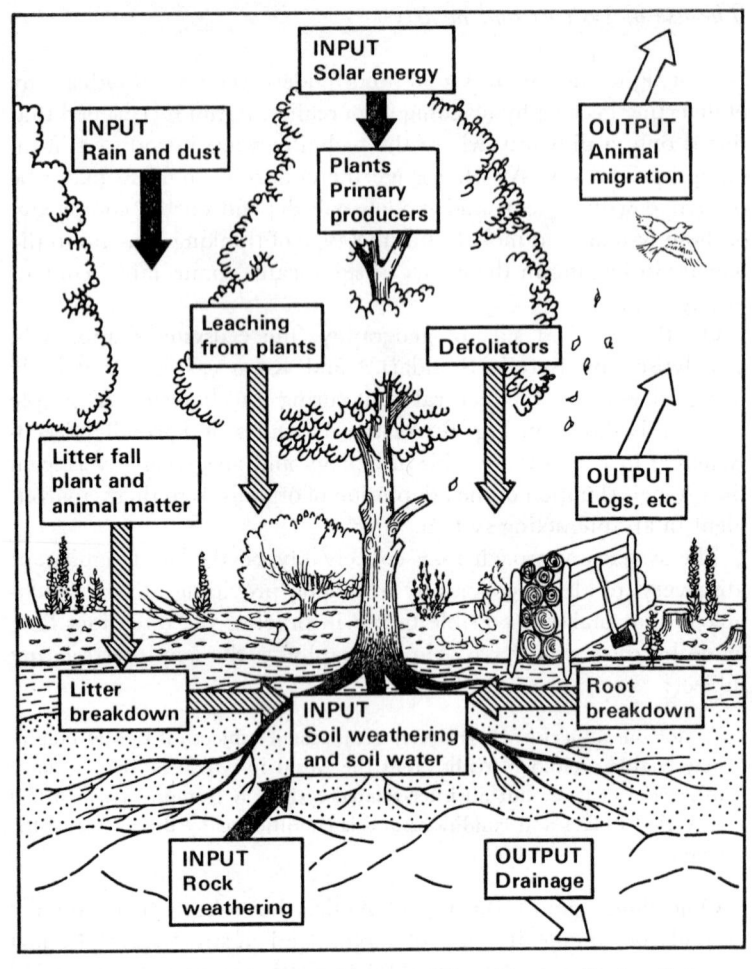

Fig. 6.1 Dynamics of a woodland ecosystem (From Harrison,[58] after Ovington, J. D., 1962, *Advances in Ecological Research*, **1**)

Simulation and gaming

Models and systems are simulations of reality. Their role is largely a cognitive one, and they help in structuring content in a meaningful way. The use of simulation and gaming is also important in cognitive terms, but contains in addition a role-playing component that has a more direct social significance.

Many simulation situations in geography take the form of introducing hypothetical states or islands, or turning real maps on their heads to produce unfamiliar shapes. Using these, children are invited, sometimes with inadequate evidence to hand, to decide on optimal locations for steel works, atomic power stations, airports, paper mills, using information and understanding acquired from previous work. In Bloom's terms, simulation exercises explore application, analysis and evaluation skills. Properly used, they can provide evidence as to whether geographical concepts have been acquired.

A further step is the use of geographical games.[63] They can be solely games of chance, which are not necessarily educationally valueless, so long as they are seen as motivational starting points and not as ends in themselves. More significant, however, are role-playing games, in which the children are placed in the position of decision makers.[64, 65]

Walford has made appropriately modest claims for such activities. Their advantages include the fostering of high levels of motivation, the possibility of learning from peers through co-operative activity, the isolation of important geographical principles (as in models), the opportunity of putting children in the roles of decision makers, and the conscious highlighting of chance factors in decision making—an antidote to determinism.

Walford emphasises the unwisdom of overdoing the use of games. They are time-consuming and are certainly no panacea for controlling dissident classes; they can become competitive pieces of entertainment in which the basic educational objective is lost. Unless carefully simplified, they may have the power to reinforce distorted or even error-laden learning. It has also been found difficult to measure whether learning in this way is more efficaceous than in other ways, bearing in mind the expenditure of scarce time which gaming activities usually involve.

Behavioural geography in school

The time-honoured notion of moving from the familiar to the unfamiliar is clearly related to the 'mental maps' of the child, starting with his 'action space': the home, the classroom and routes to school and other places. He has, in addition, secondhand 'mental maps' of other places and peoples.

There are as yet relatively few perception studies applied to classroom use. Preliminary examples include those of Cole and Beynon,[66] and Walford.[67] The Bristol Schools Council *Geography 14–18* project has designed materials to throw light on people's differential 'frames of reference',[68] materials that are deliberately ambivalent and subjective, posing problems that invite value judgements, but at the same time demand that the subjective basis of the judgements made should be explicit and open to discussion.

Gould and White have illustrated the potentiality of using short classroom questionaires for exploring children's 'images of Britain'. A convincing case is made for reproducing such studies for classroom use in order to promote intellectual understanding of environments and peoples and social awareness. Our decisions and attitudes are held to be based on personal 'perceptual filters',[69] which are entrenched early in life (page 16) and often productive of distortion. Thus unfavourable stereotypes are born.

While the time is not yet ripe to make confident predictions, this relationship between children's cognitive maps (pages 132–5) and their attitudes to other places and peoples may become more thoroughly understood in the future through investigations taking place at the frontiers between psychology and geography. It is certainly not too early to suggest that classroom activity should be planned to encourage children to explore their environmental perceptions,[70] especially if we agree with Gould and White, that a particular aim of geography is

> to make us see ourselves as others see us; to break down the stifling parochialism, the boundary thinking, the Us-Themism; to create awareness of what location in an information space implies for forming images and judgements. Only when we realise the way in which our collective perceptions are controlled and biased by our locations in streams of information can we begin to break out of the judgemental prison in which we are all trapped in greater or lesser degrees.[71]

Issue-based geography

It has been suggested that geography's recent emphasis on values and behavioural approaches has enhanced the role it is able to play in environmental education.[72] How it relates to other disciplines in fulfilling this function is the subject of the next chapter.

Papers in *Geography*[73] and the *Bulletin of Environmental Education*[74]

(1970) have respectively drawn attention to the way in which schools could be involved in, and develop attitudes towards, community affairs. On the global scale, a whole series of international organisations have advocated and provided materials for the study of world problem issues.[75] There are manifest dangers in an over-zealous concentration on such issues, and certainly evidence from the past would indicate that indoctrination is counter-productive. The aim to train better citizens is of long standing. Perhaps all that is new is a realisation of the difficulty of the task, and of the need to provide a cognitive base and practice in the range of skills required in values education[76] (pages 10–11). This move away from the objective stance clearly poses difficult questions for the teacher. To what extent should he remain neutral in discussing the world's great human issues?[77]

The use of conceptual approaches in schools

Two of the implications for school geography which Ambrose draws from 'frontier' developments are the need for a shift of emphasis towards value-based content, and from factually-based to concept-based modes of study.[78] Again, recent trends in geographical thinking are matched by those of authorities in the education field such as Ausubel, Gagné, Bruner, Hirst and Phenix (Chapters 3 and 4). It has been argued that the conceptual frameworks must emerge from expert analysis of the nature of the contributing discipline. The following schemes are provided by such experts.

Schemes based on abstract technical concepts

The first scheme is an urban-oriented one, expounded by *R. E. Dickinson*, a doyen of settlement geography, whose work long pre-dates the 'conceptual revolution'. He continues to view the regional idea as *the* overarching geographical concept, but breaks it down in terms of urban areas as follows:

1. *Centrality* (or nodality), subsuming various other concepts such as gradient, spacing, etc.
2. *Economic base*, related to activities bringing income to a town.
3. *Areal base*, combining elements of (1) and (2) and subsuming

such concepts as urban field, hinterland, city region, journey to work area, etc.

4. *Segregation*, being basically the notion of zonation.
5. *Urbanised area*
6. *Areal differentials* in levels of living, economic health, resource development, etc.
7. *Community interest*
8. *Morphology* of the urban habitat.

Dickinson regards this conceptual framework, based on the ideas of Carl Sauer and Lewis Mumford, as more or less synonymous with the whole of geography and drastically needed for a school curriculum that is over-devoted to information and built on a physical environment basis.[79]

Nystuen's identification of geographical concepts has a more overtly spatial bias. The basic geographical elements are perceived as *points*, *lines* and *areas*. The division of concepts is as follows:

1. *Directional orientation* (· → ·)
2. *Distance*
   (a) *spatial*—shortest path between two points
      (i) *nominal* (nearest, furthest)
      (ii) *scalar* (metres, miles)
      (iii) *asymmetric* (eg a → b not the same necessarily as b → a, as in a one-way street system)
   (b) *temporal*—measured by travel time
   (c) *cost*—measured by travel cost
   (d) *social*—involving segregation

The fundamental geographical property is that distance is to do with separation—intensity of communication in general falls off with distance. An associated sociological concept is *propinquity*.

3. *Connectiveness* (or connectivity)—a property independent of direction or distance, capable of transformation, as in topological maps. In these, the property of connectiveness remains, but those of direction and distance change.

4. *Functional associations* of spatially separated elements in space, which are best revealed by exchanges (*flows* of people, goods, or words) taking place between the elements.

5. *Activities* (groups of people) and *processes* (non-human elements) which explain how and why the elements under study are arranged and associated in space.

6. *Site* (place) and *situational* (relative location) characteristics, there being some overlap between the two, with the relationship dependent on scale.

7. Another group of geographical concepts are related to *tensions*, which cut across many of the previously specified concepts, and include
   (a) *historical tensions*, between present activities and past arrangements;
   (b) *dimensional tensions*, reflecting the fact that geographical elements can be characterised as points, lines and areas, and tensions are created between point and area occupying activies—what is the optimal arrangement of factories (points) in space? What are the tensions between areal (eg agricultural) and point (eg manufacturing) activities?;
   (c) *time-space tensions*, such as congestion, where an activity is connected with a time deadline, creating the problem of space inadequacy.

For Nystuen, most other geographical concepts, such as pattern, accessibility, neighbourhood and so on, can be subsumed under the above categories, though he admits to probable omissions and specifies *boundary* as one of these.[80]

In a similarly spatially orientated classification, which forms the structure of his book *Locational Analysis in Human Geography*, Haggett outlines five categories or *elements*.[81]

1. *Movement*
   (a) movement and morphology (form)
   (b) movement and distance (interaction)
   (c) movement and area (field and territory)
   (d) movement and time (diffusion)
2. *Networks*
   (a) Location of routes
   (b) Density pattern of route networks
   (c) Models of network change
3. *Nodes*
   (a) Morphology of settlement patterns
   (b) Population clusters: the size continuum
   (c) Size and spacing of clusters
4. *Hierarchies*
   (a) Functional hierarchies of settlements
   (b) Specialised centres within the hierarchy
   (c) Distortion due to agglomeration
   (d) Distortion due to resource localisation
5. *Surfaces*
   (a) Surfaces and gradients
   (b) Minimum-movement models
   (c) Distortion of regular gradients.

A conceptual scheme derived from systems theory ties these elements together. Here the underlying concept is of *flows* of people, goods, money and information, and adjustments to flows. The point is made that regularities appear to exist and persist in space and time.

Perhaps the most ambitious and well publicised attempt to structure a syllabus (in this case for 14–16 year olds) in geography in conceptual terms has been made by the *American High School Geography Project*. Here five *basic* concepts are identified,[82]

    1. *Geographical facts*, specifically
        (a) their location—where things are
        (b) their subject matter (eg a village)
        (c) their position in time.
(It will be clear that the use of the terms 'basic concepts' and 'facts' is open to ambiguity.)

    2. *Spatial distribution*, which involves asking questions about the geos graphical facts—why they are there; why they have such a pattern. Thu- 'a spatial distribution is a pattern or spread of a group of geographical facts within a specified area.'

    3. *Areal association*, involving the comparison of two or more spatial distributions to establish a correlation.

    4. *Spatial interaction*, reflecting the fact that geography is not just about static subject matter, but is also concerned with movements or flows of things, people and words, between cities or countries or whatever.

    5. *Region*—an areal classification, with the items within the region being relatively homogeneous, and those without dissimilar. The region ranges in scale from, for example, a city block to an entire continent.

Additional concepts are also identified:

    6. *Central places*.

    7. *Hierarchies*.

    8. *Gravity*, the idea that the amount of interaction between two places is directly proportional to the number of people living in those places and inversely proportional to the distance between them.

    9. *Distance*, including space, time and cost.

    10. *Scale*, focusing on the problem of points versus areas—with increasing scale points on a map (eg towns) become areas on a large scale plan.

    11. *Sequent occupance*, an aspect of 'change through time'—the identification of key stages in the settlement or occupance of a given place.[83]

    12. *Spatial diffusion*, which is closely related to spatial interaction but in the time dimension, and refers to the spread of an idea or innovation and its impact on the landscape and ways of life of a people.

Schemes based on statements of principles

The abstract technical concepts which form the basis of these schemes build up to form propositions or general principles, which have already been advanced as a useful way of presenting geographical objectives, and as a framework for selecting content (pages 37–42), Two examples of such schemes are provided below in further illustration, the first taken from the AHSGP, the second drawn up by the writer. Clearly the statements in themselves should not be seen as prescriptive, though the process they exemplify is regarded as of great assistance in the cogent structuring of content.

Principles appropriate to the study of habitat and resources (AHSGP)

In the AHSGP these are in fact referred to as 'major ideas', and each of those given below relates to a particular course activity in Unit 5 ('Habitat and Resources') of the project's course *Geography in an Urban Age*.[84]

1. Habitats may be classified according to the degree of change imposed by man. Every habitat consists of a large number of independent units.
2. Cultural traditions, technology and population affect the ways in which man uses different environments.
3. Terrain conditions relate to patterns of settlement in different ways, depending on the technology of the settlers and the population pressure on the area.
4. Because resources are defined in terms of needs and technology, conflicts arise over resource use.
5. Many adjustments to floods (hazards) are possible. Each alternative or combination has benefits or costs which must be evaluated.
6. The water balance affects many different kinds of human activity in an area.
7. The volume and character of wastes is affecting the quality of the environment. A relationship exists between economic consumption and waste production. Waste disposal decisions can affect ecological systems and cause imbalances.

Principles as a basis for the study of recreation and tourism

1. The presence of attractive coastal, mountain and other types of scenery provides a setting for physical and mental refreshment for

people during their leisure time. The need for such refreshment, and the degree of affluence required to meet this need, is most characteristic in advanced industrial societies.

2. In general, holiday makers tend to move from
   (a) inland areas to the coast;
   (b) lowland areas to the hills and mountains;
   (c) urban areas to rural areas (or from less to more attractive urban areas—resorts).
3. Such movements have been facilitated by
   (a) improved access and increased mobility resulting from technological change: foot → stagecoach → railway → automobile → aeroplane;
   (b) increased affluence and amount of leisure time.
4. Technological change has also affected the balance of competition between resorts, eg
   (a) 19th century—resort growth where rail links were established;
   (b) 20th century:
      (i) resort growth through motor contact;
      (ii) resort growth through air contact;
      (iii) switch from mass holidaying at home, to package tours abroad, made possible by improved information flows (travel agencies, telephones, cable, etc).
5. Tourist areas compete for custom on the basis of
   (a) scenic attractions
   (b) climatic attributes
   (c) quality of access.
6. Their success also reflects human decision making in terms of
   (a) provision of facilities, such as hotels and entertainments, designed to attract a particular clientele;
   (b) subjective perceptions and preferences of consumers (influenced by the nature of the facilities provided, and by advertising through the mass media).
7. The tourist industry may form a vital component in the national resource base. Consequently, the influence of governmental decision making and intervention may be crucial.
8. This resource base has the disadvantage in many cases of being subject to cyclical fluctuations:
   (a) seasonal, with different weather conditions concentrating the demand on particular seasons;
   (b) long-term financial cycles (reduction of money spent on holidays representing a possible means of cutting costs in times of financial stringency).
9. Partly because of this seasonal basis, many tourist resorts have other urban functions, often as residential areas for commuters or retired people.
10. The tourist industry exemplifies space-time tensions, being the

seasonal equivalent of the diurnal 'rush-hour' in large towns, with associated traffic and pedestrian congestion.
11. The tourist industry carries with it particularly heavy environmental costs, in the degradation of coastal, mountain, moorland and forest areas, by campers, hikers and motorists. The study of leisure, therefore, is an important component of environmental education.[85]

Such an outline brings out the range of objectives to be pursued. It draws in varying degrees on all geography's traditions, though with special reference here on the man/environment and spatial views. A strong areal studies component could be added and the earth science basis should not be ignored. Other schemes might well give different weight to each tradition. These frameworks of principles and concepts make it more likely that the overall content chosen is balanced and of intellectual and social worth.

Priority readings

1. EYRE, S. R. 'Determinism and the ecological approach to geography' in *Geography* (1964), **49**, pp. 369–76.
2. WATTS, D. G. *Environmental Studies* (Routledge & Kegan Paul), Chapter 2, pp. 20–47.
3. EVERSON, J. 'Field work in school geography' in WALFORD, R. (ed.) *New Directions in Geography Teaching* (Longman), pp. 69–84.
4. LONG, M. & ROBERSON, B. S. *Teaching Geography* (Heinemann), Chapter 7, pp. 99–120; Chapter 8, pp. 121–7.
5. FITZGERALD, B. P. *Developments in Geographical Method*, No. 1 in *Science in Geography* series (Oxford University Press).
6. THOMAS, P. R. 'Education and the new geography' in BALE, J., *et al.* (eds.) *Perspectives in Geographical Education* (Oliver & Boyd), pp. 67–76.
7. WALFORD, R. *Games in Geography* (Longman), Chapters 1–3, pp. 1–40.
8. GOULD, P. & WHITE, R. *Mental Maps* (Penguin Books), Chapter 7, pp. 173–92.
9. 'Teaching about the third world: a report of a symposium' in *Geography* (1975), **60**, pp. 52–8.

Questions for investigation and discussion

1. With reference to the statement by a nineteenth-century public school headmaster (page 76) regarding the respectability of geography as a secondary school subject, outline arguments you might use to refute similar suggestions from a headmaster or colleagues today.

2. Obtain a textbook of pre-World War I or inter-war vintage, and write critical reviews, (a) as though you were a teacher at that time, (b) from a point of view which would be more typical of today.
3. Set up the following role-playing simulation exercise with your colleagues:
    (a) Divide into groups of five or six, with each group representing the geography department of a large school. Assume that two of the staff are experienced 'hard-core traditionalists', in a position to control the purse strings but 'bending' a little in the face of innovatory new examination syllabuses. One or two more are 'enlightened' traditionalists, wishing to know more about the 'new geography', but lacking confidence to establish it in the school off their own bat. The final members of the staff are young but inexperienced teachers very anxious to introduce new methods.
    (b) Having decided which of the three types of role each individual is going to play, each of you should note down carefully before the exercise aspects of the personality and geographical viewpoint of the person he or she is going to assume.
    (c) The actual situation is that your sceptical head of department has agreed that, as a one-year experiment, an innovatory new syllabus can be introduced for the first years. The 'actor' or 'actors' playing the 'innovator(s)' should have a hand-out of the new syllabus they propose ready.
    (d) The role-playing exercise should simulate a departmental meeting at which the issues are thrashed out. The 'actor' playing the head of department should make a summary of the discussion and outline his conclusions.
4. Discuss the potential advantages and disadvantages of adopting idiographic as against nomothetic approaches in geography courses (a) at first form and (b) at sixth form level.
5. List and define the abstract technical and abstract vernacular concepts (refer back to page 39) contained in the statements of principles appropriate to geography courses on pages 97–9.
6. Refer to Chapter 7 in Gould and White (Priority reading No. 8).
    (a) Discuss in general its implications for school geography, relating this discussion to the conclusions emerging from the earlier consideration of stereotyping (pages 14–16).
    (b) Describe in detail how you would build the principles outlined in that chapter into a lesson or course unit for a particular age group in a secondary school.

References

1. CHARLTON, K. (1973) 'Aims in education: an historical approach' *London Educational Review*, **2**, 11.

2. BERNSTEIN, B. (1971) 'On the classification and framing of educational knowledge' in YOUNG, M. F. D. (ed.) *Knowledge and Control: New Directions for the Sociology of Education* (Collier-Macmillan, London), 47–69.
3. For a brief but useful introduction to the literature, see GOPSILL, G. H. (1956) *The Teaching of Geography* (Macmillan, London, 4th edition, 1973), 20–1.
4. See VAUGHAN, J. E. (1972) 'Aspects of teaching geography in England in the early nineteenth century' *Paedagogica Historica*, **12**, 131.
5. RAVENSTEIN, E. G. (1885) 'The aims and methods of geographical education' in *Report of the Proceedings of the Royal Geographical Society in Reference to the Improvement of Geographical Education* (John Murray, London, 1886), 165.
6. KELTIE, J. S. (1886) 'Report to the council', *ibid*, 24.
7. RGS (1886) 'Opinions of headmasters of English schools as to the value of geography and the position it ought to have in schools and universities', *ibid*, 92.
8. MARCHANT, E. C. (1964) 'Geography in education in England and Wales' *Geography*, **49**, 185.
9. FITZGERALD, B. P. (1974) *Developments in Geographical Method* Vol. 1 in *Science in Geography* series (Oxford University Press), Preface.
10. ROBERSON, B. S. (1963) 'A study of the kind of geography taught in secondary modern schools' *Educational Review*, **16**, 15.
11. HERBERTSON, A. J. (1913) 'The higher units: a geographical essay', reprinted *Geography* (1965), **50**, 335.
12. JAY, L. J. (1965) 'A. J. Herbertson: his services to school geography' *Geography*, **50**, 356.
13. PICKLES, T. (1939) *The World* (Dent, London, 1946 edition), 35.
14. HARRIES, S. G. (1967) 'Models of geographical teaching' in CHORLEY, R. J. & HAGGETT, P. (eds.) (1967) *Models in Geography* (Methuen, London), 777.
15. JAY, L. J. (1965), *op. cit.*, 358.
16. EYRE, S. R. (1964) 'Determinism and the ecological approach to geography' *Geography*, **49**, 370–1.
17. See SIMONS, M. (1966) 'What is a geographical factor?' in BALE, J., *et al.* (eds.) (1973) *Perspectives in Geographical Education* (Oliver & Boyd, Edinburgh), 170–80.
18. VAUGHAN, J. E. (1972), *op. cit.*, 133.
19. SYMONS, J. (1852) *School Economy* (Woburn Press Reprint, London, 1971), 100–1.
20. BURROWS, F. R. (1900) 'The teaching of geography in preparatory schools' in *Preparatory Schools for Boys: Their Place in English Secondary Education*, Board of Education Special Reports on Educational Subjects, Vol. 6 (HMSO, London, 1900), 228.
21. JAY, L. J. (1957) 'Sketch maps and geography teaching: the emergence of a technique' *Researches and Studies* (University of Leeds Institute of Education), **15**, 59.
22. KIRK, W. (1963) 'Problems of geography' *Geography*, **48**, 363.
23. BALCHIN, W. G. & Coleman, A. M. (1965) 'Graphicacy should be the fourth ace in the pack' in BALE, J. *et al.* (eds.) (1973), *op. cit.*, 81.
24. BALCHIN, W. G. (1972) 'Graphicacy' *Geography*, **57**, 194–5.
25. PERSONNE, E. (1959) 'L'observation directe en geographie: les classes-promenades' in SORRE, M. (ed.) *La Geographie* (Cahiers de Pedagogie Moderne, Editions Bourrelier, Paris), 68.
26. JOLLY, W. (1879) *Education: its Principles and Practice as Developed by George Combe* (Macmillan, London), 453–5.
27. WATTS, D. G. (1969) *Environmental Studies* (Routledge & Kegan Paul, London), 20–47.
28. *Ibid*, 44–7.

29. BALL, N. (1964) 'Richard Dawes and the teaching of common things' *Educational Review*, **17**, 62–4.
30. *Report of the Committee of Council on Education* (1876–7) 'Report of Rev. G. Steele on the Preston District' (HMSO, London), 577.
31. DAVIS, W. M. (1902) 'Field work in physical geography' in JOHNSON, D. W. (1909) *Geographical Essays by William Morris Davis* (Constable, London, 1954 edition), 239.
32. BARNARD, H. C. (1935) *Observational Geography and Regional Survey* (Le Play Society, London), 10.
33. LAURIE, S. S. (1888) *Occasional Addresses on Educational Subjects* (Cambridge University Press), note on 96–7.
34. REYNOLDS, J. B. (1901) 'Class excursions in Wales and England' *The Geographical Teacher*, **1**, 33. Though see also ORFORD, E. J. (1906) 'Home geography in London' *The Geographical Teacher*, **3**, 264–6.
35. BLYTH, W. A. L. (1965) *English Primary Education*, Vol. II (Routledge & Kegan Paul, London), 100, referring to CONS, G. J. & FLETCHER, C. (1938) *Actuality in School: An Experiment in Social Education* (Methuen, London), 1–18.
36. Cadbury Brothers, Ltd. (1943) *Our Birmingham* (Cadbury Brothers, Ltd., Birmingham), 54–5.
37. DAVIS, W. M. (1902) 'The progress of geography in the schools' in JOHNSON, D. W. (1909), *op. cit.*, 61.
38. LYDE, Professor (1912) 'Discussion on the homework of the geography class' *The Geographical Teacher*, **6**, 200–1.
39. Quoted in BRIGHAM, A. P. & DODGE, R. E. (1933) 'Nineteenth century textbooks of geography' in WHIPPLE, G. M. (ed.) (1933) *The Teaching of Geography* National Society for the Study of Education (University of Chicago Press), 10.
40. FITCH, J. G. (1884) *Lectures on Teaching* (Cambridge University Press), 362–5.
41. *Ibid*, 364–5.
42. *Report of the Committee of Council on Education* (1878–9) 'Report of H. W. G. Markheim on the Northallerton District' (HMSO, London), 643.
43. FITCH, J. G. (1884), *op. cit.*, 346.
44. MARCHANT, E. C. (1964), *op. cit.*, 173.
45. HUXLEY, T. H. (1877) *Physiography* (Macmillan, London), Preface viii.
46. HICKMAN, G. M. (1950) 'The sample study—a method and its limitations' *Journal of Geography*, **49**, 151–9.
47. ROBERSON, B. S. & LONG, M. (1956) 'Sample studies: the development of a method' *Geography*, **41**, 248–59.
48. BLOOMFIELD, E. R. (1971) 'New roles for case studies in geography' in BIDDLE, D. S. & DEER, C. E. (eds.) (1973) *Readings in Geographical Education*, Selections from Australian and New Zealand Sources, Vol. 2, 1966–72. (Whitcombe & Tombs, Sydney, for the Australian Geography Teachers' Association), 228.
49. MACKINDER, H. J. (1943) 'The development of geography' *Geography*, **28**, 70.
50. SCARFE, N. (1969) 'Curriculum planning in geographic education' *New Zealand Journal of Geography*, **47**, 20.
51. THOMAS, P. R. (1970) 'Education and the new geography' in BALE, J. *et al.* (eds.) (1973), *op. cit.*, 73.
52. BARTRAM, H. (1912) 'The correlation of elementary practical geometry and geography' in *The Teaching of Mathematics in the United Kingdom*, Board of Education Special Reports on Educational Subjects, Vol. 26, (HMSO, London), 80.
53. As explored in COLE, J. P. & BENYON, N. J. (1968 and 1972) *New Ways in Geography* series (Basil Blackwell, Oxford).
54. FITZGERALD, B. P. (1973) 'Scientific method, quantitative techniques and the teaching of geography' in WALFORD, R. (ed.) (1973) *New Directions in Geography Teaching* (Longman, London), 93.

55. EYRE, S. R. (1964), *op. cit.*, 369–76.
56. STODDART, D. R. (1965) 'Geography and the ecological approach: the ecosystem as a geographic principle and method' *Geography*, **50**, 242–51.
57. RENNER, J. M. (1970) 'Ecosystem studies and geographic education' *Journal of Geography*, **69**, 404–7.
58. HARRISON, C. M. (1969) 'The ecosystem and the community in biogeography' in COOK, R. V. & JOHNSON, J. H. (eds.) (1969) *Trends in Geography* (Pergamon Press, Oxford), 39.
59. DARROCH, A. (1906) 'The teaching of geography' *Scottish Geographical Magazine*, **22**, 486.
60. WALFORD, R. (1973) 'Models, simulations and games' in WALFORD, R. (ed.) 1973), *op. cit.*, 95–106.
61. SLATER, F. A. (1974) 'The use of models in classroom geography' *Classroom Geographer*, December 1974, 10.
62. See MARSDEN, W. E. (1974) *Changing Environments in Britain* Book 3. *Food Supplies/Conservation* (Oliver & Boyd, Edinburgh), 12–13, 22.
63. See WALFORD, R. (1969) *Games in Geography* (Longman, London).
64. TAYLOR, J. L. & WALFORD, R. (1972) *Simulation in the Classroom* (Penguin Books, Harmondsworth, Middlesex), 18–20.
65. WALFORD, R. (1968) 'Decision making' in BALE, J. et al. (eds.) (1973), *op. cit.*, 218–20.
66. COLE, J. P. & BEYNON, N. J. (1972), *op. cit.*, Book 3, 40–5.
67. WALFORD, R. (1973) 'Perception of a Local Environment' in WALFORD, R. (ed.) (1973) *op. cit.*, 29–33.
68. HICKMAN, G. *et al.* (1973) *A New Professionalism for a Changing Geography* (Schools Council, London), 6–7.
69. GOULD, P. & WHITE, R. (1974) *Mental Maps* (Penguin Books, Harmondsworth, Middlesex), 45.
70. See DONNELLY, P. A. (1972) 'Perception studies in geography' *Geographical Education*, **1**, 343–9.
71. GOULD, P. & WHITE, R. (1974) *op. cit.*, 186.
72. EMERY, J. S., *et al.* (1974) 'Environmental education: the geography teacher's contribution' *Journal of Geography*, **73**, 11. See also SHORTLE, D. (1971) 'Environmental quality and geographical education: charting a course for the 1970s' *Geographical Education*, **1**, 253–77.
73. GRIMSHAW, P. N. & BRIGGS, K. (1970) 'Geography and citizenship: pupil participation in town and country planning' *Geography*, **55**, 307–13.
74. STORM, M. (1970) 'Schools and the community: an issue based approach' in BALE, J. *et al.* (eds.) (1973), 289–304.
75. For a convenient summary, see 'Teaching about the third world: a report of a symposium' *Geography* (1975), **60**, 52–8.
76. See BLACHFORD, K. R. (1972) 'Values and geographical education' in BIDDLE, D. S. & DEER, C. E. (eds.) (1973), *op. cit.*, 42–50.
77. See LEACH, D. C. (1972) 'Teaching geography and teacher neutrality' *Classroom Geographer*, December 1972, 3–5; and, in reply, CLARK, R. (1973) 'Neutrality and commitment in teaching geography' *Classroom Geographer*, January 1973, 19–23.
78. AMBROSE, P. J. (1973) 'New developments in geography' in WALFORD, R. (ed.) (1973), *op. cit.*, 80–1.
79. DICKENSON, R. E. (1967) 'Urban concepts' *Times Educational Supplement*, 26 May, 1967, 1800.
80. NYSTUEN, J. D. (1963) 'Identification of some fundamental spatial concepts' in BERRY, B. J. L. & MARBLE, D. F. (eds.) (1968) *Spatial Analysis* (Prentice Hall, Englewood Cliffs, N.J.), 35–41.
81. Based on chapter headings and subheadings in HAGGETT, P. (1965) *Locational*

Analysis in Human Geography (Edward Arnold, London). See also BALE, J. (1976) *The Location of Manufacturing Industry* (Oliver & Boyd, Edinburgh), Chapter 1, for a similar type of conceptual framework.
82. THOMAS, E. N. (1965) 'A structure of geography: a proto-unit for secondary schools' in American High School Geography Project (1968) *The Local Community: A Handbook for Teachers* (Collier-Macmillan, London), 4-9.
83. See, for a British example, MARSDEN, W. E. (1972) 'An approach to "sequent occupance" for schools: a British case study' *Journal of Geography*, **71**, 340-8.
84. American High School Geography Project (1965) *Geography in an Urban Age*, Unit 5: *Habitat and Resources*, Teacher's Guide (Collier-Macmillan, London), iv-v.
85. See, for example, Schools Council *Geography for the Young School Leaver*, project kit (1974) *Man, Land and Leisure* (Nelson, London, for the Schools Council). The project was based on Avery Hill College of Education and co-directed by R. Beddis and T. Dalton.

7 Curriculum Integration and Geography

'Integration' is one of the most elusive terms in the curriculum literature. The opening sentence of Warwick's book on the subject: 'There is of course no such thing as "Integrated Studies" '[1] is not entirely paradoxical. Subject integration is also a thorny issue, and much of the controversy is generated by the fact that it means so many different things to different people.[2]

Integration in practice

Warwick identifies various forms of integration, classified according to the degree of structuring that is present.

(a) At the *unstructured* end of the spectrum, the approach is one 'in which the subjects as such do not make an appearance at all and in which children are free to develop their own individual and group approaches to large open-ended themes.'[3]

(b) The first step towards a more formalised position is termed *'theme teaching'*. Here the subjects are present in the background to give shape to the integrated scheme. The situation is a lightly structured one with balanced subject inputs.

(c) *Faculty teaching* describes the structuring of individual subjects into faculties such as 'humanities', 'creative arts', etc. The contribution of each subject is balanced, and within each faculty a 'common-core' syllabus is evolved through discussion. One of the subject departments concerned may take a leading role. The approach is more formal than (a) and (b), with content and direction controlled by the teachers. Team teaching procedures may be used. The timetable is blocked, formally recognising the existence of an integrated arrangement.

(d) *Related studies* refer to situations in which there is no formal timetable recognition of faculty groupings. History, geography and other subjects continue as timetable labels. Integration takes place to the extent that subject heads find out what others are doing, when they are doing it, and the order in which they are doing it. Cross-referencing is carried out and joint lessons or exchanges of teachers may be arranged.[4]

Warwick presents these as the most common forms of integration, though not the only ones in use. He acknowledges that they are largely organisational categories within which idiosyncracy of practice prevails, and he argues the need for a theoretical underpinning of such integrated schemes.[5]

Theoretical distinctions

Discussion at the theoretical level is helpful in sorting out the pros and cons of different types of integrated approach, and of these against the use of single subjects. Illustrations of the theory will, however, be made through reference to a theme that is a popular project topic in schools, namely 'The Sea'.

Pre-disciplinary enquiry

The most extreme form of integration is associated with the view that school subjects are subversive to child-centred education. In their place, a centre of interest, enquiry-based approach is advanced. It is based on a long-established concept of education which places the child at the centre, to be introduced to work in school relatively painlessly through contact with familar objects and scenes, prior to moving outwards to the less familiar (pages 84–5). From a preliminary stimulus, which may be in the form of a visit or some interesting material collected by the teacher or child, a project is developed on individual or group lines, often ending up with a public wall display.

Such enquiry is essentially pre-disciplinary. It accords well with children's needs at a particular stage of development, when it is guided experience which contributes to conceptualisation rather than formal criteria of understanding. Lawton has stressed, however, that such pre-disciplinary work is not non-disciplinary.[6] The children will often know whether it is English, geography, history or arithmetic they are using in building up their topic. They should be working, without perhaps being aware of it, within a framework ultimately based on a structure of knowledge understood and applied by the teacher. It is certainly not appropriate that the teacher's work should be pre-disciplinary.

If the claims made for this type of study are thus limited there is little cause for disagreement. The claims are often much wider than this, however, and form part of a progressive ideology antipathetic to academic subjects, which are described as mere 'rows of books in libraries'.[7] A subject stereotype of narrowness, academicism, encyclopaedism and accidental or dubious origins is presented, in antithesis to the values associated with child-centred education.

The philosophic basis of this argument rests on the notion that knowledge is a 'seamless cloak' and that in consequence the fragmentation introduced by subject-centred approaches and, by implication, the whole idea of curriculum planning are undesirable. Proponents of this view, however, do not substantiate it by first making clear what they mean by the unity of knowledge, and Pring dismisses it as being in the nature of an 'emotional craving'.[8]

There is a complementary idea that there is also unity in method. Knowledge is seen as only worthwhile when the child relates new facts and principles to his own scheme of understanding. In terms of initial motivation this is, of course, acceptable. But Pring suggests that there is more to it than this: no less than a 'theory of meaning'. Knowledge 'out there', away from the child's needs, is often viewed as pointless. This thesis he finds unacceptable on the grounds that (a) language and ways of knowing are essentially public and it is part of the job of the teacher to initiate children into common worlds of meaning, and (b) the idea that truth is relative to its usefulness in enquiry is an invalid view of knowledge (pages 48–9).[9]

The polarisation of 'child-centred' and 'subject-centred' reveals, in any case, a confusion of two separate dimensions. A subject-centred curriculum may be child-centred or not according to the nature of the classroom procedures used. The integrationist believes that topics should start from experiences familiar to the pupils. This has, in fact, been a long-standing and widely accepted teaching principle, fully applicable to subject-centred curricula (page 84). A case that rests heavily on evidence of bad practice in subject-centred curricula can easily be met by advocating a reform of subject teaching from within.[10] Presumably there are stronger arguments in favour of integration than this.

The association of enquiry-based learning with a progressive ideology is used to legitimise what are essentially pre-disciplinary approaches in the secondary school, where their place is much more arguable. Far from 'unity of knowledge' becoming a reality, a loosely-knit and somewhat arbitrary collection of materials and ideas often emerges. Thus Warwick makes use of a case study of a secondary school project on 'The Sea'. Part of the 'starter session' to the project was described as 'remarkable for the variety of material, including ship's cannon, sails, innumerable shells, seaweed, uniforms, and models which we had managed to accumulate'; and was categorised as 'an exhibition of the things associated with the sea.'[11] It is difficult to envisage how topics which have so wide a scope that it is hard to be irrelevant can readily contribute to the development of thinking skills, though they may be effective in promoting motivation, psycho-motor skills and a certain type of creative work.

This choice of example is open to the charge of condemning a system on the evidence of bad practice. But the critique is one of principle. The success of an educational operation is seen here as depending on the skill with which the teacher gradually and unobtrusively builds in opportunities for the exercise of thinking skills. *At the appropriate stage*, what has been described as pre-disciplinary enquiry can contribute to this objective. The criticism is thus addressed generally to those who seem to perceive enquiry-based, unstructured approaches as educational panaceas, universally applicable.

Combined studies

An intermediate stage between separate subject approaches and full integration is provided by 'combined' or 'related' studies, which Warwick regards as 'a legitimate first step to any closer liaison.'[12] This is in effect a pragmatic solution, involving a limited degree of co-operation between staff in organisational terms, and a complementary rather than a truly integrated approach to themes in the structural sense. Reverting to the previous example of 'The Sea', a 'combined studies' operation might be organised as in Fig. 7.1.

A lot of work undertaken under Warwick's 'faculty teaching' label (page 105), and much that is regarded as truly integrated, probably is more in the nature of combined studies teaching of this type.

A major disadvantage of combined studies approaches is that

integration is *implicit*. The student is left to do the integrating. Unless the material is very carefully arranged and cross-referenced, integration in any true sense is unlikely to be achieved. Assessments need to be designed to check whether it has taken place.

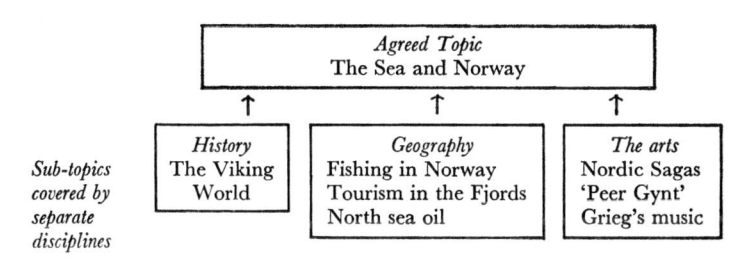

	Agreed Topic The Sea and Norway	
Sub-topics covered by separate disciplines	*History* The Viking World	*Geography* Fishing in Norway Tourism in the Fjords North sea oil	*The arts* Nordic Sagas 'Peer Gynt' Grieg's music

Fig. 7.1

Inter-disciplinary enquiry

Within the structure of knowledge broad *fields of experience* can be recognised. Interpretations of what these fields are differ, but in practice they include the sciences, the humanities and the creative arts, among others. Pring raises the question of what integrating basis there is in, for example, the humanities?

> ... we are bound to ask in what way does this theme or this area of study *itself* give a basis for structuring or organising knowledge other than in the worked out disciplines of thought. How does a child classify what he observes if not within the conceptual scheme that owes its formal structure to the basic and differentiated forms of knowledge?[13]

There are also in the structure of knowledge complex conceptual connections between the various forms (page 51). In addition to concepts intrinsic to particular disciplines, there are many inter-disciplinary connections, especially in areas such as the social sciences (pages 112–18), which share many broad concepts.

An important justification for integrated studies lies in the possibility of exploring these broad fields of experience and their inter-connections.[14] There is a strong case, however, for referring to this process as *inter-disciplinary enquiry*. This is taken to refer to the use of a number of disciplines in conjunction to focus on a problem of an intellectual, moral or practical nature. It is useful to distinguish this from the looser concept of *integration*, which is conveniently used to define the process by which subjects are grouped in the school curriculum. Inter-disciplinary enquiry would be one of the variants of integration in this sense, but not the only one. In inter-disciplinary enquiry the integrity of the disciplines is maintained. They are seen as means to an end, but not as redundant.

True inter-disciplinary enquiry is concerned with *inter-action* rather than mere juxtaposition. At the organisational level it implies detailed co-operation between staff in which agreed statements of objectives are spelled out and course structures jointly planned. The purpose of the exercise is to bring together the concepts, principles and methodologies of different disciplines in an attempt to come to grips with problem issues which could not be grasped as effectively by individual disciplines alone.

A preliminary task is to identify 'problems' that require such study. These need not be solely real-life social and environmental problems, though these will figure prominently in such schemes. In real-life planning, a team of researchers will be brought together to exercise their skills on, for example, urban traffic or rural conservation issues. In the classroom, simulated problems of this kind can usefully be introduced. Links have to be established at two levels, as illustrated in Fig. 7.2 through the unifying theme 'Using the North Sea's resources wisely', which is a topic given a value-laden, problem orientation.

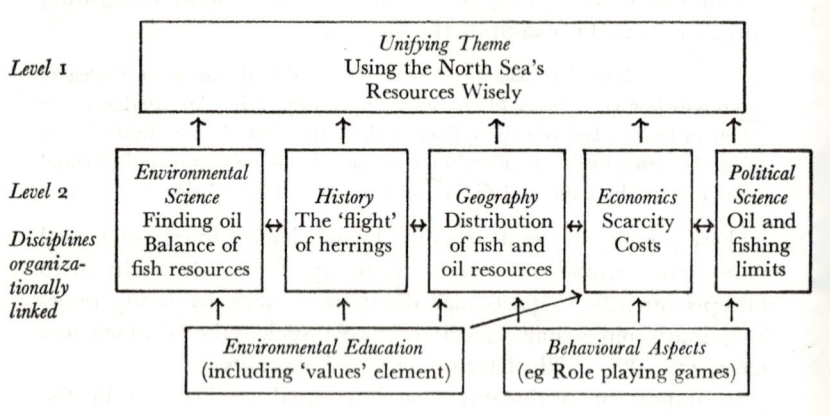

Level 1	\multicolumn{5}{c}{Unifying Theme — Using the North Sea's Resources Wisely}
Level 2 — Disciplines organizationally linked	Environmental Science — Finding oil, Balance of fish resources	History — The 'flight' of herrings	Geography — Distribution of fish and oil resources	Economics — Scarcity, Costs	Political Science — Oil and fishing limits
	\multicolumn{3}{c}{Environmental Education (including 'values' element)}	\multicolumn{2}{c}{Behavioural Aspects (eg Role playing games)}

Fig. 7.2

The degree of co-operation that such a scheme implies provides potentially for a fruitful cross-fertilisation of ideas that can be highly enjoyable and, given a proper division of labour, even time-saving in the long run. Such activities necessitate a fresh look at objectives, highlight the need for support from in-service provision, and may hopefully lead to a more professional approach, in which practice is underpinned by theory. Holly's contention that the 'good specialist is, in the end, defeated by his own specialism'[15] is speculative, but not so wide of the mark as not to draw attention to the fact that high subject expertise *can* lead to self-satisfaction and closing of minds. The need for new thinking can blow a lot of cobwebs away.

Further support for the fully-fledged integration that interdisciplinary enquiry represents, comes from Bernstein, who shows it to have important social consequences for the school. He identifies two types of curricula: *collection* and *integrated*, and two general concepts pertaining to the structuring of the curriculum: *classification* and *framing*.

(a) A *collection-type* curriculum is where the contents are insulated from one another, as in subject-centred approaches.

(b) An *integrated-type* is as described above.

(c) *Classification* is proposed as a term to describe the degree of boundary maintenance between the contents.

(d) *Framing* is used to refer to the relationship between teacher and taught, defined as *strong* in formal, highly structured situations, and *weak* in informal, lightly structured situations.[16]

Oversimplification is clearly present, in that strong classification and framing are linked with collection type curricula, and weak classification and framing with integrated type. It is not difficult to find subject departments which maintain firm boundary definitions, but adopt weakly framed teaching styles. Bernstein accepts that there are variants, but maintains that framing is only allowed to weaken after a long period of conditioning to the school ethos, as in the sixth form; and classification only after a long period of initiation into subject loyalties (which in fact often does not occur until post-graduate level). Weakened classification and framing is also allowed for less able children 'whom we have given up educating.'[17]

Bernstein regards the collection code as providing for those who go on to the sixth form and beyond 'order, identity and commitment', but for those not doing so 'it can sometimes be wounding and seen as meaningless.'[18] The integrated code, on the other hand, reduces the authority of subject content and the discretion of teachers, and shifts the balance of power from teachers towards pupils. There is also a reduction of hierarchical orientation at staff level, with a greater stress on horizontal contacts between staff than on the vertical between a head of department and his assistants. Acts of teaching become more visible.[19] The teacher is less isolated within the walls of his classroom.

A further argument for inter-disciplinary enquiry stems from changes which have taken place in subjects themselves, which at university level are actively 'de-classifying'. Geography is a good example. It would be ludicrous to accept the philosophy of the 'new geography' without acknowledging that movements 'at the frontier' are largely in favour of convergence with other disciplines. The conceptual revolution in the subject points firmly in the direction of inter-disciplinarity (page 69).

This has happened because so many of the issues the new methodology is addressing itself to are those for which inter-disciplinary treatment is necessary, a point which may well constitute the strongest of the arguments for inter-disciplinary enquiry. Thus Hirst and Peters have noted the role of integrated approaches of this type in equipping people adequately to make practical and moral judgements. This requires the ability to recognise the relevance of very diverse considerations, and to bring them together in a responsible judgement. They see conclusive arguments for having both independent and integrated approaches in school curricula:

> Just as it is hard to see how the distinctive character of logically distinct modes of knowledge and experience can possibly be understood without some separate systematic attention to them, so it is hard to see how, without the use of properly designed integrative units, the complex interrelations of the domains can be adequately appreciated.[20]

Problems and resolutions

1. *Structuring knowledge: geography, history and the social sciences*

In the 'broad fields of experience' that the humanities and social science areas represent, considerable problems are posed by the complex nature of the relationships between the constituent elements. The purpose of this section is to try to tease out some of the connections between history, geography and the social sciences. History and geography have a manifestly close relationship. As Kant observed, geography is concerned with relations among things that coexist in space while history is concerned with sequences of natural events in time, with history presupposing geography and geography dependent on historical knowledge for explanatory purposes.[21] One of the major contradictions in Hirst's original formulation of the 'forms' and 'fields' of knowledge (pages 50–1) lay in his allotment of history to the forms and geography to the fields. They are similarly distinguishable from the 'pure' social sciences, in that they are *both* 'fields' according to Hirst's earlier criteria; whereas the social sciences might with greater justification be described as 'forms' of knowledge. History and geography are alike in rather similar ways. These include their

(a) synthesising element, which contrasts with the more analytical approaches of the social sciences;

(b) propensity for 'mutating' concepts derived from the other disciplines (page 51), particularly from the social sciences;

(c) characteristic methodologies and tools of enquiry, with traditionally a stress on idiographic as distinct from nomothetic approaches (page 59). This distinction is, however, now breaking down, particularly in geography.

From the geographer's standpoint, a second caveat has been lodged against the interpretation of the nature of geography which Hirst accepted, as the study of man's relationship with his environment (page 50). Earlier discussion made clear the shift, at the frontier of knowledge at least, in geography's relationships from the humanities towards the social sciences. Mikesell notes that the interests of geographers are not evenly or randomly distributed across the whole spectrum of their enterprise, and that the community of geographers 'now includes a substantial, if not dominant, group of scholars who hope to see their subject ranked alongside anthropology, economics, political science, psychology and sociology as a social or behavioural science.'[22]

Social scientists are also aware of the interfaces of their disciplines with history and geography, but do not seem quite clear as to what it is history and geography are offering. 'One searches the list [of methods, points of view and approaches] in vain for a substantive concept to identify with history or geography, as "culture" is related to anthropology, "power" to political science, and "scarcity" to economics', laments Morrissett.[23] It would seem that as yet social scientists are unaware of the fact, or unable to accept, that geography at least *has* such a distinctive characteristic in its peculiar involvement with the spatial dimension though, as we have seen, there is the danger of gross over-simplification in seeking a single, catch-all, distinctive 'key concept'.

The following are usually accepted as the main social sciences:

(i) *Anthropology*, which is the study of social and cultural systems of total societies and social organisations, with the notion of 'culture' as a central concept.

(ii) *Sociology*, which is the study of the relation of individuals or groups to society as a whole, with central concepts such as 'role', 'social class' and 'ideology'.

(iii) *Economics*, a study in which the central idea is the 'scarcity' concept.

(iv) *Political science*, which is a study of the way in which society organises itself to resolve value conflicts, in which 'power' is a high level concept.

(v) *Psychology*, which is the study of behaviour. [24, 25]

The ideas which the social sciences are interested in are often the concern also of historians and geographers. Heater, for example, identifies a number of sociological concepts which he sees not only as well illustrated, but in need of illustration, by history, namely leadership, decision making, the role of the individual, ideology and international relations. [26]

Similarly in geography, no valid study of, for example, land reclamation in the Netherlands could neglect the basic economic concept of scarcity; nor could a study of primitive societies omit reference to anthropological, sociological (and also ecological) concepts; nor could a study of spatial perception of environmental hazards ignore ideas from the behavioural sciences.

There are many trans-disciplinary concepts, which figure prominently across the social sciences/history/geography spectrum, though some may be identified as more important in some areas than others. (See Fig. 7.3.)

Examples of Broad Social Science Concepts	Economics	Geography	History	Sociology
Hinterland	/	//	/	/ (catchment area)
Feudalism		/	//	/
Community	/	/	/	//
Trade	//	/	/	/

/ denotes important // very important

Fig. 7.3

History and geography can usefully be seen as disciplines drawing together, or synthesising, elements of the social sciences, each making a distinctive contribution, with history looking at the world from a chronological or 'vertical' viewpoint and geography from a chorological or 'horizontal' viewpoint. The relationships can be illustrated as in Fig. 7.4.

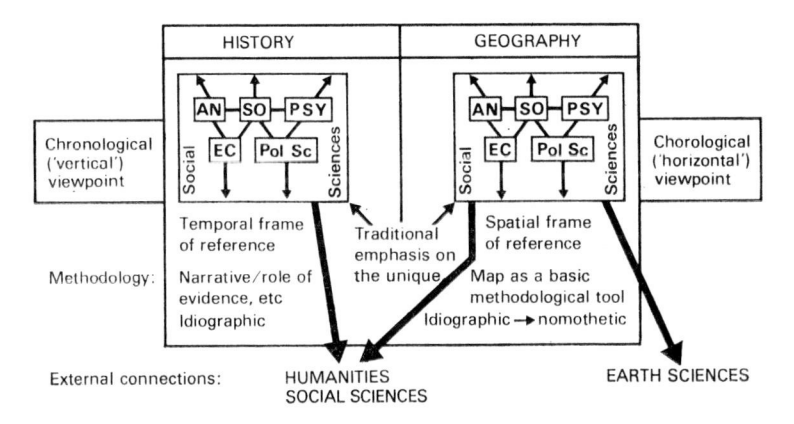

	HISTORY	GEOGRAPHY	
Chronological ('vertical') viewpoint	Social [AN–SO–PSY] [EC] [Pol Sc] Sciences	Social [AN–SO–PSY] [EC] [Pol Sc] Sciences	Chorological ('horizontal') viewpoint
Methodology:	Temporal frame of reference Narrative/role of evidence, etc Idiographic	Traditional emphasis on the unique	Spatial frame of reference Map as a basic methodological tool Idiographic → nomothetic	
External connections:	HUMANITIES SOCIAL SCIENCES		EARTH SCIENCES

Fig. 7.4

The diagram shows also the connections of history and geography outside the social sciences. Both subjects, and especially history, have connections with the humanities, which are taken to include literature, the fine arts, and religious and moral education; while geography, though tending to shift away from the humanities, especially at university level, retains a strong association with the 'earth sciences'. These include geology, hydrology, oceanography, meteorology, pedology and here, for the sake of convenience, ecology, though strictly this is one of the biological sciences.

Translating this into a hypothetical school situation, in which the spectrum of knowledge is divided into a series of areas of study broader than the traditional disciplines, the situation is no less complicated. Fig. 7.5, illustrating the relations of geography in particular, demonstrates this complexity.

The diagram suggests that there are four subject areas which have intrinsically strong 'integrating' tendencies, namely ecology, geography, history and English, all of which except ecology are standard subjects in the curriculum. While the methods used in these subjects may in practice be narrow, the spread of content which they cover certainly is not.

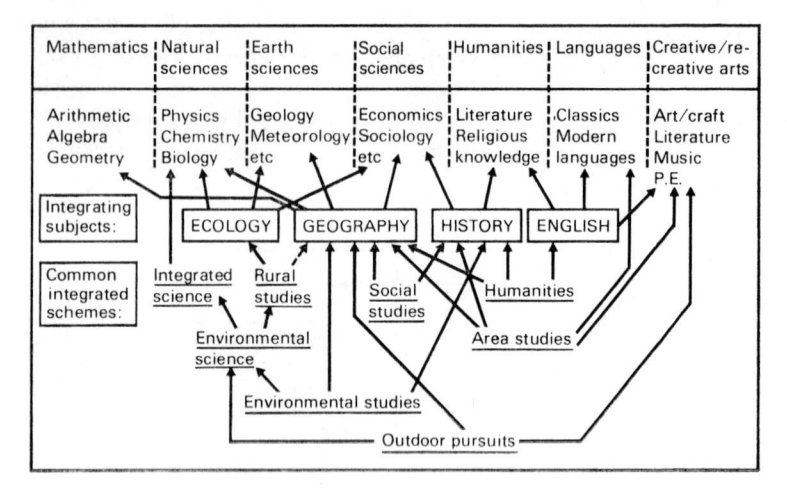

Fig. 7.5

The connections of geography are particularly wide-ranging. It is commonly found in the following types of 'integrated scheme':

Environmental science: The physical elements of geography, with ecology (or biology), geology, meteorology, pedology (soil study) and so on.

Environmental studies: Both physical and human aspects of geography, local history, ecology (or biology), and perhaps a social science component (for example, archaeology).

Social studies: Largely human aspects of geography, with history and the social sciences. (Here the 'new' social studies should be distinguished from the immediate post-war version, in which 'civics' seems to have been the main 'social' component.)[27]

Humanities: The human aspects of geography, with history, religious knowledge and English.

Outdoor pursuits: the physical aspects of geography, with earth sciences, ecology (or biology) and physical education.

Area studies: Not so much local studies (see environmental studies) as studies focused on large-scale units such as European or American studies, drawing on regional geography, history, literature and other creative arts, languages and the social sciences.

In practice, geography is most frequently involved today in two broad types of scheme. The first is *environmental studies* in which it often lies in the middle of a sandwich between biology and history. Such schemes are now tending to broaden out in both areal and social terms to provide an issue-based *environmental education*, in which the environment is not only used for education, but education is seen as a means of promoting conservation of the environment. Wheeler regards this as 'a pragmatic involvement in environmental problems and teaching strategies'[28] rather than as something emerging from the frontiers of knowledge.[29]

The second type of scheme perhaps reflects the fact that there are more teachers of history and religious knowledge in the schools than of economics and sociology, so that a large number of integrated schemes with which geography is associated are part not of a social sciences, but a *humanities* package. It is used as a means of introducing children to their cultural heritage, and often includes, in the early stages of the scheme, geological, ecological and anthropological components as part of an evolutionary study. In such schemes, an authentic geographical component is easily lost.

In more theoretical terms, Cootes has advocated the need to distinguish clearly between the humanities and social sciences, arguing that attempts to integrate them in the timetable are liable to work to the detriment of both. Each have characteristic groups of objectives, methodologies and criteria for truth. The humanities are largely idiographic in nature, focusing upon the doings and achievements of individuals and unique events in a temporal or spatial context, in contrast to the central nomothetic tendency of the social sciences.[30]

Scrimshaw draws a broad distinction between the humanities and the social sciences on the grounds of the type of language they use: ordinary ('vernacular') in the case of the humanities, and specialised ('technical') language in the case of the social sciences. The language of the humanities is vaguer and more qualitative, while that of the social sciences is clearer and more consistent, in theory at least. He sees a need for both in any social education programme.[31]

Further, if 'social relevance' is an objective, Cootes suspects that the inherent qualities of the humanities may be lost sight of, as when English teachers have to select literature on the grounds of its 'relevance' rather than its aesthetic qualities. Equally, social science teaching can be distorted through being included in a humanities programme, in which general concepts such as 'conflict' may be reduced to the level of 'social speculation' to fit in with a humanities-type, 'old-time' social studies approach.[32]

Cootes argues that geography and history do not fit neatly into either the social sciences or humanities. Thus the part of history which is concerned with posing moral questions about the actions of people and with describing the unfolding drama of these actions through time, belongs to the humanities. Another part of history seeks to explain, in terms analogous to the social sciences, unique events through general theses. As we have seen, geography, though increasingly social science-orientated (page 113), retains a strong link with the earth sciences and continues to serve the humanities.

It may be, however, that this inability to fit conveniently into a grand logical design is an advantage in curriculum terms, for geography and history, drawing on a wide range of concepts from the social sciences, are to an extent inherently inter-disciplinary. Thus economic, social and political concepts may be transmitted under their aegis even though the mother subjects do not have a place in the timetable. The social scientist would, of course, ask concernedly how effectively these ideas are being transmitted, whether the coverage is broad enough and the analysis deep enough.

2. *Structuring in an inter-disciplinary framework*

One of the problems in many topic-based studies, such as those with wide scope like 'The Sea', is that the topics in themselves are not integrative, and do not in any detailed way provide criteria for choice of content, except at the level of distinguishing, say, between sea, land and air. Three problems are posed: those of balance, sequence and focus.

The problem of balance

The balance between elements in the structure of knowledge is met to some degree in traditional curricula. It may be more difficult to achieve in integrated curricula where there is a more amorphous spread of content to be incorporated, and where negotiation on what goes into the course is conducted on a personal basis. In these circumstances, decisions can be affected by the personal power of one individual, by a clash of personalities and by an unbalanced range of subject expertise. A dominant historian may over-emphasise the temporal, or a geographer the spatial dimension. For such reasons, a balance across the particular field of experience may be prejudiced.

It may be that historians and geographers feel that, at least up to sixth form level, they themselves are able to handle what they see as the relevant aspects of subjects such as economics, sociology, political science, ecology and geology. This is a hazardous assumption if it reflects a belief that the teacher need be only one step in front of the children. While many geography and history graduates have undertaken courses in these related subjects, the range of skills that is reasonably required is often beyond the compass of a single person.[33]

The 'pure' social scientist cannot be expected to accept that the geographer or historian will guarantee a balanced infusion of *his* particular contribution to an inter-disciplinary package. There is a real fear that many concepts germane to major areas of the humanities and social sciences will not be authentically presented. It cannot, in addition, be justly argued that 'pure' social science content is less important in principle than that of history and geography.

Thus the problem of balance to a considerable extent boils down to being a practical one. For the time being, there are many more skilled practitioners of history and geography than of the social sciences. Where geographers and historians alone make up the 'social education' team, it is incumbent upon them to think in inter-disciplinary terms, seeing as far as they are able that at least the broad perspectives these related disciplines have to offer are introduced. Admittedly, in any ideal sense this is not enough.

The problem of sequence

The problem of sequencing material is already a difficult one in geography, where the core concepts and principles often do not build on each other, but are of parallel importance, yet have strongly overlapping tendencies. The task becomes extremely complex when subjects such as geography are joined with similar subjects. Thus Graves notes that 'developing a worthwhile course on IDE [inter-disciplinary enquiry] lines must be an extraordinary difficult task, since the topics chosen must not only enable the dove-tailing of various disciplines in some coherent pattern, but each succeeding topic chosen must build upon the previous topic in such a way that principles and concepts learnt are gradually enriched and developed.'[34] There are also the methodological skills which each separate subject tends to stress. It is clearly more straightforward, for example, to build a logical sequence of map-reading skills into a geography curriculum than into an integrated one.

Sumner has similarly exposed this problem in the context of economics, and suggests that one solution is to emphasise the contribution of various disciplines in turn, retaining the concepts from other areas which are necessary to the topic under discussion.[35]

One of the most widely advocated methods of sequencing is Bruner's 'spiral curriculum' idea in which major concepts are revisited at different stages, each later stage involving a higher degree of complexity.[36] This is, of course, also a useful concept for a subject-centred curriculum. There would seem to be a need for an interlocking set of spirals in a broad social studies arrangement.

The problem of focus

As we have noted (page 108), a broad topic such as 'The Sea' or 'Homes' does little in itself to prevent an arbitrary selection of content. Even where certain aspects are emphasised through the introduction of disciplinary criteria, there may still be a lack of focus. Hence a project on 'Homes' can include 'Roman settlements' from history, 'igloos and kraals' from geography, baroque architecture in art and craft, 'safety in the home' in home economics, and 'homes in Victorian novels' in English literature. Other criteria need to be brought to bear to enable a coherent choice to be made. These may be found in area-based and concept-based schemes.

Area-based schemes

Area studies of different types can help in this way, though if used alone the areal component can be as diffuse as any topic. Care has also to be taken that such arrangements do not become another label for geography, for the geographer's skills are likely to be especially valuable in the areal mode of study.

Local studies at various scales, even detailed *site studies*, are a good way of focusing the contributions of particular disciplines. Many integrated schemes at all stages of schooling are based on the stimulus of local studies in the field (pages 81–4). Yet a number of well-known educationists have been disturbed by the potential of such schemes for engendering parochialism. Taba sees local studies as 'ethnocentric' when the prior need is to develop a 'cosmopolitan' viewpoint.[37] Bruner is sceptical of studies based on 'the familiar world of home, the street and the neighbourhood' and 'the friendly postman,'[38] and draws attention to the difficulty of generalising from the familiar.

Concentric studies are a useful foil, the principle being to use the locality as a base from which to move out over the world concentrically, say from local to regional, then to national, then to global levels, widening the focus on a particular topic or concept (page 85). Masterton has illustrated this principle effectively in an environmental studies context, taking as a starting point, for example, a local peak, and moving out from direct studies on the spot to indirect studies of hills and mountains in the wider world, striving to fuse at each stage the contributions of various disciplines.

Studies of large-scale areas, such as European and American Studies, are becoming more popular, and to some extent a focusing principle is provided. These, too, can be part of a concentric scheme,[39] and be used to explore similarities and differences between areas. Dufour provides an example from the Indian sub-continent, which is mentioned here to illustrate that such schemes are not just geography under a different label. Thus under *cultural topics* he includes religions, the caste system, music and instruments, architecture and buildings, dress; under *political topics* Independence, Gandhi, political groups in India and Pakistan; under *economic topics* the village, food production, foreign investment and aid, and so on.[40]

Concept-based schemes

An alternative to the topic- or area-based study is the more fully organised method of employing broad concepts as a basis on which work can be structured in a truly inter-disciplinary way. Bernstein regards as necessary for real integration the presence of a 'relational idea, a supra-content concept, which focuses upon general principles at a high level of abstraction. . . . Whatever the relational concepts are, they will act selectively upon the knowledge within each subject which is to be transmitted.'[41] These concepts are likely to be expressed at a high level of generality. They are often in the nature of commonsense or vernacular concepts, by definition trans-disciplinary (see 'Key concepts', page 40).

Several examples may be used to illustrate differing interpretations of this type of process. First, Bruner's well-known and anthropologically orientated *Man: A Course of Study* is organised round three recurrent questions.

> What is human about human beings?
> How did they get that way?
> How can they be made more so?

In pursuit of these questions, five great 'humanising forces' function as over-arching themes, namely tool-making, language, social organisation, the management of man's prolonged childhood, man's urge to explain the world.[42] The inter-penetration of these themes is emphasised. The contributions of the social and behavioural sciences, the humanities and the natural sciences demonstrates that the ambition of the scheme is to furnish a near-total curriculum.

It was suggested earlier that the use of statements of principles and generalisations rather than bare concept terms is a helpful way of structuring content, as well as providing a source of objectives (pages 38–9). A familiar topic such as *Leisure* can be thus transformed from a loose thematic label to a basis for a scheme that is problem-orientated and cogently structured. Lawton and Dufour have outlined such a scheme on this topic.[43]

QUESTIONS TO BE EXPLORED	GENERALIZATIONS TO BE ENCOURAGED
1. *What is leisure?*	Leisure is the name we give to activities which we undertake in time which is separate from work and other essential human activities. It is a difficult concept, especially related to complex society (since small-scale societies see no distinction between work and other activities and leisure). Also some people may relax and derive satisfaction and entertainment from their work.
2. *How can we distinguish types of leisure and recreation?*	We can distinguish these varieties by dividing them into two groups—participating and non-participating.
3. *How have leisure and recreation changed?* Selected examples of various types of leisure, recreation and sport.	Leisure has changed as a result of changes in the technological and cultural stages of the society. Leisure varies over time and between societies (historically and comparatively).

4. *What patterns of leisure and recreation can we discern today?* Case-studies of the organisation techniques and popularity of a limited number of pursuits. Special study of television, based on professional research findings and pupils' own enquiries.	Statistics confirm that patterns are becoming more varied; more people from a broader cross-section of class backgrounds are taking up a wide variety of participatory activities, eg horse-riding, canoeing, sailing, and driving into the countryside (associated with car-ownership). Television has established itself as a major domestic form of entertainment. Related to this, cinema attendance declined.
5. *How may leisure change in the future?*	With greater technological development in industrial societies we can expect: (i) a change in the technology of entertainment; eg an increase in cassettes as opposed to records; (ii) that taste in leisure and recreation will be less clearly related to social class and similar factors. (iii) an increase in the time available for leisure and recreation owing to increasing automation: this will manifest itself in shorter hours of work and early retirement.

It is interesting to compare this with a previously outlined geography scheme based on the same topic (pages 97–9). There is the same stress on the use of principles or generalisations as a means of selecting important content. Both can be regarded as interest-based and relevant. While there are overlaps, the slants are very different. One of the schemes is presented as part of a disciplinary and the other an inter-disciplinary framework. Both are, however, wide-ranging in their content and ideas, though neither cover a comprehensive range of relevant concepts. A truly sociological component is as conspicuous by its absence from the first scheme as a geographical one is from the second.

Another useful trans-disciplinary concept is that of *frontier* or *barrier*, which has important connotations in geography, history and the social sciences. In geography we might think of a physical frontier such as a watershed; in history of a national frontier, possibly changing over time; in economics of trade barriers; in anthropology/ethnology of cultural or ethnic differences; in sociology of social divides or class barriers; in political science of party divisions, or ideological divides such as communism versus capitalism.

Gould has argued strongly in favour of looking to such broad concepts as 'barriers' as integrating themes.

> What sense does it make for example, to discuss tariffs in economic geography, administrative boundaries in political geography, linguistic constraints in cultural geography, housing constraints in urban geography, and so, wearily, on? The important point is that there are *barriers* to all sorts of human flows across geographic space, including the barrier of distance itself, suitably warped and twisted by transportation and communications technology. Show the beginning student how to handle, think about, measure and analyse barriers, and you have given him a higher order concept that means he will never be able to think about this aspect of human spatial organisation with quite the same naïveté again. . . . There is a genuine question of intellectual *efficiency* here . . . an area of the traditional curriculum . . . where much consolidation and pruning is possible, to reduce the usual over-blown list while sharpening the contents.[44]

Within a single subject field, the concept of barrier is thus seen to invoke a range of meanings. Even within one subject, however, the notion does not in itself provide a non-arbitrary structuring mechanism unless other criteria are applied. The spatial dimension is here regarded as a co-integrating theme.

The dangers are more evident in an inter-disciplinary scheme. An attempt to resolve the problem in a wider setting is presented in relating the idea of 'barriers, divides and frontiers' to an area studies framework, here European studies.

European studies: 'Barriers, divides and frontiers'
1. Conflicts between groups and nations are associated with *division*: with, for example, social divides, economic barriers and political frontiers among other things.
2. *Political frontiers* reflect divisions between nation states and isolate and protect people of similar national identity.
3. Such frontiers may reflect *natural geographical obstacles* such as rivers, marshes and mountain ranges.
4. *Artificial barriers* may be built as a substitute or reinforcement for natural barriers: eg Hadrian's Wall, the Maginot and Siegfried Lines, the Berlin Wall.
5. *Religious differences* have an ideological basis, and are the product of long standing historical contexts, though with less well developed geographical expression than national frontiers, eg north and south Germany, Ulster and Eire.

6. *Ethnic divides* result from migration of peoples and are often a cause of serious internal conflicts within otherwise ethnically homogeneous states, eg Jews in Europe, displaced persons, migrant workers.
7. *Linguistic divides* are serious barriers to communication, both between and within states, but compare Belgium and Switzerland.
8. *Social divides* are common within all countries, and operate at individual and group levels (social class divides): they also have ideological overtones (eg capitalist versus communist systems).
9. *Economic barriers* reflect different resource bases, and the need to protect home industries and markets from overseas competition. Countries may join to erect communal barriers against outsiders, eg the European Economic Community and Comecon. Economic differences also operate at group and individual levels.
10. *Cultural differences* In many ways Europe has a 'common culture', but many regional and national differences occur in terms not only of language, but also of architecture, customs and life styles.
11. National, cultural and social differences lead to the formation of 'inferior images' or *stereotypes*. Other significant concepts in this area include *patriotism* and *propaganda*.

This provides only a general framework for a large curriculum unit. Depending on the scope of the unit, each of these major principles needs to be broken down further. Then each of the sub-principles require further unpacking before lesson units emerge (pages 38-48).

3. *Subject-specific skills and concepts*

Emphasis has been placed on connections between disciplines and important groups of concepts which are trans-disciplinary. There remain, however, many relatively specific concepts, not to mention a wide range of skills and tools of enquiry, that would appear more conveniently tackled in school within the bounds of a particular discipline. Some subjects feel this need more than others, mathematics and modern languages being cases in point. But even in subjects which lend themselves to integration, including history and geography, many by no means reactionary teachers would still make a claim to have some time to cover essential skills and basic concepts and principles. This claim is here accepted, and reinforces Hirst's and Peters' argument for both independent and integrated approaches in the school curriculum (page 112).

4. *The role of the teacher*

The imposition of integrated schemes can pose serious problems for teachers whose range of intellectual and social skills is narrow. The commitment of teachers to integrated codes is a crucial factor in whether or not they are successful. Bernstein spells out the issues:

> There must be consensus about the integrating idea and it must be very explicit. . . . Integration codes . . . weaken specific identities . . . [and] require a high level of ideological consensus and this may affect the recruitment of staff. Integrated codes at the surface level create weak or blurred boundaries, but at bottom they may rest on closed explicit ideologies. Where such ideologies are not shared, the consequences will become visible and threaten the whole at every point.[45]

Teachers used to working under traditional schemes require a process of socialisation into the integrated code, for the procedures of the new code will need to be as much internalised as those of the old. It is well known that integrated schemes in both intellectual and organisational terms are more difficult to work than traditional schemes. As Bernstein writes:

> The collection code is capable of working when staffed by mediocre teachers, whereas integrated codes call for much greater powers of synthesis and analogy, and for more ability to both tolerate and enjoy ambiguity at the level of knowledge *and* social relationships.[46]

A further problem is that 'socialisation' of teachers seeking a 'progressive badge' may be quick and superficial, bringing an ideological commitment to dispense with the disciplines, rather than a positive perception of their role in an integrated code. This point is made in Shipman's investigation of the working of a Schools Council 'integrated' project. Despite regular statements by the project team that their objective was to make productive use of subject contributions in an integrated situation, those teachers with whom the idea had caught on persisted in seeing the process as a 'breaking down' exercise.[47]

Conclusions

A cool appraisal of some of these problems may lead a particular school to conclude that it is either undesirable or impractical to reorganise on an integrated basis; or that the disadvantages outweigh the advantages. In these circumstances there is a desperate need for reform from within existing subjects. In subjects such as geography there is every opportunity to 'think inter-disciplinary', to see boundaries as permeable, and to co-operate with other teachers at least at the 'combined studies' level.

This may be thought to savour too much of a pragmatic, safety-first solution. Yet in the light of the state of knowledge, current levels of professionalism, other burdens being placed on teachers (such as mixed ability grouping) and lack of in-service provision and other resources, a holding position may be the defensible policy for many secondary schools. It is possible to be in favour of the principle of inter-disciplinary enquiry, yet be held back by a discouraging lack of evidence that in practice the problems that it poses have even been perceived as problems, let alone solved.

There seems no reason why what seems a useful and even necessary solution, that is to use concurrently both independent and integrated approaches, cannot be achieved in terms of timetabling. But how do we ensure that when it takes place it becomes more than a progressive publicity label? The critical factor is again the quality and commitment of the headteacher and his staff. This is so weighty a variable that the subject-centred versus integrated curriculum question itself can be seen as not the most crucial educational issue of the day. Both systems can work well given the right staff and an adequate backing of resources. Where these are not present, the system less difficult to operate may be the appropriate, though one hopes the interim, choice.

Priority readings

1. WARWICK, D. (ed.) *Integrated Studies in the Secondary School* (University of London Press).
2. NAISH, M. 'Geography in the integrated curriculum' in GRAVES, N. J. (ed.) *New Movements in the Study and Teaching of Geography* (Temple Smith), 55–71.
3. BULL, G. B. G. 'Interdisciplinary enquiry: a geography teacher's assessment' in BALE, J., et al. (eds.) *Perspectives in Geographical Education*, 258–66.
4. MUSGROVE, F. 'The contribution of sociology to the study of the curriculum' in KERR, J. F. (ed.) *Changing the Curriculum* (University of London Press Unibooks), 96–109.
5. BERNSTEIN, B. 'On the classification and framing of educational knowledge' in YOUNG, M. F. D. (ed.) *Knowledge and Control* (Collier-Macmillan), 47–69.

6. LAWTON, D. *Social Change, Educational Theory and Curriculum Planning* (University of London Press Unibooks), 139–61.
7. WHITE, J. P. *Towards a Compulsory Curriculum* (Routledge & Kegan Paul), Chapters 3–5, 25–72.
8. WILLIAMS, M. (ed.) *Geography and the Integrated Curriculum: a Reader* (Heinemann).

Questions for investigation and discussion

1. Contrast the nature and functions of the generalisations which are intended to act as guides to choice of content in a course unit on 'Leisure' as laid out on pages 97–9 (chapter 6) and pages 122–3.
2. (a) Draw up a similar series for an inter-disciplinary course unit in the social sciences (including history and geography) on a major social/environmental topic, such as pollution, migration, population growth, etc.
   (b) Show how the topic you choose might be differently treated in
      (i) a pre-disciplinary type course;
      (ii) a geography course;
      (iii) a combined studies course.
3. (a) Is it useful from the curriculum point of view to distinguish between 'humanities', 'social studies' and 'environmental studies' as faculty labels? Provide criteria for the choice of label, or justify your arguments if you think it is not useful to distinguish them.
   (b) Indicate how well you think different approaches to geography fit in with the different forms of integrated schemes.
4. Refer to the following quotations:
   '[Geography is] the true meeting place of the natural and human sciences, meaning by the latter Economics, Sociology and History. Enthusiasts even tell us that, so far from being an unscientific collection of facts in which no principle or cause or law can be found, it is the science of sciences, bringing together the laws which are found in all, and showing their operation as causes in the sphere of human life.' (1910)[48]
   'Many curriculum courses in colleges of education and university departments of education do in fact induct student teachers into subject ideologies and utopias. Unvalidated claims are made for the subject's potency and effectiveness in attaining particular ends. Well established subjects usually make do with an unsystematic collection of parables and heroic myths.' (1968)[49]
   (a) Assess the relative strengths of the opposing cases presented above.
   (b) Attempt a critique of the stance taken in this chapter in the light of the second quotation.

(c) To what extent are the diverse views taken by Bull and Bernstein on integrated curricula (see Priority readings Nos 3 and 5) related to those in the above quotations.

References

1. WARWICK, D. (ed.) (1973) *Integrated Studies in the Secondary School* (University of London Press), 1.
2. *Ibid*, 1.
3. *Ibid*, 2.
4. *Ibid*, 3.
5. *Ibid*, 3.
6. LAWTON, D. (1969) 'The idea of an integrated curriculum' *Bulletin of the University of London Institute of Education*, **19**, 8.
7. WATTS, D. G. (1969) *Environmental Studies* (Routledge & Kegan Paul, London), 18.
8. See PRING, R. (1973) 'Curriculum integration: the need for clarification' *New Era*, **54**, 61–4.
9. See PRING, R. (1971) 'Curriculum integration' in PETERS, R. S. (ed.) (1973) *The Philosophy of Education* (Oxford University Press), 141–6.
10. See KIRK, G. (1973) 'A critique of some arguments in the case for integrated studies' *Scottish Educational Studies*, **5**, 95–102.
11. WARWICK, D. (ed.) (1973), *op. cit.*, 19 and 36.
12. *Ibid*, 3.
13. PRING, R. (1971), *op. cit.*, 133–4.
14. *Ibid*, 146–8.
15. HOLLY, D. (1973) *Beyond Curriculum* (Hart-Davis MacGibbon, London), 172.
16. BERNSTEIN, B. (1971) 'On the classification and framing of educational knowledge' in YOUNG, M. F. D. (ed.) (1971) *Knowledge and Control: New Directions for the Sociology of Education* (Collier-Macmillan, London), 48–54.
17. *Ibid*, 58.
18. *Ibid*, 59.
19. *Ibid*, 62.
20. HIRST, P. H. & PETERS, R. S. (1970) *The Logic of Education* (Routledge & Kegan Paul, London), 72–3.
21. See MAY, J. A. (1970) *Kant's Concept of Geography and its Relation to Recent Geographical Thought* (University of Toronto Press), 151.
22. MIKESELL, M. W. (1969) 'The borderlands of geography as a social science' in SHERIF, M. & SHERIF, C. W. (eds.) (1969) *Interdisciplinary Relationships in the Social Sciences* (Aldine Publishing Co., Chicago), 227. See also CLARKSON, J. D. (1970) 'Ecology and spatial analysis', *Annals of the Association of American Geographers*, **60**, 712. For a strongly contrary view, see BLACHFORD, K. R. (1973) 'Myths in geographical education' *Geographical Education*, **2**, 20.
23. MORRISSETT, I. (1967) 'The new social science curricula' in MORRISSETT, I. (ed.) (1967) *Concepts and Structure in the New Social Science Curricula* (Holt, Rinehart & Winston, New York), 9.
24. See LAWTON, D. & DUFOUR, B. (1973) *The New Social Studies* (Heinemann, London), Chapter 4.
25. See SENESH L. (1967) 'Organizing a curriculum around social science concepts' in MORRISSETT,, I. (ed.) (1967), *op. cit.*, Chapter 3.

26. HEATER, D. (1970) 'History and the social sciences' in BALLARD, M. (ed.) (1970) *New Movements in the Study and Teaching of History* (Temple Smith, London), 142.
27. For discussions of these distinctions, see, for example, LAWTON, D. & DUFOUR, B. (1973) *op. cit.*, 5–16; and CANNON, C. (1964) 'Social studies in secondary schools' *Educational Review*, **17**, 18–30.
28. See MARTIN, G. & WHEELER, K. (1975) *Insights into Environmental Education* Oliver & Boyd, Edinburgh), preface.
29. See also the journal *Bulletin of Environmental Education* (BEE), published by the Town and Country Planning Association.
30. COOTES, R. J. (1972) 'Integrated humanities in the secondary school curriculum—a philosophical critique' (Unpublished M.A. Dissertation, University of London), 5 and 9–10.
31. SCRIMSHAW, P. (1975) 'The language of social education' in ELLIOTT, J. & PRING, R. (eds.) (1975) *Social Education and Social Understanding* (University of London Press), 72 and 83.
32. COOTES, R. J. (1972), *op. cit.*, 5–6.
33. See, for example, the skills embodied in BRIDGES, D. (1975) 'Education and international understanding' in ELLIOTT, J. & PRING, R. (eds.) (1975), *op. cit.*, 104–18.
34. GRAVES, N. J. (1968) 'Geography, social science and inter-disciplinary enquiry' *Geographical Journal*, **134**, 392–3. See also NAISH, M. (1972) 'Geography in the integrated curriculum' in GRAVES, N. J. (ed.) (1972) *New Movements in the Study and Teaching of Geography* (Temple Smith, London), 64–5.
35. SUMNER, H. (1974) 'Integration and sequence in economics for 8–13 year-olds' in WHITEHEAD, D. (ed.) (1974) *Curriculum Development in Economics* (Heinemann, London), 99–100.
36. BRUNER, J. S. (1960) *The Process of Education* (Vintage Books, Random House, New York, 1963 edition), 13 and 52–4.
37. TABA, H. (1962) *Curriculum Development: Theory and Practice* (Harcourt, Brace & World, New York), 273.
38. BRUNER, J. S. (1966) *Toward a Theory of Instruction* (Harvard University Press, Cambridge, Mass.), 93.
39. See MASTERTON, T. (1969) *Environmental Studies: a Concentric Approach* (Oliver & Boyd, Edinburgh), 11.
40. DUFOUR, B. (1973) 'Teaching about development and other countries' in LAWTON, D. & DUFOUR, B. (1973), *op. cit.*, Appendix 1, 489.
41. BERNSTEIN, B. (1971), *op. cit.*, 60.
42. BRUNER, J. S. (1966), *op. cit.*, 74–5.
43. LAWTON, D. & DUFOUR, B. (1973), *op. cit.*, 240.
44. GOULD, P. R. (1973) 'The open geographic curriculum' in CHORLEY, R. J. (ed.) (1973) *Directions in Geography* (Methuen, London), 266–7.
45. BERNSTEIN, B. (1971), *op. cit.*, 64.
46. *Ibid*, 65.
47. SHIPMAN, M. D. with BOLAM, D. & JENKINS, D. (1974) *Inside a Curriculum Project* (Methuen, London), 46.
48. ARCHER, R. L., LEWIS, W. J. & CHAPMAN, A. E. (1910) *The Teaching of Geography in Elementary Schools* (A. & C. Black, London, 3rd. edition, 1918), 2.
49. MUSGROVE, F. (1968) 'The contribution of sociology to the study of the curriculum' in KERR, J. F. (ed.) (1968) *Changing the Curriculum* (University of London Press), 103.

8 Pupils and Teachers

First you must understand how children think.[1]

The previous four chapters, in concentrating upon the subject context of geography and the frameworks in which it may be placed, have tended to remove the discussion one step away from what the educational process is primarily about, namely the interaction between pupils and teachers. The purpose of this chapter is to redress the balance and draw attention to critical variables which the geography teacher, in common with other teachers, has to keep in the forefront of his mind: namely, the pupils' abilities and attitudes, which affect their capacity and willingness to learn.

The focus will be on factors affecting classroom learning, based where possible on evidence derived from research into geographical learning. It must be stressed that most of the psychological factors considered are general rather than subject-specific, though general research on spatial cognition, for example, has special interest for geography teachers. In addition, general ideas on such topics as concept formation, have a particular application in different subject areas. A more detailed basis for understanding these psychological factors than can be provided here is, however, necessary. Readers are, therefore, advised to use this chapter as a springboard into general introductory texts in the field, such as Stones (1966)[2], Ausubel and Robinson (1969)[3] and Child (1973).[4]

Relationship to aims and objectives

A recurrent emphasis in earlier sections of this book has been on the need to promote *meaningful learning* (pages 10, 28, 32–3, 75–7). The development of personal autonomy was proposed as the overarching educational aim (pages 9–10), seen as a particularly useful idea in its reconciling of the cognitive and affective aspects of learning. The growth of personal autonomy is built on the acquisition and application of thinking skills. 'Thinking' is in turn linked with the infusion of 'meaning'. Unless words have common meanings, communication and, therefore, social interaction is difficult. Thus personal development cannot be divorced from social development.

> ... true human communication presupposes a generalising attitude, which is an advanced stage in the development of word meanings. The higher forms of human intercourse are possible only because man's thought reflects conceptualized activity. ... The conception of word meaning as a unit of both generalizing thought and social interchange ... permits ... systematic study of the relations between the growth of the child's thinking ability and his social development.[5]

Meaningful learning in geography

Two particular problems face pupils in the early stages of studying geography. One is that so much of reality has to be shown at second hand. Children are inevitably required to perceive and interpret patterns on maps and photographs, less often on the ground,[6] which poses complex perceptual problems. The second relates to the interest of geography in spatial patterns. Spatial understanding involves coming to grips with macro-environments, which again creates problems of conceptualisation. The nature of the development of children's spatial concepts is, therefore, of great concern to the geography teacher.[7]

Developmental theories of learning

Blaut and Stea have pointed out that 'environmental learning' deals with comprehension of different environments on a different scale from that usually dealt with in psychological research on perception. 'It appears that this form of learning must incorporate the cognitive representation of geographical space, and we have chosen to call such representations ... *cognitive maps*.'[8] How do such cognitive maps develop?

In contrast to most other interpretations, Blaut and Stea see the child as a map-maker as early as the age of three, in that he can assemble a set of landscape-feature toys (houses, cars, trees, etc), into a map-like model of a macro-environment. Ability to do this is interpreted as an 'adaptive relation to early macro-environmental experience.'[9] Such early learning is only possible because the child is able to 'make use of small-scale surrogates or simulations of the environmental situation', such as toys.[10]

At the age of five or six, Blaut and Stea maintain that pre-literate children, of mixed social and ethnic background, can cope with simple map-like representations, can read an aerial photograph and abstract to semi-iconic (representational) map signs. Their tests involved five to six year olds, for example, identifying roads on a vertical aerial photograph, tracing the outlines of homes with red crayon and roads with yellow and solving a simple annotated navigational problem.[11]

In consequence of this research, Blaut and Stea recommend that advantage should be taken of this early cognitive mapping ability, especially with those children who have more difficulty in handling information conveyed by the printed word. They see the notational system or language of the map as a better means of teaching a child the concept of abstract symbols. But the ability must be harnessed if it is not to decay.[12] This research is interesting in reinforcing Balchin's advocacy of a training in graphicacy,[13] and also in appearing to conflict with conclusions drawn from some well-known developmental theories of learning.

The best known of these is *Piaget's*, in which four major stages of development, linked with mental age ranges, are identified. It is emphasised that while these stages are invariant in sequence, the chronological or mental ages associated with them are not fixed.

Stage	Mental Age Range
(i) *Sensori-motor*	0–2 years

Through this stage, the child develops from being capable only of reflex activity, to being able to co-ordinate actions and internalise thoughts.

(ii) *Pre-operational*	2–7 years

The child is able to 'think' at elementary levels, can represent the world in terms of symbols, though his operations are intuitive, egocentric and only partly co-ordinated. This is the stage at which Blaut and Stea have shown that children are able to manipulate materials to form a 'cognitive map'.

(iii) *Concrete operations*	7–11$\frac{1}{2}$ years

At this stage the child is capable of logical thought, but his reasoning is tied to concrete experience and is dependent on perceptual facts around him.

(iv) *Formal operations*	11$\frac{1}{2}$ years onwards

Here the individual is able to follow an argument at the level of abstract ideas, without need of concrete props. He can reason hypothetically and deductively, so that the process is sometimes referred to as hypothetico-deductive reasoning.[14]

Bruner similarly postulates different *systems of representation* in cognitive development, also sequential. The first is *enactive*, 'learning by doing'; the second *iconic*, dependent on visual or other sensory organisation; and the third *symbolic*, representation in words or language, resulting in an immense power to 'generate meaning'.[15] It is noticeable that Blaut and Stea's work was based on a blend of the enactive and iconic, leading to the use of a set of symbols less abstract than the written word.

Spatial cognition

These theories are applicable to an important aspect of human learning, the development of *spatial cognition*. In this, there is a move from *action-in-space* to *perception of space* to *conceptions about space*, which represents a progression from an egocentric, undifferentiated view, to something that is more differentiated and distanced from the individual.

Spatial concepts are associated with notions of distance, directions, and relationships between objects in space. In the early organisation of space by children, *topological* rather than Euclidean or projective understanding is acquired.[16] Hence the first spatial properties which can be represented are to do with proximity, spatial succession, and surrounding or enclosure, rather than with the continuity of lines or absolute distances.[17]

After the egocentric stage, an intermediate stage of *fixed systems of reference* is needed as a means of orientation to a macro- or large scale environment. Co-ordination is by reference to familiar landmarks such as the home. Thus children can deal better with *route maps*, mentally tracing their route of locomotion through an area, than with overall *survey maps*, which are representations of a general configuration of objects. The 'local' scheme of things has a definite relationship with the child's physical world: the 'out-there' scheme does not. This is a period of *domicentricity*.[18]

A deep sense of familiarity with the home area is necessary as a basis for moving outwards. Maps and photographs can be orientated by finding home first.[19] The process of moving out from this personal territory is known as *decentration*. Piaget's work suggests that at the first stage of decentration children, of about 6–7 years, usually know of their own town and their own country, but the two are mutually exclusive, and the local tends to assume dominant importance. At the second stage, from 8 to 10 or 11 years, the two scales of territory are associated, but the reasoning is often inconsistent, and logical territorial relationships are not clearly understood. Consistent explanations begin about 12 years of age, when children are able to complement verbal explanations with graphical explanations.[20]

Stoltman summarises research which indicates that, apart from age, decentration ability is associated in different areas with socio-economic disparities, travel, and variations in national curricula. His work suggests that American elementary school children decentrate later than Swiss, which he sees as a consequence of the stronger tradition of local studies in Europe, and the relative neglect of social studies and geography in American elementary school grades.[21]

Improved decentration is associated with more comprehensive and reliable information inputs. These influence perceptions of various places and in turn spatial preferences. Research carried out in Sweden shows children of $7\frac{1}{2}$ years old unable to give preferences, as they were unfamiliar with maps and had little information to guide them. The striking aspect of the perception surface of $9\frac{1}{2}$ year olds was the strong dome of desirability round the home town, Jonkoping. By $11\frac{1}{2}$ years, the 'mental map' of the group had become more differentiated, with high preference values for the south, and particularly for holiday areas. A further experiment asking the children to write down names of towns and cities they could remember showed an expansion and refinement of information surfaces, with a strong emphasis at first on the local area, large nearby towns and the capital, Stockholm.[22] Gould and White's maps of school-childrens' 'images of Britain' reveal similar development, with strong local preferences, but with particular areas such as the south-west generally being regarded as desirable.[23] An important extrapolation is that without adequate information inputs, local preferences and prejudices, will tend to harden (see pages 12–16 and 91–2).

'Theoretical space' is a concept which can only be acquired at the formal operations stage. It requires an understanding of cardinal directions and conventional map forms, which provide a co-ordinated frame. At this stage there is an ability to abstract and hold on mentally to straight lines, angles, curves and distances. When linked with a stable concept of number, the child can thus measure and organise the space he knows. 'Once he can envision space, or the objects occupying it, in the framework of a co-ordinate system, he is no longer so bound to the space he has experienced directly.'[24] Co-ordinate systems and Euclidean frames of reference are prerequisite to the understanding of conventional maps.

Satterly suggests that far more training is needed to increase perceptual skills if map drawing and map interpretation achievement are to reach satisfactory levels. He points particularly to the problems children find in interpreting the contour organisation of a landscape as a whole (ie true 'topographical' or 'survey' mapping) as distinct from discrete features, of correlating oblique photographs with maps and of orientation of maps in the field. He emphasises the need to start with large-scale maps of the home area.[25] Sandford has shown that children have similar problems with atlas maps, especially problems of scale and generalisation. Again, starting with large scale maps is advocated.[26]

As the stages of development are sequential and not associated with fixed points in chronological age, it cannot be assumed that by the time children have reached the secondary school they are at or even near the formal operations stage. In terms of spatial cognition, they may be at a more or less advanced stage than they are in respect of other skills. Many adults are in the same situation. In their own field of expertise they can employ hypothetico-deductive reasoning without difficulty, but in an unfamiliar field require concrete props. At the beginning of the secondary school stage at least, the geography teacher should still be thinking in terms of moving from the familiar to the unfamiliar, the near to the far, the concrete to the abstract, and generally be sensitive to each pupil's stage of readiness to undertake a particular learning task.

Forming concepts in geography

Early stages

Meaningful learning is linked with the formation of concepts (page 32). A major group of concepts encountered in the early stages of geography teaching are those concrete 'vernacular' concepts (page 41) which relate, for example, to physical features of the landscape, such as 'river', 'valley', 'hill', 'mountain' and so forth.

In the development of a concept such as 'mountain', the first step involves associating the percepts which provide the incoming data, making possible the distinguishing of the concept 'mountain'. Imperatore has outlined such a scheme (Fig. 8.1).[27]

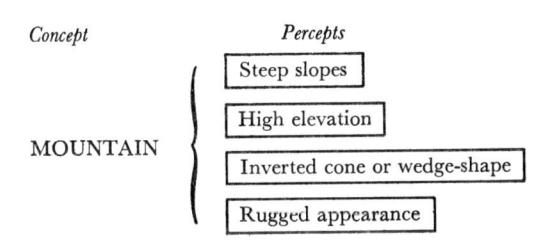

```
Concept              Percepts
                  ┌─ Steep slopes
                  │
                  │  High elevation
   MOUNTAIN   ────┤
                  │  Inverted cone or wedge-shape
                  │
                  └─ Rugged appearance
```

Fig. 8.1

There are not enough criteria here, in fact, to 'fix' the concept with certainty. In a child's eyes, the four given above might refer to a pyramid. Thus 'natural origin' and perhaps even details of height might need to be added.

We need more evidence than this, however, to be in a position to accept that an adequate level of conceptualisation has been achieved. Meaningful learning requires something more than the ability to verbalise the word 'mountain', or even state that 'Everest is a mountain' or 'the Himalayas are a range of mountains'. Evidence is needed that the child can identify exemplars and non-exemplars of particular criteria, from descriptions, in distinguishing them on photographs or in the field.

The basic concept of 'mountain' should not be difficult to establish, given proper stimulus materials. It is the task of the geography teacher to enrich the concept, perhaps by pursuing distinctions or contrasts between different types of mountains in terms of appearance, human occupancy and origin. Lunnon provides examples of how the basic concept of 'mountain' can be enriched at primary school level.[28]

(a) Basic concepts (as in the Imperatore scheme).
(b) Building on these: such ideas as snow covering, in some cases all the year round; grouping into peaks and ranges; association with specialised activities.
(c) At a later stage: height measured above sea level; altitudinal zonation; formation and erosion of mountains; historical significance—frontiers and passes.
(d) Differences in mountain landscapes and occupations over the world.

In an interesting piece of research, Hannam uses a matrix in which percepts and other criteria are matched against *levels of conceptualisation*, in this case in the analysis of children's developing grasp of the concept of a valley (Table 8.1).

Table 8.1

Criteria		Levels	
Long profile	Awareness	Simple detail	Complex detail
Cross profile	,,	,,	,,
Process	,,	,,	,,
Spatial sense	Limited part of valley	Whole of valley	Extended landscape sense
Verbalisation	Limited common language	Clear common language	Genetic/generic terminology

Thus, in the case of the cross profile, conceptualisation is presented as advancing from awareness of the simple curve to a range of possible variations within the valley form. Three examples of different levels of conceptualisation emerged, and each is represented below by a quotation typical of the quality of response when asked to talk about valleys and illustrate ideas by modelling in sand.

Level 1—Awareness
Land that dips in the middle, into a sort of curve, and dips into the middle where you find stream and villages there.

Level 2—Simple detail
A river runs in a valley . . . they are V-shaped or U-shaped . . . supposed to be a flat floor, steep side.

Level 3—Complex detail
This is embodied in longer accounts, of which the following is an example:

This would be a young valley . . . very steep cross section going in and out, what we call interlocking spurs . . . very steep sides, more vertical than lateral erosion, something like this—this is more gorgelike . . . then you get your middle valley, the mature valley, much wider curve, and the meander rather than the sharp curves you get in the younger stages . . . you'd get the river cliff . . . and the final stage, it's not so distinguishable, it's spread out.'[29]

Later stages

At the secondary school stage, we are concerned with the transition from and interaction between concrete and formal operations stages, and increasingly with the latter. Rhys confirms that:

> The limitations imposed by concrete operational thought are gradually removed during the years from 12 to 15, when the adolescent develops an ability to make use of propositional operations within a conceptual system which can be equated with a self-contained 'structured whole' . . . the adolescent's power of operational thought is no longer confined to practical problems and concrete situations, since he can now make use of hypothetico-deductive reasoning to deal with problems and possibilities which he has not encountered before.[30]

Rhys outlines a sequence of 'response levels' during the immediately pre-adolescent and the adolescent period, on the evidence of a piece of research which uses geographical exemplars.

1. *Approximately to age* 11 Patterns of analysis of geographical illustration material showed 'inability to comprehend the environmental context under review, where answers revealed tautology, irrelevance and denial of premises', and in which answers were frequently 'related to personal experience and individual preferences, with scant consideration given to the reality of the situation.'
2. *Approximately to* $12\frac{1}{2}$ *years* Reality orientated, but tending to focus only on a single piece of evidence. Dominated by the content and unable to look outside it.
3. *Approximately to* $13\frac{1}{2}$ *years* Difficult to distinguish from second stage, but items of evidence combined to give limited deductive analysis.
4. *Approximately* $14\frac{1}{2}$ *years and upwards* A more sophisticated, elaborate and comprehensive analysis and judgement based on hypothetico-deductive reasoning. Able to go outside the content of the passage and evoke possible hypotheses from his own experience.[31]

In Peel's view, this process is associated with a fundamental change from descriptive to explanatory thinking.[32] He uses the example of a short 'environmental' story, presented to children at the sort of age levels given above, and presents a range of responses to this stimulus material from the first to the fourth of these levels.

> Only brave pilots are allowed to fly over high mountains. This summer a fighter pilot flying over the Alps collided with an aerial cableway, and cut a main cable causing some cars to fall to the glacier below. Several people were killed and many others had to spend the night suspended above the glacier.

The questions asked of the children were:

1. Was the pilot a careful airman?
2. Why do you think so?
3. What do you think about the happening in the story?

A fourteen and a half year old replied 'He was either not informed of the mountain railway on his route or he was flying too low also his flying compass may have been affected by something before or after take-off this setting him off course causing collision with the cable.'

This responder is clearly looking outside the content, drawing on his own experience, and invoking a plausible, though not necessarily correct hypothesis, representative of the final stage of reasoning described above.

In contrast, an eleven and a half year old replied 'The people must also be brave to stay the nights suspended above the glacier. The pilot must be not only brave but a good driver.' Here the comments are tangential to the question, the judgements partial and circumstantial, rooted in the content, and invoking no valid outside concepts.[33]

The general principle that if pupils do not acquire propositional thinking during adolescence they are hardly likely to at all is too often insufficiently acted upon at the secondary level. Slater found in her research, for example, that many children were unable to think abstractly about their environment, even though in Piagetian terms at the formal operations stage of development. The root of the problem seemed to lie in the fact that underlying geographical concepts were not being taught. They do not emerge from an engagement with learning masses of content alone. Exercises requiring application, problem solving, simulation and role playing were all recommended.[34]

The school, as Vygotsky has urged, is the responsible body for presenting demanding, problem-orientated tasks to the adolescent.

> With assistance every child can do more than he can by himself—though only within the limits set by the state of his development . . . the only good kind of instruction is that which marches ahead of development and leads it . . . [35]

Individual differences

The discussion so far has centred on aggregates—the general qualities of the population of children as a whole at different stages of development. This is vital knowledge for the teacher, but does not solve his main classroom problem, namely the presence of children in the same group with widely differing abilities and attitudes. The problem is exacerbated by the increasing tendency to de-stream, which presents the class teacher with mixed-ability and mixed-attitude groups.

1. *Ability differences*

Whether geography as a subject taps particular intellectual abilities or a special 'intelligence' appears still to be an open question. Research completed to date seems to have provided few definite conclusions. Veness suggests that geography could be expected to call on a wide though not full range of intellectual skills.[36] The most 'relevant' ability would seem to be 'spatial ability', yet Taylor's research, for example, provided no evidence that spatial ability entered into attainment in geography.[37] Similarly Mullins, in summarising research in the field, revealed conflicting evidence on spatial ability but a consensus that general verbal ability was of considerable significance and, supporting the comment by Veness, that other abilities, such as number facility, memory and reasoning might enter into success in particular aspects of geography.[38]

This conflicting evidence, and possible relation of success in geography to verbal ability, is less than surprising when it is realised how strongly verbal a subject geography is when traditionally taught, with only a certain lip-service paid to its spatial component. In practice some degree of innate spatial ability would seem to be needed to cope with the sort of perceptual problems highlighted earlier (pages 132–6). Once assumptions of minimum levels of literacy, numeracy and graphicacy have been made, however, there are no grounds for believing that a wide ability range cannot be coped with in geography. It may be that ability differences are not the most important factor in explaining differences in attainment.

2. *The time factor*

Most teachers would agree that time is an important component in learning. Carroll goes further and maintains that it is the crucial component. The 'learner will succeed in learning a given task to the extent that he spends the amount of time he *needs* to learn the task.'[39] Time refers of course not to elapsed time, but time spent in learning. Apart from basic pupil ability and the quality of teaching, the variables for successful learning are directly linked with the time factor.

(a) *Aptitude*—the *time needed* by a learner to learn a task. Children of high aptitude for a particular task can master it more quickly than those of low aptitude.

(b) *Opportunity*—the *time allowed* for learning. Lack of time causes inefficient learning, and may incite rote learning. Opportunity is a variable under teacher control, though teachers would argue that the pressure of external examinations makes time very scarce. Over-inflated syllabuses are a deleterious influence in education, for 'one of the most aversive things which a school can do is not to allow sufficient time for a well-motivated child to master a given task before the next is taken up.'[40]

(c) *Perseverance*—the time the learner is *willing* to spend in learning, which is clearly linked with motivation.

3. *Different learning styles*

It is well known that some children are *convergent thinkers*, respond well to disciplined and structured activity, and are at ease with situations where questions are closed and there is one unique answer. Others are *divergent thinkers*, and their work tends to be more original and spontaneous. They are happier with open questions, and like to follow their thoughts in different directions.[41] Similarly, some children are *reflective* and thoughtful, and give more correct answers; while others are *impulsive*, giving quick and often erroneous answers, and are generally satisfied with lower quality performance than the first group.

Kagan has argued that 'pedagogical procedures should acknowledge this interaction between the preferred strategy of the learner and the material to be acquired, and tailor the presentations of materials to the psychological requirements of the task and the cognitive pre-disposition of the learner.'[42] To handle such differences and build up valid pupil profiles, there is a need to use a variety of techniques in any assessment procedure (see page 171–2).

4. Differences in motivation

For learning to take place, a 'meaningful learning set' must be established, that is there must be some intent to learn successfully.[43] Motivation is a complex phenomenon, and is related to the achievement of basic human needs. Leaving aside physiological needs, there are three basic needs or drives affecting children's motivation.[44]

(a) *The cognitive drive*, which has to do with curiosity, the desire to know and understand. Learning activities are seen as rewarding things in themselves. Motivation of this type is therefore *intrinsic*.

(b) *The achievement drive*, which is linked with ambition, the competitive spirit, the earning of status in terms of current prestige, and the willingness to defer present satisfaction to achieve future ends, usually career goals. It is an *extrinsic* form of motivation, promoting an instrumental view of the educational process, as a preparation for later life. As Booth expressed it over 100 years ago:

> It must be borne in mind by those who are engaged in discussing the improvements of education, that the great mass of the public hold it to be not an end but a means to an end: for its intrinsic advantages they are little solicitous; to its adventitious adjuncts they chiefly look.[45]

The achievement drive is closely associated with fear of failure, which can range from extreme neuroticism to a gentle concern. In the performance of straightforward tasks, mild anxiety is regarded as a positive motivational force. But where learning tasks are difficult, anxiety impairs discrimination and performance deteriorates.[46]

The single minded pursuit of examination success can have crippling academic consequences in that in many subjects, of which geography is a prime example, it can be achieved through rote learning strategies. This can result in the creation of the 'articulate idiot', defined by Bruner as 'the student who is full of seemingly appropriate words but has no matching ability to use the ideas for which the words presumably stand.'[47]

(c) *The affiliation drive*, which is associated with the desire to please. The growing child interacts with parents, teachers and friends. He has a need to please one or more groups—which one varying with the different stages of development. In adolescence the desire to affiliate with the peer-group becomes stronger. While the desire to 'please teacher' may be weaker than in the primary school, alienation is far from inevitable at the secondary stage; the teacher's influence is of equally great importance.

The influence of the teacher

Teacher-pupil relationships

Pupil alienation is more likely with the authoritarian teacher on the one hand and the weak teacher on the other, than with one who is generally calm, cheerful and sympathetic, fair, more inclined to praise than blame, and intent on running without fuss an orderly class and creating a 'learning environment'. It is widely agreed that the extremes of rigid authoritarianism and permissiveness should be avoided. Over-strict discipline arouses sullenness, fearful reaction and inhibits response to questions and class discussion. It is the death of intrinsic motivation. Absence of discipline problems is no proof that pupils are in reality involved in their work. On the other hand, a riotous classroom atmosphere is totally disruptive of learning.

While there are members of staff whose control is weak even in the most placid of grammar schools, discipline problems are generally seen as concentrated in the lower streams of schools where the range of ability in the intake is great, especially in inner city areas. In such schools, breakdown of relations between teachers and pupils is widely publicised. Keddie sees as an important contributing factor to such breakdown low *teacher expectation*, and argues that teachers develop stereotyped ideas about different classes. Even though their vocabulary outside the classroom may seem a progressive one, their attitude towards different classes varies, with a 'reciprocity of perspective' between teachers and 'A' stream-type pupils, while 'C' stream-type are labelled deviant and unteachable—whether or not the school is streamed.[48]

Teacher expectations communicate themselves to pupils through all sorts of cues the teacher gives out, and produce the phenomenon of the self-fulfilling prophecy. If teachers expect poor pupil performance they get it. Wiseman regards the identification of teacher expectation as a major variable affecting the performance of children as 'the single most significant outcome of educational research' in recent times.[49] Similarly, Pidgeon regards the relatively large differential between the most and least able pupils in England, as compared with other countries, as 'due in no small part to the expectations of their teachers for such a differential performance.'[50] On the other hand, Eysenck denounces the 'self-fulfilling prophecy' as 'an educational myth' in the sense that IQs can be changed in the direction expected of them.[51]

The balance between a democratic, sympathetic atmosphere, and one in which order prevails, is difficult to achieve in the presence of disruptive elements. It must not be forgotten, of course, that there is also an insidious and equally anti-educational alienation present in the often orderly atmosphere of the grammar school, where 'successful' achievers parrot their way through 'O'- and 'A'-level examinations without an original thought in their head and not the slightest inner commitment to the area of study in which they are engaged.

In achieving a balance between democracy and structure, between a libertarian outlook and good practical management, a relevant concept may be that of *pedagogic control*, advanced by Holly.[52] This refers to decisions taken by the teacher in relation to the organisation of learning. The direction exercised by the teacher is of materials, learning resources and framework rather than of pupils. The strategy is based on structured independent learning, and must be powered by cognitive and affiliative drives, as well as achievement drives, on the part of the pupil.

The teacher's skills

The two main roles of the teacher in the classroom have been identified as *communicator* and *entrepreneur*.

The teacher as communicator

The communication skills are related particularly, though not exclusively, to class teaching techniques. While the principle of pedagogic control is linked particularly with individualised learning, it is difficult to envisage a situation in which class teaching skills could be regarded as redundant.

The component skills of the teacher as communicator

Allen and Ryan have identified a whole series of contributing skills.[53]
A. *Stimulus variation*
  1. *Movement*—the need to attain a happy medium between maintaining a static desk or board position and being distractingly peripatetic.
  2. *Gestures*—head, hand and body movements, consciously or naturally generated: but NOT nervous mannerisms (eg chalk-wagging).
  3. *Focusing*—calling attention to a particular point, eg 'Pay special attention to', 'Listen carefully to', 'Take a good look at this'.
  4. *Interactional styles*—three main patterns help to break up teacher monologues:
     (a) *teacher-group*—'global' questions to class as a whole;
     (b) *teacher-student*—individual questioning;
     (c) *student-student*—directing replies from (a) or (b) to another student, involving students in discussion.
  5. *Pausing*—use of pregnant pause—stopping action and rallying attention to enable re-focusing.
  6. *Shifting sensory channels*—switching of the primary mode of communication, as from oral to visual, or from verbal exposition to use of blackboard, overhead projector, cine- or slide projector.
B. *Set Induction*
  Defined as a pre-instructional technique, preparing class for an activity—more than a brief introduction to a topic.
  Involves:
  1. *achievement of attention*
  2. *clarifying goals of instruction*
  3. *identifying pupil's present knowledge and skills*
  4. *heightening attention* through use of real-life or other striking analogy; a demonstration, etc.
C. *Closure*
  1. *Closure* is achieved when the major purposes of a lesson or a section of it are achieved.
  2. *Intermediate closure* can be used, the teacher drawing attention to what has been achieved so far. Closure involves more than a quick summary, for it requires the pulling together of major points, acting as a link between old and new knowledge. It should be used, therefore, both at intermediate

points in the lesson, and at its end. The end of a lesson might well represent an intermediate closure if the unit of work is not complete.

D. *Non-verbal cues*
1. *Silence* The teacher can take advantage of momentary silences:
   (a) *after an introductory statement*—silence to allow class to think about purport of question;
   (b) *after a question from pupil*—the teacher ponders to give weight to it;
   (c) *after asking a question to class*—allow moment for an answer before butting in with another question;
   (d) *after pupil response*—momentary silence to encourage development of statement.
2. *Facial expressions*—smile, frown, serious, quizzical look—NB use of eyes as well as mouth.
3. *Body movement*—refers to purposeful movement, eg moving towards a responding student—'I want to hear this'; tactical move towards offending pupil as means of quietly defusing a situation.
4. *Head movements*, eg hand to ear ('speak up'), nod ('yes'), shake ('no'), cocked ear ('I'm listening').
5. *Hand gestures*, eg pointing to student, beckoning, motioning to stop.

E. *Reinforcement*
Refers to rewarding desired behaviour.
1. *Positive verbal*—ranges from a bland 'correct' to an enthusiastic 'excellent'—can be overdone—'fabulous', 'fantastic', etc are not usually appropriate. Words can be varied in intensity. The major point is that it should be apposite to the situation—an enthusiastic 'good' to every mediocre reply destroys its value when a good answer really appears.
2. *Positive non-verbal*—eg
   (a) teacher nods hard, smiles, etc
   (b) „ writes answer on board
   (c) „ puts a connected slide on the projector.
3. *Positive qualified*—should be used for a worthy but not wholly accurate answer—a qualified 'yes, but . . .' may give a cue or some form of prompt. Involves 'probing' (see questioning).
4. *Delayed reinforcement*—where the teacher emphasises positive aspects of response by redirecting class attention to earlier contributions by a student.

The tactful use of reinforcement techniques is important in bringing into the lesson quieter pupils who are generally slow to come forward with answers.

5. *Negative reinforcement* can be used to dampen down undesired behaviour—shouting out of answers, etc.

F. *Questioning skills*

Perhaps the most vital component skill lies in the teacher's questioning skills. As Manson maintains:

> Teachers should be able to ask good questions. A teacher should be able to ask provocative questions which will stimulate interest and prompt discussion. A teacher should be able to phrase insightful questions which will promote thinking and expedite problem solving. A teacher should be able to construct valid and reliable test questions which will permit him to make an accurate assessment of learning. And a teacher should be able to pose thoughtful and clarifying questions which will help students recognise and assess their attitudes and value commitments.[54]

Manson thus proposes a typology of questions adopted from the Bloom taxonomy. He takes the Bloom 'abilities' as a 'process dimension', which he places in a matrix (Fig. 8.2) against a 'knowledge dimension' which includes facts, concepts and generalisations (see pages 37–42), and gives examples of the sorts of geographical questions that are appropriate in each section of the matrix. This type of specification is important in drawing attention to the range of questions that are available, and perhaps highlights how little of this range, usually in the bottom left hand corner of the matrix, is actually used as normal practice.

Good questioning will therefore include, as appropriate, the following attributes:

(a) asking questions fluently and precisely;
(b) gearing questions to the pupil's state of knowledge;
(c) involving a wide range of pupils in the question-answer session;
(d) focusing questions on each category in the taxonomy of abilities;
(e) asking probing questions—not accepting each answer as of equal value;
(f) redirecting questioning to allow accurate and relevant answers to emerge;
(g) using open-ended as well as closed questions, so that creative thought and value judgements are invited.

In line with earlier discussion (page 37), it is suggested that four broad groups of questions should be envisaged: *recall questions, comprehension questions, problem-posing questions* and *open-ended (creative) questions.*

		Facts	Concepts	Generalizations
THE PROCESS DIMENSION	Judging		Is the concept 'threshold' sufficiently precise to permit measurement?	Assess the validity of the friction of distance principle by comparing it with 'the real world'.
	Synthesizing		Develop a procedure through which you could teach the idea of 'a nested hierachy' to high school students.	Formulate several testable hypotheses deriving from the assumptions of central place theory.
	Analyzing		Outline the form of scientific explanation used in developing central place theory.	'If there were no Great Lakes, Chicago would still be a large city.' What assumptions seem to be implicit in that statement?
	Solving		Given a population distribution map and the assumptions of central place theory, construct the most probable urban hierarchy.	How would a reduction in transport costs affect the range of a good?
	Understanding		Explain what is meant by 'a nested hierarchy'.	Draw a graph showing the relationship between threshold level and range of a good.
	Remembering	The originator of central place theory was.....	State the definition of 'range of a good'.	List the assumptions of central place theory.
		Facts	*Concepts*	*Generalizations*

THE KNOWLEDGE DIMENSION

Fig. 8.2

Micro-teaching An increasingly used method of developing communication skills among student and in-service teachers is through the use of a procedure known as micro-teaching. This is defined as 'a scaled down teaching experience',[55] diminished in terms of class size (say 8–12 pupils), lesson length (say, up to ten minutes), lesson content (say, building up a single concept) and number of component skills practised (say, just a concentration on the use of probing questions). Additional characteristics may be the use of the student peer-group as the class instead of actual pupils, and the video-taping or audio-taping of the lesson as a valuable way of providing feed-back.

In addition, transcripts may be taken to make possible closer and more analytical feed-back, either on a personal basis to the student or on a group basis. A short section from an actual geography micro-teaching lesson is given in Fig. 8.3 (pages 152–3). Alongside the transcript there are columns for coding the component skills (pages 146–8). The questioning skills are numbered 1 to 4 in the order: recall, comprehension, problem-posing and open-ended questions, as given above. In addition, space is left for general comments of a more qualitative nature.

This particular lesson is clearly in a formal mode, associated in this case with a CSE unit the student was given to teach. The use of a snatch of the lesson can only give a flavour of the undertaking as a whole. Later on in the 'micro-lesson', this particular student began to use the names of individual pupils in questioning, and to ask rather more open-ended questions, about perceptions of the quality of life in Broken Hill for example (though in the event this tended to reinforce a gross stereotype of what it was like to live in a 'hot, dry climate', where 'you could sunbathe all the time'). The general tone of the questioning showed a conscious desire to accommodate to the level of a not very able CSE class, covering what was for them a fairly abstract and difficult topic. But the danger of over-simplifying to the point of distortion was not avoided. Attempts were also made to relate the physical concepts to human occupancy, and to compare the environment of south-east Australia with that of Britain.

The technique is valuable in its property of exposing to the student problems which he might otherwise not readily be aware of. Once the basic skills have become 'habitual', a more general, qualitative approach is appropriate. Micro-teaching can clearly become narrowing and stereotyped if over-used.

A note on note-taking A class-teaching strategy equally as pervasive as the question-answer session is the provision of notes. A distinction must here be made between teacher-dictated *note-taking* and pupil *note-making*. While it is hoped that pupils understand notes they take down from the teacher, they are commonly associated with rote learning and reproduction in a test or examination. Similarly, independently made pupil summaries can be copied out more or less verbatim from a book, and perhaps be even less meaningful than dictated notes.

If pupil-made notes are to embody a constructive synthesis, a range of materials is needed and requisite skills must be previously developed. Howe argues that in the right circumstances individual note-making, involving the coding of information by the learner in his own words, can make particular sense to him.[56] But prerequisite to this process is the understanding of the original material, and ability to apply a structure whereby the main ideas can be transformed and collated into a meaningful and smaller-scale synthesis. It is a difficult undertaking to accomplish well.

The teacher as entrepreneur

The teacher of today is increasingly immersed in more complex situations than in the past, when his normal task involved didactic class teaching of his own subject in a relatively small school to a homogeneous ability group, geared to the requirements of a single external examination.

Teachers are increasingly being expected to grapple with:
(a) individualisation of learning;
(b) pupil participation in group work;
(c) team teaching and interdisciplinary work;
(d) mixed ability groups;
(e) more than one type of external examination;
(f) a great variety of educational materials and audio-visual gadgets;
(g) large schools with complex organisational structures.

Skilled management is vital in coping with the onerous demands which ensue. Bailey has discussed some of the management problems faced by the geography teacher, who, in addition to the problems already mentioned, needs to have a grasp of the range and, not least, cost-effectiveness of his resources—books, descriptive extracts, maps, photographs, film strips and slides, tapes, instruments, fieldwork

Topic: Climate and farming in south-east Australia
Objective: To revise the concept of *rain shadow* with reference to SE Australia
Class: 5th year CSE (Mode III course section on SE Australia) pupils in an inner city comprehensive school
Materials: Atlases; blackboard; CSE booklet in worksheet form
The start of the micro-lesson (the last 10 minutes or so of a lesson on the topic)

	A	B	C	D	E	F	General Comments
	(refer to component skills pp. 146–8)						
TEACHER Now we've just been having a look at the map on page 5 (of the booklet). Have you got it?		1					
And we're trying to account for the distribution of rainfall.		2					
Now can you tell me what is wrong with that map? . . . I've already pointed it out.		4					
PUPIL It's the rainfall's not right.							
TEACHER Good. Now what's wrong with it? . . . (a)	3					3	(a) Accepts vague reply with blanket approval, but probes further.
Can you remember, we drew section across SE Australia on board? . . .	6						
What place was that (draws dot for Sydney) ?(b)					1→3		(b) Relying on general address to class—'global' questions.
PUPIL Sydney.							
TEACHER OK . . . and here we have (marks dot on board)?					2	1	
PUPIL Canberra.							
TEACHER Canberra . . . and that little place (marks on dot)?					2	1	
PUPIL Hay.							

Video tape needed to be able to record

TEACHER	Hay ... and what was the last one (marks on dot) ?				2	
PUPIL	Broken Hill.					1
TEACHER	Broken Hill (marks on dot). We've already located these on the atlas so we know roughly where they are. Right ... now what did we say about the rainfall on the coast by Sydney? (points to board)	3 6			2	2
PUPIL	It's higher.					
TEACHER	Higher ... good. And what do those maps tell you? They're wrong, aren't they?(c)				1→3	3 (c) Repeats earlier probe.
PUPIL	Yes, miss.					1
TEACHER	OK The thing is, as we were reading in the text, the rainfall by Sydney is high (pointing to the board). Can you remember roughly how high?	3/6				
PUPIL 1	48 inches. *(simultaneously)*					
PUPIL 2	50 inches				1	
TEACHER	Good ... 48 to 50 inches. We had both, didn't we? About 50" (writes on board).(d) Compared with Britain which only has about 30". So it's high.(e)	6 3				(d) Rightly receives both replies within acceptable range of accuracy—but 2 pupils reply simultaneously. (e) Use of familiar example but in rather 'gross' way.

Fig. 8.3 Micro-teaching transcript:

equipment, and means of storage and techniques of filing.[57] Similarly, Davis notes the problem of organising for a four-period day, which is time-economic, but poses problems of organising lessons and breaking them down into manageable but varied units.[58]

The greatest difficulty is associated with managing mixed-ability groups, often containing reluctant learners and children who are way behind their age group in intellectual skills. For the reluctant learner, two coping strategies which are often advanced are stimulating interest and reinforcing success. For the mixed-ability situation, and in effect even streamed classes contain some range of ability, the individualisation of learning is necessary.

Stimulating interest It is often argued that disadvantaged pupils are alienated from school because didactic methods and a content derived from 'high culture' are imposed upon them. A preferred strategy is held to be the stimulus of interest through relevant materials, relevant being taken to mean applicability to the child's social and environmental situation.

Bearing in mind our original statement of aims, a more tenable definition of 'relevant' would be relevant to the child's intellectual, and through this personal, development. The idea that there should be an 'interest-based curriculum' for some, and 'real education' for others has increasingly been criticised.[59] Entwistle has exposed as illusory the view that intellectual skills are separable from interest (ie often local and community) based content.

> The notion that solutions to problems which have eluded entire communities (sometimes for centuries) may be within the grasp of fifteen-year-old leavers—especially those less able pupils for whom integrated social studies are often prescribed—is dangerous.[60]

Wall, too, has suggested that the use of 'interest' as a means of motivation must be viewed with caution, because stated interests are often transitory, and may also be merely the surface expression of deeper needs.[61] The general conclusion would seem to be that the stimulus of interest should be regarded as a goal in the teaching of *all* groups of children, and that the interest of children should form a starting point and an important, but not the only, criterion in the selection of content. The geography teacher of today knows, however, that his subject has to be positively well taught, and that the material alone, however 'socially relevant', is no guarantee in itself of gaining interest. As Marland writes:

> Pupils can be as resoundingly switched off by the relevant as the obscure;

they can be as bored by the apparently child-centred as by the adult-dominated.[62]

Reinforcing success An alternative strategy is advanced by, among others, Ausubel and Robinson. They suggest that 'the best way of motivating an unmotivated pupil is temporarily to by-pass the problem of motivation and to focus on the cognitive aspect of teaching . . . [and] to rely on the cognitive motivation that is developed retroactively from successful educational achievement.'[63] Academic success must be seen as achievable from an early stage, as a result of which the teacher 'can establish a motivational beachhead for the crucial pre-adolescent stage when alienation from school would normally reach sizeable proportions.'[64]

Wall, too, is clear that: 'Success, if frequent enough, leads the pupil to set appropriate goals' while 'continued failure' leads him to aim too low (to ensure a relative success) or unrealistically high in a despairing attempt to maintain a self-concept of being capable enough. . . . Failure in a general context of success has a different meaning from failure which is one more of a long chain.'[65]

Bloom and colleagues regard the main job of the teacher as fostering successful learning, and advance the concept of *mastery learning*. They suggest that 'given sufficient time [page 142] and appropriate types of help, 95% of students can learn a subject with a high degree of mastery', and affirm that, leaving out the top 5% and bottom 5% of the school population, the ratio of time required between the slow and the quick learner is 6 to 1. They suggest tentatively that with effective teaching this can be reduced to 3 to 1.[66]

For internal assessment purposes, Bloom and colleagues see the normal curve of distribution as a subversive influence. If results equate with this curve, they should be seen as symptomatic of unsuccessful teaching, with large numbers of children inevitably seeing themselves as having failed. Bloom recognises the difficulty of applying this concept in a realistic way in the secondary school, for by this stage many children have already experienced a long string of failures. 'It is unlikely that mastery learning can be attained in a given term by students who have had a long history of learning difficulties',[67] particularly in subjects where sequential learning is important.

It may be, therefore, that in the first stages of the secondary school it would be expedient quietly to manipulate standards *in the short term* in order to avoid the debilitating effects of consistent early failure. This is not to advocate any long term lowering of standards, but to provide the springboard which might lead to an overall raising of standards through a stimulus to intrinsic motivation. Two key strategies in this process are the effective use of feedback and the individualisation of learning.

Feedback The concept of reinforcing success is inextricably linked with feedback. For it to foster intrinsic motivation it must (a) as we have seen, reflect generally successful learning, and (b) provide *detailed* diagnosis of success and failure 'not as reward and punishment, but as information.'[68]

Again, the reinforcing success concept does not mean 'going soft'. There needs to be correction of errors, clarification of meanings and removal of misconceptions individual by individual. Such diagnosis is 'a continuous and perennial task'.[69] Each pupil ideally needs clarification of (a) how near his answer was to an entirely correct one (if there is one); (b) what was the magnitude and direction of the error(s); (c) in more general terms, why or how the answers were right or wrong; and a specification of remedies.

Feedback in the form of detailed comments is required, therefore, preferably discussed personally by teacher and pupil. More time will need to be spent with weaker pupils. How is this to be found? Two possible ways are to spend less time in class teaching (by using worksheets, page 157) and in marking essays (page 184). But cooperative ventures between schools and within departments in a school are the crucial need permitting 'division of labour'.

If marks have to be assigned, it is preferable that they should be related to the individual's own potential, and not aggregated at the end of term to allow class rankings. Apart from its subversive influence on the pupils lower down in the form, it may well be that a pupil of a particular ability and attitude near the top of a weak class may be underachieving, while one near the bottom of a strong class may be working his heart out.

It has been shown that the detailed feedback of school achievement *to parents* is of equal importance. Again, the positive effect of successful feedback is emphasised. Banks and Finlayson maintain that the deterministic notion of a linear cause and effect relationship between home and school, (ie good middle-class homes lead to high parental aspirations and good school achievement; difficult working class environments lead to low aspirations and poor achievement) is a dangerous distortion. Their research suggests that parental aspirations may be a *consequence* as well as a *cause* of school achievement. Hence if pupils fail the 11+, are placed in low streams, get bad reports, show unwillingness to do homework and a generally poor attitude towards school, the message comes through clearly to parents, who gradually lower their aspirations and expectations for their children's futures.[70]

Teachers are often heard to say of parents' evenings 'the parents whom we really wish to see do not turn up', meaning in effect they are wishing to provide some negative feedback. It is not surprising that many parents prefer not to come into school to hear a catalogue of their child's inadequacies year after year.

Individualising learning Individualising learning was advanced over forty years ago by Courtis as 'the master trend in education'.[71] More recently, Gagné is but one who concludes that processing of information is an idiosyncratic process, and affirms 'that individualized instruction represents the route to efficient learning.'[72] The main burden of the argument in this chapter has been shifting towards this position. No other strategy seems as relevant in the context of mixed ability classes.

The usual tactic is to make use of worksheets, which should contain enrichment exercises for those who work more quickly, and also reinforcement exercises for those who find the initial tasks difficult. Examples of individualised worksheet materials are provided in Chapter 15. The application of individualising instruction to geography teaching is no new discovery. In the late 1920s, for example, Pearce was giving practical advice on how to cope with the organisational demands which it made. In her girls' secondary school she divided the geography curriculum into a number of assignments:

> typewritten and duplicated, so that every girl has an assignment for herself. . . . Every assignment contains—something practical to do, something to read, something to prepare for 'group work' . . . and some problems to solve. As the work goes on, the variation in individual speed of the slowest and quickest members of the form in completing an assignment is certainly a plea for continuation of the plan. In the early days of the experiment it was found that the quick ones were getting too far ahead with set work for convenience when testing came. . . . To obviate this difficulty and yet keep all busy and interested, additional optional exercises were added to the assignment. . . .
>
> The two hours (per week) devoted to geography in school are divided into two periods, a long one of 80 minutes and a short one of 40. The long period and the homework time are given to 'individual' work while the shorter lesson is for class work. This short period we call the 'conference'. It is spent sometimes in oral recapitulation and discussion of work prepared by pupils in the assignments and its amplification and elaboration by the teacher.

Miss Pearce went on to describe her assessment procedures, including carefully kept record cards to check on the individual pupil's progress.

> It would be ideal to correct each girl's written assignment in her presence, but this being obviously impossible with large classes, the correction must be done when the pupil is not present. Having completed their assignment, each girl checks it against a 'model' answer prepared by the teacher, providing a means of self-assessment, writing down 'ways in which I can improve my assignments'.[73]

Summary of guidelines

The practical implications of the various insights into pupil learning and teacher influence considered in this chapter can be summarised in the following guidelines. These are not, of course, panaceas.

1. In the early stage of the secondary school course, the content should be rooted as far as possible in reality, starting off with matters within the experience of the children.
2. As other criteria dictate that not all work should be confined to the local environment, a concentric structuring of the syllabus is valuable, exploring vital principles first in the home area, before extending these outwards to the national and global levels. The use of contrasted case study material is highly appropriate.
3. To infuse 'familiarity', such studies should as far as possible be presented as 'fieldwork in the classroom', with the help of visual and other first-hand materials.
4. Similar perceptual problems have to be overcome in atlas, other type of map and photograph interpretation. Here, too, introduction of maps and photographs of familiar scenes should precede that of the unfamiliar. Large-scale maps should be introduced before small-scale ones.
5. As far as possible, independent learning should be catered for, for example through the use of worksheets, though it is important that worksheets should be seen as only one of a variety of appropriate devices. Worksheets can well reflect the core material of work units, in addition to which enrichment activities need to be provided for more able pupils.
6. The nature and purpose of the work should be clear to the pupil. At all times it should carry meaning through stimulating concept formation.

7. Due attention should be paid to both vernacular and technical concepts and the functional links between them. In geography, fortunately, both types loom large.

8. No attempt should be made to achieve a descriptive and comprehensive 'world coverage', or otherwise overload syllabuses, as adequate time is necessary to make possible meaningful learning. More limited, in-depth approaches are to be preferred.

9. At the adolescent stage considerable effort should be devoted to fostering critical, explanatory thinking, through activities which can diagnose whether understanding, application and problem-solving tasks have been successfully achieved. Concepts should be revisited at progressively higher levels.

10. Spaced recall is advantageous in helping to fix concepts that need to be retained over a considerable period.

11. Positive motivation of the pupil through, in the first place the use of interesting starter-material, but more generally through the promotion of successful learning, is critical.

12. Diagnostic feedback to pupil and parent, giving precise information about the quality of performance, is also a vital factor in motivation (unless it serves purely to reinforce failure).

13. Teachers who exhibit warmth *and* orderliness, and provide a democratic but structured classroom atmosphere are more likely to promote favourable attitudes than authoritarian or over-permissive teachers.

14. In the contemporary situation a high degree of managerial expertise and much effort is required of teachers. Problems can be reduced by co-operative ventures within and between schools.

Priority readings

(see also page 131)

1. TAYLOR, P. H. 'The contribution of psychology to the study of the curriculum' in KERR, J. F. (ed.) *Changing the Curriculum* (University of London Press Unibooks), Paper 4, pp. 79–95.
2. BRUNER, J. S. *The Process of Education* (Vintage Books, Random House, New York), Chapters 3–5, pp. 33–80.
3. VENESS, T. 'The contribution of psychology' in GRAVES, N. J. (ed.) *New Movements in the Study and Teaching of Geography* (Temple Smith), pp. 75–82.
4. SANDFORD, H. 'Perceptual problems' in GRAVES, N. J. (ed.) *op. cit.*, pp. 83–92.

5. RHYS, W. 'The development of logical thinking' in GRAVES, N. J. (ed.) *op. cit.*, pp. 93–106.
6. BLAUT, J. & STEA, D. 'Mapping at the age of three' *Journal of Geography* (1974), **73**, pp. 5–9.
7. BLAUT, J. M. & STEA, D. 'Studies in geographic learning' in BALE, J., *et al.* (eds.) *Perspectives in Geographical Education* (Oliver & Boyd), pp. 87–100.
8. SATTERLEY, D. J. 'Skills and concepts involved in map drawing and map interpretation' in BALE, J. *et al.* (eds.), *op. cit.*, pp. 162–9.
9. GOULD, P. & WHITE, R. *Mental Maps* (Penguin Books), pp. 69–92.

Questions for investigation and discussion

1. For a piece of research on the development of pupil thinking in geography, Rhys set an exercise on Prairie farming, providing a set of oblique aerial photographs of the Prairie area, including one showing a small market centre surrounded by apparently endless plain. The question was asked: 'Why has this small town grown up just here, where the railway and road cross each other?'
The following are three replies:
   A. 'It would be situated in the middle and have the same amount of land on either side.'
   B. 'Because you can get the wheat here by road and rail, and seeing as how the railway goes straight through it can pick up all the wheat from the farms.'
   C. 'Because the land is flat and they build on flat land usually.'[74]
   (a) Refer to he diffe rent response levels as outlined by Peel and Rhys (pages 139–40). Try to place the above statements in the appropriate response level.
   (b) Outline the limitations of each statement.
   (c) What further information and understanding would pupils need to bring to bear to give an adequate answer to the question?
2. (a) Draw up a simple structure for the teaching of the concept 'site' OR 'hinterland', specifying the materials you would use.
   (b) Outline a set of 'probing questions' you would employ to assess whether the concept had been grasped.
3. A child in your class writes an unusually fluent essay on 'Factors affecting the growth of steel manufacturing in the north-eastern states of the USA'. What evidence would you seek to check whether the understanding was real, or whether the words were a façade covering a mere regurgitation of notes?
4. Your headmaster tells you that parents of a bright fourth form class have been complaining that their children are not getting as many notes

in their geography lessons as in other subjects. The headmaster warns you that if the 'mock' results are not satisfactory, he might have to transfer you to other work. Justify your actions, explaining how you would reassure your headmaster.

5. You are given the task of organising a course in geography and related studies for a non-examination group of 5th form pupils. Draw up what you would consider to be a suitable framework for selecting content in the light of the criteria suggested in this chapter.
6. Specify what is meant by and assess the relative importance of each of the following teacher activities: (a) gaining and maintaining attention; (b) concentrating on factual recall; (c) provision of visual cues; (d) structuring content; (e) providing feedback; (f) specifying objectives; (g) organising group work; (h) individualising learning. Use geographical illustrations where possible.
7. (a) Would you regard the component skills detailed on pages 146–8 as purely general teaching skills, or in some cases more applicable to certain subjects than others? Justify your conclusions.
   (b) Are there any skills (leaving aside knowledge and expertise in the subject) which you would identify as particularly necessary to a geography teacher that are neglected on this list?

References

1. Title of an article by GRAVES, N. J. in the *Times Educational Supplement*, 28 April, 1972, 61.
2. STONES, E. (1966) *An Introduction to Educational Psychology* (Methuen, London).
3. AUSUBEL, D. P. & ROBINSON, F. G. (1969) *School Learning: an Introduction to Educational Psychology* (Holt, Rinehart & Winston, New York).
4. CHILD, D. (1973) *Psychology and the Teacher* (Holt, Rinehart & Winston, London).
5. VYGOTSKY, L. S. (1934) *Thought and Language* (MIT Press, Cambridge, Mass., 1962), 7.
6. SANDFORD, H. (1972) 'Perceptual problems' in GRAVES, N. J. (ed.) (1972) *New Movements in the Study and Teaching of Geography* (Temple Smith, London), 83.
7. RHYS, W. (1972a) 'The development of logical thinking' in GRAVES, N. J. (ed.) (1972), *op. cit.*, 95.
8. STEA, D. & BLAUT, J. M. (1970) 'Toward a developmental theory of spatial learning' in DOWNS, R. M. & STEA, D. (eds.) (1973) *Image and Environment* (Edward Arnold, London), 51.
9. BLAUT, J. M. & STEA, D. (1974) 'Mapping at the age of three' *Journal of Geography*, **73**, 9.
10. STEA, D. & BLAUT, J. M. (1973) 'Some preliminary observations on spatial learning in school children' in DOWNS, R. M. & STEA, D. (eds.) (1973), *op. cit.*, 228.
11. BLAUT, J. M. & STEA, D. (1971) 'Studies in geographic learning' in BALE, J., et al. (eds.) (1973) *Perspectives in Geographical Education* (Oliver & Boyd, Edinburgh), 87–98.

12. STEA, D. & BLAUT, J. M. (1973), *op. cit.*, 233-4.
13. See BALCHIN, W. G. & COLEMAN, A. M. (1965) 'Graphicacy should be the fourth ace in the pack' in BALE, J. *et al.* (eds.) (1973), *op. cit.*, 78-86.
14. See HART, R. A. & MOORE, G. T. (1973) 'The development of spatial cognition: a review' in DOWNS, R. M. & STEA, D. (eds.) (1973), *op. cit.*, 260-1.
15. BRUNER, J. S. (1966a) *Toward a Theory of Instruction* (Harvard University Press, Cambridge, Mass.), 10-12.
16. RHYS, W. (1972a), *op. cit.*, 93-4.
17. ALMY, M. (1967) 'The psychologist looks at spatial concept formation: children's concepts of space and time' in BALL, J. M., *et. al.* (eds.) *The Social Sciences and Geographic Education* (John Wiley, New York), 72.
18. See HART, R. A. & MOORE, G. T. (1973), *op. cit.*, 276-80.
19. See BAYLISS, D. G. & RENWICK, M. (1966) 'Photograph study in a junior school' in BALE, J. *et al.* (eds.) (1973), *op. cit.*, 119-30.
20. See STOLTMAN, J. P. (1972) 'Territorial decentration and geographic learning' in ADAMS, W. P. & HELLEINER, F. M. (eds.) (1972) *International Geography 1972*, Vol. 2. (22nd International Geographical Congress, 1972) (University of Toronto Press), 1036.
21. *Ibid*, 1037.
22. GOULD, P. R. (1973) 'The black boxes of Jonkoping: spatial information and preference' in DOWNS, R. M. & STEA, D. (eds.) (1973), *op. cit.*, 236-43.
23. GOULD, P. R. & WHITE, R. (1974) *Mental Maps* (Penguin Books, Harmondsworth, Middlesex), 69-91.
24. ALMY, M. (1967), *op. cit.*, 78.
25. SATTERLEY, D. J. (1964) 'Skills and concepts involved in map drawing and map interpretation' in BALE, J. *et al.* (eds.) *op. cit.*, 162-8.
26. SANDFORD, H. (1972), *op. cit.*, 85-92.
27. IMPERATORE, W. (1970) 'On the nature of concepts' *Journal of Geography*, **69**, 176.
28. LUNNON, A. J. (1969) *The Understanding of Certain Geographical Concepts by Primary School Children* (unpublished M.Ed. thesis, University of Birmingham), 15.
29. HANNAM, R. (1969) 'An analysis of some geographical concepts and their development in the learning processes of the individual mind' (unpublished Ph.D. thesis, University of Leeds), 125-7. (Table 8.1 appears on p. 125 of thesis.)
30. RHYS, W. (1972a), *op. cit.*, 99.
31. RHYS, W. (1972b) 'Geography and the adolescent' in PEEL, E. A. (ed.) (1972) 'The quality of understanding in secondary school subjects' *Educational Review*, **24**, 186-8.
32. PEEL, E. A. (1972) 'Understanding school material' in PEEL, E. A. (ed.) (1972), *op. cit.*, 171.
33. PEEL, E. A. (1965) 'Intellectual growth during adolescence' *Educational Review*, **17**, 172-4.
34. SLATER, F. A. (1970) 'Content and concepts in geographical education' in BIDDLE, D. S. & DEER, C. E. (eds.) (1973) *Readings in Geographical Education: Selections from Australian and New Zealand Sources*, Vol. 2, 1966-72. (Whitcombe & Tombs, Sydney, for the Australian Geography Teachers' Association), 84.
35. VYGOTSKY, L. S. (1934), *op. cit.*, 103-4.
36. VENESS, T. (1972) 'The contribution of psychology' in GRAVES, N. J. (ed.) (1972), *op. cit.*, 75.
37. TAYLOR, C. C. (1960) 'A study of the nature of spatial ability and its relation to attainment in geography' *British Journal of Educational Psychology*, **30**, 270.
38. MULLINS, P. G. (1967) 'An alternative form of examination in geography at GCE 'O' Level' (unpublished M.Ed. thesis, University of Manchester), 8-10.

39. CARROLL, J. B. (1963) 'A model of school learning' *Teachers College Record*, **64**, 725.
40. *Ibid*, 728.
41. GUILFORD, J. P. (1956) 'The structure of intellect' *Psychological Bulletin*, **53**, 274.
42. KAGAN, J. (1966) 'Developmental studies in reflection and analysis' in *Personality, Growth and Learning: A Source Book* (Open University Press, Longman, 1971), 55.
43. AUSUBEL, D. P. & ROBINSON, F. G. (1969), *op. cit.*, 53.
44. *Ibid*, 357–8.
45. BOOTH, J. (1857) *How to Learn and What to Learn* (Bell & Daldy, London) 24.
46. VERNON, M. D. (1969) *Human Motivation* (Cambridge University Press),146.
47. BRUNER, J. S. (1960) *The Process of Education* (Vintage Books, Random House, New York, 1963), 55.
48. See KEDDIE, N. (1971) 'Classroom knowledge' in YOUNG, M. F. D. (ed.) (1971) *Knowledge and Control: New Directions for the Sociology of Education* (Collier-Macmillan, London), 133–60.
49. WISEMAN, S. (1973) 'The educational obstacle race: factors that hinder pupil progress' *Educational Research*, **15**, 90.
50. PIDGEON, D. (1970) *Expectation and Pupil Performance* (National Foundation for Educational Research, Slough) 117.
51. EYSENCK, H. J. (1973) 'A better understanding of IQ and the educational myths surrounding it.' *Times Educational Supplement*, 18 May, 2.
52. HOLLY, D. (1973) *Beyond Curriculum* (Hart-Davis MacGibbon, London), 145.
53. ALLEN, D. & RYAN, K. (1969) *Microteaching* (Addison-Wesley, Reading, Mass.), 15–23, 126–9.
54. MANSON, G. (1973) 'Classroom questioning for geography teachers' *Journal of Geography*, **72**, 24.
55. ALLEN, D. & RYAN, K. (1969), *op. cit.*, 2. See also STONES, E. & MORRIS, S. (1972) *Teaching Practice: Problems and Perspectives* (Methuen, London), 79–101; WRAGG, E. C. (1975) *Teaching Teaching* (David & Charles, Newton Abbot). 103–36; and BROWN, G. (1975) *Microteaching: a Programme of Teaching Skills* (Methuen, London).
56. HOWE, M. J. A. (1972) *Understanding School Learning: a New Look at Educational Psychology* (Harper & Row, New York), 64–6.
57. BAILEY, P. J. M. (1972) 'The organisation and management of geography departments in secondary schools' *Geography*, **57**, 226–31. See also BAILEY, P. J. M. (1975) *Teaching Geography* (David & Charles, Newton Abbot), 83–96.
58. DAVIS, D. (1971) 'Comprehensive geography' *Times Educational Supplement*, 5 March, 31.
59. See, for example, SHIPMAN, M. (1969) 'Curriculum for inequality' in HOOPER, R. (ed.) (1971) *The Curriculum: Context, Design and Development* (Oliver & Boyd, Edinburgh/Open University Press), 105; SEAMAN, P. (1972) 'The changing organisation of school knowledge' in *Innovation and Ideology* (1972) (Open University Press), 32; WHITE, J. P. (1973) *Towards a Compulsory Curriculum* (Routledge & Kegan Paul, London), Chapters 3–5; LAWTON, D. (1973) *Social Change, Educational Theory and Curriculum Planning* (University of London Press), 140–2.
60. ENTWISTLE, H. (1970) *Child-Centred Education* (Methuen, London), 109–10.
61. WALL, W. D. (1958) 'The wish to learn: research into motivation' *Educational Research*, **1**, 29.
62. MARLAND, M. (1973) 'Preference shares' *Education Guardian*, 11 September 1973, 18.
63. AUSUBEL, D. P. & ROBINSON, F. G. (1969), *op. cit.*, 447

64. *Ibid*, 445.
65. WALL, W. D. (1968) *Adolescents in School and Society* (National Foundation for Educational Research, Slough), 58.
66. BLOOM, B. S., *et al.* (1971) *Handbook on Formative and Summative Evaluation of Student Learning* (McGraw Hill, New York), 51.
67. BLOOM, B. S. (1968) 'Mastery learning' in BLOCK, J. H. (ed.) (1971) *Mastery Learning: Theory and Practice* (Holt, Rinehart & Winston, New York), 55. See also BLOOM, B. S. (1971) 'Mastery learning and its implications for curriculum development' in EISNER, E. W. (ed.) (1971) *Confronting Curriculum Reform* (Little, Brown & Co., Boston, Mass.), 17–55, and DETHEUX, M., *et al.* (1974) 'From compensatory education to mastery learning' *London Educational Review*, **3**, 41–50.
68. BRUNER, J. S. (1966b) *On Knowing* (Harvard University Press, Cambridge, Mass.), 90.
69. TABA, H. & ELKINS, D. (1966) *Teaching Strategies for the Culturally Disadvantaged* (Rand, McNally & Co., Chicago), 66.
70. BANKS, O. & FINLAYSON, D. (1973) *Success and Failure in the Secondary School* (Methuen, London), 65.
71. COURTIS, S. A. (1930) 'Individualization in education' *University of Michigan School of Education Bulletin*, **1**, 52.
72. GAGNÉ, R. M. (1967) 'Learning theory, educational media, and individualized instruction' in HOOPER, R. (ed.) (1971) *op. cit.*, 312.
73. PEARCE, M. (1929) 'An individual method in the teaching of geography' *Geography*, **15**, 298–302.
74. RHYS, W. (1972b), *op. cit.*, 193–4.

Section 3 Assessment

9 Purposes and Techniques of Assessment

Distinction needs to be made between what have been termed 'summative' and 'formative' assessment procedures.[1]

Summative assessment is most starkly represented by the external examination, but would also include internal end-of-term or end-of-year tests which function as pilot tests for an external examination. This form of assessment is likely to be *norm-referenced*, meaning that it is related to a set of norms, or average performances, drawn from an appropriate population, which act as a kind of bench-mark against which the pupils can be measured.

Formative assessment is a monitoring procedure undertaken on a continuing basis. It is *criterion-referenced*, meaning that the pupils are expected to attain appropriate levels of knowledge and understanding. The aims provide the criteria, and all should be able to 'pass the test'[2] if sufficient effort is made, even though this has the consequence of distorting the normal curve of distribution (see page 155).

The purposes of summative assessment

1. *Placing or grading of candidates*

The first intention is to measure the candidates' achievement as accurately as possible so as to place them in a rank order. The measure may be expressed as marks or grades. The placing may serve some specific vocational goal, such as selecting a limited number of candidates in a competitive situation, in which case the number of 'passes' is constrained by the number of places available. This *competitive* type of test is different from the *qualifying* GCE type, in which large numbers of candidates pass if they achieve the standards laid down. The result is taken as evidence that the candidate has satisfactorily completed a course of study. The selection of the pass/fail line is on a normative basis.

2. *Predicting future achievement*

This second type of placing also has a predictive function, for it is qualifying a candidate on the upper side of a pass/fail line, in some relatively diffuse way, as fitted to undertake a wide range of future activities. A high placing is presumed to be diagnostic of greater chances of later success than a low placing. The examination, therefore, acts as 'a clue to future achievement'.[3] Prediction is likely to be more accurate where future is linked with previous learning. A high 'A'-level grade in geography, for example, is thought to predict a good honours degree in that subject. But there is not a direct correspondence, as other variables are involved, such as the personality of the student and the methods of teaching adopted in the school. A hard-working but unimaginative pupil, therefore, effectively spoon-fed in school, might well achieve good 'A'-level results, but find himself lost in the more open situation of the university, and under-achieve there just as he had over-achieved at school.

Even more problematical is the situation where a 'transfer of training' is needed. Possession of a good honours degree is no guarantee that a graduate in geography will make a satisfactory teacher of the subject, nor a good town planner, nor a successful manager in industry. On the other hand, a string of 'O' or 'A' levels is usually diagnostic of hard work. If an employer is looking for 'clerkly diligence', he might find conventional examination success generally reasonably predictive of the quality he wants! Those whose demand is for originality and initiative might well find the examination process has militated against the development of such attributes.

The purposes of formative assessment

The major purpose of formative assessment is *monitoring*. It is designed to provide continuing feedback on the progress of the individual pupil and of the class as a whole, diagnosing weaknesses and suggesting appropriate remedies. While summative assessment provides a once-off, global feedback, that from formative assessment is regular, detailed and precise, so long as the appropriate instruments are used.

Two other functions are served by both *formative and summative assessment*:

(a) *To provide incentives and as a result raise standards.* Assessment procedures are in many circumstances a stimulus to effort on the part of both pupils and teachers, and thereby a means of raising standards. Summative assessment encourages *extrinsic* motivation, in that a long-term reward in the shape of improved occupational prospects beckons. Formative assessment, if correctly applied, can promote *intrinsic* motivation as well.

(b) *To assess the effectiveness of teaching.* The teacher must be held accountable to some extent for the success of his pupils, bearing in mind the constraints pointed out in the previous chapter (see page 151). In the case of formative assessment, the feedback on success or otherwise will tend to be personal to the teacher. In the case of summative assessment it is public, and likely to be regarded as testimony by both headteachers and parents as to the success of the teaching.

An historical perspective on external examinations

In contrast to the low repute in which external examinations stand with many writers on education today, their genesis in this country has been described as 'one of the great discoveries of nineteenth-century Englishmen'.[4] They were introduced to serve the sorts of purposes just discussed, and in response to certain inadequacies and malpractices in the previous system.

At the ancient universities, for example, the introduction of honours degrees was designed to encourage a long-overdue raising of standards. Similarly, external examinations were used to enhance the status of the newly established middle-class secondary schools. In the field of science and technical education the need to fix standards was also regarded as a priority in the second half of the nineteenth century.

Examinations were also seen as necessary incentives. As James Booth, Treasurer of the Royal Society of Arts, one of the pioneering examining bodies, then put it (1857):

though you catch your boys and impound them in your schoolrooms, you cannot force them to learn. But once hold out to your pupils the inducement that every hour they give to hard labour, to real hard work, will tell on their future advancement and prospects of life; mark what a face of reality it will put on all they are doing, how their attention will be awakened.[5]

The desire to raise standards was associated with the growth in the national demand for white-collar and skilled manual workers in administration, commerce and industry. The India Act of 1853 opened appointments in the Indian Civil Service to competition. In the Home Civil Service, there was limited competition from 1855, and open competition from 1870. For middle-class schools, the highly influential 'Locals' of the universities of Oxford and Cambridge were established. By the end of the century, even children from the elementary school system were finding a wider range of occupational opportunities made available to them. A scholarship ladder was slowly being erected.

In the technical and scientific sphere, in which the evidence of international exhibitions had shown Britain to be lagging behind the continent, a proliferation of examining bodies grew to meet the demand for higher standards of inventiveness and workmanship. In the long run, this proliferation came to cause great strains on the schools. In the early 1900s, for example, a school might have needed to prepare a pupil for ten or more different examinations. The position was rationalised by the establishment of the School Certificate system which followed World War I.[6]

In promoting occupational mobility, examinations were thus a mechanism of social engineering. Booth saw them as enabling competition rather than conspiracy to be the arbiter of promotion, and assured the public: 'Our examinations will be conducted with the most rigid impartiality, and with the greatest strictness.'[7] This meritocratic (ability plus effort) concept was clearly preferable to the process of patronage which had operated before. In the event, it has served to replace one privileged group by another, with consequences later summarised by Montgomery (1965).

> There was little lasting disgrace in failing an examination in the mid-nineteenth century, when only a small élite was generally involved. A century later, nearly everyone was examined and graded at one level or another, and opportunity for promotion was becoming steadily more available to those who passed the tests. But the sense of failure was to be savoured . . . by correspondingly large numbers.[8]

There is not space here to recount the attempts which have been made in this century to ameliorate the consequences of undue concentration on external examination requirements. There seems to be an in-built dilemma in that however well intentioned its statements of aims, the examination in practice tends to determine rather than follow the school syllabus. Yet those who regard this as inevitable, and argue for the radical step of abolishing external examinations, have still to demonstrate an alternative which would not place reliance on family influence, financial advantage, and the good favour of teachers. Is a reformist rather than a revolutionary solution practicable? To paraphrase Elvin,[9] if the present external examining system represents the 'thesis', and the values of progressive educationists the 'antithesis', can a compromise 'synthesis' be found, that reconciles to an acceptable extent conflicting principles?

Gearing examinations to educational aims and objectives

A reformed examination system would need to respond to the criteria discussed in the contexts of aims and objectives, the contribution of the subject and, particularly, the needs of the pupil.

1. *The pupil*

To take the pupil first, the system must not serve to reinforce failure, and particularly early failure. In the internal context, while there is every need to monitor progress and be critical of individual deficiences, it is potentially damaging to publicise overall class rank lists. Apart from the fact that they reinforce a sense of failure for many pupils, a child near the bottom of a 'good' form might be working nearer his optimum than one near the top of a weaker form (see pages 155–6).

At later stages in the secondary school, choices have clearly to be made, and it is increasingly widely being accepted, in grammar schools as elsewhere, that these should be made on grounds of subject interest. This does not in itself do away with the streaming principle, of course, as different subjects have different statuses (page 47).

There remains the intractable problem of the so-called non-examination pupil. There is an increasing feeling that all pupils should end up with their 'bit of paper'. Hence Eggleston expresses the hope that improved technology may be able to produce examinations

> that serve the whole curriculum and all students who follow it. . . . And it may well be true that the wider use of examinations . . . may well take us further forward in the pursuit of social justice envisaged by the advocates of comprehensive education. Certainly the present arrangement where 'non-examination' classes are identified as and identify themselves as examination failures even before the examinations are taken makes nonsense of the view that those who do not take the examinations are in some way liberated and unoppressed.[10]

2. *The curriculum*

A second major issue is whether the examination system can be made responsive to curriculum change, rather than acting as a reactionary force. A rationalisation for resisting change is often given as the constraints on time imposed by the examination syllabus. It is thus increasingly argued, though not without dissent, that effective reform must start with the examination system.

Thus Morris has insisted: 'If we are to reform the work of the schools we must begin by reforming the content of our examinations, by seeking explicitly to identify our desired objectives in teaching, and then by embodying these in suitable instruments of assessment.'[11] Macintosh sees the examinations boards as having an important change of role to undertake in moving into the sphere of curriculum development and evaluation[12] and, in a later statement with Smith, suggests that 'teachers can exploit the hitherto neglected potential of the existing examination system to provide more appropriate evaluation than in the past. In this way they can aid course development and a freer curriculum, the term used in this book for curriculum which is directly related to the expressed needs of the pupil.'[13]

Whitfield, too, argues that the examination system can provide the dynamic for improvement. 'Why should we therefore hesitate to marshal our expertise to fulfil our educational aims through a sensitively reformed examinations system?'[14] Kelly maintains that 'examinations can be used to aid curriculum development and a teacher's diagnostic work without undermining their value as examinations *per se*',[15] on the basis of experience of a Nuffield 'A'-level project. Similarly, the Bristol Schools Council *Geography 14–18 Project* has found it impossible to divorce curriculum innovation at this level from the inevitable priority which the school gives to preparing children for examinations and accept that 'examination questions dominate the goals of both teachers and pupils and thus can be used constructively.'[16]

In geography, testimony as to the positive impact of an examination innovation can be found in the great leap forward which has taken place in fieldwork in school since it became a required element in most CSE syllabuses in the mid-1960s.[17] While the motivation for undertaking fieldwork thus became extrinsic, it seems fair to say that once triggered off many teachers, despite their initial scepticism, found it both practicable and enjoyable and applied the method in lower forms of the school as well. Not least, geographers could now demand from their head-teachers, what they had previously been reluctant to grant, a slot in the timetable for this purpose.

The assumption is, therefore, that an external examination system can be reconciled with the broad aims of education, and play something more than a narrowly intrumental role. To do this it must be explicitly related to these aims, which is only possible if, in addition to a change in intent (and there have been these before), there is a *change in technique*. Thus, if the aim is to develop critical and imaginative thinking, there is little point in relying on a monolithic assessment device that manifestly tests neither.

Part of such a technology must lie in extending the range of types of assessment. Assessment by means of once-and-for-all written papers not only sets a premium on literary ability, which it may not be the prime intention of the examination to test, but also favours a particular type of learning style (see page 142). There is a need to assemble more rounded *pupil profiles*, based on tests which take account of factual knowledge, thinking skills, creative work and overall effort in course work.

Techniques of assessment

A range of techniques of assessment is available both for formative and summative purposes. Each technique should be evaluated to ensure that it plays the role for which it is best suited. Certain types of assessment 'fit' certain subjects better than others. Different types of assessment procedure may also perform different functions within a subject field.

The following techniques of assessment will be investigated in varying detail, illustrated by geographical examples, in the chapters which follow:
A. Essay-type assessment
B. Objective questions, particularly multiple-choice
C. Structured questions
D. Assessment of course work
E. Assessment of attitudes.

The special emphasis given to multiple-choice assessment is not because it is seen as the most important but because, apart from having a specialised value, it is also in general the least known, the most misunderstood and most frequently maligned technique.

For a fuller discussion of techniques of assessment, readers are advised to consult recent texts such as those written or edited by Hudson (1973),[18] Macintosh (1974)[19] and Thyne (1974).[20]

Priority readings
(see also references above)

1. WISEMAN, S. & PIDGEON, D. *Curriculum evaluation* (National Foundation for Educational Research).
2. WHEELER, D. K. *Curriculum Process* (University of London Press Unibooks), Chapter 10, pp. 267–87.
3. LONG, M. & ROBERSON, B. S. *Teaching Geography* (Heinemann), Chapter 17, pp. 362–81.
4. GRAVES, N. J. 'School Examinations' in GRAVES, N. J. (ed.) *New Movements in the Study and Teaching of Geography* (Temple Smith), pp. 171–5.

Questions for investigation and discussion

1. (a) Refer back to Chapter 2 and the statement of basic aims of education. Discuss the extent to which the presence of conventional external examinations (a) inhibits, or (b) fosters the achievement of these aims.
   (b) How much weight do you attach to the arguments (page 170) that a reformed examinations system can be an influence favouring curriculum innovation?
2. (a) Guy and Chambers see examinations constituting an infringement of human rights, including the basic human 'right to privacy'. They see them as maximising differences, putting the pupil in a position

of duress, and causing distress 'for what pupils are being forced to do . . . is to display their abilities in a public contest or suffer the consequences of being thought to lack such abilities.'[21]

(b) 'To control the matriculation examination of a country is to control its educational system; to develop tests that are widely used for selection and prediction purposes is to determine which human qualities are prized and which are neglected; to develop instruments that are frequently used to classify and describe human beings is to alter human relations and to affect a person's view of himself.'[22]

Assess the validity of these judgements, and discuss their implications as possible guides to practical action.

References

1. SCRIVEN, M. (1967) 'The methodology of evaluation' in TYLER, R. W. et al. (eds.) (1967) *Perspectives of Curriculum Evaluation* (Rand McNally, Chicago), 43. (It should be pointed out that Scriven used the terms 'summative' and 'formative evaluation'. The term 'assessment' is inserted here in line with consistent usage in this book.)
2. WISEMAN, S. & PIDGEON, D. (1970) *Curriculum Evaluation* (National Foundation for Educational Research, Slough), 85.
3. Educational Testing Service (1958) *Selecting an Achievement Test: Principles and Procedures* (Princeton, New Jersey), 19.
4. ROACH, J. (1971) *Public Examinations in England, 1850–1900* (Cambridge University Press), 3.
5. BOOTH, J. (1857) *How to Learn and What to Learn* (Bell & Daldy, London), 22.
6. See GRAVES, N. J. (1972) 'School Examinations' in GRAVES, N. J. (ed.) (1972) *New Movements in the Study and Teaching of Geography* (Temple Smith, London), 171–3.
7. BOOTH, J. (1857) op. cit., 20.
8. MONTGOMERY, R. J. (1965) *Examinations* (Longman, London), 271.
9. ELVIN, L. (1969) 'The positive roles of society and the teacher' in PETERS, R. S. (ed.) (1969) *Perspectives on Plowden* (Routledge & Kegan Paul, London), 87–8.
10. EGGLESTON, S. J. (1973) 'Guidance and examinations—central components of educational technology' *Cambridge Journal of Education*, **3**, 70–2.
11. MORRIS, B. (1972) 'Examinations as instruments of educational reform' in MORRIS, B. (ed.) (1972) *Objectives and Perspectives in Education* (Routledge & Kegan Paul, London), 82.
12. MACINTOSH, H. G. (1970) 'A constructive role for examining boards in curriculum development' *Journal of Curriculum Studies*, **2**, 32–9.
13. MACINTOSH, H. G. & SMITH, L. (1974) *Towards a Freer Curriculum* (University of London Press), viii.
14. WHITFIELD, R. (1972) 'Curriculum objectives, examinations and curriculum change' *Cambridge Journal of Education*, **2**, 86.
15. KELLY, P. J. (1971) 'A reappraisal of examinations' *Journal of Curriculum Studies*, **3**, 126.
16. HICKMAN, G., et al. (1973) *A New Professionalism for a Changing Geography* (Schools Council), 8.

17. CULLEY, A. (1972) 'The present state of fieldwork in secondary schools' *Geography*, **57**, 27.
18. HUDSON, B. (ed.) (1973) *Assessment Techniques: an Introduction* (Methuen, London).
19. MACINTOSH, H. G. (ed.) (1974) *Techniques and Problems of Assessment* (Edward Arnold, London).
20. THYNE, J. M. (1974) *Principles of Examining* (University of London Press).
21. GUY, W. & CHAMBERS, P. (1973) 'Public examinations and pupil's rights' *Cambridge Journal of Education*, **3**, 88.
22. BLOOM, B. S. (1970) 'Towards a theory of testing which includes measurement-evaluation-assessment' in WITTROCK, M. C. & WILEY, D. E. (eds.) (1970) *The Evaluation of Instruction: Issues and Problems* (Holt, Rinehart & Winston, New York), 25.

10 Essays

The writing of essays has dominated both the internal and the external examination scene in Britain over the last hundred years, a phenomenon which would seem to indicate that they have great advantages as means of assessment. Reservations about this widespread use are far from new. In the 1920s Ballard was writing of the essay: 'my scepticism goes further than denying it is a good means of measuring the pupil's knowledge of geography, history and science: I deny that it is a good means of measuring anything.' At the same time: 'Let it not be thought that in pointing out the weakness of the essay as a means of assessment I wish to speak lightly of it. I do not. My thesis is not that the essay is not good enough for a school examination, but rather that a school examination is not good enough for the essay.'[1]

The broad contention being advanced in this chapter is that in practice, if not in intent, a large number of geography essay titles can be reduced in essence to a single one, prefixed 'Write about' or 'Write all you know about'[2] It must be stressed that the focus of the critique is very largely directed at the use of the extended essay for purposes of mass examination of pupils in geography.

The disadvantages of essays as means of assessment

These can be looked at in terms of reliability and validity, appropriateness to the field of geography, effective use of teacher time and adequacy of feedback.

1. *Reliability*

The reliability of a test refers to whether it will give consistent results if repeated under similar conditions at a later date. It is a particularly important quality in terminal assessment, and is bound up with the discriminating power of the test. Essay methods of examining diminish reliability in a number of ways.

(a) *Problems of scoring*

Essay marking is a notoriously subjective and unstable procedure. Not only do different examiners mark to different standards, the same examiner confronted with the same essay at different times is also likely to mark it inconsistently. In justice it must be said that the major examining boards go to great lengths to make essay marking as fair as possible. Where impressionistic marking is necessary, multiple marking, shown to improve reliability considerably, is increasingly being adopted.[3] In subjects such as geography, however, points marking is generally used, based on schemes previously agreed with chief examiners as part of an elaborate interchange of information between the board, the chief examiner and his assistants.[4]

A crucial problem presents itself at the end of the process, however. A pass-fail line needs to be drawn through a large and closely-grouped cluster of candidates. To do this fairly is a manifest impossibility, and particularly so with essay tests. 'Unfortunately, though the margin of error involved can be calculated in respect of tests wholly of the objective type, no method of calculating it in respect of essays seems yet to have been devised.'[5]

(b) *Attenuation of the mark range*

There is a general tendency in essay marking to limit the range of marks allotted. If an essay is marked out of 10, the subjective marker usually works within a range such as 3/10 to 8/10, giving an effective mark range of 5. Such attenuation may not be important in formative assessment, but in a terminal test it lowers powers of discrimination and thus of reliability.

(c) *The effects of a limited number of questions*

Almost by definition, an essay test involves the candidate in answering a limited number of questions. The effect of this limitation is again to lower powers of discrimination. Ebel, quoting Posey, shows that a 10-question test is much less effective than, say, a 100-question objective test in discriminating between students, in this example using the cases of three students who had learned 90 per cent, 70 per cent and 50 per cent of what they should have learned on the course. (see Fig. 10.1).

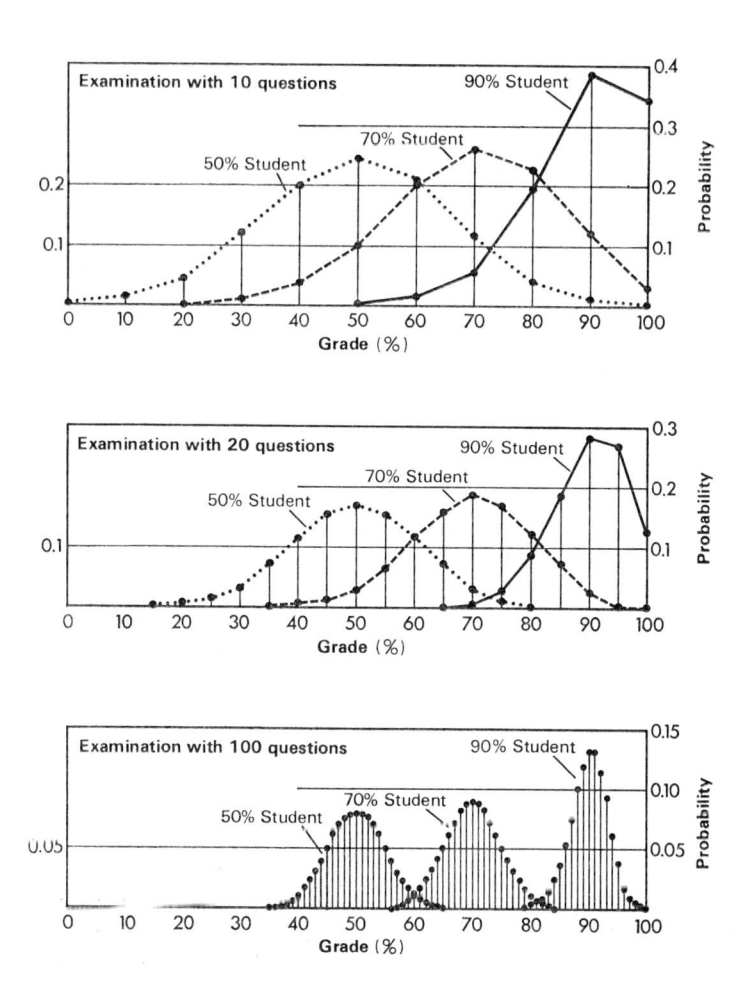

Fig. 10.1 Relation of the number of questions in an examination to the sharpness of discrimination of different levels of ability (Reprinted with permission from *Journal of Engineering Education*, **33**, 1932)

On the ten question test, the '50 per cent capable' student has 24/100 chances of scoring 50 per cent; 20/100 chances of scoring between 60 and 40 per cent; 12/100 between 70 and 30 per cent; 5/100 between 80 and 20 per cent; and 1/100 between 90 and 10 per cent, suggesting a tremendous potential overlap between the three students at these different levels, and thus the likelihood of large sampling errors. In contrast, on the 100-question test, the '50 per cent capable' student had only 1 chance in 100 of scoring over 70 per cent. There is, therefore, relatively little chance of overlap between the three candidates.[6]

2. *Validity*

In educational terms, validity is an even more important quality in a test than reliability. Does the test achieve what it sets out to achieve? Four types of validity have been identified. *Content validity* refers to whether the content of the test is adequately related to the teaching and learning that has previously taken place. It refers not only to factual content, but also to the more general objectives of the course. *Construct validity* refers to whether the test fairly measures the attributes of the candidate which it is ostensibly designed to measure. *Concurrent validity* means that the test should accurately correlate with some other established test or criterion obtained at the same time (such as teacher ratings); while *predictive validity* means that the test should adequately predict some later measure of performance. Only the first two types will be discussed here.

Content validity

Content validity is influenced by a number of factors.

(a) *A limited number of questions* Apart from diminishing a test's discriminating power, a limitation in the number of questions means that it cannot adequately sample the syllabus. It may well be that a large number of questions will be set on the paper to cover the syllabus reasonably well. But the candidate can only choose four or five, which do not adequately sample the work he has done.

Inevitably, an element of chance is introduced, which varies between schools and between candidates from the same school, according to whether or not the questions fit particular sections of the syllabus which have been more thoroughly covered than others, which have been studied more recently and so on. The choice element also has implications in terms of construct validity (page 182).

(b) *Choice of questions* The fact that the candidates are given this choice means that they are effectively sitting different examinations. The degree to which prior coverage will match the questions set will vary from school to school according, for example, to whether the teacher determines to cover the syllabus at all costs, however superficially, or whether he chooses the educationally more desirable in-depth approach (page 159).

(c) *What ability is being tested?* Perhaps the most crucial aspect of content validity is whether the test accurately reflects the objectives of the course. These will presumably require testing more than ability to recall facts. Essays have always been presented as the most effective means of assessing higher level abilities such as synthesis and creative work. This point is accepted, providing that the questions genuinely do demand these qualities and, more important, this is recognised in the marking scheme. A warning note, however, has been sounded by Bruce (1969), a former secretary of the University of London School Examinations Council.

> In recent years teachers have justifiably criticised the amount of unaided recall tested by GCE papers and have demanded more testing of understanding, of ability to organise material and all the other highly esteemed skills. Examiners in English literature responded by weighting the marking in favour of candidates who could organise material rather than those who simply showed they had read their set books and remembered the narrative. The results were a disaster for all concerned although the extent of the débâcle was never fully revealed because it is a principle in examining that the whole age group of one year cannot differ fundamentally from that of another year.[7]

Whether this was the predictable consequence of a unilateral change in marking procedures, or whether the implication is that children of this age group are unable *en masse* to measure up to more stringent requirements, is a fundamental question. In geography, it seems highly doubtful whether questions can be set under mass examination conditions truly to assess creative abilities. Can they, however, be set to indicate conclusively whether a candidate understands and can apply his material, whether he can meet the challenge of problem-posing questions and substantiate any judgements he makes, in addition to organising his material and expressing it in a coherent way?

It has been argued that the problem could be overcome by using more searching titles than the standard 'Write a geographical account'.[8] It is at this point, however, that the sort of gap between intent and practice to which Bruce alluded appears. Let us take a hypothetical question, and a hypothetical, though not untypical, 'O'-level answer. The question is intended to be more searching than the 'write an account of' kind. Assume that twelve marks are allotted to it. The objective of the course and of the examination is to do more than assess factual recall, so presume a maximum of four marks for factual details relevant to the question, leaving eight marks for direct evidence of higher level abilities. The question is 'Assess the importance of tourism to the economy of Switzerland'. The answer is as follows:

> Switzerland is one of the most mountainous countries in the world. It lies within the Alps and therefore has snow and glaciers all the year round. Beautiful scenery is found round Lake Constance and Lake Geneva. These lakes are between high mountains with many geographical features which influence tourists. Agriculture and small industries are provided in the Berne area.
> On the Alpine slopes skiing is an attraction to tourists. Numerous hotels are built side by side with the tourist resorts. Clocks and watches are the main industries, with highly qualified engineers and skilled workers. The large towns of Switzerland are easily accessible. Huge tunnels of 10–12 miles long are constructed under the Simplon Pass and other passes into Italy. Railways link with other countries—France, Italy and Germany. Rivers are also made use of.

It would presumably be agreed that the basic requirement of the question has not been met, though there is a minimal knowledge, and a hint that the topic *has* been covered in class. But any relationship between tourism and the Swiss economy is left implicit. To be able to answer such a question adequately, a candidate needs to have mastered far more than recall skills. Let us turn to an answer that ostensibly meets these 'higher level' requirements.

> Switzerland is one of the most mountainous countries in the world, in the heart of Alpine Europe. The Alps are glaciated, and contain spectacular peaks (eg the Matterhorn), U-shaped valleys (eg the Lauterbrunnen) and still-existing glaciers (eg the Aletsch). Along the fringe of the Alps attractive lakes such as Geneva and Lucerne are present.
> The Swiss have taken advantage of their natural scenery by providing facilities for winter sports enthusiasts and for summer tourists, by providing hotels, camping sites, aerial cableways and mountain cabins in areas such as the Bernese Oberland. Many tourist resorts such as Davos have grown

in the Alpine region and on its fringes. Switzerland lies in the centre of Europe and is well served by land, air and water connections, as along the Rhine valley. Many tourists come from Britain and northern Europe and enter the country via Basle. An electrified rail system can take them all over the country. The Alpine road system is one of the engineering marvels of Europe, and penetrates most valleys.

Many mountain valleys rely on tourism to supplement their people's income. Local people serve as mountain guides and skiing instructors, or run hotels, restaurants and souvenir shops. Farms take in visitors and sell dairy produce to the tourist resorts. A year round income may be provided. Switzerland is an isolated country with few natural resources, apart from hydro-electricity. But it makes full use of the skill of its people, and depends particularly on its tourist industry to keep it prosperous, as the foreign currency brought in by visitors is a valuable 'invisible export' for the Swiss economy.

This would be a good 'O'-level answer, containing an adequate factual base, and the ability to organise material, selected in accordance with the limits of the question. But what if the teacher has 'spotted' this question, and all the efficient learners in the class have produced a similar response on the basis of his set of notes? What evidence is there then that the desired abilities are genuinely those of the candidate? One would be more certain if the content of the answers from different candidates in the group varied. It must be concluded that even questions which at face-value demand more thought than the 'Write a geographical account' type, cannot readily provide satisfactory evidence of higher-level abilities in a mass examining situation. To secure content validity a more specific instrument than the essay is needed if we are to know with any degree of certainty whether the desired objectives are being achieved.

Construct validity

Various factors conspire to make it difficult also for an essay examition to achieve construct validity.

(a) *Difficulty levels of questions* As has been noted, the choice element means that different candidates are sitting different examinations. This is not only the case in respect of prior content coverage, but also because of the varying degrees of difficulty of questions. Some candidates will make a wiser choice than others, thus introducing a further variable into the situation.

Ebel argues that the presence of options brings in 'factors of judgement extraneous to the ability being measured.'[9] Research by Taylor and Nuttall has reinforced the fact that while most candidates choose questions wisely in the sense of matching them to previously acquired knowledge, a significant minority do not, and most of them figure in the lower grades. Taylor and Nuttall's study showed that approximately 25 per cent of the candidates could have improved scores had they chosen different questions.[10] There are additional factors, too, such as whether the questions 'wisely chosen' on the criterion of previous study, were in the event easy questions to score on; and also the degree of training in 'choosing wisely' given previously by the teacher. Different candidates start from different baselines, and an important anomaly in this context is that some teachers know the marking schemes because they serve as assistant examiners in marking GCE scripts. From experience they can advise their pupils on the sort of questions to select or avoid. Others have not this advantage.

(b) *The wording of questions* Many essay questions are vaguely or ambiguously worded. In a situation where so many of the directives such as 'analyse', 'assess the importance of', 'discuss' or 'describe and explain' are translated down to an all-embracing 'write about' there may be safety in numbers. Where words do mean something however, and those in the question have some influence on the marks being allotted, varied understanding by candidates of ambiguities in questions may well mean marks being awarded for accomplishing different tasks. Where this occurs the marks are strictly non-comparable.[11] In geography examinations, for example, the directive 'compare and contrast', or merely 'compare', produces considerable differences in interpretation. These may have punitive consequences for those candidates whose conception, or whose teacher's conception, does not equate with the one intended by the examiner.

(c) *Communication skills* The basic purpose of a geography examination is to assess achievement of geographical understanding. Yet it is difficult for an examiner in marking essays to ignore such 'non-geographical' qualities as contrasts between tidy and untidy, grammatical and ungrammatical, compact and rambling work and so on. The situation is even more delicate in internal examining, where the pleasant and co-operative pupil starts off with a halo round his script. It is not being argued that cosmetic qualities should not be assessed, but that they should be assessed separately, and certainly not several times over in the same examination.

Essays also have a culture bias. The literary associations of the essay are part of a tradition of artifice, thought appropriate to the cultivation of an élite. While the importance of prose writing as a form of communication, which this tradition stresses, should not be devalued, it is not the only form of communication. Over-emphasis on the essay has the pernicious effect of loading the dice heavily against certain groups, exacerbating the difficulties of so-called 'socially disadvantaged' pupils. Prose-writing is not a form of communication which comes naturally to them and the disadvantage is hammered home by repeated use of the procedure in different subjects in the same examination. It is difficult in these circumstances to decide whether deficiencies have arisen from lack of innate ability in the subject or from problems of communication in 'standard English'.[12] In this way again the essay is not fairly measuring the basic attribute it was introduced to measure.

3. *Appropriateness to the needs of geography*

Geography has been taught largely as a literary subject over a long period of time. Its place in the scientific tradition has been neglected. Fuller attention to graphicacy and, in respect of recent trends, numeracy would seem vital. The increasing interest in behavioural geography, and in games and simulations, has also made it necessary for geography teachers to think more seriously of the contribution of oral skills. All these factors combine to suggest that at best the extended essay should be seen as a peripheral rather than central feature of assessment.

Dury has argued strongly that the 'literary tradition' by its very nature inhibits the clear exposition of geographical content:

> repeated practice both in the reading and writing of elaborate prose, without explicit consideration of the purpose both of the writer and of the reader, is capable of maintaining in geography a tradition of manner to which geographical subjects are rarely suited. . . . To say technical things in non-technical language demands a large number of words, and very elaborate structural manipulations of the language.[13]

Similarly, in school there has grown over the years an examination-type English in which blandness and the neatly turned phrase take precedence over spontaneous if rougher expression.[14] While this problem is no doubt more apparent in 'English composition', neutralised, parroted prose is a ubiquitous feature in geography as well.

It is, of course, inconceivable that verbal communication should be neglected in geography. But there are a number of ways in which it might be encouraged without strict adherence to the rules of essay writing in their classic form. The use of short paragraphs focused on a specific topic, sub-headings and the 'report' format all spring to mind.

4. *The effective use of teacher time*

The most time-consuming activity of the average teacher of subjects such as geography is probably the marking of essays. Few regard it as one of the more enjoyable aspects of their work. Is it truly a purposive as distinct from a ritual activity?

A GA committee in the 1960s, considering the use of essays in 'A'-level geography courses, was clear, however, that the burden of marking must 'be borne with fortitude, for most will agree that the teacher has no better method of encouraging clear thinking, with lucidity and conciseness of expression, and no surer way of developing among his pupils an intellectual discipline and a fuller and richer geographical understanding.'[15]

The previous discussion makes clear the writer's opinion that this statement seems to contain a near reversal of the actual state of affairs. The pressures on geography teachers in the 1970s (page 151) reinforce the point that, unless essay marking can be shown to be an effective use of teacher time in terms of feedback to the pupils, its continuing widespread use should be brought into question.

5. *The question of feedback*

Constraints of time make it almost inevitable that feedback from essays cannot be adequate at the individual level. Overloaded teachers have hardly time to do more than 'administrate' work: check that it has been completed, correct obvious errors, and append a short generalised comment at the end. The children are more usually interested in the mark than the comment. There is little time to dwell on underlying meanings and on the special weaknesses of individual children. If the essay is to have real value, the teacher must be able to work with the individual child in a tutorial capacity, the essay preferably being marked in his presence. The one-to-one tutorial system of the Oxbridge college is the optimal one for the formative use of essay procedures, but this is a pipe-dream in the normal school situation. Only in the small sixth form are the conditions remotely comparable.

Claims continue to be made for essay forms of assessment both on general and on subject-specific grounds. Biddle outlines the benefits of the essay as providing a better method of assessing geographical skills and higher-level cognitive abilities, as leading to a more desirable approach than objective questions to the content of geography, and as a means of developing styles of study appropriate to tertiary education.[16] None of these assertions is substantiated, but it is interesting that Biddle's associated examples of 'preferred' types of question[17] are, in fact, partly-structured data-response questions (see pages 228–9). These do have a desirable degree of specificity, a quality not usually characteristic of the standard extended essay, which is the form that has been the focus of criticism in this chapter.

Priority readings

1. PRITCHARD, D. F. L. 'Essays' in HUDSON, B. (ed.) *Assessment Techniques: an Introduction* (Methuen), Chapter 3, pp. 66–91.
2. SHERIDAN, W. 'Open-ended questions' in MACINTOSH, H. G. (ed.) *Techniques and Problems of Assessment* (Edward Arnold), Chapter 1, pp. 1–6.
3. GRAVES, N. J. 'School examinations' in GRAVES, N. J. (ed.) *New Movements in the Study and Teaching of Geography* (Temple Smith), pp. 175–9.

Questions for investigation and discussion

1. On the whole, the authors quoted in the Priority readings take a more positive view towards the essay than the one presented in this chapter. On the basis of this reading, work out your own check-list of the advantages and disadvantages of essay assessment.
2. What do you think is the import of Ballard's comment (page 175) that a school examination 'is not good enough for the essay'? Is it a valid point in your opinion?
3. 'All too often standard English is represented by a style that is simultaneously over-particular and vague. The accumulating flow o. words buries rather than strikes the target. It is this verbosity that is

most easily taught and most easily learned, so that words take the place of thought, and nothing can be found behind them.'[18]

With reference if possible to particular examples, would you regard this comment as legitimate (a) in general terms (b) in the geographical context?

4. Examine the following 'O'-level essay question and the answer which follows:

'Explain why New South Wales and Victoria are the most fully developed parts of Australia.'

> New South Wales and Victoria are the most densely populated states in Australia. The first reason for this is historical. These were the first parts of Australia to be colonised and therefore the people who settled here were more likely to remain because they would not wish to change residence.
>
> The most important factor is their climatic advantage. The climate is suitable for whites while in Queensland it is too wet and hot, and in Western Australia and South Australia too hot and dry. In Tasmania it is too cold and wet. The highest temperature is around 70 degrees Fahrenheit at the coast and it decreases to the west. The rainfall varies from 30″ at the coast to 10″ inland.
>
> This climate is also suitable for grass to grow thus making this part of Australia the most important sheep rearing region. Cattle rearing is also suited to the climate of the coastal areas, while sheep are mainly in the interior. The wheat-growing region corresponds with the sheep farming, but is not as important. Thus farmers are more concentrated in this area of Australia. There is no part of Australia better for farming.
>
> Furthermore, there is much mineral wealth in this part of Australia. Gold is found in Victoria, coal at Sydney and Newcastle, and other minerals like silver, copper and iron in Broken Hill. These are all factors that help the south-east of Australia to be more populated.
>
> The excellent harbours of Melbourne and Sydney serve the hinterland, and allow the export and import of goods. There are many other large towns where population is concentrated. The nearness of this part of Australia to overseas trading countries is also important.
>
> The artesian wells also help in the arid area. The Murray-Darling Downs is the most important agricultural region. The land is well drained by these two rivers.
>
> The influence of the sea reduces the heat of the climate. This is the most fully developed part of Australia. It has a good network of railways so that the rich hinterland is served properly.

(a) Mark the above essay in three ways; (i) according to your general impression of it; (ii) by a previously worked out points marking scheme; (iii) more rigorously, according to the following principles: maximum

25% of marks for recall of facts; no marks for information contained in a passage not brought to bear on the question; at least 40% of marks reserved for relation with other less developed parts of Australia. (Total 20 marks.) In each case compare your marks with those of colleagues.
(b) Do this and the other essays quoted in the chapter lend any weight to Bruce's statement (page 179) and if so, in what way?
(c) To what extent do these essays confirm or refute the view that for mass examining in geography the essay does not make possible an adequate assessment of varying abilities.

References

1. BALLARD, P. B. (1923) *The New Examiner* (University of London Press, 1949 edition), 52-3, and 66.
2. See also HARTOG, P. J. (1936) 'English composition at the School Certificate Examination; and the "Write anything about something for anybody" theory' in International Institute Examinations Enquiry (1936) *Essays on Examinations* (Macmillan, London,) 131.
3. Schools' Council (1966) *Multiple Marking of English Compositions* (Examinations Bulletin No. 12. (HMSO, London), 27.
4. BLACK, E. L. (1962) 'The marking of GCE scripts' *British Journal of Educational Studies*, **11**, 63-9.
5. CHRISTOPHER, R. (1969) *The Work of the Joint Matriculation Board* (JMB Occasional Publication No. 29, Manchester), 23.
6. EBEL, R. L. (1965) *Measuring Educational Achievement* (Prentice Hall, Englewood Cliffs, N.J.), 88-90. Based on POSEY, C. (1932) 'Luck and examination grades' *Journal of Engineering Education*, **23**, (unpaginated offprint).
7. BRUCE, G. (1969) *Secondary School Examinations: Facts and Commentary* (Pergamon Press, Oxford), 19.
8. See GRAVES, N. J. (1972) 'School Examinations' in GRAVES, N. J. (ed.) (1972) *New Movements in the Study and Teaching of Geography* (Temple Smith, London), 175-8.
9. EBEL, R. L. (1965), *op. cit.*, 115.
10. TAYLOR, E. G. & NUTTALL, D. L. (1974) 'Question choice in examinations: an experiment in geography and science' *Educational Research*, **16**, 149.
11. See MADAUS, G. F. & MACNAMARA, J. (1970) *Public Examinations: A Study of the Irish Leaving Certificate* (Educational Research Centre, St Patrick's College, Dublin), 84.
12. See LABOV, W. (1969) 'The logic of non-standard English' in KEDDIE, N. (ed.) (1973) *Tinker, Tailor: The Myth of Cultural Deprivation* (Penguin Books, Harmondsworth, Middlesex), 34-44.
13. DURY, G. H. (1963) 'Geographical description: an essay in criticism' in BIDDLE, D. S. (ed.) (1968) *Readings in Geographical Education: Selections from Australian Sources*. Vol. 1, 1964-1966 (Whitcombe & Tombs, Sydney, for the Australian Geography Teachers' Association), 93 and 103.
14. See BROWN, J. (1966) *Objective Tests: Their Construction and Analysis* (Longman London), 4.
15. Geographical Association (1967) 'The evaluation of sixth-form essays in geography' *Geography*, **52**, 52.

16. BIDDLE, D. S. (1966) 'Examinations in geography in New South Wales' in BIDDLE D. S. (ed.) (1968), *op. cit.*, 274–5.
17. BIDDLE, D. S. (1971) 'The quest for reliability in marking responses to essay questions in geography' in BIDDLE, D. S. & DEER, C. E. (eds.) (1973) *Readings in Geographical Education: Selections from Australian and New Zealand Sources*. Vol. 2, 1966–1972. (Whitcombe & Tombs, Sydney, for the Australian Geography Teachers' Association), 419–23.
18. LABOV, W. (1961), *op. cit.*, 44.

11 Multiple Choice

Objective forms of assessment

The preceding critique of the essay is not a preamble to an uncritical acceptance of objective tests, and in particular multiple choice tests, as instruments of assessment. It will, in fact, be argued that the use of such tests should be confined to the purposes for which they are best suited.

While the climate of opinion is not as unfavourable to objective tests as in, say, the 1950s, the attitudes of teachers and others are still cautious. There is still a feeling that objective tests are academically suspect, which is not surprising when many of the examples in print are so trivial. It must not be thought, however, that objective tests are a new and fleeting trans-Atlantic fashion. Morris records that as early as the first half of the nineteenth century, in the quest for impartiality and objectivity, 'the ingenious were at great pains to devise novel ways' of meeting these ends. Jeremy Bentham stipulated, for example, that all questions should have one correct answer only.[1]

There is now a wide variety of texts discussing the general rationale of objective tests, and it is suggested that readers sample Vernon (1964),[2] Brown (1966),[3] Macintosh and Morrison (1969),[4] Hudson (1973),[5] Bonney Rust (1973),[6] Macintosh (1974),[7] and Thyne (1974).[8] The intent of the following section is to discuss the rationale mainly in the geographical context. Fewer texts have attempted this, though exceptions include Senathirajah and Weiss (1971),[9] and Salmon and Masterton (1974).[10]

Types of objective test

Two basic types can be identified:
 1. *Supply or completion* type items, in which the candidate is

required to supply or complete the answer, part of which is given.

Eg The capital of Australia is . . .

An increasingly used example of this kind of question is the *insertion type*.

Eg Manchester's original site lay on the east bank of the River I.......... A sandstone bluff provided firm ground for a Roman fort, named M.......... and later for a S.......... market place. The river separates the city of Manchester from the city of S.......... Manchester today covers much of the 'bay' of lowland between the uplands of R.......... to the north and the P.......... to the east.

The trouble with such items is that if they are truly objective they are likely to test only factual knowledge. They can, however, be applied to circumstances in which more than one correct answer is possible, and higher level abilities can thus be assessed. But they then become increasingly subjective (though far less so than the essay). Hence the supply type of item will be left for the time being, and returned to in the section on structured questions.

2. *Multiple choice* items are the 'purest' type of objective test, in which the candidate is constrained to choose a correct answer from a number of supplied alternatives.

A terminology has been devised to describe multiple choice questions, which are generally referred to as ITEMS, and is illustrated by a simple geographical example below.

STEM	The capital of Australia is		
OPTIONS or RESPONSES	A Canberra	KEY	(Correct answer)
	B Melbourne		
	C Perth	DISTRACTORS	(Incorrect answers)
	D Sydney		
	E Wellington		

The STEM is, therefore, the first part of the item and sets out the task to be undertaken. The OPTIONS are made up of a number of DISTRACTORS and one correct answer, the KEY.

It will be clear that this item leaves no room for subjective interpretation. The basic problem in multiple choice writing is to maintain such lack of ambiguity while associating the procedure with higher-level educational objectives, which has not, of course, been done in the example used above.

Advantages of multiple choice tests

1. *Improved reliability*

The proper use of multiple choice tests improves reliability in a number of ways.

(a) The scoring does not depend on subjective interpretation. This is true both for internal and external assessment. In the latter, items can be marked and the results analysed by computer.

(b) The large number of items sharpens the discrimination of the test (see pages 177–8), which can be further improved on the basis of information derived from pre-testing items.

(c) Standardisation of scoring over a period of time and between schools or regions is made possible, thus making comparisons more valid.

(d) While errors are bound to occur, the degree of error can be calculated.

2. *Improved content validity*

As has already been noted, reliability in itself is not enough, for it tells us nothing about what is being measured and whether it is worth measuring. Properly set multiple choice tests have the added advantage of enhancing content validity for the following reasons.

(a) The use of a large number of short items allows an *adequate sampling of syllabus content* (which, of course, carries the corollary that over-inflated syllabuses must be reduced when multiple choice testing is used, if over-pressure is not to result).

(b) *All the candidates sit the same examination,* as no choice of questions is offered. Thus a 'core syllabus' is needed. If a mistake is made, or a particular point is not known or understood, the omission does not of itself carry serious penalties, as it can do in an essay paper with few questions, each carrying a large number of marks. The element of luck in whether the questions match recent content coverage is reduced.

(c) The examiner, through drawing up a test specification beforehand (see page 209) *knows what abilities he is intending to test.* Later illustrations will indicate how multiple choice items can be written to assess a wide, though not full, range of abilities (pages 210–15). They are particularly useful in assessing 'thinking skills'.[11]

3. Improved construct validity

To repeat the definition, construct validity refers to whether a test in fact measures the attributes it purports to measure. Objective tests have some advantage here, for they focus more directly on the skills which have been prespecified. It was noted that with the essay there is a heavy bias towards literary skills, measurement of which is not the prime purpose of a geography test. It must, of course, be accepted that such extraneous factors are not entirely absent from objective tests. Some people temperamentally find it difficult to read every word with the care, a quality a multiple choice test demands. Such tests are more congenial to convergent than divergent thinkers (see page 142). The differing traits of students is a major reason for using a wide range of methods, including multiple choice, in assessment.

4. The provision of detailed feedback

Perhaps the most important advantage of multiple choice tests is that if correctly used they allow the provision of detailed feedback (pages 156–8). The following feedback is usually provided, in addition to such general data as means and standard deviations:

(a) The *facility index*, registering the relative ease or difficulty of the item.

(b) the *discrimination index*, registering the degree of discrimination of the item.

(c) the overall percentage responding to each option in each item.

(d) the proportions from different groups of students, arranged in order from the highest to lowest group on the overall result of the test, responding to each option.

Such feedback is of importance in formative assessment, making possible a precise diagnosis of the strengths and weaknesses both of the class as a whole and of individual children.

5. Pre-testing

In summative assessment in particular, multiple choice items should always have been pre-tested. This allows for the identification of flaws in items, which can then either be modified or rejected. Good items can be stored for later use (see pages 223–4). The pre-testing procedure provides initial feedback, and the use of validated items improves the validity and reliability of the test as a whole.

Disadvantages

It will become clear that, in the author's view, many of the arguments often advanced against multiple choice testing can readily be countered. Critics of the system sometimes seem to base their case on the principle that the present system is satisfactory and anything new must therefore be near-perfect. The position taken here is that much in the present system is highly unsatisfactory and that *for certain purposes* multiple choice methods are preferable to other methods.

The following are frequently cited disadvantages.

1. *Unsuitability for more able pupils*

The trivial image of multiple choice tests has no doubt been responsible for the feeling that they are inappropriate for use with more able children. There is the associated fear that such children, finding some items too easy, will not take them at face value, look more deeply into the item than is warranted, and end up with the incorrect answer. While this may occasionally happen, there are no empirical grounds for believing that isolated miscalculations of this type distort the effective working of a test as a whole. Clearly some children will find objective tests less congenial than others: there seems no evidence that they will be drawn from the more able.

What might of course happen is that a multiple choice test intended to assess higher level abilities will not be found as straightforward as essay tests by those children who have hitherto relied on diligent but unintelligent learning of notes to gain high marks. Conversely, it is also possible that (a) pupils who have been designated less able through difficulties they have found in extended prose writing, and (b) relatively able pupils who resent the chore of assimilating for a once-off event large masses of factual content, may find multiple choice tests to their advantage.

2. Mere intelligence tests

The criticism is sometimes made that multiple choice tests are 'mere intelligence tests', or 'just tests of logic'. This of course contains an an element of truth, but less of fair criticism. It seems high time that tests in geography *should* assess intelligence and logic. Whether there is such a thing as 'geographical intelligence' or 'geographical logic' is, however, an issue that will be side-stepped (see page 141).

3. Too much reading in the examination room

Some teachers complain about the amount of reading time that is needed in a multiple choice test, with its complex rubrics, lengthy stems and numbers of options. A properly designed multiple choice test will provide enough time for the candidates to undertake the necessary reading, however. If rubrics are obscure even after pupils have become acclimatised to them, if stems are verbose and options ambiguous, this is a criticism if the item writers rather than of the principles underlying the test.

It would seem appropriate, of course, to demand that candidates should read questions carefully, and weigh the importance of words. Multiple choice tests require reading and thinking in the examination room,[12] in contrast to conventional essay examinations, where there is a tendency to do too much writing and not enough thinking.

4. Introduce false information

There are also those who take exception to the deliberate introduction of false information, which must be part and parcel of any multiple choice test. This may be because it is thought in cognitive terms to lead to confusion, and in moral terms to be a minor form of deceit. Neither of these charges seem to be legitimate. The children know beforehand that false information is to be used, and that there is a reason for providing it. The positive justification is that in this way children can be asked, among other things, (a) to distinguish exemplars from non-exemplars of concepts, thus providing the first piece of evidence in assessing whether a concept has been grasped (page 33); and (b) to make distinctions of varying degrees of fineness, and not purely black and white ones.

It is also timely that children should be placed in situations which suggest that they should not believe everything they read, and face the challenge of making decisions on the basis that some of the information presented is inaccurate, incomplete, irrelevant or even loaded: to look at the small print in fact.

5. *Backwash effect on schools*

It is argued that multiple choice external examinations are likely to have adverse backwash effects on school curricula, leading, for example, to a proliferation of mock tests. An immediate rejoinder would be that the situation could hardly be worse than under the present system, where in some subjects in some schools children have four years of notes to 'swot up' before their 'O' levels are taken.

But that is not enough. The vital point is that *if* multiple choice tests are used to assess meaningful rather than rote learning and *if* the need is accepted to reduce the size of syllabuses to enable this to be a realistic aim, then the effects might be relatively beneficial. Clearly some 'coaching' for multiple choice tests will take place, but this is likely to be true for all types of external assessment. At the same time, the use of items assessing higher level abilities will take some power away from the teacher who at present gains splendid results by providing a 'good set of notes', and will place more onus on the conceptual grasp of the learner.

6. *Decline in the ability to write continuous prose*

'Every teacher is a teacher of English' is a widely held maxim of geography, as of other, teachers. Many genuinely fear that a widespread development of multiple choice testing will lead to a decline in the ability to write continuous prose. This does not take account of the detail of the argument, however. Two points must be stressed. The first is that few would advocate that multiple choice items should constitute the sole, or even the major, means of assessment. The second is that while geography teachers should properly feel a responsibility for fostering good English, assessment of this ability should be by a separate, purpose-built instrument.

7. Encouragement of guesswork

The problem of guesswork is a significant one, about which there are, understandably, qualms. It is certainly the case that by blind guessing a candidate may theoretically gain 20 per cent of the marks on a five-option, and 25 per cent on a four-option test, 33 per cent on a three-option, and 50 per cent on a two-option (true-false) item test. The criticism is valid enough to reinforce the need for four- and preferably five-option item tests, though not all agree that the latter is necessary. It is also the reason why true-false tests as such are not included in this book.

Guesswork can be allowed for, however, and appropriate corrections made by the simple application of a formula. Ebel has argued persuasively that correction for guesswork is unnecessary, for the following reasons:[13]

(a) Scores corrected for guessing usually arrange pupils in the same rank order as uncorrected scores.

(b) A respectable score on an adequate objective test cannot be achieved by blind guessing.

(c) Well-motivated examinees, given adequate time and prior guidance, will guess blindly on few if any items.

(d) Ordinarily no educational ill will ensue if pupils are encouraged to make intelligent guesses where these are appropriate, as where the candidate has a good general idea but is not entirely certain of the correct answer. Where the point of difficulty is one of factual content, the presence of the right answer among the options may well 'jog the memory'. It is much less likely to in the case of the blind guesser. Vernon, too, supports this view,[14] suggesting that children should be encouraged to make intelligent guesses when in doubt. At the same time, the futility of blind guesswork should be made explicit beforehand.

Ebel exposes the fact that guesswork is not confined to objective tests, and points to the analogous ruse of *bluffing* in essay-type examinations[15]—that is the transformation of the question set into the one the candidate wishes to answer. Many questions in geography are open to such transformation. In some cases the ensuing irrelevance is blatant and involves heavy penalties. But where there is a mixture of material, some partly, some remotely and some not at all focused on the question, the penalty is largely one of consuming scarce time, for marks are not normally deducted for inclusion of irrelevant material.

8. *Unfavourable attitudes of children*

There seems to be no empirical evidence to support the case that multiple choice questions are more disliked by children than other forms of assessment. The writer has conducted an exercise in which the attitudes of over 500 children to a series of multiple choice tests were sought.[16] A wide range of opinion, ranging from abusive and hostile to considered and insightful comment, was forthcoming. The strongest antipathy was over the question of guesswork. There were many accusations that the test was unfair on the grounds that on a lucky day a candidate could do well merely through guessing. It is thus vital that careful preparation is made for multiple choice tests. Apart from making sure that children understand the rubrics, the consequences of blind guesswork, as well as lack of knowledge and understanding, should be spelled out to the children.

The following examples of children's opinions are expressive of the range which emerged from the attitude test, though no attempt has been made to respect the balance between favourable and unfavourable attitudes.

> Very good and a pleasure to do.

> This type of question is easier to answer than essay questions. The answers can jog your memory, so a photographic mind is not quite as essential as in essay questions.

> I find the tests easier than essay tests, requiring less factual knowledge. This type of test also causes less anxiety during revision.

> Much better for people who find it difficult to put their thoughts into writing.

> Multiple choice gives a bigger variety of questions. This tests your more general knowledge over all the subjects you have studied.

> I think they sound easier than they are.

> I think Multiple Choice questions are good for assessing progress only with an accompanying Essay type paper, because although they *are*

interesting, more of our *own* thinking needs to be assessed to give a broader outlook of our ability.

They're not bad until they get to 3-type and 4-type questions. Some of them are very confusing, but they really do make you think because my brain's always sore afterwards!

Progress cannot be assessed accurately using multiple choice methods. To some extent luck is a factor influencing the final mark. eg A pupil knows 30 questions in a multiple choice. The other 20 are just guesses but by the law of averages he should obtain an extra 4 marks.

The method is *time-wasting, energy-wasting* and a *total failure*. The geography of the pupil is not really being tested at all, you could put a pen in a monkey's hand and tell it to tick anything it liked and the chances are that it would get a higher score than a pupil through sheer good luck. Thank goodness this rubbish is not in the 'O'-level curriculum.

9. *Difficulty of writing*

Good items are very difficult to write. While it is relatively easy to construct straightforward and often trivial factual recall items, those testing higher level abilities are much more difficult to think out and express unambiguously. The problems can be met to some extent by the organisation of workshops where expert advice is given to groups of teachers, whether by examining boards, teachers' centres or other organisations making in-service provision. In this as in the pre-testing of items, mutual help is not just an advantage, it is a prerequisite.

10. *Time involved in writing*

In contrast to the essay test, which is quick to construct, but time-consuming to mark, a heavy burden of time is involved in the writing of items and construction of multiple choice tests, though marking is easy. This does not imply that the two procedures cancel each other out. Having had experience of both, my personal feeling is that writing and reviewing of items is a more constructive and enjoyable exercise than the marking of essay scripts. More important, once good items have been identified by review and pre-testing, they can be stored for later use, thus progressively reducing the consumption of energy.

11. *Subjectivity in writing*

A subjective element is sometimes present in the writing of items, particularly those which set out to test more than factual recall. Items may reveal personal idiosyncrasies in construction, some of which may be undesirable. The problem can usually be resolved by the use of reviewing panels in external examinations, by critical colleagues in the case of internal tests, and by the provision of item banks, which make it possible to draw on a wide range of items, written by a considerable number of people.

12. *Testing the whole spectrum of 'abilities'*

Multiple choice items do not adequately test the whole range of abilities, though they cover much more than factual recall. It is not easy nor is it particularly appropriate to assess the skills of synthesis, and to a lesser extent, evaluation by this means. Creative thought requires other forms of assessment. This is a good reason for restricting the use of multiple choice items in an assessment, though not for their exclusion altogether.

Types of multiple choice items

Four frequently used types of multiple choice item are discussed here. Unfortunately, no consensus on nomenclature yet exists. The terms employed in this text, with alternatives which can be found elsewhere, are as follows:

This text	*Alternative(s)*
1. Simple selection	Multiple choice; simple completion
2. Multiple selection	Multiple completion
3. Relationship analysis	Assertion-reason
4. Classification	Matching pairs

1. Simple selection

The term 'simple selection', is preferred to 'multiple choice'. Where several types of item are being used it is confusing to use the generic term for one of the species also. 'Simple selection' is preferred to 'simple completion' on the obvious ground that the candidate is required to select rather than complete an answer. The word 'simple' should not be taken literally, of course, for this type of item is not necessarily easier than other types.

Examples of the five-choice item are used consistently here, even though some argue in favour of the four-choice type on the grounds that it is often difficult to find fifth options. Where there is difficulty, recourse can be made to using a different item format which provides a better fit for the task to be set. Five-choice items also go some way to minimising the problem of guesswork. If there is a bad option in a four-choice item, for example, it effectively reduces it to a three-choice type. A five-choice item can more safely 'carry' a poorly functioning option.

In addition, the other types of items described below also include five choices, as it seems desirable to keep to a consistent pattern. Having said this, there appears to be no strong empirical evidence that would categorically uphold the case of five-choice as against four-choice items.

The *rubric* associated with simple selection items runs:

Choose the correct response from the five options presented.

2. Multiple selection

Multiple selection items are a more complex variant of the simple selection type. After the stem, as in simple selection, a set of options is provided. Unlike simple selection, however, where only one of these options can be the key, multiple selection items can have one *or more* options (or even none at all) correct. Usually three or four options are offered. The candidate has then to choose a specified permutation of options as the key.

The following is an example of a *three-option multiple selection* item:

STEM Market gardening is a farming activity characterised by
OPTIONS   1   small holdings
            2   intensive cultivation
            3   cereal growing

CHOICES   A if 1, 2 and 3 are correct
          B if 1 and 2 only are correct   (KEY)
          C if 2 and 3 only are correct
          D if 1 only is correct
          E if 3 only is correct

A *four-option variant* would be:

STEM   Market gardening is a farming activity characterised by
OPTIONS   1 cereal growing
          2 small holdings
          3 intensive cultivation
          4 vegetable growing
CHOICES   A if 1 only is correct
          B if 1 and 3 only are correct
          C if 1, 2 and 4 only are correct
          D if 2 and 3 only are correct
          E if 2, 3 and 4 only are correct   (KEY)

There is nothing sacrosanct about the above permutations, and others are available, including 'none of these'. Each option must figure at least twice in the set of choices, however, otherwise there are circumstances in which the candidate, by knowing one only of the options, could achieve the correct answer without knowledge of any of the rest. The correct options must, of course, be arranged to fit the specified permutations. It is strongly urged that once a permutation has been agreed, it should be used consistently. The above permutations are the ones used in this text.

Multiple selection items have certain advantages over simple selection in a subject such as geography, in which there is often more than one correct explanation of a situation. Thus in the sort of question involved with a series of factors explaining the growth of a settlement or an industry, the use of a simple selection type means that the item writer has to find four incorrect options (distractors) to go with the key; alternatively he has to use a negative in the stem: 'Which of the following has NOT helped in the growth of, etc.'

A criticism of multiple selection items is that the rubrics are too complicated, particularly for 'O'-level or CSE candidates. While some worried comments were made by children in the attitude test previously referred to (page 197) about the greater complexity of this type, there seems no empirical evidence to hand that this concern is warranted, in the sense that certain types of items are intrinsically more difficult than others. But understanding of the rubrics must be established before the test.

The *rubrics* for multiple selection items may be given as follows:

ONE or MORE of the three (or four) possible options provided is (are) correct. Decide which of the options is (are) correct, then choose according to the following code.

The codes are as set out above.

3. *Relationship analysis*

These are often referred to as *assertion-reason* items. In that they consist of two statements, one an assertion and the second a reason for that assertion, this label is a logical one. The fact that it is not used here is to do with the nature of geography, in that in an assertion-reason format the connecting word 'because' is placed between the two statements, giving the semblance of a simple linear relationship between them and often a deterministic one at that. In the relationship analysis format, the word 'because' is not present, and the emphasis is focused on whether or not some relationship exists.

The *rubric* for a relationship analysis item runs:

Here a statement in a left hand column is followed by a statement in a right hand column. Decide whether the first statement is true or false. If both statements seem to be true, you also have to decide whether the second one is a correct explanation of the first.

Hence the statements might be:

Statement 1	*Statement 2*
The most important industrial axis in Britain now lies between London and Bristol	The completion of the M4 has improved communications between London and Bristol

The following code has then to be used for the choice of answer:

	Statement 1	*Statement 2*	
A	True	True	Statement 2 is a correct explanation of Statement 1
B	True	True	Statement 2 is NOT a correct explanation of Statement 2
C	True	False	
D	False	True	(KEY)
E	False	False	

It will be apparent that the relationship analysis item is a sophisticated version of the true-false type.

Probably more objections have been advanced by geographers against this type of item than others. It is all too easy to 'stretch' the relationship or non-relationship between the two statements too far, and the question becomes artificial. Not all geographical relationships fit well into this format by any means. In addition, it can be argued that items for which the key is 'B' require a more refined judgement than the rest. This type of item has therefore to be used cautiously.

4. *Classification*

Classification items are often grouped in sets of three. The *rubric* might run as follows:

> Here questions are grouped, each group of questions relating to five headings, labelled A to E. For each numbered question following you have to select the heading which matches up with it. Each heading may be used once, more than once, or not at all.

The following is an example:

> Questions 1 to 3 refer to people either on the move, who have moved or who have been forced to move.
>
>   A   Commuters
>   B   Deportees
>   C   Nomads
>   D   Pilgrims
>   E   Shifting cultivators
>
> Which of the above categories is most applicable to
> Q.1.   Masai tribesmen in Kenya   (Key: C)
> Q.2.   Jordanian Arabs in Mecca   (Key: D)
> Q.3.   Ugandan Asians in Leicester   (Key: B)

The so-called 'headings' are in effect the options. The five headings could of course generate five questions, though in this case the item becomes a straight 'matching' type. A heading or option can be used more than once, and if it is so indicated in the rubric it is important that on occasions this should occur. More than five headings can be presented, but five are chosen here to preserve an overall five-choice pattern.

Classification items are particularly useful in geography, especially for use with maps, graphs and other types of stimulus material. The time spent in preparing such material may well demand more than one associated item, though the geographical content embodied must be important enough to justify setting more than one question on it.

Principles of writing multiple choice items

One of the main problems met with in constructing multiple choice tests is the finding of good items. Dunstan observes that:

> Skill in item writing consists in large measure of adeptness in isolating a key element of the content being tested, associating it with a particular ability which is to be tested, and combining these two into a precisely described test situation.[17]

In addition, subject expertise is required, and an ability to apply a series of technical skills. The following guidelines may prove useful.[18]

1. *Writing the stem*

The purpose of the stem is to set out the task to be undertaken in a clear, concise and unambiguous way. The stem may be in the form of directions, a question or an incomplete statement and may be associated, indeed should be frequently associated, with verbal, numerical, graphical or visual stimulus material.

(a) In general, *the stem should contain as much of the wording as possible*. Ideally the candidate, if knowledgeable, should be in a position to have a good idea of the answer before reading the options. This is not an invariable rule, however, for it might on occasions be preferable to use a brief stem such as 'A conurbation is' followed by a series of finely distinguished definitions; rather than give the definition in the stem, followed by 'this refers to: a metropolis; a built-up area; a conurbation, etc', which may require a less refined judgement. While the general rule is a reasonable one, the ultimate test is: which arrangement leads to the provision of the better evidence of understanding.

(b) *Negatives should be used with caution* though no harm need ensue from their occasional presence. This type of problem crops up most frequently in simple selection items, where it tends to be easier to find four positive factors with the negative factor providing the key. In these circumstances it is often preferable to rephrase as a multiple selection item (page 200). Double negatives, in stem and options, should always be avoided, as these create ambiguity.

(c) The stem and options should be in *grammatical relationship*, in terms of singulars and plurals and of tenses, for example. One of the arts of multiple choice writing is to invest the item with a natural flow between stem and options. So many read awkwardly and arbitrarily. A problem occurs in writing the stems of multiple selection items, however. A stem such as 'Which of the following countries are members of the EEC' is not acceptable because in theory it gives away the fact that any choice which involves a single option only is pre-determined as incorrect (D and E in a three-option type; A in a four-option type). A theoretical alternative is to rewrite as 'Which of the following countries is (are) a member(s) of the EEC', clearly far too clumsy to be acceptable (though a straight 'is (are)' without further complications is a reasonable compromise). A better solution is to use a stem such as 'Member countries of the EEC include...', which also has the benefit of being more compact.

Trouble over tenses occurs in items where there is a strong 'change over time' component. The writer must avoid using the present tense to relate to factors no longer operative, yet at the same time cannot say in the stem that something *is* present and give in the options a reason that *was* present. An alternative might be to insert a phrase such as 'The growth of... has been helped by', or make the question relate solely to present-day factors.

(d) *Vagueness* should be avoided. A perennial problem occurs in such subjects as geography where relationships between phenomena are rarely explainable in black and white terms. Thus descriptions such as 'most important', 'best describes' need to be used very carefully, and are particularly hazardous where distinctions between the options are finely graded. Other difficult cases include 'past', 'present' and 'recent', and here more definite alternatives are desirable, requiring the stating of a precise period of time. Equally, it is possible to be *over-precise*, particularly in using exact dates or figures, as it is rarely important whether a particular event occurred, say, in 1968 or 1969.

From the geographical point of view, perhaps the most objectionable sort of vagueness is that related to stock phrases such as 'suitable climate', 'good soils' and 'nearby markets', still prevalent in the 'O'-level literature. These should be used exceptionally and preferably not at all. Avoidance of 'because' as a connecting word between stem and options is also recommended in view of its deterministic overtones.

(e) While the stem should not be too lengthy, it is legitimate to include an extended piece of *stimulus material*, perhaps in the form of a descriptive extract. If it is above a certain length, requiring more reading time than the average, it might be preferable to set two or more items upon it, depending also on whether the content is weighty enough to carry such extra questions. The stimulus material need not, of course, be in verbal form.

(f) The stem should preferably contain a *central theme* or idea, which should be significant in respect of the general objectives of the course. The basic intention behind the item should be thought through beforehand. Thus if the objective is to assess an understanding of the concept of the site of a settlement, material which might be diffusely related to the settlement, but not to the site concept, should be excluded.

2. *Writing the options*

As with the stem, the options should be worded clearly, concisely and unambiguously.

(a) It is desirable to arrange the options in a *logical* order, where possible. This is particularly the case where there is a numerical or chronological order. Less critical, but sometimes advocated, is the alphabetical ordering of options, such as a set of geographical place names. This is less easy to do in multiple selection items, where the ordering of the options has to match with the permutation of choices that has been specified.

(b) The options should be *parallel*, in grammar and, where possible, in content. Achieving parallelism may shorten the verbiage by allowing words that would be repeated in all the options to be confined to the stem. Insistence on such parallelism serves the useful function of tidying up loosely expressed items.

(c) The options should not contain *specific determiners*, that is elements in the options which might give away the key. The most frequent type of specific determiner is probably that in which the key is a longer and more qualified statement than the distractors. The key might also be specifically determined if the four distractors are parallel in content but the key option is not. Another type is where there is a verbal association between a word in the key and a crucial element in the stem.

(d) The options should not *contradict, overlap or call attention to each other*. One distractor cannot subsume another. It would be tautologous, for example, to use as one distractor 'less than 50 per cent', and for the next 'less than 60 per cent'. Similarly, an item could not include as options 'growth of wheat' and 'growth of cereals'. The problem of overlap frequently occurs in classification items. Thus the options may be in the form of a set of urban functions, including, say, 'fishing port' and 'holiday resort'. If one of the questions posed was which of the set of five functions was characteristic of Fleetwood, or Lowestoft, the answer could be either of the above options.

(e) The distractors should be *plausible*, and based where possible on commonly held misconceptions. These can in fact be collected from previous experience and introduced as appropriate into items. Highly heterogeneous options are sometimes a cause of implausibility. In general, homogeneous options are more plausible as distractors, but serve to make the item more difficult. Judgement is needed to match the level of discrimination required to the abilities of the group of candidates.

(f) The distractors *should not contain catches*. They are designed to attract the indolent, careless and misinformed, and the rote learner, but not to perplex. They should not therefore be based on misspelling. Nor should they be flippant or designed to display the cleverness of the item-writer. There are clearly marginal cases. Would it be legitimate, for example, to introduce the Rhône as a distractor into an item for which the key was the Rhine? Or Minneapolis into an item about Megalopolis? If in doubt, the distractor should *not* be included.

(g) None of the distractors should be *justifiable as the key*. But multiple choice items should not be confined to situations where there is purely a black or white answer, otherwise they become mere vehicles for assessing the recall of specific facts. In items testing higher level abilities it is quite appropriate that distractors should contain *elements* of truth, whereas the key contains the *central* truth. It is, however, particularly important that items of this type should be carefully vetted by reviewers, and pre-tested to make sure that there is, indeed, not more than one legitimate answer to the question.

3. *The item as a whole*

Having considered the stem and the options, the item writer and later the reviewers should re-examine the question as a whole, taking note of the following more general criteria. (a) *Does the item as a whole contain an integrating theme*, or some other form of inner logic? Or does it embody merely a loose and jumbled collection of geographical information? Items of the latter type can be rejected even before they are pre-tested.

(b) *Would the material be better set in a different format?* This has already been discussed in the example of 'factors' types of items, in which it was indicated that multiple selection is often more appropriate than the simple selection format (page 201). Experience soon tends to suggest how particular content can be most neatly matched with a particular format. The availability of a variety of types of items is thus a distinct advantage. It should be added that some geographical topics and materials are better not forced artificially into the multiple choice format at all, and should be set in another form, such as the structured question.

(c) *Is the item as a whole a fair test of what it sets out to accomplish?* Apart from the question of trickery, it is vital to ensure that items reflect the 'state of readiness' of the candidates and their prior experience. Background information on previous coverage by the candidates of essential content (facts *and* concepts) in class is important to the item writer.

(d) *Is the item testing significant knowledge?* Perhaps the most vital question to ask is whether the item, however technically adept it appears, is really testing knowledge worth testing. This must be judged on the basis of criteria derived from the subject context and from general educational aims and objectives.

Is it, for example, appropriate to reject all items testing purely factual content? This cannot be answered in isolation. In each test a prior specification (pages 209–10) should have been drawn up in which the balance of items testing recall, comprehension and higher level abilities will have been decided. An item testing knowledge of geographical place names is correspondingly more questionable in a test in which fifty items of its type have been set, than in one in which five is the limit. More important, however, is whether the factual knowledge in the item can potentially contribute to some wider end. Items listing names of capes and bays or heights of mountains above sea level could not be justified in anything but an end of term, light-hearted quiz. The criterion of 'significance', of course, involves both the cognitive and social relevance of the content.

(e) *Are the stem and options in conjunction functioning in the same general frame of reference, or at the same level of generality?* It is disconcerting and not uncommon to find items in which the stem leads the reader to believe the item is specific to a particular geographical region, and then find no evidence of information peculiar to that region in the options. For example:

> Which of the following constitutes a handicap to wheat farmers in East Anglia?
> A   Cold winters
> B   Heavy rainfalls in autumn
> C   Poor soils
> D   Lack of sunshine
> E   Lack of nearby markets

Apart from the fact that any choice from the above selection is dubious as an answer, the stem has invited us to look for details peculiar to East Anglia, whereas the options suggest it is an item about a highly generalised stereotype of wheat farming.

The introduction of location-specific information in the options does, of course, mean including extra words, but this is a price which needs to be paid. Even when this condition is met, however, there is no guarantee that criterion (d) has been met also. Hence while a generalised stem on world wheat farming, followed by options containing generalisations about fertile soils, level land, nearby markets, large labour supplies and suitable climate, might respond to criterion (e), it does not to the more important criterion (d). A proliferation of such 'factors' items should in any case be avoided as much as one of pure factual recall items. In fact it is often difficult to disentangle the two.

Test specifications

The role of the test specification is a vital one, namely to gear assessment procedures explicitly to the basic objectives of the course. If the examination is to have positive backwash effects on the course work it should promote meaningful learning. It should not be possible for rote learning to achieve a satisfactory result. Thus the number of questions which can be answered by factual recall alone should be strictly limited.

The first stage of the specification is thus to negotiate the proportion of marks to be allotted to various abilities, which will presumably include recall, basic comprehension and higher level abilities.

Technical skills, such as map drawing, might be added as a separate category. It may be concurrently decided that three forms of assessment will be used, say (a) multiple choice, (b) structured questions and (c) course work.

A matrix can then be drawn up to match the *abilities* against the *test type* dimension, in which the proportion of marks allotted can be filled in (Fig. 11.1).

Test type (or Content)	Abilities				Total
	(1)	(2)	(3)	(4)	
(a)					
(b)					
(c)					
Total					100

Fig. 11.1

A futher matrix is then needed for each type of assessment, to match *abilities* against *content*. This is relatively easy to do in multiple choice and structured question tests, where an adequate sampling is possible. The degree to which the content is broken down will vary. The result should achieve a balance between adequate sampling—which needs a reasonably detailed breakdown of content—and flexibility, for the more the scheme is broken down, the more inflexible it will become. For internal test purposes it may be useful to have a highly detailed breakdown for each important topic. Here, in fact, course content, learning activities and the assessment procedure are all part of the same formative process.

At this level of detail, it is also important to break down the ability levels into their component parts. The following type of scheme might be drawn up.

1. *Recall*

(a) Recall of specific verbal geographical facts.
(b) Recall of locations on maps.
(c) Recognition of straightforward features on maps and photographs.

2. *Interpretation*

Interpretation of information on maps, photographs, tables and graphs.

3. *Evidence of comprehension*

(a) Distinguishing exemplars from non-exemplars of basic concepts.
(b) Distinguishing relevant from irrelevant factors.
(c) Perceiving comparisons/contrasts.
(d) Perceiving causes/consequences.
(e) Discriminating patterns and distributions in space.
(f) Discrimination related to dynamic aspects of reality—movement/access/distance, etc.

4. *Higher level abilities*

(a) Application of concepts to new situations.
(b) Problem-solving.

Abilities such as synthesis, creativity and, to some extent, evaluation will in all probability not be included in a multiple choice test, though they should in the assessment procedure as a whole.

For application and problem solving, the presentation of *stimulus material* unfamiliar to the candidate is usually needed. It may well be desirable to draw up another specification to check that a balanced range of stimulus materials has been used.

The construction of test specifications is thus a multi-stage and multi-dimensional process. It is a means of formalising a principle that good teachers have been practising informally for a long time, namely of achieving a balance. More important, and this has often been omitted, it is a means of bringing out into the open the objectives of the course, and of matching the assessment procedure to them.

Assessing different 'abilities' through multiple choice tests

As we have noted, contrary to popular opinion, multiple choice tests possess the important attribute of being able to assess effectively a wide, though not the full, range of intellectual abilities (page 199). Here three broad types of ability will be considered, namely recall, basic comprehension and 'higher-level abilities' (including application and problem solving),[19] 'creativity' being omitted because it is not appropriately assessed in this way.

1. *Recall*

While Bloom's knowledge category has been equated with 'remembering' many of his knowledge sub-categories, such as knowledge of classifications (1.23), principles (1.31), theories (1.32) and so on, cannot justifiably be separated from 'higher' mental processes (page 32). The main exception is knowledge of specific facts (1.12), in which most items set will be recall items (page 190). There are also other cases, such as knowledge of conventions (1.21), in which recall items can be set. Most attempts to set recall items which slavishly follow all the Bloom 'knowledge' sub-categories tend to be artificial.

2. *Comprehension*

Whether an item can be placed in this category depends on whether it provides evidence that a basic understanding of a concept or principle has been acquired. For example, can exemplars be distinguished from non-exemplars of concepts?

Take the following example:

A conurbation is defined as

A   a large and ancient city surrounded by open country
B   an urban area containing a large number of factories
C   a continuous built-up area formed by the merging of towns (KEY)
D   a large area of open land surrounded by large towns
E   a series of towns in a region functioning as an urban hierarchy

The question obviously contains a knowledge element, but should not in consequence be immediately placed in the recall category. The term 'conurbation' is a concept, and the candidate is being asked if he can discriminate between exemplar and non-exemplar definitions of the concept. If he can do this, evidence of the first stage of conceptualisation is provided. The item thus belongs to the comprehension category. It demands knowledge *with* understanding. Plausible distractors tend to expose unintelligent memorisation, and thus properly set questions of this type can justifiably be inferred as assessing comprehension.

3. *Higher-level abilities*

This heading is used to cover application, analysis and, to a limited extent, evaluation in Bloom's terminology.

The following item might be asked:

On the basis of the evidence provided by the meteorological chart for oo hours [not given here], the main weather characteristics in the next 24 hours at place x are likely to include
1 cold nights
2 early morning dew
3 strong winds
4 afternoon sunshine

This demands the ability to 'apply' an understanding to a new circumstance, namely a synoptic chart not seen before.

Application items in geography can take the form of
(a) presenting information illustrating a familiar concept in an unfamiliar way;
(b) applying abstract classroom knowledge to a real-life situation;
(c) applying concepts learned in the context of a specific geographical area to one not previously encountered;
(d) applying concepts learned in a real geographical situation to a deliberately simulated hypothetical one.

Fig. 11.2 (page 214) is an illustration of the last category. It is a rudimentary example of an application item which might be criticised on geographical grounds, for example, that there is an element of determinism involved with a stress on traditional geographical factors. But it serves as a means of assessing basic ability to 'apply' a particular idea to do with industrial location. In an internal test the children could, of course, be asked to justify their decision.

Such items are essentially problem-posing questions.

Analysis questions in geography generally involve presenting the student with stimulus material he has not seen before, in the form of a verbal, visual or graphical communication, or a combination of them. He is expected to scrutinise the material and abstract

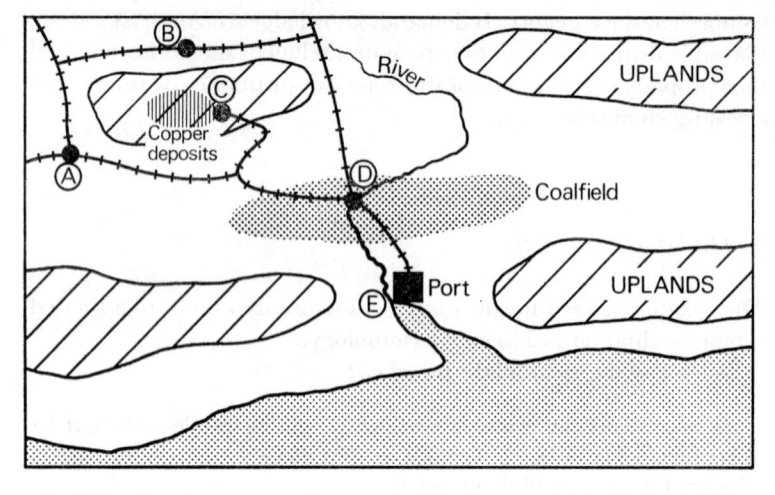

Refer to the above map. The most advantageous site for an ore smelter would be at

    A
    B
    C
    D
    E

Fig. 11.2

from it the cues that provide evidence for selecting an answer. The following is an example.

> Although the Cairngorms have on average the highest snowfall totals in Britain, the ski-slopes are unlike those of the Continent in that, for a considerable part of the season, they rely on long lasting snow beds rather than general snow cover. These snow beds are concentrated in the corries, in which drifting snow accumulates. Some of them are 'semi-permanent' and bear no relation to snow conditions outside the immediate confines of the corries or to snow conditions at the nearest ski-resorts which all lie at considerably lower altitudes. Thus, although the roads in the Aviemore area, altitude 210 metres (700 feet) may be relatively snow-free during the average winter, there is usually a good covering of snow on the actual ski-slopes. This is not altogether surprising when it is realised that the half-way stage of the White Lady ski chair-lift in the Cairngorms is at an altitude of 750 metres (2 500 feet) and the top of the chair-lift is at an altitude of about 1 080 metres (3 600 feet).
>
> Which of the statements below does(do) *not* necessarily follow from the information given in the above paragraph?

1. The roads of the Aviemore district are rarely snow-bound in winter.
2. The longest lasting snow beds are found in the Cairngorm corries.
3. The best ski slopes are at altitudes above 750 metres (2 500 feet).
4. There is a continuous general snow cover over the Cairngorm summits throughout each winter.

(Key C: 2 and 3)

The candidate is here required to make some semantic distinctions, between the different meanings of the statement on roads made in the passage and in option 1. Relationships described in the extract need, in fact, to be analysed for each of the options. The length of the passage ideally requires that more than one item be set on it.

Item analysis

Item writing should be followed up by *reviewing* and *pre-testing*. The results of the pre-testing should be analysed both for the test as a whole and item by item. This analysis provides detailed *feed-back* for teachers and pupils, and also identifies useful items which can be *banked* for later use.

The *reviewing* process can profitably be started by the writer himself, looking again at the items some time after they have been written in accordance with the criteria previously laid down (pages 204–9). In an external examination, this is followed by a review by other item writers, and then by a panel, which results in the acceptance, rejection or modification of items. Internally, the reviewing can be undertaken by colleagues. Reviewers should not be given the keys, for a major test of the item is whether it suggests the same answer to different people.

Analysis

Methods of statistical analysis of pre-tests are provided in publications by the National Foundation for Educational Research,[20] the Educational Testing Service,[21] and in a text edited by Macintosh.[22] These can all be used by teachers even if they do not have access to computers, and lack understanding of advanced statistical techniques. An application of procedures for analysing classroom tests in the context of geography has been provided by the writer in a recent issue of *Geography*,[23] and the description of techniques given there will not be repeated here. The procedures are straightforward, and provide detailed item-by-item information that is vital to the feedback process. This detailed feedback is probably the main educational justification of multiple choice tests.

Feedback

The following details are provided for each item:

1. Its *facility index* (FI), referring to the degree of ease or difficulty of the item. Facilities in the 40–70 per cent range are regarded as highly acceptable, and those between 25 and 80 per cent usable for an external test. For a criterion-referenced internal test, of course, values of 80–100 per cent might be sought.

2. *Its discrimination index* (DI), referring to how well an item discriminates between high and low groups of candidates. This is a much more important quality in an external than in an internal test. The values sought will vary with sample size. In the examples which follow, those of 0.23 and over can be used with confidence, and over 0.20 with caution.

Statistically successful items are not necessarily good items geographically. Conversely, there may be occasions when the use of statistically doubtful items is justified. But the presence of too many of these will diminish the reliability of the test.

3. *The functioning of the distractors.* For each option, details are given of the *percentage* of candidates choosing the key and each of the distractors. This information is given in three columns, the first covering the *high group* (the top 27 per cent of the candidates); the second the *low group* (the bottom 27 per cent), and the third the *total entry*.

In addition, the *key* of each item; the *item type* (labelled SS, MS3, MS4, RA and CL, in accordance with the information on pages 200–3); and the *ability* it is meant to test (labelled I, II and III, covering respectively recall, basic comprehension and higher level abilities, as discussed on pages 212–14) are given. A *verbal commentary* is provided with each example to illustrate the nature of the feedback which can be obtained. All the examples which follow demonstrate outcomes of the pre-testing procedure undertaken in preparation for the author's texts *Multiple Choice and Structured Questions in Geography* (1975).[24]

Examples

1. 'Huerta' cultivation is characteristic of

A	the Ebro Basin	17	25	(16)
B	the Lombardy Basin	0	13	(5)
C	northern Portugal	7	17	(13)
D	Sicily	3	13	(8)
E	the Valencia area	73	30	(57)

FI	51%	DI	0.43	OM* 0	2	(1)

Key: E
Type: SS
Ability: I

* OM refers to candidates omitting to do the particular item

Comments

(a) The distractors have functioned well, all attracting candidates from the low group, which gives the item its good discrimination value. Only 'A' has impressed the high group, who thus are well aware that huerta cultivation is characteristic of Spain.

(b) The item is at about the right level of difficulty for an external examination, though in questions such as this the facility index can vary widely according to whether the content has been previously covered. For an internal test, a higher facility index might well be wanted.

(c) The item belongs to category I because the association between huerta cultivation and the Valencia area is a matter of recall. No evidence is provided of whether the candidate understands what huerta cultivation is, and why it is associated with the Valencia area.

2. Which of the following states of the USA has the highest proportion of negroes in its population?

A	California	2	5	(6)
B	Florida	8	8	(7)
C	Mississippi	66	40	(53)
D	New York	22	42	(31)
E	Texas	2	5	(3)

FI	52%	DI	0.26

Key: C
Type: SS
Ability: I

Comments

(a) The distractors have functioned reasonably well, 'D' being particularly strong, presumably because candidates have confused New York City and New York State.

(b) While answerable and intended as a straight recall item, candidates might just be able to respond correctly on the basis of first principles. Even though they do not actually know that Mississippi is the correct answer, by associating that state with the 'Old South', they may select the right key. Here an element of intelligent guesswork may be present.

(c) Both this and the previous item are associated with interesting or important geographical content. The information involved can function as a means to a wider end, and is thus not without educational worth. On these grounds a limited number of recall items can be justified.

3. The Carron iron works, Grangemouth oil refinery, the Clydeside shipyards and the Linwood car plant represent four significant stages in the development of manufacturing industry in the central lowlands of Scotland. In which order were they built?

A	Clydeside-Carron-Linwood-Grangemouth	20	24	(27)
B	Carron-Clydeside-Grangemouth-Linwood	63	22	(43)
C	Clydeside-Linwood-Grangemouth-Carron	3	18	(7)
D	Grangemouth-Linwood-Clydeside-Carron	0	10	(3)
E	Carron-Clydeside-Linwood-Grangemouth	14	18	(18)

FI 43%   DI 0.40   OM 0   8   (2)

Key: B
Type: SS
Ability: II

Comments

(a) This item, perhaps predictably, has proved to be fairly difficult, even though the topic formed part of the detailed 'home region' study of the candidates concerned. It has discriminated very well indeed.

(b) All the distractors have functioned well. The fact that they have all attracted 10 per cent or more of the candidates from the low group is indicative of guesswork. On the other hand, only 'A' and 'E' have attracted many of the high group. This difference has given the item its good discrimination.

(c) It is clear that there is a crucial knowledge component here, but also that it is highly unlikely that the item could be answered by factual recall alone. To answer it safely, the candidate is helped by some general understanding of the notion of technological change in manufacturing industry as applied in this particular area.

4. London suburbs such as Camberwell and Hampstead were able to grow rapidly in the late nineteenth century

The construction of rail and tube systems enabled Londoners to live further away from their place of work in the city centre

A	52	29	(42)
B	22	22	(23)
C	3	20	(11)
D	17	22	(19)
E	6	5	(4)
OM	0	3	(1)

FI 41%   DI 0.22

Key: A
Type: RA
Ability: II

Comments

(a) The discrimination of the item is moderate, largely because a relatively high proportion of the high group have been attracted by options 'B' and 'D'.

(b) Over 75 per cent of the total entry has identified the first statement, correctly, as true (ie those choosing 'A', 'B' and 'C'); and over 80 per cent the second, also correctly, as true (in choosing 'A', 'B' and 'D'). Nearly 25 per cent of the entry (choosing 'B') has not perceived the relationship between the two statements as being a true one, however.

(c) The item is related to an important area of content, including concepts about sequent occupance and movement (commuting). For a local group of candidates it could prove very much a 'general knowledge' item, of course.

5. Market gardening is a farming activity characterised by

1	small holdings	A	4 6	(4)
2	intensive cultivation	B	68 40	(57)
3	cereal growing	C	9 24	(15)
		D	15 22	(20)
		E	4 6	(3)
		OM	0 2	(1)

FI 54% DI 0.28

Key: B (1 and 2 correct)
Type: MS4
Ability: II

Comments

(a) The item is of ideal 'facility' for terminal examining purposes, and discriminates satisfactorily.

(b) The distractor, 3, present in 'A', 'C' and 'E', has attracted 22 per cent of the candidates as a whole, and 36 per cent of the low group. 18 per cent ('C' + 'E') have not associated market gardening with small holdings, and 23 per cent ('D' + 'E') not with intensive cultivation.

(c) This item is asking for demonstration of one of the early stages in the grasp of market gardening as a concept, namely ability to distinguish exemplar from non-exemplar characteristics of the process.

6. Clear skies at night in winter in Britain may be followed by

1	the killing of fruit blossom	A	3 8	(7)
2	difficulty in gathering in hay crops	B	8 34	(19)
3	a series of accidents on motorways	C	5 5	(8)
		D	20 29	(29)
		E	61 24	(36)
		OM	3 0	(1)

FI 42% DI 0.37

Key: E (3 only correct)
Type: MS3
Ability: III

Comments

(a) As with many items that prove rather difficult, this one discriminates well.

(b) All the distractors are working, and mostly in the right direction. The item has proved very difficult for the low group. Choice 'D' (1 only) is the most popular apart from the key.

(c) This would imply, together with choice 'B' (1 and 2) perhaps inadequate reading of the stem, for if the words 'in winter' are not taken account of, 1 would be correct. This is an example of an item presented in category III which does not include stimulus material unfamiliar to the candidate. But it does present him with an unfamiliar situation, and the need to apply understanding of a relationship between physical geography and human responses to it.

Questions 7 to 9 refer to the world map, Fig. 11.3, and relate to selected examples of areas in which
- A some of the earliest cities in the world grew up
- B the Industrial Revolution first took hold
- C settlement was stimulated by a 'Gold Rush'
- D population densities are among the highest in the world
- E the presence of mining settlements breaks up generally sparse population densities

To which of the above can the groups of areas marked on Fig. 11.3 be matched?

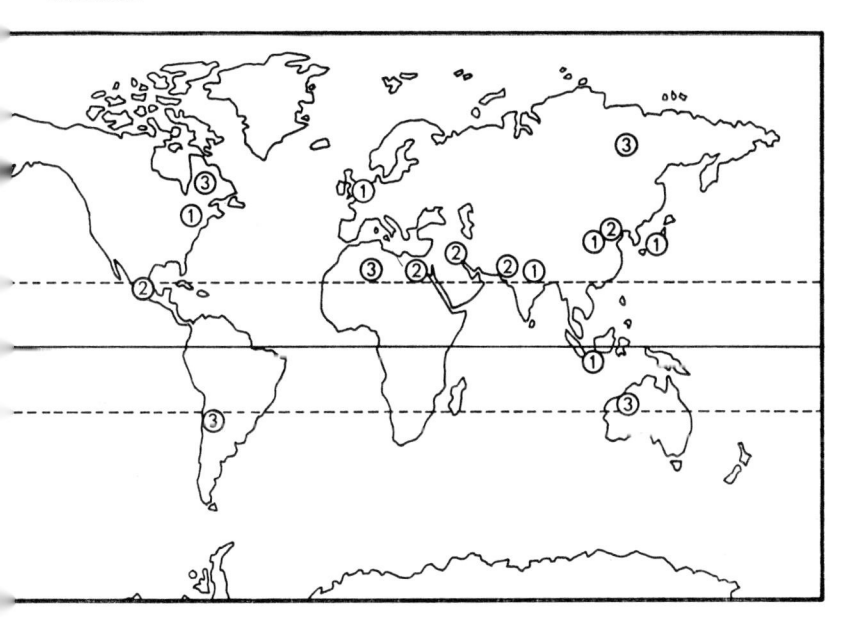

Fig. 11.3

7. Group 1

			A	7	13	(16)
			B	3	13	(10)
			C	0	9	(7)
			D	87	58	(63)
			E	0	0	(1)
FI	73%	DI	0.30	OM	3	7	(3)

Key: D
Type: CL
Ability: II

8. Group 2

			A	64	12	(37)
			B	5	18	(10)
			C	13	20	(16)
			D	13	20	(26)
			E	5	20	(8)
			OM	0	10	(3)
FI	39%	DI	0.53			

Key: A
Type: CL
Ability: II

9. Group 3

			A	0	15	(8)
			B	3	8	(4)
			C	29	27	(28)
			D	0	18	(9)
			E	65	22	(47)
			OM	3	10	(4)
FI	44%	DI	0.42			

Key: E
Type: CL
Ability: II

Comments

(a) The discrimination power of all three items in the group is very good.

(b) In Q.7 distractor 'E' is hardly working at all, but all the others are and, except for 'C' in Q.9, are working in the right direction. The set as a whole has proved very suitable for the high group but, apart from Q.7, difficult for the low group.

(c) The questions demand a certain broad cultural knowledge and the result, from groups covering both GCE and CSE ability ranges, is pleasing. The items require an appreciation of general world distributions and, though basic knowledge is needed, more than factual recall is involved.

Item banking

Multiple Selection BRITISH ISLES Weather Study *5th Year* *Ability level* I, II, ⅠⅠⅠ (Highest ability) *Christmas Term (1973)* *Difficulty* 1, 2, 3 (Fairly difficult) (see F I) *94 in group*				

Clear skies at night in winter in Britain may be followed by		(%)		
		H	L	T
1. the killing of fruit blossom	A	3	8	(7)
2. difficulty in gathering in hay crops	B	8	34	(19)
3. a series of accidents on motorways	C	5	5	(8)
E: (3 only correct)	D	20	29	(29)
	E	61	24	(36)
	OM	3	0	(1)
	FI	42%		
	DI	0·37%		

Comments:
1. Item on the difficult side, but shows very good discrimination.
2. Item seeks understanding of relationship of weather (as a hazard) to human activities. Popularity of B (1 and 2 correct) and D (1 only correct) is noticeable among low group. Option 2 (present in A (1, 2 and 3 correct), B (1 and 2 correct) and C (2 and 3 correct)) has cut little ice with high group.
3. $> \frac{1}{3}$ high and $\frac{3}{4}$ low group chose responses including option 1—did they read stem?

Fig. 11.4 Specimen of a completed index card for item banking system. NB Results of future tests can be inserted on reverse side of card.

The results of reviewing and particularly of pre-testing will have shown which items are worth keeping, and will have given a considerable amount of information about them. Such items can be 'banked' for future use.[25, 26, 27] A convenient way of doing this is to use a card index system. As so much information is involved, large cards of 8″ by 5″ size are perhaps the most appropriate. The following information is worth including.
1. Content classification (topic of study)
2. Type of item

3. Purpose for which item has been written, and/or purpose and date on which it has been used
4. Ability being tested
5. The item itself
6. Its facility index (on pre-test/test(s))
7. Its discrimination index (on pre-test/test(s))
8. Percentage of candidates choosing different options
9. Comments on the working characteristics of the item

Fig. 11.4 (page 223) is an example of such a card, filled in to illustrate how it can be used in practice.

Priority readings
(see also p. 189)

1. HUDSON, B. 'Objective tests' in HUDSON, B. (ed.) *Assessment Techniques: an Introduction* (Methuen), Chapter 5, pp. 122–56.
2. ARGENT, B. 'Short answer questions and objective items' in MACINTOSH, H. G. (ed.) *Techniques and Problems of Assessment* (Edward Arnold), Chapter 3, pp. 19–47.
3. MORRISON, R. B. 'Item analysis and question validation' in MACINTOSH, H. G. (ed.), *op. cit.*, Chapter 4, pp. 48–57.
4. Secondary Schools Examinations Council, *The Certificate of Secondary Education: An Introduction to Objective-type Examinations*, Examinations Bulletin No. 4 (HMSO).
5. The Schools Council, *The Certificate of Secondary Education: Trial Examinations—Geography*, Examinations Bulletin No. 14. (HMSO).
6. Schools Council, *Question Banks: their Use in School Examinations*, Examinations Bulletin No. 22. (Evans/Methuen).
7. SALMON, R. B. & MASTERTON, T. H. *The Principles of Objective Testing in Geography* (Heinemann).

Questions for investigation and discussion

1. 'In geography a danger which exists in every form of examination is the tendency to test knowledge of facts rather than conceptual knowledge.'[28]

    (a) Clarify the distinction between knowledge of facts and conceptual knowledge.

    (b) In the light of this statement, examine a major contention in this chapter that multiple choice tests are potentially a more potent means of assessing conceptual knowledge than essay methods.

(c) Is the danger highlighted by the statement greater in geography than in other subjects?

2. 'Its sole *raison d'être* is that marking can be done by computers and is therefore cheaper.'

'It would be disastrous indeed if this ill-conceived multiple choice test were to restrict English teachers from introducing pupils to the real pleasure of learning about humanity.'

'... a most soul-destroying and pointless exercise ... crippling to sensitivity and pleasure. ...'

(a) Attempt an informed justification or refutation of these comments in letters to the *Education Guardian* (May 1972) on the introduction of an 'O'-level multiple choice test in English.

(b) Do the arguments shift if one is talking in terms of (i) geography (ii) the physical sciences?

3. Refer to the examples of multiple choice items given below:

(a) For each identify (i) the key (ii) the ability level being tested.

(b) Refer to the principles of writing multiple choice items (pages 204–209), and outline the flaws, technical and geographical, in each of the examples.

A *Simple selection*

1. Blackpool, the most popular and important tourist centre of north-west England, attracts annually to its hotels, boarding houses, and camping sites
   - A 1 000 000 visitors
   - B 12 000 000 visitors
   - C 4 000 000 visitors
   - D 8 000 000 visitors
   - E 100 000 visitors

2. The Merseyside conurbation is
   - A the area of Liverpool and Birkenhead
   - B at the lower end of the Mersey estuary
   - C the built-up area on either side of the Mersey estuary
   - D the towns north of the Mersey
   - E the urban area within 15 miles of Liverpool

B *Multiple selection*

Bolton has not suffered from severe unemployment in recent years despite the decline in the cotton industry, because it has been able to attract new industries, such as engineering firms, food processing firms and mail order companies, among others. Which of the factors given below have caused this?

1. Because it is at a focus of major roads with good access to the motorway system
2. Because it is near Manchester
3. Because the cotton mills are still in good order

(Refer to page 201 for code.)

C *Relationship analysis*

1. The best growing area for barley and oats in Britain is East Anglia — Barley and oats require a sunny climate and fertile soils
2. Iron ore mining has increased in the Jurassic scarplands to become England's main producer with 10 million tonnes in 1971 — There is an important market for the ore in the nearby steel-making centres

D *Classification items*

Twentieth-century towns are often divided on the basis of their size, functions and sphere of influence, and in many cases have joined together to form an urban sprawl or conurbation. The following are among the functions towns assume.

    A Market towns
    B Packet stations
    C Railway junctions
    D Residential suburbs
    E Ecclesiastical functions

Which of the above matches which of the following towns?

1. Canterbury
2. Chicago
3. Esbjerg

4. (a) Draw up a test specification for a terminal examination at the conclusion of the first year of a secondary school geography course.
(b) Explain the rationale behind your specification.
(c) Isolate a topic from this specification, and write on it one or two items testing each of the three abilities noted on pages 212–3.

References

1. MORRIS, N. (1961) 'An historian's view of examinations' in WISEMAN, S. (ed.) (1961) *Examinations and English Education* (Manchester University Press), 29.
2. VERNON, P. E. (1964) *The Certificate of Secondary Education: An Introduction to Objective-Type Examinations* (Secondary Schools Examinations Council, Examinations Bulletin No. 4, HMSO, London).
3. BROWN, J. (1966) *Objective Tests: Their Construction and Analysis* (Longman, London).
4. MACINTOSH, H. G. & MORRISON, R. B. (1969) *Objective Testing* (University of London Press).
5. HUDSON, B. (ed.) (1973) *Assessment Techniques: An Introduction* (Methuen, London), Chapter 5.
6. BONNEY RUST, W. (1973) *Objective Testing in Education and Training* (Pitman, London).
7. MACINTOSH, H. G. (ed.) (1974) *Techniques and Problems of Assessment* (Arnold, London), Chapters 3, 4 and 13.

8. THYNE, J. M. (1974) *Principles of Examining* (University of London Press), Chapters 14–16.
9. SENATHIRAJAH, N. & WEISS, J. (1971) *Evaluation in Geography: A Resource Book for Teachers* (Curriculum Series/10: The Ontario Institute for Studies in Education, Toronto).
10. SALMON, R. B. & MASTERTON, T. H. (1974) *The Principles of Objective Testing in Geography* (Heinemann, London).
11. See, for example, GRAVES, N. J. (1971) *Geography in Secondary Education* (Geographical Association, Sheffield), 77–8.
12. MACINTOSH, H. G. & MORRISON, R. B. (1969), *op. cit.*, 74.
13. EBEL, R. L. (1965) *Measuring Educational Achievement* (Prentice Hall, Englewood Springs), 76.
14. VERNON, P. E. (1964), *op. cit.*, 7.
15. EBEL, R. L. (1965), *op. cit.*, 98.
16. This was associated with the pre-testing of items for MARSDEN, W. E. (1975) *Multiple Choice and Structured Questions in Geography*, Books 1 and 2. (Oliver & Boyd, Edinburgh).
17. DUNSTAN, M. (1966) 'A reply to some criticisms of objective tests' in HEYWOOD, J. & ILIFFE, A. H. (eds.) (1966) *Some Problems of Testing Academic Performance* (University of Lancaster Department of Higher Education, Bulletin No. 1), C3.
18. See TITTLE, C. K. & MILLER, K. M. (1976) *Examination Techniques* (Independent Assessment and Research Centre, London). The author here acknowledges a debt to Dr Miller and colleagues for ideas derived from association with workshop sessions of the IARC.
19. For more detailed attempts to explore the Bloom taxonomy through multiple choice items in geography see SENATHIRAJAH, N. & WEISS, J. (1971), *op. cit.*, Chapters 6 and 7; and SALMON, R. B. & MASTERTON, T. H. (1974), *op. cit.*, Chapter 10.
20. NUTTALL, D. L. & SKURNIK, L. S. (1969) *Examination and Item Analysis Manual* (National Foundation for Educational Research).
21. Educational Testing Service (1964) *Short-cut Statistics for Teacher-made Tests* (ETS, Princeton, New Jersey).
22. MORRISON, R. B. (1974) (a) 'Item analysis and question validation' (b) 'The application of statistics to assessment' both in MACINTOSH, H. G. (ed.) (1974), *op. cit.*, 48–57; and 146–56.
23. MARSDEN, W. E. (1974) 'Analysing classroom tests in geography' *Geography*, **59**, 55–64.
24. See MARSDEN, W. E. (1975), *op. cit.*, 6.
25. WOOD, R. & SKURNIK, L. S. (1969) *Item Banking* (National Foundation for Educational Research).
26. Schools Council (1971) *Question Banks: their Use in School Examinations*, Examinations Bulletin No. 22. (Evans/Methuen, London).
27. WOOD, R. (1974) 'Question banking' in MACINTOSH, H. G. (ed.) (1974), *op. cit.*, 208–20.
28. GRAVES, N. J. (1972) 'School Examinations' in GRAVES, N. J. (ed.) (1972) *New Movements in the Study and Teaching of Geography* (Temple Smith, London), 186.

12 Structured Questions

Their nature

All structured questions have in common the fact that the candidate has to supply the answer. This marks them off from multiple choice items. At one extreme, structured questions may be *objective* (pages 189-90). As we have seen, these can be presented in *completion* form ('The capital of France is . . .') or in the form of a direct question ('What is the capital of France?'). They cannot be marked as objectively as multiple choice items, however, even where the ability being tested is purely factual recall. The question of spelling for example, can produce some marginal cases, though normally minor spelling errors will be accepted.

An extension of the completion question is the well-known *insertion* type, as for example 'The climate of southern Italy consists of . . . summers and . . . winters.' As such questions are open to more than one interpretation, for younger children at least some would advocate putting in further cues, such as the first letters of the key words. 'The climate of southern Italy consists of h . . . d . . . s . . . and w . . . w . . . w . . .'. The dilemma is apparent in that the clearer and more objective the question becomes, the more likely it is to be concentrating on factual recall. The structured test is as prone as the multiple choice to a surfeit of such questions.

Another form of structured question asks the candidate to define, in a phrase or a sentence, an important geographical concept. He might, alternatively, be asked to give reasons for the growth of a particular town or industry, or describe the scenery of a particular area. Such questions can also be set in essay tests, but in the structured format direct guidance might be provided as to the number of reasons to be given, or indirectly, by leaving an appropriate amount of space on the paper for the answer. Where structured questions are no more than essay questions broken down into three or four component parts, they are sometimes referred to as *partly structured* questions.

The most desirable type of structured question, and one widely used not only in geography but also in the physical sciences, is that which is prefaced by stimulus material, providing data which the candidate has to interpret or analyse. Such questions are often termed *stimulus* or *data response* questions.

The advantages of structured questions

1. As with multiple choice items, the student has a clearer and more detailed idea of what is required of him than in the case of essay questions. This is, of course, less true of the partly structured question. The marking is fairly easy, though not as straightforward nor as expeditious as with multiple choice tests. Structured tests are also rather less difficult to set than multiple choice.

2. From the student's point of view, the answers have to be produced rather than selected. Some would favour this in principle. Partial credit can be given for answers, which is not usually permitted in multiple choice tests. Again, many teachers favour allowing for partial credit.

3. In terms of reliability and validity, structured tests have the advantage over essay tests. They discriminate 'more rigorously' than essays.[1] They allow the syllabus to be more effectively sampled, though less so than is the case with multiple choice tests. A test specification can be drawn up to show the balance of 'content' and 'abilities' being assessed. Higher level abilities, as we have seen, are often best tested through the use of stimulus materials, and it is sometimes easier to set structured questions than multiple choice items on such materials. Like multiple choice items, structured questions are not easily linked with creative work or that asking for a synthesis. But, these apart, they can be used to assess a wide range of abilities.

4. Structured questions are highly flexible. They can be presented in worksheets as part of normal classroom activity, in internal tests or in external examinations. If well structured, they will give the teacher much of the detailed feedback that can be gained from a multiple choice test. There can be a close and meaningful kinship between the formative procedure and the terminal test.[2] The final examination can be more precisely geared to the objectives of the syllabus.

5. As they have many of the advantages of multiple choice items, structured questions can be commended to teachers who find multiple

choice tests uncongenial. They can be looked upon as useful a compromise form between multiple choice items and the extended essay.

Principles of writing structured questions[3,4]

Many of these follow from the points made above.

1. An important quality is the *balance* of the test as a whole in terms of *abilities* to be assessed. The ease with which superficial questions can be set on the one hand, and the time required to collect materials for thoughtful data response questions on the other, can too easily lead to a test top-heavy with factual recall questions. A test specification is *pre-requisite*.

2. This can help also to balance out the content and ensure the test has content validity. A dilemma may arise here, however, for in many cases it is preferable to relate a series of questions to stimulus materials looking for an *in-depth* analysis which might mean less adequate sampling of the syllabus as a whole. The preferred solution is to have a test which contains both multiple choice *and* structured questions, the former to cover content validity in particular.

3. The importance of introducing *stimulus materials* has already been mentioned. Their main purpose is to encourage less stress on the storage and recall of specific facts from previous learning, and more on the application of concepts in new circumstances. The problem-solving situation should be kept to the fore.

4. The purport of structured questions should be quite *clear* to the candidate. It is desirable that the questions should be *specific*, so that the candidate knows the scope of the answer expected. This might be accomplished by specifying the *number of facts* or factors that are expected in the candidate's response by leaving an optimal *number of lines* for answering the questions, and also by providing information on the *weighting of marks*. The objection may be made that this is rendering the questions more 'closed'. The answer is not to exclude closed questions, however, but to ensure on the test as a whole a balance between closed and open questions.

5. The writer of structured questions should undergo the discipline of *writing out the answers* for himself. He can easily over-estimate the degree of clarity of his questions or under-estimate their level of difficulty. New light might also be shed on the worthwhileness of the questions. Mathews regards seeing 'the information and the questions *through the eyes of the candidates*'[5] as the most important criterion of all.

Examples of structured questions

1. *Blackburn district map*

    (a) In the space provided at the foot of Fig. 12.1 draw a section to show the relief of the land from A to B.
    (b) On the map shade in the areas *over* 375 m high.
    (c) In the space provided name:
      (i) River 1 .... (ii) River 2 ....
      (iii) River 3 .... (iv) River 4 ....
      (v) Hill 5 .... (vi) Hill 6 .... (vii) Hill 7 ....
      (viii) Upland 8 .... (ix) Town 9 ....
      (x) Town 10 .... (xi) Town 11 ....
      (xii) Town 12 ....

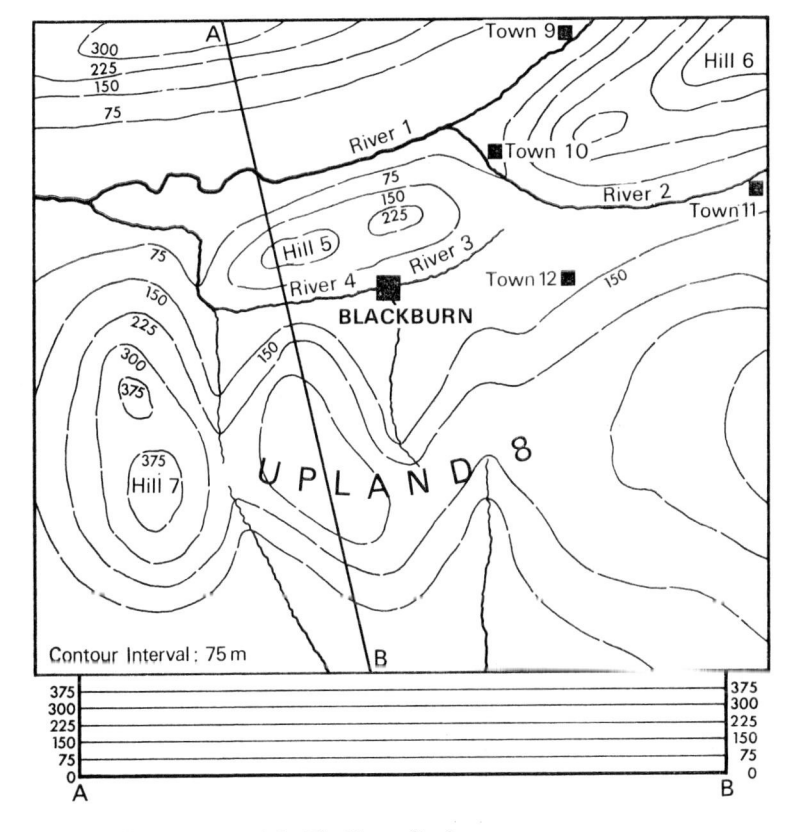

Fig. 12.1 Contour map of the Blackburn district

(d) In travelling as the crow flies from Blackburn to Town 10, you would be moving in a .... direction.
(e) Towns 11, 12 and Blackburn itself were traditionally linked with the .... branch of the cotton industry.
(f) Name the inventor of an important piece of textile machinery in the eighteenth century who was associated with Blackburn, together with the name of his invention. Inventor .... Invention ....
(g) Give *three* reasons, apart from this invention, for the expansion of the cotton industry in Blackburn after 1770.
   (i) ....
   (ii) ....
   (iii) ....
(h) Since the beginning of the twentieth century, the cotton industry has declined. Other countries, such as .... and ...., which were once markets for Lancashire cloth, have developed their own textile industries. The early development of the industry in Lancashire meant that it was working with .... machinery. Since the late 1950s the decline has been even more rapid as a result of the .... Act of 1959.
(i) State *two* important provisions of the Act of 1959.
   (i) ....
   (ii) ....
(j) Name two industries that are located in old cotton factories in Blackburn.
   (i) .... (ii) ....
(k) Despite the decline, textile manufacturing is still important in towns such as Blackburn. Indicate *two* changes which have taken place in most textile factories which remain in operation.
   (i) ....
   (ii) ....

Comments

The question is intended as part of a terminal test for a junior form in a secondary school. The focus is a local one, and the format is one frequently used at this level. The main criticism of the questions might well be that there is too much emphasis on recall of facts. In the sub-sections asking for 'reasons', the nature of the questioning is unlikely to produce evidence of real understanding. None requires 'application'.

In defence, it might be argued that at this level it is proper to assess some build up of factual knowledge, especially that which has a local relevance and is part of the culture of the area. But this could still be contrasted with material pertaining to other parts of Lancashire's textile region, for example, to see if understanding of basic concepts can be applied in the context of a somewhat similar area.

The layout is clear to the pupil. The marking scheme is not given. Whether this should be provided at this early stage is a matter of judgement for the teacher. It is necessary, however, to warn the children not to spend too long over drawing the section, which can bring severe penalties if time is not left to complete the test.

2. *Snowdonia map and photograph*

1. (a) Give the grid references of:
    (i) Dolwyddelan Castle..........
    (ii) a disused railway terminus.......... *Knowledge*
    .... 2 marks
   (b) What is featured, on the evidence of photograph and map, at
    (i) GR 626568? ....slope *Comprehension*
    (ii) GR 622567? ....valley 2 marks
2. Draw a section to show the rise and fall of the land along easting 70 from northing 64 to northing 54. *Skills/Application* 4 marks (deduct $\frac{1}{2}$ for each error)
3. State two ways in which the long profile and the cross profile of the Llanberis valley differ. *Comprehension* 2 marks
    (a) ....
    (b) ....
4. State two pieces of evidence shown on the photograph which prove that it could not have been taken over south-eastern England *Application* 2 marks
    (a) ....
    (b) ....
5. You are invited to set up a nature trail in the area of one of the grid squares on the map. The area has to fulfil a number of conditions. It must (a) lie largely within $1\frac{1}{2}$ km of a youth hostel; (b) adjoin a lake; (c) have the majority of its area covered by woodland; (d) lie largely below 300 metres (1 000 feet). *Analysis:* 4 marks (Deduct 1 for each criterion not fulfilled)
   The square is: .... (give 4 figure grid reference).

6. Assume a plot of land has come into the market on the north-east shore of Llyn Peris. You are thinking of building a holiday cottage on this site. State two advantages and two disadvantages of the site which would affect your decision whether to build or not.

Analysis/ Evaluation
4 marks

Advantages (a) ....
(b) ....
Disadvantages (a) ....
(b) ....

Total
20 marks

Comments

This question is related to a well-known examination map extract of the Llanberis area of Snowdonia. The other piece of stimulus material is a photograph taken from the top of the pass and looking down-valley towards the sea. Neither of these materials is included here, but the purport of the questions will be clear.

The test is aimed at 15–16 year old candidates, in the 'O'-level and perhaps also CSE ability ranges. The weightings and the ability levels tested are both provided. The arrangement of 'abilities' departs from the procedure used elsewhere in this text, where the Bloom terminology is not adhered to as closely as it is here.

3. *A partly structured question—Italian maps and tables*

On the basis of the information provided in the maps (Figs. 12.2 and 12.3) and tables (tables 12.1–12.5), and your own knowledge of the growth of the Italian autostrade network in the 1963–73 period:
(a) Outline the extent and discuss the adequacy of motorway provision in Italy in 1971 as compared with other West European countries.
(b) In the light of the condition of the Italian economy over this period, what was the justification for under-writing the masssive cost of providing this motorway network?
(c) Analyse the impact of motorway provision on various parts of Italy, with special reference to the Mezzogiorno.

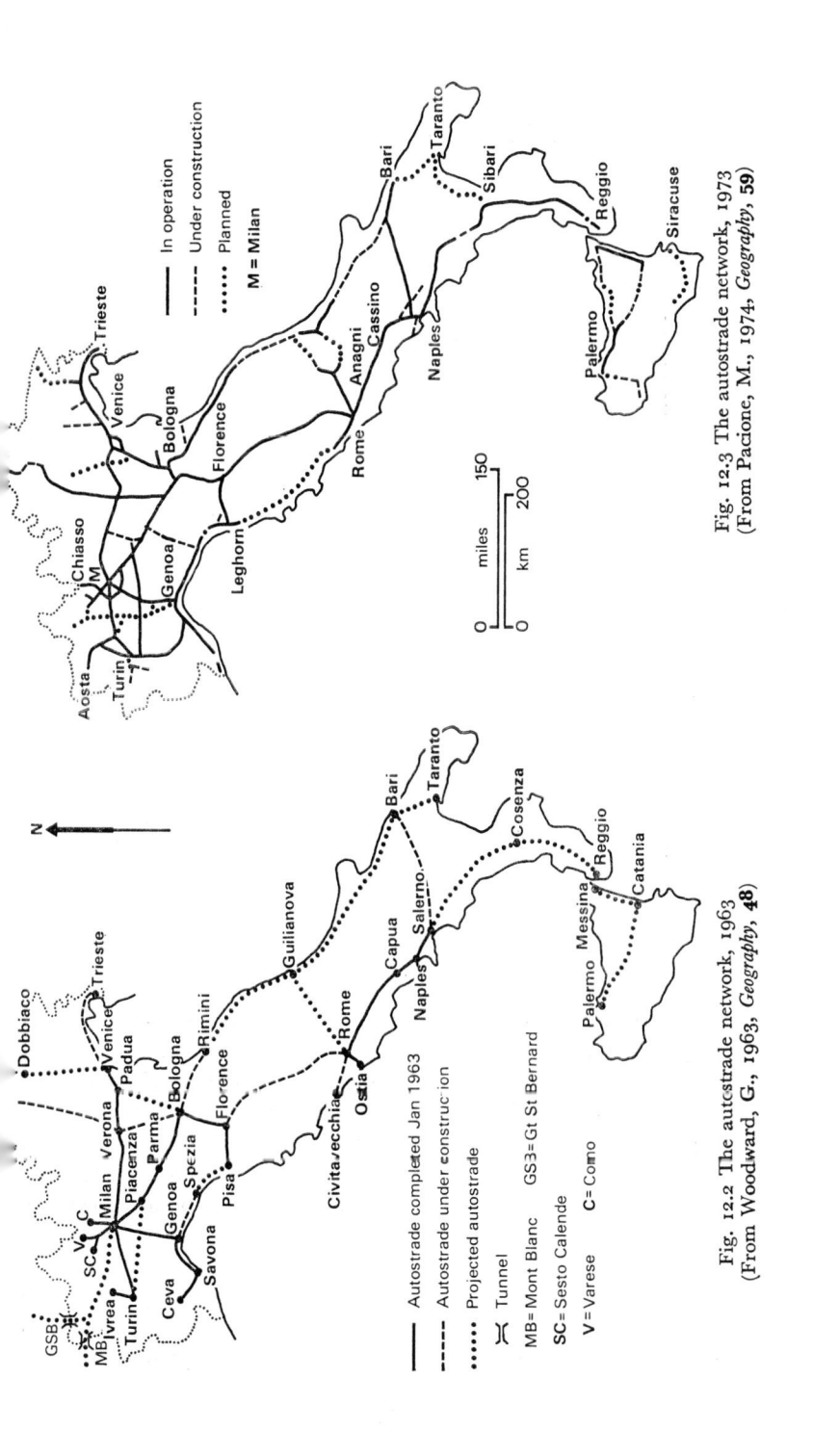

Fig. 12.2 The autostrade network, 1963 (From Woodward, G., 1963, *Geography*, **48**)

Fig. 12.3 The autostrade network, 1973 (From Pacione, M., 1974, *Geography*, **59**)

Table 12.1 Length in km of motorways in European countries and numbers of vehicles in circulation

Country	Motorway length (1971)	Vehicles in circulation (1970)
Belgium	482	2 185 775
France	1 538	13 710 000
West Germany	4 453	14 297 652
Italy	3 907	9 862 574
Luxembourg	10	101 348
Holland	979	2 533 000
Austria	489	1 505 584
Great Britain	1 232	13 220 000

Table 12.2 Vehicles in circulation in Italy

Year	No.	Index	Year	No.	Index
1962	3 580 222	100	1968	8 976 558	251
1964	5 319 294	149	1969	9 862 574	276
1966	7 057 113	197	1970	11 298 500	316

Table 12.3 Length in km and class of road in use

Year	Autostrade	Index	Other state roads	Index
1955	510	100	176 559	100
1960	1 136	223	190 357	108
1965	1 705	334	197 760	112
1970	3 907	766	281 082	159

Comments

The questions are obviously inviting the candidates to write short essays. They differ from the classical essay format in that the overall topic is broken down into major components. The provision of data means that the candidate does not have to rely solely on recall of large quantities of facts for gaining marks. Some processing is needed and presumably the candidate could achieve an adequate mark on the basis of this alone. But further background knowledge and understanding of the issues behind the data can enhance greatly the quality of the response.

There is a danger that the conventional essay reply may be replaced by an equally undesirable superficial translation into verbiage of the cartographic and statistical material provided. Much

Table 12.4 Changes in provincial population 1951–71 by areas

Area	No. of provinces	No. of provinces		Provinces with autostrade	Provinces with autostrade		Provinces without autostrade	
		+	−		+	−	+	−
North	38	29	9	33	24	9	3	2
North-central	15	9	6	11	7	4	2	2
South-central	15	6	9	11	5	6	1	3
South	10	5	5	4	1	3	4	2
Sicily	9	4	5	3	2	1	2	4
	87*	53	34	62	39	23	12	13
Per cent	100	60·9	39·1	71.3	62.9	37.1	48	52

+, population increase; −, population decrease.
* Excluding three provinces of Sardinia.

Table 12.5 Volume of traffic using roads (millions of vehicles/km)

Year	Autostrade	Index	Other state roads	Index
1955	0·6	100	36·3	100
1960	2·3	383	49·2	136
1965	8·0	1 333	80·2	221
1970	17·0	2 833	149·9	413

Source of Tables 12.1–12.5: M. Pacione 'Italian Motorways', *Geography*, **40**, 1964, 35–7.

is to be said for bringing the objectives of the exercise into focus, and making clear to the candidates and their teachers the basis of the marking scheme. The analysis of the material could be more incisively assessed by adopting a fully structured format, though some might argue that skills of synthesis are better tested by this partly structured format or even a single essay. It is vital that the writer of questions such as this should have identified his objectives, and that they should be built into the marking scheme. It is necessary that the message gets through to the candidate, for example, that the first part of question (a) carries less weight than the second half, and that credit will be given for drawing on the whole range of materials provided, and especially for cross-referencing between them.

Priority readings

1. NEALE, P. D. 'Structured questions' in HUDSON, B. (ed.) *Assessment Techniques: an Introduction* (Methuen) Chapter 4, pp. 92–121.
2. MATHEWS, J. C. 'Structured questions' in MACINTOSH, H. G. (ed.) *Techniques and Problems of Assessment* (Edward Arnold), Chapter 2, pp. 7–18.
3. SENATHIRAJAH, N. & WEISS, J. *Evaluation in Geography: A Resource Book for Teachers* (The Ontario Institute for Studies in Education), Chapter 8, pp. 60–77.

Questions for investigation and discussion

1. Comment on the advantages and disadvantages of using structured questions as against (a) essays (b) multiple choice tests.
2. Refer to the materials provided (pages 235–7) for the partly structured question. Write a fully structured question on these materials, justifying each of the sub-questions asked, outlining the abilities being tested and justifying also a specified marking scheme.
3. (a) Use an Ordnance Survey 1:50 000 or 1:25 000 extract, preferably along with a photograph of part of the area covered, and draw up a structured test, specifying the abilities to be tested and the weighting of marks.

   (b) Try to translate your questions into multiple choice form, and indicate cases in which it is not easy to do so.

References

1. FERGUSON, C. M. & GARRETT, S. (1975) 'Stimulus material in "O" Level history' *Educational Research*, **17**, 92.
2. MATHEWS, J. C. (1974) 'Structured questions' in MACINTOSH, H. G. (ed.) (1974) *Techniques and Problems of Assessment* (Edward Arnold, London), 7.
3. NEALE, P. D. (1973) 'Structured questions' in HUDSON, B. (ed.) (1973) *Assessment Techniques: An Introduction* (Methuen, London), 103–11.
4. MATHEWS, J. C. (1974), *op. cit.*, 16–17.
5. *Ibid*, 17.

13 Other Types of Assessment

The assessment of course work

This section concentrates on course work which is undertaken as part of an external examination requirement. It is abbreviated because much general advice on the subject is available from various sources. Readers are advised to consult texts by Hudson,[1] Macintosh,[2] Nuttall and Willmott,[3] as well as a number of Schools Council Bulletins, particularly Nos. 1 and 5.[4,5,6] There are, in addition, various reports published by GCE and CSE examining boards, which are available to schools in the areas of these boards and give advice on the content and assessment of course work.[7,8]

Advantages of assessing course work

1. Course work assessment is a vital element in building up a *cross-profile* of the pupil. A well-balanced assessment requires a multiple choice test; papers covering structured, partially structured and, some would insist, essay questions; and also a piece of course work assessment. In geography the course work will often take the form of a detailed fieldwork project, or a similar venture based on first-hand library sources.

2. This type of assessment may shed a new light on the work of those who are not at their best in a situation where rigorous time constraints operate, as in the conventional examination. It caters for different *learning styles*, can provide due reward for the offerings of both convergent and divergent thinkers, and may also be used to assess a greater variety of communication skills than the purely verbal.

3. Assessment of course work is probably the best means of providing evidence of the candidate's *creative abilities and skills of communication*. It is particularly helpful in geography also because it allows for the consideration of work related purely to the local area,[9] which is difficult in a conventional written paper.

4. The knowledge that course work will be assessed is a stimulus to effort *over a period of time*. More important, there is considerable evidence that, even among pupils whose conventional work is undistinguished, the interest of a properly guided, in-depth personal field study often takes over, leading to enhanced pride in work and consequently higher standards than are manifested in other parts of the assessment. Fieldwork is obviously not the only type of course work. There is, however, much less to be said for examining externally course work in the form of a file built up of notes made in lessons and other material based on second-hand sources. The assessment of such work should be formative, providing continuing feedback inside the school.

So long as the project is properly chosen, course work assessment has educational advantages that are difficult if not impossible to replace by other modes. Apart from advantages accruing to the pupils, such work is almost invariably more enjoyable to mark than the mass examining of essays.

Problems of assessing course work

1. The major problem of assessing course work is to ensure standardisation between schools. This is usually done by a process of *moderation*. After the preliminary internal assessment, moderation may be undertaken by staff drawn from local consortia of schools, a practice adopted by a number of CSE boards. At a later stage, samples of course work are moderated by qualified subject specialists appointed by the board.

It is highly desirable that course work should also be assessed at GCE level, but the scale of operations at which the major boards work make moderation on a personal basis difficult. Despite a certain amount of opposition from teachers, some boards are trying to establish the principle of *statistical moderation* by correlating achievement on course work with that on conventional written papers.[10] Empirical evidence suggests that, so long as the sample from a school is not too small, such correlation exists. One way of meeting the objections is to use the statistical correlation as a *screening* mechanism only. This means that the internal assessments of course work are left as they are, so long as there is no major discrepancy between a particular school's marks on the written papers and its course work assessment.

2. In internal marking, it is difficult for the teacher to dissociate his *view of the pupil* from the pupil's work. There can easily be a hidden mark for co-operative attitudes and neatly presented work, qualities which the teacher may well be wishing to assess. If so, the fact should be publicised. There is also a tendency to bunch marks in internal assessment, which is particularly the case in fieldwork projects, where it is unlikely that much work of an exceptionally low standard will be submitted. The project might be looked upon as an insurance policy for the weaker candidates. On the positive side, the interest this type of work generates will also tend to push up standards.

3. There is also the danger of judging a project rather in terms of its *weight and cosmetic appearance* than its inherent geographical qualities. Thus it is important that the criteria for marking are carefully laid out, with separate marks specified for presentation. Even if no direct penalties for irrelevance are imposed, some sort of procedure is needed to ensure that work that is compact and to the point is ranked higher than diligent but rambling accounts.

4. A related problem is posed by differences in *quality of teaching* and *teacher expectation* which can emerge starkly in course work. The problem is obviously not confined to this type of assessment alone, but it can cause embarrassment and even acrimony at meetings where studies of highly disparate quality are being publicly moderated by local consortia of teachers.

5. It may also be difficult to judge how *individual* the work being presented is: how much there is in it of the rest of the peer group, of relations and friends, and especially of the teacher himself. Guidelines are laid down by some examining boards, but all must rely in the last resort on professional integrity. The main problem in geography fieldwork projects is that some of the objectives and methods can best be approached by group study. In geomorphological fieldwork, for example, the measuring of slopes demands the co-operation of more than one person. Teachers are likely to be anxious unless clear directives can be given on this issue and perhaps marginal test cases decided. It may be that the preliminary collection of data could be a joint effort, but all the processing thereafter should be individual.

For reasons such as these, internal assessment is unpopular with some teachers, though many who have been engaged in the moderation process in CSE examinations have come to regard it positively as a fruitful means of cross-fertilisation of ideas, of reducing isolation and even of initiating co-operation.

But resistance is still strong, as indicated by the comments of the Incorporated Association of Assistant Masters on the Schools Council Bulletin 23.

> It must be stated that there are many teachers who firmly believe that the truly external examination is the only one which has any real standing in the academic world. Many feel that teachers are not necessarily the best assessors of their own pupils and regard this as an intolerable burden. . . . It must not be believed that all teachers believe in the efficacy of the Mode III type examination and, indeed, many do suggest that the time is now ripe for a critical survey of all its aspects and implications to be made.[11]

6. Teachers also find it difficult to cope with the *internal administrative problem* of organising 4 000 word assignments for whole classes of pupils. There is the added constraint of the potential 'drowning' of local farms, villages and shopping centres by hordes of juvenile researchers.[12] Then there is the burden of moderation. The working of consortia, though a valuable means of co-operation between teachers, is none the less another time-consuming exercise.

This question of imposing additional strain on teachers must be seen in the light of earlier comments in connection with 'the teacher as entrepreneur' (page 151). It is a problem which jeopardises many otherwise well thought out and educationally desirable schemes. Increased course work assessment requires additional resources, not only in expanding the moderating service (and is it financially impossible to engage a professional corps of full-time moderators at the regional level?), but in enhancing teacher expertise in all forms of assessment procedure. As Macintosh puts it, it is necessary for teachers 'to recognise that competence in assessment is an integral part of their professional duties, and indeed of their professionalism, and this means more pre- and in-service training. It means also that assessment must be regarded by teachers as an integral part of the total educational process and not as something alien to it.'[13]

Principles of organising and assessing project work

Many of the CSE boards give useful advice on the sort of topics which are suitable, and in some cases also on methods of assessment. One characteristic example is that of the South Western Examinations Board, part of whose 'Field Notebook' section of the course is set out below.

FIELD NOTEBOOK

The field work syllabus has deliberately been made as wide as possible to allow individual schools to follow topics related to their local areas or to the special interests of their teachers. In all cases the results of the field work should be presented by (a) maps, sketches and other means, eg models, and (b) a summary of findings in written or diagram form. The notebooks in which field work is written up must reveal evidence of individual work and must be available at all stages of moderation.

Assessments will be made on the basis of: (*a*) Observation in detail and depth, (*b*) Logical recording and variety of methods and presentation of material, (*c*) Personal effort, (*d*) Originality (within the scope of the school situation), (*e*) Conclusions and/or relevance to other work. Assessments should always be based on the Board's Standard Five Point Scale.... The final assessment, also based on the Five Point Scale, will be made subjectively, taking account of the assessments given for the individual aspects.

Any topic may be chosen for study in the field. The following list is for assistance and guidance only:

A farm study: position, size, water supply, field division, crop rotation, livestock, labour, machinery, buildings, markets, transport, power supplies, changes in farming pattern.

A local industry (manufacturing): site, raw materials, labour, buildings, markets, transport, by-products, special problems, changes.

A quarry or mine (china clay, slate, coal): site, local rocks, relief, water supply, processes, products, uses, markets, changing pattern of industry.

A village study: location, types of buildings, materials (stone, brick, wood), roofing (thatch, tile, slate), use of buildings. . . .

Where schools have, in many cases, not undertaken fieldwork before, these are valuable guidelines, indicating criteria of assessment (though not in this case the weighting) and providing suggestions for suitable content. It must be said, however, that this method of presenting possible topics might, all too easily, encourage the mere collection of data; information is given on methods of presentation, but not very much on methods of processing.

The following are useful general criteria to be kept in mind.

1. The topic should be on a *local* scale, though not essentially pertaining to the local area of the school. If parents agree, there is no reason why the choice could not be of an area visited on holiday, or where relatives or family friends live. The *small scale, in-depth* study, such as an analysis of a bend in a local stream, usually lead to more interesting and personal work than grandiose projects such as 'Aspects of the Geomorphology of the Wye Basin,' where the content tends to be second-hand and cumulative.

2. Although the topic should clearly be *geographical*, it would be a pity if this were narrowly interpreted. While the norm would be a fieldwork project it would seem quite legitimate to study, for example, the changing patterns of journeys to work, based on research in the library using census materials rather than in the field. There are also many interesting historical geography topics that would necessitate concentration on library research. The 'geographical test' is not whether studies are undertaken in the field, but whether the processing of the information is geographical.

3. The material should, of course, be largely *first-hand*. Thus reliance on brochures from industrialists, travel agencies and the like, though perhaps useful in providing illustrative detail, should not be the central resource base. Above all, the scissors and paste method of using such material, involving the copying out of verbal sections, and a lack of annotation or 'translation' of the data contained in maps, diagrams and photographs, should be penalised. Where second-hand material is used, it should be *properly referenced*. There is no reason why pupils from the fourth form upwards cannot be taught as part of the techniques of presentation an appropriate way of attributing material to its sources.

4. A wide range of *methods of presentation* should be encouraged, maintaining a balance between verbal, numerical, graphical and cartographical forms. Properly used, this will do more than give an attractive presentation; it will help to spotlight the structure and sequence of the material.

5. The question of *structure* is very important. A recommended method is to use the problem-solving scientific approach advocated by, among others, Cole and King[14] and Everson.[15, 16] The process is as follows:

(a) Start with a *problem* (one, of course, that is worth looking into). This might, for example, be to do with reasons for variation in the density and nature of traffic on the local by-pass, the main road through the village, and the minor road past the school.

(b) Advance a *hypothesis*, or hypotheses, such as one related to differences between internally and externally generated traffic, eg traffic is heavier on the by-pass than on the other two roads because it is mainly generated by two nearby larger towns which the by-pass serves to connect (which introduces the question of the gravity model, if the teacher wishes to take a more sophisticated approach).

(c) Decide *what information is needed*, which would include maps of the local area, traffic counts, a census of types of vehicles, with details of place of origin (for which the *AA Book* giving a list of vehicle registration numbers and place of registration might be legitimate as a rough guide for younger forms).

(d) *Collect* and roughly code this information, using base maps, observation, field notebooks, and so on, in a neat enough form for it to be easily interpreted later.

(e) *Store* the information on maps, graphs, matrices and so on. More advanced work may require the coding of the information in a form susceptible to computerisation.

(f) *Process* the information, analysing and trying to interpret the evidence which emerges, ie testing the hypothesis. At more advanced levels, correlation will not be intuitive, and may be based on statistical tests of significance and so on.

(g) Consider whether the results justify accepting the hypothesis or not. Clearly at earlier stages the teacher will tend to guide the children towards hypotheses that are likely to be supported by the evidence. The degree of rigour insisted upon for the acceptance of the hypothesis will also vary with age. If the hypothesis falls, a new one might be set up and tested. If it is established, it might lead on to some further generalisation, about traffic patterns in this case.

This method is no panacea. It does not guarantee good work, and can become as stereotyped and mechanistic as any other method. Much depends on the generative power of the problem posed. If this is not worthwhile, the product is likely to be no better than traditional accounts which merely accumulate verbal information. Creativity should not be stifled by a rigid insistence on particular methods of processing. There is no inherent reason why this scientific approach should inhibit creative work, however, unless creativity is to be equated with 'the arts' and lack of structure, which would be an unfortunate interpretation. The best work will tend to hide the skeleton, but a framework will still be there.

6. Another useful device is the *comparative study*. This is the technique used in the local traffic example just mentioned. As has been noted, the use of contrast is a powerful way of highlighting concepts.[17]

7. *Assessment* should accurately reflect these guidelines. Marks should be allotted for:

(a) the appropriateness of the choice of topic and how well it is justified;

(b) the quality of the observation and the collection of data;

(c) the accuracy and clarity with which the material is used within a defined framework;

(d) the validity of the interpretations and conclusions reached in the light of the evidence collected;

(e) the quality of the presentation, which should not be purely a stock cosmetic matter, but relate also to qualities of individuality (a departure from a stock presentation scheme obviously provided by the school may be evidence of additional worth and should be given credit).

The assessment of attitudes

Information on attitudes is vital in at least three ways:

(a) in the direct sense that interest in a subject is essential to efficient learning;

(b) because a teacher ought to have feedback on whether such aims as stimulating interest, awareness, appreciation, involvement and so on, have been achieved in some degree;

(c) because positive attitudes towards something may have more predictive validity than success in a written paper that is regarded by the pupil as his final commitment to a subject area.

A certain scepticism regarding the assessment of attitudes is understandable, for they are relatively intangible and difficult to test. An attempt to assess attitudes quantitatively has been made in the experimental 'A'-level chemistry syllabus of the JMB, in which student attitudes to practical work are judged according to a number of criteria: willingness to co-operate in the normal routine of laboratory work; persistence and resourcefulness; enthusiasm.[18] There are good reasons, however, for not giving marks for attitudes, the most obvious being that it is incompatible to provide extrinsic reward for something by definition intrinsic. In addition, favourable attitudes figure already as a hidden element in marks ostensibly allotted for intellectual worth.

Further, demonstration of enthusiasm can be a fairly superficial characteristic. 'Liking geography' may really mean 'liking the geography teacher', or liking the success that comes with a certain facility in the subject, or merely disliking it less than other subjects.[19] The interest may prove to be transitory when a less congenial teacher or section of the course appears.

The promotion of favourable attitudes *is* a basic aim of schooling, however, and it is difficult to achieve. Many teachers would agree that it is easier to attain good examination results than to foster positive attitudes towards a subject and to school in general.

Dimensions

Attention has already been drawn (pages 34-7) to Kratwohl's 'Affective Domain' and Carswell's detailed application of it to geography in school. Here a more general approach is taken. The following manifestations of 'positive attitudes' are identified.

1. *An interest in activities which take place in geography lessons*

This type of interest has been investigated by Long,[20] whose research suggests that secondary school children prefer group work, projects, drawing and fieldwork, to such activities as writing essays, studying OS maps and taking notes. This type of feedback is not sufficient reason for discontinuing activities towards which reactions have been negative, for example to OS map work in geography, but it should lead the teacher to think of more acceptable methods of study.

An investigation by Booth of children's attitudes towards history[21] showed similar findings. Two additional points emerged.

(a) Children were asked to distinguish between activities they found interesting and those they found useful. They were shown to dislike 'learning facts', for example, but found the process useful.

(b) Activities the children said they liked, such as writing projects, local studies and the use of visual aids, were those least employed by history teachers.

Investigations such as these can be undertaken quite easily by practising teachers. The feedback they provide can suggest ways of varying activities as a boost to interest.

2. *Attitudes toward the world outside*

As these relate closely to the aims of teaching geography (pages 14-16) discussion here will be brief. The point that geography teachers should make use of issue-based approaches is reiterated. These need to be linked with the provision of an information base and the practice of relevant skills. In this way it is at least more likely that more refined judgements will be made than would be the case were they based on popular stereotyping, ignorance or disinterest. The assessment of such attitudes must, however, be indirect, geared to finding whether the pupil possesses the requisite knowledge and skills for making critical judgements, and to seeing how well he justifies them. But there is a real dilemma if, for example, unacceptable attitudes in human terms are skilfully communicated and justified. In this case it would seem more appropriate to regard the unacceptable part of the communication as material for later discussion, rather than as something to be formally assessed.

3. An 'internalisation of the values geographers hold'

This phrase is used by Carswell, and interpreted in a rather narrow, academic way.[22] He identifies three aspects as of paramount importance in such a diagnosis:

(a) a propensity to use maps;

(b) a belief in the virtue of direct observation based on fieldwork and primary source materials;

(c) a yearning for comprehension, in the sense of a need to make syntheses, as in the 'regional approach'.

The 'internalisation of what values geographers hold' can also be interpreted as meaning their skills will be used in trying to achieve certain desired ends, such as social justice (see page 68). The geography teacher obviously hopes values such as these will be acquired by his pupils. We need to remind ourselves, however, of the danger of instilling an enclosed subject ideology (see page 128).

Means of assessing attitudes

There is general agreement that a variety of evidence is helpful.[23]

1. Participant observation

This is the most obvious but can be the least controlled of the approaches to assessment of attitudes. It is dangerous to engage in a facile correlation of observed behaviour and inner attitude. Thus skilled observation of non-verbal cues in class (degree of attention, distractability, etc) is an important component in the process of assessment of attitudes. Face-value interpretation of, for example, overtly expressed interest or of individuals voluntarily staying behind after hours must be viewed with caution, as it may be evidence of a strong desire to please the teacher rather than intrinsic love of the subject. On the other hand, the presence of numbers of children consistently in the geography room in dinner hours, engaged in voluntary and purposeful activity, is not just pleasing to observe, but is probably diagnostic of a situation in which positive attitudes have developed. Conversely, absence of such activity may merely mean that school sanctions bar children from staying in school at lunch-time, or that a large proportion of children go home for dinner. The value of skilful participant observation is that the wide range of possible diagnostic variables is taken into account and weighted.

It should, however, be undertaken systematically. Carswell[24] and Styles[25] have applied the Kratwohl 'affective' taxonomy to this end. The following is an abstraction of some of their ideas.

(a) *Varying types of 'approach behaviour'*

(i) willingness to listen
(ii) willingness to answer questions
(iii) willingness to read assigned literature
(iv) willingness to initiate discussion
(v) voluntary acquaintance with geographical literature
(vi) reaction associated with enjoyment
(vii) initiatives taken which are compatible with commitment.

These various behaviours can be linked with more general aspects such as regularity of attendance and reliability in completing course work. The degree to which 'approach' behaviours exceed 'avoidance' is symptomatic of success.[26]

(b) *Engagement in external activities*

It is hoped that this build up of positive attitudes will transfer to related activities outside the classroom, such as joining the school geography society, borrowing travel books from the local library or subscribing to geographical or travel magazines, selecting TV documentary programmes as preferred watching and, particularly, outside involvement in social and environmental activities.

Systematic observation of such qualities may provide significant feedback to the teacher on the success of his teaching. While not formally assessed, it can be commented upon in reports and references.

2. *Questionnaires*

A more systematic way of collecting information is the use of the questionnaire, which can test, for example, the degree to which pupils find a course interesting and/or helpful. Such questionnaires are increasingly being used, and even demanded, at student level. Various techniques are available. A standard British reference source is A. N. Oppenheim.[27] A handy technique for classroom use is the Likert scale, employed by Booth, for example, in which pupils are asked to rank each class activity along two five-point scales, as rough measures of the interest and usefulness of the course.[28] (See Table 13.1.)

Table 13.1

Activities	Attitudes									
	Interest					Use				
	1	2	3	4	5	1	2	3	4	5
Activity A										
Activity B										
etc										

1. very enjoyable
2. enjoyable
3. indifferent
4. dislike
5. strong dislike

1. very helpful
2. helpful
3. indifferent
4. unhelpful
5. very unhelpful

Based on the results of the class as a whole, simple percentages can be worked out and plotted on a bar graph, showing the proportion of pupils choosing each category for each activity. Where a formal piece of research is being undertaken, more sophisticated statistical processing can be used.[29]

3. *Sentence completion*

Perhaps linked with the questionnaire, the pupil on completing a course or an activity might be asked to answer a series of questions, which have been organised in a pointed way by the teacher.

> The most enjoyable aspect of the fieldwork at Malham was..........
> The least enjoyable aspect of the fieldwork at Malham was..........
> On leaving school, my connection with geography is likely to be........

The device can also be used to assess the formation of attitudes to various aspects of local, national and international issues.

4. *Interviews and discussions*

Much evidence on attitudes to course work can emerge from individual interviews,[30] or from group or class discussion, designed for this purpose.

5. *Role-playing*

Though little used in conventional geography teaching, the introduction of structured role-playing activities is potentially a valuable means of eliciting evidence of empathy on the part of pupils—the degree of senstivity to the feelings of others. This may well be an important outcome of the increasing use of role-playing games, in which questions of values can emerge strongly.

Assessment of attitudes is a sphere in which the sensitive teacher treads softly. Any publicity attached to such assessment should be of a group and not an individual nature, and even then there are dangers of negative teacher assessments of a group's attitudes being reciprocated by classes in the 'self-fulfilling prophecy' (see page 144). New and more open classroom procedures which lay more stress on the attitudinal component are a threat to privacy. As Bernstein has observed, weakened classification and framing (see page 111) can be intrusive, causing more of the pupil 'to be made public—more of his thoughts, feelings and values.'[31] While this conflict of principle needs to be considered, the balance of advantage is still in favour of bringing into the open the attitudes dimension.

Priority readings
(See also page 239)

1. MACINTOSH, H. G. 'Internal assessment' in HUDSON, B. (ed.) *Assessment Techniques: An Introduction* (Methuen), Chapter 6, pp. 157–90.
2. ROGERS, T. J. 'Course work and continuous assessment' in MACINTOSH, H. G. (ed.) *Techniques and Problems of Assessment* (Edward Arnold), Chapter 9, pp. 157–71.
3. HALE, D. E. 'Moderation' in MACINTOSH, H. G. (ed.) *op. cit.*, Chapter 11, pp. 186–96.
4. Secondary Schools Examinations Council *The Certificate of Secondary Education: Some Suggestions for Teachers and Examiners* Examinations Bulletin No. 1. (HMSO), pp. 18–26.
5. MATHEWS, J. C. 'The assessment of attitudes' in MACINTOSH, H. G. (ed.) *Techniques and Problems of Assessment* (Edward Arnold), Chapter 10, pp. 172–85.
6. LONG, M. 'The interests of children in school geography' *Geography*, **56** (1971), pp. 177–90.
7. JONES, G. W. 'Children's choice of geography' *Geography*, **59** (1974) pp. 351–4.
8. HAMILTON, D. *Curriculum Evaluation* (Open Books, London).

Questions for investigation and discussion

1. Assume you are in a school which has opted for the Mode III procedure in CSE geography.
(a) Ensure that you are clear what Mode III is, and the nature of the regulations relating to it.[32]
(b) Outline briefly the content of your proposed syllabus, assuming that it lasts for two years.
(c) Outline its educational aims and objectives.
(d) Specify how you would employ different modes of assessment for different purposes.
2. Distinguish the roles of the conventional external examiner, the moderator and the internal assessor of work for an external examination.

3. Outline the criteria you would give to your pupils in preparation for project work for an external examination. Produce a hand-out which exemplifies these criteria in the context of a local case-study.
4. Outline strategies you would adopt to ensure that (a) particular field-work sites were not overloaded with pupils,[33] and (b) that safety regulations were observed.[34]
5. Over the course of a term's work, keep a check-list of observations which shed light on whether the attitudes of the pupils you teach are positive or negative. Assess variations between different classes.
6. Draw up a questionnaire, on the lines shown on page 250, in order to make a more formal assessment of pupil attitudes to a year or a term's course (or even an individual project or piece of fieldwork) you have undertaken.
7. If you felt strongly motivated as a teacher to undertake rigorous and consistent assessments of attitudes, how would you arrange for pupils not to feel threatened by such measurements?
8. Is it possible or desirable to attempt to assess the change in children's attitudes to other peoples as, for example, on 'loaded' topics such as the racial geography of New York or the social geography of Belfast?

References

1. See. MACINTOSH, H. G. (1973) 'Internal assessment' and KENNEDY, J. B. (1973), 'Moderating procedures' in HUDSON, B. (ed.) (1973) *Assessment Techniques: An Introduction* (Methuen, London), 157-90, and 191-214 respectively.
2. See ROGERS, T. J. (1974) 'Course work and continuous assessment' and HALE, D. E. (1974) 'Moderation', in MACINTOSH, H. G. (ed.) (1974) *Techniques and Problems of Assessment* (Arnold, London), 157-71 and 186-96 respectively.
3. NUTTALL, D. L. & WILLMOTT, A. S. (1972) *British Examinations: Techniques of Analysis* (National Foundation for Educational Research).
4. Secondary Schools Examinations Council (1963) *The Certificate of Secondary Education: Some Suggestions for Teachers and Examiners*, Examinations Bulletin No. 1, (HMSO, London).
5. The Schools Council (1965) *The Certificate of Secondary Education: School-based Examinations*, Examinations Bulletin, No. 5, (HMSO, London).
6. The Schools Council (1975) *Continuous Assessment in the CSE*, Examinations Bulletin No. 31 (Evans/Methuen Educational, London).
7. For example, Associated Lancashire Schools Examining Board (1971) *Examination Objectives and Techniques*, Report No. 5 (ALSEB, Manchester) pp. 24-36.
8. North-Western Secondary Schools Examination Board (1970) *Geography: Field Work and its Assessment*, Pamphlet No. 9. (NWSSEB, Manchester).
9. See HICKMAN, G. et al. (1973) *A New Professionalism for a Changing Geography* (Schools Council, London), 28.
10. See, for example, KENNEDY, J. B. (1973) 'Moderating procedures' in HUDSON, B. (ed.) (1973), *op. cit.*, 210-11.
11. Incorporated Association of Assistant Masters (1972) 'A common examination

at 16+: Association comments on Schools Council Bulletin 23' *AMA*, **67**, 229.
12. See MOTTERSHEAD, R. & OWEN, M. D. (1972) 'Some problems arising in fieldwork in modern geography' *Geography*, **57**, 232-4.
13. MACINTOSH, H. G. (1973) 'Internal assessment' in HUDSON, B. (ed.) (1973), *op. cit.*, 159.
14. COLE, J. P. & KING, C. A. M. (1968) *Quantitative Geography* (Wiley & Sons, London), 18-19.
15. EVERSON, J. (1969) 'Some aspects of teaching geography through fieldwork' in BALE, J. *et al.* (eds.) (1973) *Perspectives in Geographical Education* (Oliver & Boyd, Edinburgh), 197-210.
16. For an example of an application of the Everson scheme, see RAWLING, E. (1975) 'Supermarket for Llandovery—an exercise in field research' *Teaching Geography*, **1**, 7-10.
17. See BRUNER, J. S. (1966) *Toward a Theory of Instruction* (Harvard University Press, Cambridge, Mass.), 93.
18. Joint Matriculation Board (1973) *Experimental Scheme for the Internal Assessment of Practical Skills in Chemistry (Advanced)* (JMB, Manchester), 3 and 7.
19. See JONES, G. W. (1974) 'Children's choice of geography' *Geography*, **59**, 354.
20. LONG, M. (1971) 'The interests of children in school geography' *Geography*, **56**, 177-90.
21. BOOTH, M. B. (1969) *History Betrayed?* (Longman, London), 137-70.
22. CARSWELL, R. J. B. (1970) 'Evaluation of affective learning in geographic education' in KURFMAN, D. G. (ed.) (1970) *Evaluation in Geographic Education* (Fearon Publishers, Belmont, California), 111.
23. See, for example, PARLETT, M. (1974), 'The new evaluation' *Trends in Education*, **34**, 16-17.
24. CARSWELL, R. J. B. (1970), *op. cit.*, 113-15.
25. STYLES, E. (1972) 'Measurement of affective educational objectives in geography' in BIDDLE, D. S. & DEER, C. E. (eds.) (1973) *Readings in Geographical Education: Selections from Australian and New Zealand Sources:* Vol. 2, 1966-72. (Whitcombe & Tombs, Sydney, for the Australian Geography Teachers' Association), 415-16.
26. CARSWELL, R. J. B. (1970), *op. cit.*, 108.
27. OPPENHEIM, A. N. (1966) *Questionnaire Design and Attitude Measurement* (Heinemann, London).
28. BOOTH, M. B. (1969), *op. cit.*, 139.
29. OPPENHEIM, A. N. (1966), *op. cit.*, 120-54.
30. See MATHEWS, J. C. (1974) 'The assessment of attitudes' in MACINTOSH, H. G. (ed.) (1974), *op. cit.*, 180-1.
31. BERNSTEIN, B. (1971) 'On the classification and framing of educational knowledge' in YOUNG, M. F. D. (ed.) (1971) *Knowledge and Control: New Directions for the Sociology of Education* (Collier-Macmillan, London), 66.
32. Refer to ROE, P. E. (1971) 'Examining CSE geography' *Geography*, **56**, 105-11.
33. Refer to MOTTERSHEAD, R. & OWEN, M. D. (1972) *op. cit.*, 232-4.
34. Refer to Schools Council (1972) *Out and About: A Teacher's Guide to Safety on Educational Visits* (Evans/Methuen, London).

Section 4 Synthesis: The Geography Curriculum

14 Frameworks

There are various ways of structuring geography syllabuses. From the subject point of view, traditional alternatives are the *regional* and the *systematic* approaches. The objective of both is to achieve a world coverage. The two approaches are not mutually exclusive. In the regional structure the sub-divisions reflect systematic categories, each region being studied in terms of its physical and human aspects and, it is hoped, their inter-relation. In the systematic approach, examples are taken from different regions, and these can range from a superficial mention to detailed case studies.

Another method of structuring is to look beyond geography, and make use of broad categories which are not subject-specific, which can be applied to any field of study. Two possible approaches are the *topic-based* and the *concept-based*. These are particularly necessary where geography is part of an integrated scheme. As has been noted, the problems of balancing and focusing such broader schemes are intense (pages 118-21). Both topic and concept approaches need a further selective mechanism if they are not to be too general to provide a cogent structure.

In geography such mechanisms are to hand. Thus a topic can be given an areal or a systematic orientation, exemplified through a detailed *case-study* or, often better still, *contrasted* case-studies. The case-study may be, say, 'Lapland', with an integrating theme such as 'How the Lapps adapt themselves to a hostile environment', which embodies various important concepts. An alternative is to give it a stronger conceptual thrust: something to do with the 'perception of hazards', for example, illustrated by the study of the Lapps.

The concentric approach

It is doubtful, however, whether a single study is enough to establish important concepts. To help with this, geographers often use a *concentric approach*,[1] which has the complementary advantage of

Legend

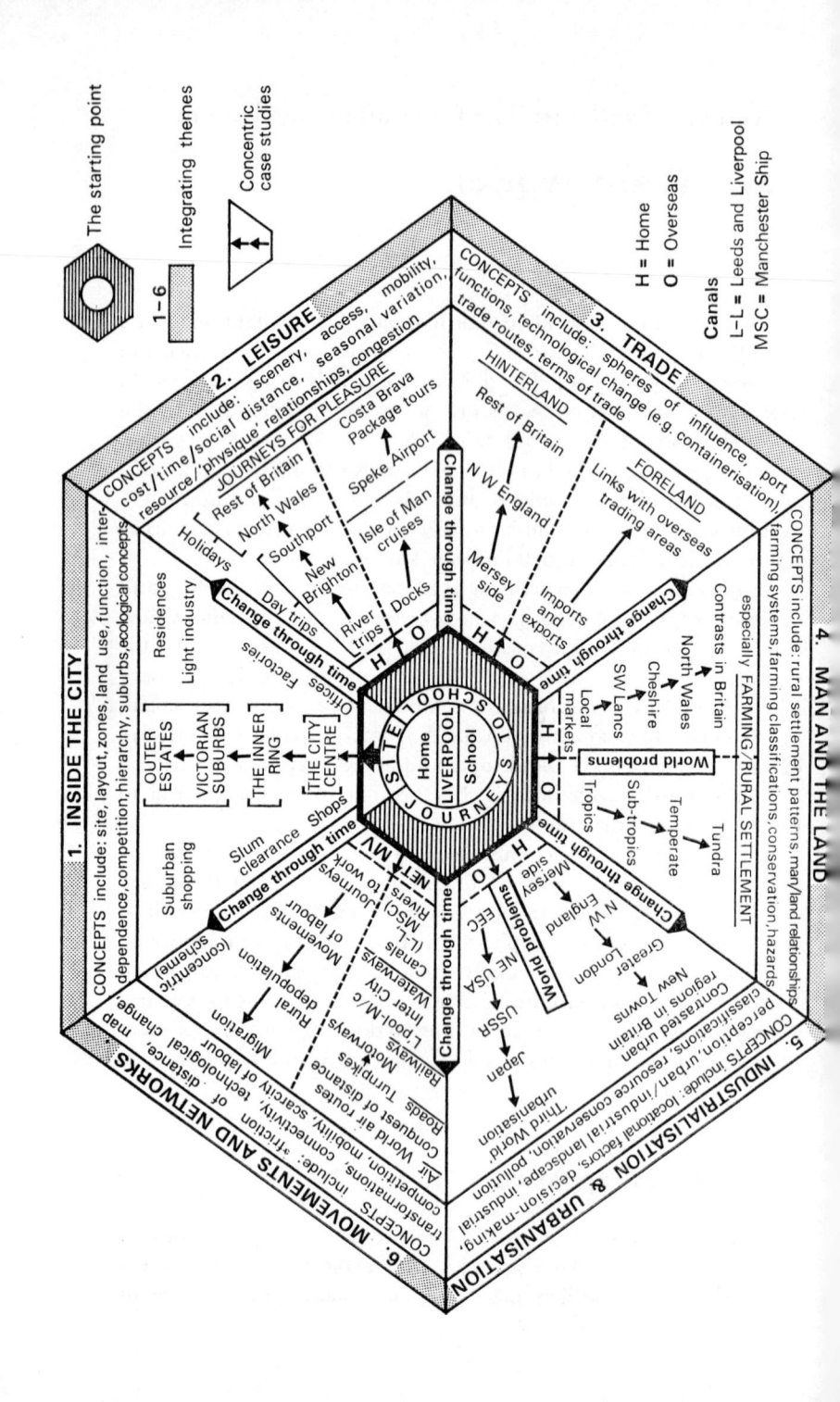

- The starting point
- 1–6 Integrating themes
- Concentric case studies

Canals
L–L = Leeds and Liverpool
MSC = Manchester Ship

H = Home
O = Overseas

---

1. INSIDE THE CITY

CONCEPTS include: site, layout, zones, land use, function, interdependence, competition, hierarchy, suburbs, ecological concepts

- THE CITY CENTRE
- THE INNER RING
- VICTORIAN SUBURBS
- OUTER ESTATES

Offices, Factories, Light industry, Residences
Shops, Slum clearance, Suburban shopping (concentric scheme)

Change through time

2. LEISURE

CONCEPTS include: scenery, access, mobility, cost/time/social distance, seasonal variation, resource/'physique' relationships, congestion

JOURNEYS FOR PLEASURE

- Costa Brava / Package tours
- Rest of Britain
- Speke Airport
- North Wales
- Isle of Man cruises
- Southport
- New Brighton
- Holidays
- Day trips
- River trips
- Docks

3. TRADE

CONCEPTS include: spheres of influence, port functions, technological change (e.g. containerisation), trade routes, terms of trade

HINTERLAND
- Rest of Britain
- NW England
- Merseyside

FORELAND
- Links with overseas trading areas
- Imports and exports

Change through time

4. MAN AND THE LAND

CONCEPTS include: rural settlement patterns, man/land relationships, farming systems, farming classifications, conservation, hazards

Contrasts in Britain — especially FARMING/RURAL SETTLEMENT
- North Wales
- Cheshire
- SW Lancs
- Local markets

World problems
- Tundra
- Temperate
- Sub-tropics
- Tropics

Change through time

5. INDUSTRIALISATION & URBANISATION

CONCEPTS include: locational factors, decision-making, perception, urban/industrial landscape, industrial classifications, resource conservation, pollution

Contrasted urban regions in Britain
- Merseyside
- NW England
- Greater London
- New Towns

- EEC
- NE USA
- USSR
- Japan
- Third World urbanisation

World problems

6. MOVEMENTS AND NETWORKS

CONCEPTS include: 'friction of distance', connectivity, mobility, scarcity of labour, transformations, competition, technological change, map

- Migration
- Rural depopulation
- Movements of labour
- Journeys to work
- Inter-city waterways
- Canals (L–L)
- Railways
- L'pool–M/c MSC
- Motorways
- Roads, Turnpikes
- Conquest of distance
- World air routes

Change through time

Central hexagon: SITE / JOURNEYS TO SCHOOL / LIVERPOOL — Home, School obeying the sound pedagogic principle of moving from the familiar to the unfamiliar, yet avoiding the dangers of parochialism present in pure local studies approaches. It allows a selective coverage of the world to be built up, but does not entail superficial blanket description.

The model proposed in Fig. 14.1 is an attempt to integrate the major traditions of geography (though there is little reference to the earth science view). In terms of approaches, there is strong emphasis on the *three Cs*—conceptual, concentric and case-study. The model is applied to the circumstances of a school on Merseyside, and is intended to form the basis of a syllabus for the first three years of the secondary school. There should be no trouble in adapting it to the needs of other metropolitan regions, though for schools in rural and small town areas different emphases might be appropriate.

There is nothing sacrosanct in the hexagonal shape of the model. It merely forms a compact means of framing the content. Such structuring, though very helpful in this or some equivalent form, is, however, no guarantee of successful lesson units. Indeed, syllabus framing is a potentially hazardous process from the pedagogic point of view, for the cogency of the structure may reinforce the determination to cover the syllabus at all costs.

While the boundary lines give a rigid appearance, the content within is open to flexible interpretations. Though it is held important to preserve both a balance of concepts and the concentric arrangement of case-studies, the number and scope of such studies can be modified and adapted to varying constraints, such as the ability of the children, timetabling exigencies and so forth.

Commentary (on Fig. 14.1)

1. The important principle of *sequencing* is not built into the framework at this stage. In general terms, however, the depth of understanding envisaged at the 'Inside the City' (first year) stage, for example, is less than at the 'Movements and Networks' (third year) stage. Concept labels may be the same at different stages, but this does not infer unnecessary repetition, a point illustrated in the alternative 'spiral' framework suggested later (pages 261–3). The sequence of major 'integrating' themes is more or less changeable, and can be adapted to different circumstances. In a rural environment, both the order and the nature of these broad themes might need to be altered.

The sort of three-year programme the scheme could offer is:

1s *Year*
Term 1 ⎫
Term 2 ⎬   1. INSIDE THE CITY
Term 3   2. LEISURE

2nd Year
Term 4   3. TRADE
Term 5 ⎫
Term 6 ⎬   4. MAN AND THE LAND

3rd Year
Term 7 ⎫
Term 8 ⎬   5. INDUSTRIALISATION AND URBANISATION
Term 9 ⎭   6. MOVEMENTS AND NETWORKS

The first term starts with the home and the school before going out into the local urban environment. The concentric principle is already embodied, but confined to the immediate area. The true concentric arrangement begins in the third term, the summer term, envisaged as an appropriate time to deal with 'leisure'. A more systematic look at the world comes in the second year, the theme of trade leading out from the port as an introduction to the world and its environments. Here and in the third year a more overt problem-orientation is introduced. In the third year a more formal look at concepts and the spatial view is taken.

2. Other variables have still to be built into the scheme, notably the concepts, techniques and tools, and a range of materials. The techniques, tools and materials are more appropriately specified at the detailed level of planning course units, but the conceptual framework needs to be discussed here. The principles that were earlier advanced as providing a useful means of structuring content at the detailed course unit level (pages 38–9, and 97–9) need to be built into the general framework. A flexible (not verbatim) translation of the curriculum model might be as in Fig. 14.2 (pp. 260–1).

3. It may be objected that *physical geography* as such is excluded, and thus the earth science tradition neglected. Physical aspects will, of course, be integrated at appropriate points, as in studies of site and rural land use. It is likely in any case that more systematic studies of physical geography will form part of subsequent CSE, 'O'-and 'A'-level syllabuses. Another way in which physical geography can be introduced is by adopting the idea of the ecosystem in the man/land studies section.

4. The scheme requires considerable exercise of energy in *collecting materials* at the local level, in which time can be saved through co-operation, perhaps arranged through local teacher centres. At the national and global levels, once basic principles have been met, a criterion of choice may be commercial availability of materials. There is today a proliferation of case-studies covering most parts of this country and of the world as a whole. Their presentation surpasses that which can normally be produced by local duplication, and attractive presentation is important to the pupil. Despite the soaring cost of books, those with a wide range of photographs, diagrams and even coloured maps remain 'a good buy' if sensibly purchased and used. Individual teacher initiative is retained if they are seen as source books and not as course books.

5. The model is, in sum, an attempt to *integrate*:

(a) factual content and concept;

(b) the above with a variety of methods and materials;

(c) local with regional, national and global studies, in a concentric, case-study-orientated scheme;

(d) a realistic infusion of ideas from the frontiers of geography into the school setting, without throwing out of the window the traditional regard for the unique and the real:

(e) the varying traditions of geography;

(f) the intellectual and social aims which must underpin any geography course which wishes to justify its place in the school timetable.

An alternative procedure

One of the most powerful advocates of 'structuring' has been Jerome Bruner. He sees this structure developing from the forms of knowledge (page 49), 'there is an appropriate version of any skill or knowledge that may be imparted at whatever age one wishes to begin teaching—however preparatory that version may be.'[2] Thus the early childhood years may be wasted 'by postponing the teaching of many subjects on the grounds that they are too difficult.' The basic ideas of subjects 'are as simple as they are powerful. . . . A curriculum as it develops should revisit these basic ideas repeatedly, building upon them until the student has grasped the full formal apparatus that goes with them.'[3]

Fig. 14.2

Topics	Concepts include
1st Year Term 1	
1. Home and school	(a) *Site*—home/school/city
	(b) *Scale*—plans of home/classroom/playground
	(c) *Location*—latitude/longitude: 'grids'
	(d) *Distance*—journey to school (map) time/cost distance
	(f) *Functions*—related to materials—location
2. Homes and people in Liverpool	
(i) Population growth	(a) *Demography*
(ii) Inner zone—clearance	(b) *Change through time*
(iii) Victorian	(c) *Zonation*—variation in space
(iv) Outer suburbs	(d) *Socio-economic* (at very elementary level)
(v) Overspill	
Term 2	
3. Industry in Liverpool	(a) Simple *locational concepts*
	(b) *Distance*—journey to work
	(c) *Zonation*—(i) riverside (ii) industrial estates
4. Shopping in Liverpool	(a) *Hierarchies* ⎫ (i) corner shops
	(b) *Centrality* ⎬ (ii) suburban shopping centres
	(c) *Journey to shop* ⎭ (iii) CBD (mention only)
Term 3	
5. Holidays	
(i) Day trips	(a) *Journeys for recreation*—access—time/cost distance
(ii) Holidays in Britain	(b) *Ecological*—settlement/resource/physique relationships
(iii) Holidays abroad—docks—cruise; Speke—package tour	(c) *Tensions*—competition for land
2nd Year Term 4	
1. Liverpool markets	
(i) Home produce	(a) *Economics* (what is a 'market')
(ii) Produce from abroad	(b) *Centrality*
	(c) *Rural-urban interaction*
2. Farming/rural settlement	(a) The farm as part of a wider *system*
(i) SW Lancashire	(i) *biosphere*—relate to geology, relief, drainage, soils, vegetation
(ii) Cheshire	
(iii) N Wales	(ii) *economic sphere*
(iv) Contrasted areas of Britain	(b) *Rural settlement patterns*—hierarchies, etc
	(c) *Competition for land*

Term 5
3. The port of Liverpool
   (i) The docks—linked to hinterland and foreland eg southern dock (closed) northern docks Tranmere/Bidston Seaforth (container terminal)
   (ii) Overseas connections—imports/exports

   (a) *Port spheres of influence*—hinterland/foreland
   (b) *Access*—canal/road/rail/sea
   (c) *Congestion*
   (d) *Change through time*

4. Man/land relationships in overseas context
   (i) Temperate Zones

   As in topic 2

   Term 6
   (ii) Man in tropics and sub-tropics*
   (iii) Man in the tundra

   (a) Overseas farm studies/rural settlement
   (b) World problems

   As in topic 2
   Also include *demographic concepts* at a simple level
   Ecosystems approach to climatic/soil/vegetation regions

3rd Year *Term 7*

MERSEYSIDE ← BRITAIN ← OVERSEAS   EMPHASISE COMPARATIVE STUDIES

1. Industrialisation and urbanisation
   (i) Merseyside (may include some revision of 1st year work)
   (ii) NW England eg cotton/chemicals/glass
   (iii) Contrasted areas of Britain eg W Midlands, London area, N Ireland

   Term 8
   (iv) Contrasted areas abroad eg W Europe, NE USA, USSR, Japan, Third World cities

   LINK WITH CONURBATIONS

   (a) *Economic-locational factors*
   (b) *Zonation*
   (c) *Access*—link extractive industry, manufacturing and markets
   (d) *Change through time* (technological)
   (e) *Tensions* (i) *competition* for land and resources
        (ii) with *environment* (pollution)
   (f) *Decision making and perception*

   Term 9
2. Movements and networks
   (i) Communication systems†—canals, turnpike roads, motorways, railways, sea routes, air routes
   (ii) Movements of people—commuting† (microscale), movements of labour (meso-scale), migration (macro-scale)

   (a) *Topology* friction of distance—surface/time/cost/connectivity, etc
   (b) *Economics*—link with Terms 7 and 8 —competition
   (c) *Change through time*
   (d) *Differentiation of function*
   (e) Population *mobility*

* Malayan example, p. 267ff.
† Changing accessibility of Southport example, pp. 287ff.

From this emerges the 'spiral curriculum' notion, which is exemplified below in the context of urban study.[4] Other topics can also be built up in this way. Here it is envisaged that the pupils will revisit basic concepts, using progressively more advanced methods and materials, with a deeper understanding aimed at at each stage.

1st Stage (10–12 year age range)
1. *The classroom*
    (a) Its plan
    (b) Its function: simple locational ideas
2. *The school*
    (a) Its plan
    (b) School 'land use' and 'zones'
3. *Journey to school*
    (a) Introduction to large scale maps
    (b) Journey to work concepts
    (alternative: *The postman's round*)
4. *Buildings*
    (a) Building materials (extractive industry)
    (b) Age of buildings—urban growth
    (c) Simple land use classification
5. *Traffic*
    (a) Simple traffic census
    (b) Comparisons between streets
6. *A street study*
    (a) Linked with land use classification
    (b) Its place in the town as a whole
    (c) Comparison with other streets
    (d) Changes in the street over time (linked with old maps and directory material)

2nd Stage (about 14 years—linking in with, eg, CSE project)
1. *Small town study* and/or *village study* and/or *suburban area study* and/or *industrial zone study*
    (a) More detailed land use classification
    (b) Age of buildings
    (c) Simple zoning (6″ OS map)
    (d) Hierarchies
    (e) Possible industrial visit(s)
2. *Locational attributes*
    (a) Town site and situation
    (b) Physical environment of the town (smaller scale OS maps)
3. *Links between town and country*
    (a) Bus and train services: timetable analysis: journeys to work
    (b) Rural land use/farm/market studies
    (c) Rural amenities

(d) Transport networks (which could be developed as a separate study)
  (e) Spheres of influence
4. *Comparative studies*
  Other small towns, villages, etc. in local area or in Britain, as contrasted case-studies.

3rd Stage (VI form)
Full scale urban studies with examples from Western World, Communist World, 'Third' World
  1. Central area of a large town (CBD)
  2. Hierarchies—towns/shopping centres
  3. Urban fields
  4. The growth of urban functions
  5. The evolution of urban landscapes
  6. The present urban landscape and its problems
  7. Social area analysis
  8. Journeys into the city
  9. Images of towns and cities.

Texts appropriate to each of these stages, based on a conceptual approach to geography, have become increasingly available recently.[5] Within this type of approach, various interpretations are possible and to be desired.[6] But it must be remembered that a well structured framework, though a necessary preliminary stage, is not in itself a guarantee of a good course. The translation of these guiding principles into course units is the critical element.

Priority readings

1. BRUNER, J. S. *Toward a Theory of Instruction* (Harvard University Press), Chapter 4, pp. 73–101.
2. LONG, M. & ROBERSON, B. S. *Teaching Geography* (Heinemann), Chapter 14, 267–317.
3. GRAVES, N. J. *Geography in Secondary Education* (Geographical Association), Chapter V, pp. 61–76, Appendices A and B, pp. 81–4.
4. WALFORD, R. (ed.) *New Directions in Geography Teaching* (Longman), Part 2, Chapter 8, pp. 175–88.

Questions for investigation and discussion

1. In the light of the discussion in this chapter, and information derived from the priority readings above, outline the pros and cons of the different methods of syllabus construction provided.
2. (a) Draw up a set of criteria for constructing a geography syllabus which is not constrained by external examination requirements, but which has to provide a basis for meeting these requirements at a later stage.
   (b) Fill in the details of this syllabus, justifying your selection of concepts and exemplars.

References

1. The idea of different 'scales' of study (macro-, meso- and micro-) complements the concentric approach. See HICKMAN, G., et al. (eds.) (1973) *A New Professionalism for a Changing Geography* (Schools Council, London), 8–9.
2. BRUNER, J. S. (1966) *Toward a Theory of Instruction* (Harvard University Press, Cambridge, Mass.), 35.
3. BRUNER, J. S. (1960) *The Process of Education* (Vintage Books, Random House, New York), 12–13.
4. A similar idea is illustrated in a syllabus provided in GRAVES, N. J. (1971) *Geography in Secondary Education* (Geographical Association, Sheffield), Appendix E, 95, 97–8.
5. Examples might be: *1st stage* COLE & BEYNON *New Ways in Geography* (Blackwell); LINES & BOLWELL *Discovering your Environment* (Ginn); Oxford Geography Project Vol. 1 *The Local Framework* (Oxford University Press); *2nd Stage* BRIGGS, K. 'Introducing Towns and Cities' (University of London Press); MARSDEN, W. E. *Changing Environments in Britain* Book 1: Towns and Cities (Oliver & Boyd); *3rd Stage* EVERSON & FITZGERALD *Concepts in Geography* Book 1: Settlement Patterns, Book 3: Inside the City (Longman).
6. It is good to see the appearance of examples of structured syllabus construction in *Classroom Geographer* and *Teaching Geography*. See, for example, CROMARTY, D. (1975) 'Reconstructing the syllabus' *Teaching Geography*, **1**, 28–31.

15 Units

Guidelines

In the light of the preceding stress on merging theory into practice, the purpose of this concluding section is to try to demonstrate in some detail how practical course units can be underpinned by theory. It is emphasised, however, that there is no prescriptive element embodied in the actual choice of examples. The 'should' element suggests only that some type of structuring procedure such as this is needed. The following is a selective summary of guidelines which have emerged from earlier chapters.

1. In chapter 2 the general aim of education was seen to be the development of thinking skills as a means of promoting the growth of personal autonomy and, in turn, of social skills. Geography was seen as having a role to play in the whole of this process. The minimum need was made clear: to include within course units material of social import, drawn from a variety of environmental settings.

2. From a consideration of objectives (chapter 3) it was concluded that for meaningful learning to take place, careful structuring of learning activities is needed. Useful structuring elements are (a) a classification of intellectual abilities (recall, comprehension, problem-solving and synthesis/creativity) and (b) specification of levels of generality at which objectives can most constructively be stated.

3. In chapter 4 criteria were derived from an analysis of the structure of knowledge and the place of geography in it. After this there was a fuller discussion of the subject's contribution to education in chapters 5 and 6. From these three chapters guidelines emerge, such as the desirability of integrating the varying traditions of geography and the pedagogically sound ideas of the 'old' and the 'new' geography.

4. An outcome of chapter 7 was the suggestion that geography itself could be viewed to some degree as an inter-disciplinary study. Its use of concepts derived from other disciplines, especially the social sciences, is testimony to its interdisciplinary nature, a valuable

attribute in circumstances where practical difficulties prevent the adoption of fully integrated schemes. This implies that geography teachers should 'think inter-disciplinary' and see the subject playing a full role in social and environmental education. Where integrated schemes are introduced, the particular offerings geography has to make should not be lost, even if the subject does not appear as a separate heading on the timetable.

5. In terms of planning detailed course units, chapter 8, in some cases reinforcing chapter 3, offered fundamental guidelines, relating to pupils as learners and the skills of the teacher, which were laid out in detail on pages 158–9.

6. The sections on assessment (chapters 9–13) included many examples of the types of feedback different assessment procedures could supply. It will become clear that these principles and a variety of techniques of formative assessment are built into the two curriculum units which follow.

First Curriculum Unit

An Aboriginal Group in Malaya

Placing in curriculum scheme (see page 260)

> Integrating theme: **Man and the Land**
> Sub-section: Man in the Tropics
> Timing: Unit in second half of second year, taking not less than three weeks.

(In the context of individualising instruction and promoting flexibility, it is not regarded as desirable to be absolutely specific over timing of curriculum units.)

Aims

These are (a) to provide a basis for building up an informed and empathetic attitude to a vastly contrasted social group, emphasising 'common humanity' as much as the obvious differences of environment and culture; and (b) to present the issues introduced by this unit as examples of broader issues affecting the world's so-called 'primitive' peoples.

Objectives

(a) To produce an interesting and varied set of illustrative materials to heighten interest.
(b) To clarify the meaning, where necessary, of concrete 'vernacular' concepts, such as forest, jungle, peninsula, communal, craft (to take some examples from the material used).

(c) To clarify the meaning of more technical concepts required in the study, such as aboriginal, equatorial forest, convectional rainfall, ladang, hill padi, belukar, etc.
(d) To improve overall understanding of the integrating geographical theme of *adaptation of man to environment*, through focus on the following principles (which are used to structure the unit). The major concepts are in italics.

  (i) The aboriginal groups of Malaya inhabit a basically '*hostile*' *environment* (note loaded wording) in terms of relief, climate and vegetation, (using as far as is practicable an 'ecosystems' approach).
  (ii) The people are very closely integrated with, or *adapted* to this environment, which not only provides them with food, but also with shelter, tools and hunting equipment.
  (iii) The type of economy practised by such groups is largely of a *subsistence* type.
  (iv) The particular manifestation of subsistence agriculture in this case is *shifting cultivation*, built into which is an important *conservation* principle.
  (v) The aboriginal groups are highly dependent on specific *life-skills*, handed down from generation to generation: a *way of life* in which *tradition* and *family ties* are important. (Here geography steps over into anthropology.)
  (vi) The nature of the environment has induced *cultural isolation*, and helped to preserve the traditional way of life.

(e) To demonstrate that this isolation has for some years been breaking down, *technological change* and *socio-political change* promoting contact with more 'advanced' cultural groups.
(f) To demonstrate that similar changes over time are *generalisable* over the world, the tendency being for more advanced societies to drive less advanced either into more isolated areas, into extinction or into assimilation in the local society, often at a low status level.

Materials: resources for learning

These can, as appropriate, be presented in the form of *information sheets*, with exercises undertaken on separate paper, or be integrated with the exercises to form *worksheets*. It must be stressed that the layout which follows is not the clearest that could be devised. Constraints on space have meant that it has been compacted more than would be desirable in practice, where it is vital to arrange materials in an attractive and easily accessible form. Here, for example, the lines which would provide space for answering the partly structured questions are omitted. Resource material and exercises are for the most part not combined in true worksheet form.

The worksheet (page 157) has the distinct advantages of

(a) promoting pupil involvement and providing the structured guidance through which meaningful learning can take place;

(b) providing a basis through which a 'core' curriculum can be worked out, separated from 'enrichment' exercises, which seems the only realistic way of allowing pupils to proceed at their own rate, ie of individualising instruction.

(c) making possible the structuring not only of content but also of exercises designed to assess varying abilities;

(d) allowing continuing assessment and feedback between teacher and pupil, and the possibility of more time being spent with the weaker pupil;

(e) providing the basis of informed class answering of questions and general discussion.

It must be repeated that the worksheet is not regarded as *the* answer to the problems of mixed-ability teaching. If used in isolation, it can become as stereotyped and off-putting to pupils as any other method.

Underlying Principles

These are specified here as a structure for the teacher. Whether they should be included on the worksheets given to the children is an important point for discussion. Each principle is followed by assignments designed to help pupils to understand it by working with appropriate materials. The exercises include multiple choice, structured and partly structured questions and a group project, and cover a wide range of abilities.

Map 1 South-east Asia

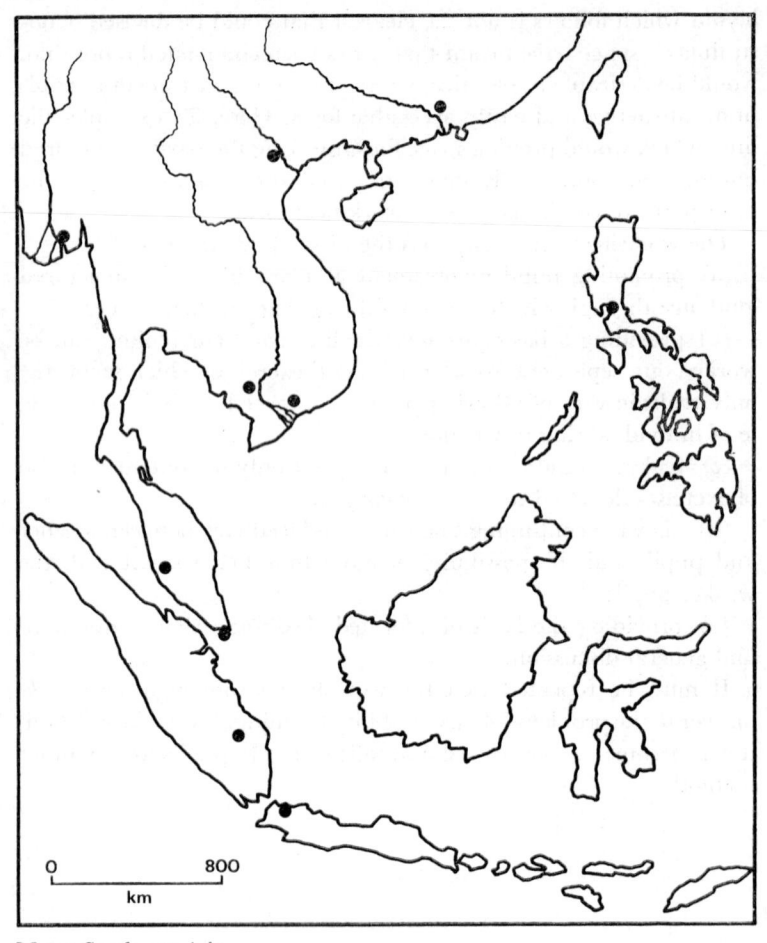

Materials required

An atlas

Other maps
1. Location map of south-east Asia
2. Physical features of Malaya and Singapore
3. Land use and towns of Malaya and Singapore
4. Density of population of Malaya and Singapore
5. Annual rainfall distribution of Malaya and Singapore

(*continued on page 273*)

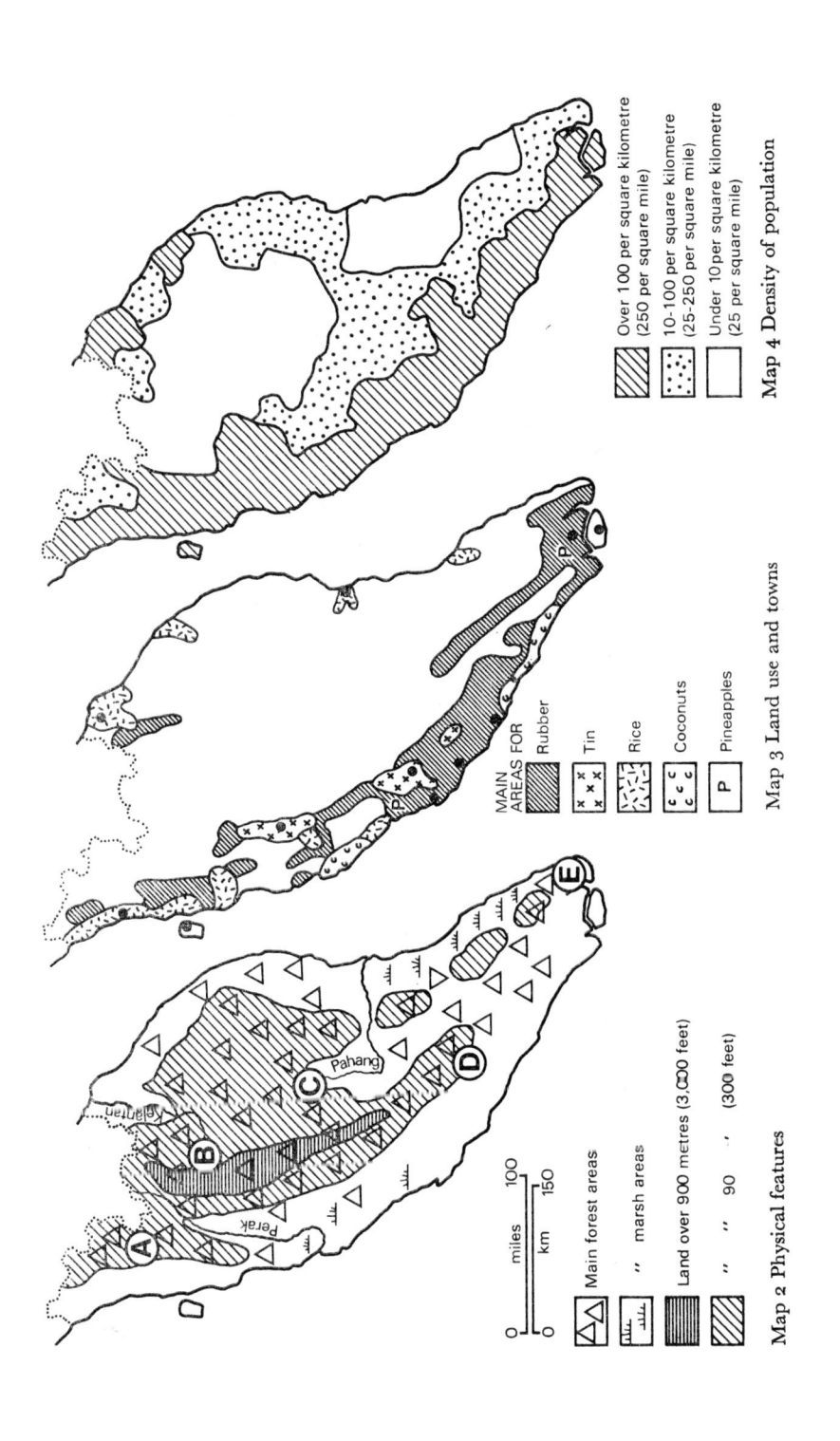

Map 2 Physical features

△△ Main forest areas
⋏⋏ marsh areas
▓ Land over 900 metres (3,000 feet)
▒ " " 90 " (300 feet)

Map 3 Land use and towns

MAIN AREAS FOR
▒ Rubber
×× Tin
⋎⋎ Rice
cc Coconuts
P Pineapples

Map 4 Density of population

▒ Over 100 per square kilometre (250 per square mile)
∴ 10–100 per square kilometre (25–250 per square mile)
☐ Under 10 per square kilometre (25 per square mile)

	Over 250mm (10")

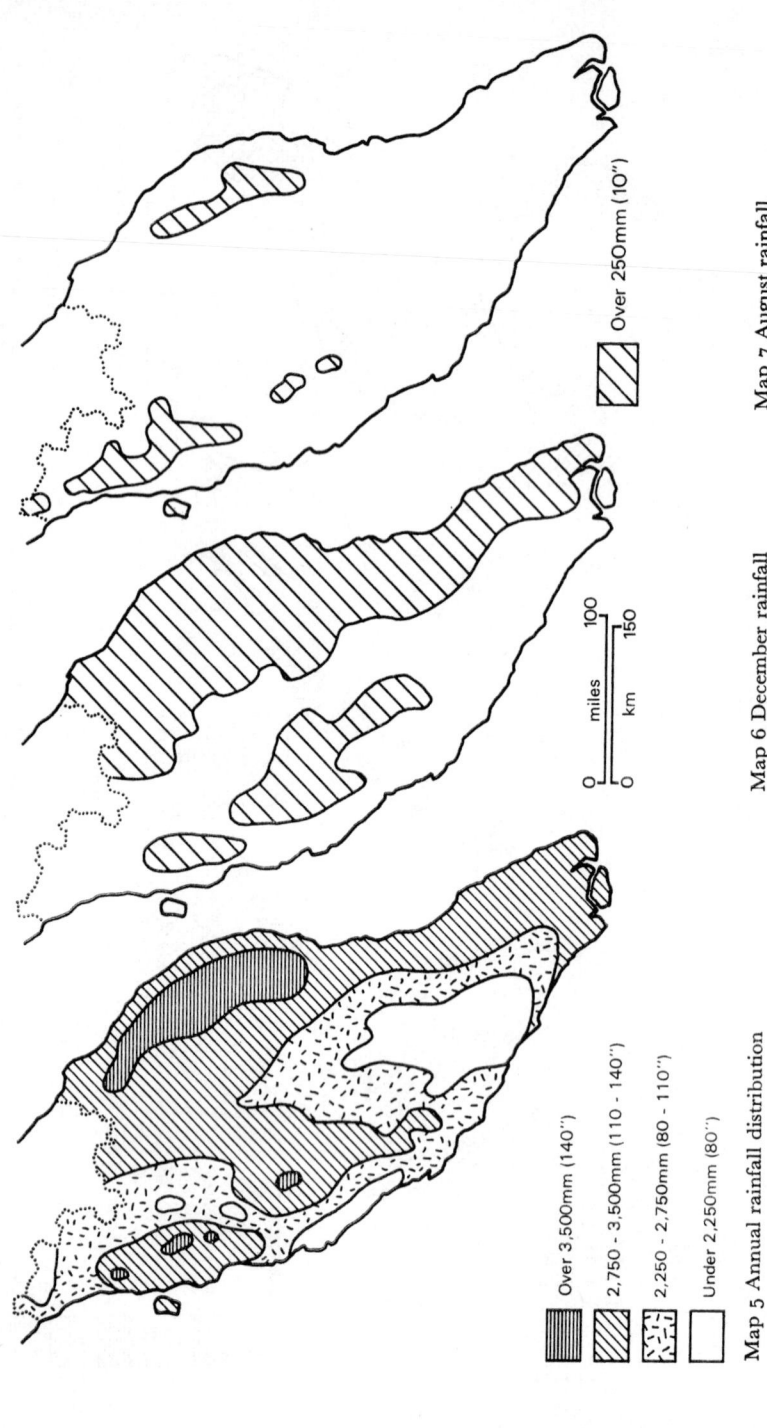

Map 7 August rainfall

Map 6 December rainfall

	Over 3,500mm (140")
	2,750 - 3,500mm (110 - 140")
	2,250 - 2,750mm (80 - 110")
	Under 2,250mm (80")

Map 5 Annual rainfall distribution

(*continued from page 270*)
  6. December rainfall of Malaya and Singapore
  7. August rainfall of Malaya and Singapore
  8. 'Awang's Saka'
  9. Kelantan—location of 'Awang's Saka'

Descriptive extracts

1. From Marion Ward's case-study 'Awang of the Temiar' in *Malaya and Singapore* (Educational Supply Association)

2. From Ooi-Jin-Bee *Land, People and Economy in Malaya* (Longman)

3. From John Slimming *Temiar Jungle* (John Murray)

Figures (graphs, tables, etc)

1. Temperature and rainfall figures of Penang (Table A)
2. Daily rainfall cycle at Kuala Lumpur (Fig. A)
3. Annual work cycle and sources of food of shifting cultivators of Malaya (Table B)
4. Plan of a Temiar longhouse (Fig. B)

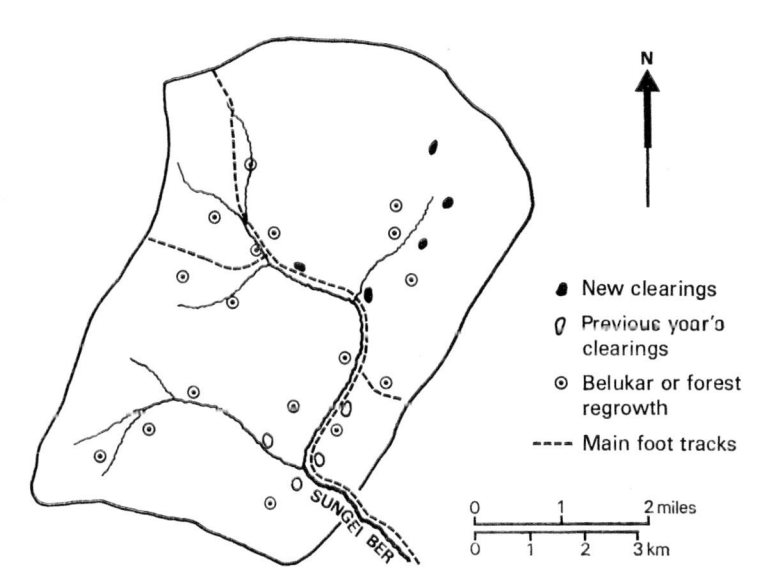

Map 8 Awang's saka (From Ward, *Malaya and Singapore*)

Photographs

1. An aboriginal ladang in the Malayan highlands (Plate 1)
2. An air-drop over the Malayan forests (Plate 2)
3. A close-up of the equatorial forest (Plate 3)

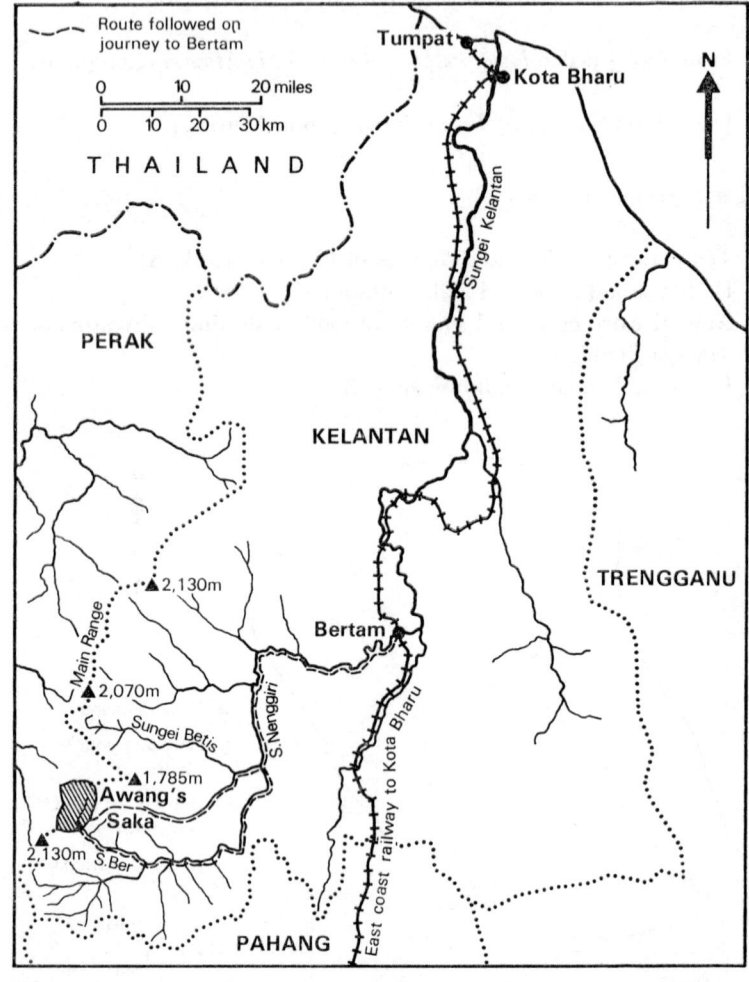

Map 9 The state of Kelantan, showing position of Awang's saka (From Ward, *Malaya and Singapore*)

Table A Climatic information

PENANG	J	F	M	A	M	J	J	A	S	O	N	D	Range Total
Temp. °C	27	27	27	28	27	27	27	27	27	27	26	26	2
°F	80	80	80	82	80	80	80	80	80	80	79	79	
Rain Inches	100 4	75 3	125 5	180 7	280 11	180 7	225 9	330 13	480 19	410 16	280 11	125 5	2790 110

Fig. A Daily rainfall at Kuala Lumpur

Fig. B Plan of a Temiar longhouse (From Ward, *Malaya and Singapore*)

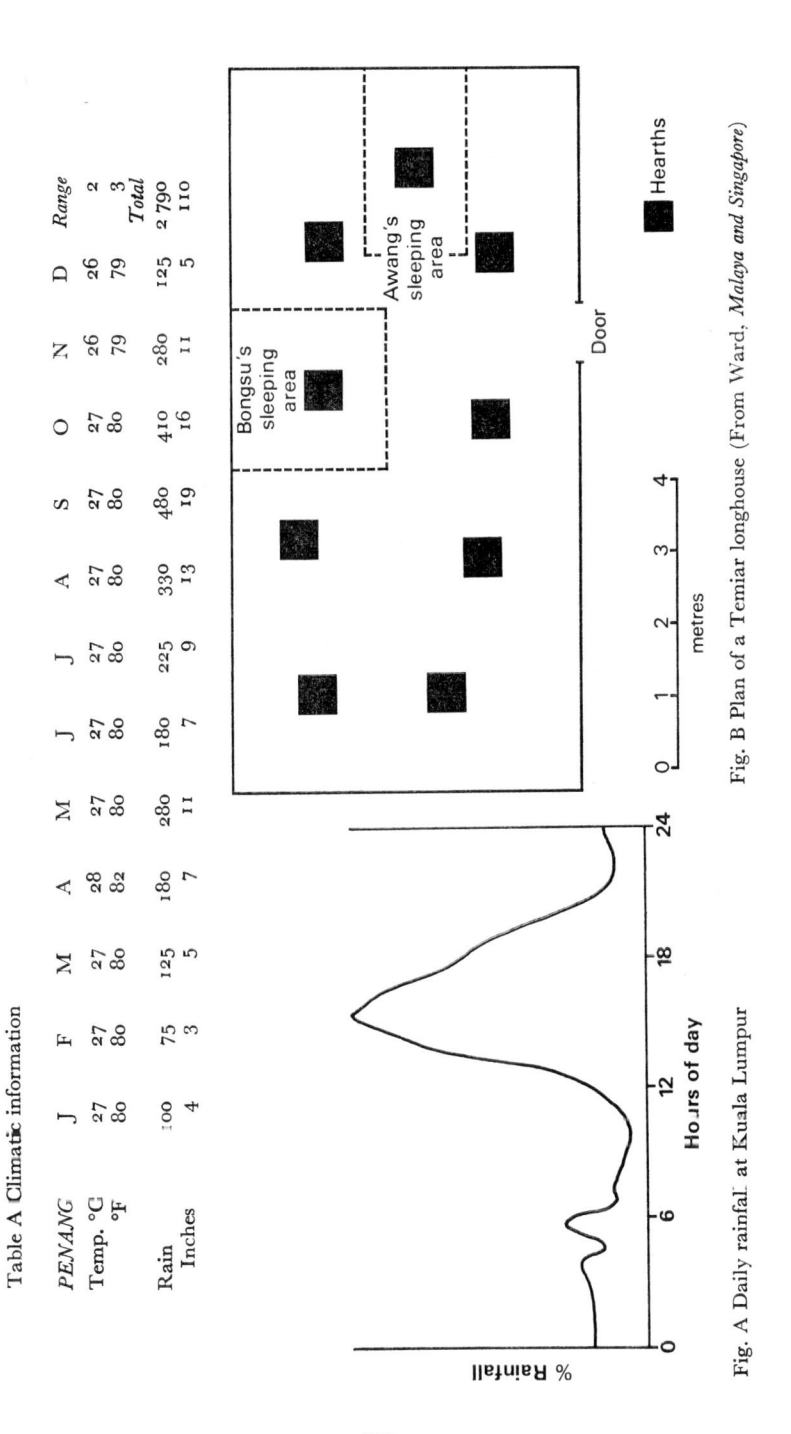

275

Table B Aboriginal shifting cultivators of Malayan highlands (including Semang, Sakai, Temiar)—annual work cycle and sources of food of shifting cultivators

PERIOD	AGRICULTURAL WORK	OTHER WORK	SOURCES OF FOOD
April-May	New LADANG (clearing) site selected and initial area of two or three acres cleared.	Some collection of jungle produce, eg bamboo.	Tapioca from last year's harvest. Food purchased in exchange for jungle produce. Animals, fish and roots.
May–June	Initial site burnt and planted to maize, tapioca and banana. Felling of main ladang started.	Temporary shelters erected, followed by erection of new houses.	As above
July–August	Main ladang burnt and planted to hill padi, tapioca, maize, yams and sweet potato.	Fruit season. Various fruits and nuts collected.	As above
September–October	Some weeding	Repair of fish traps. Some fishing.	As above, plus maize. End of fruit season.
November–December	Harvest of the main padi crop.	Durian (type of fruit) season.	As above.
January–March	None	Fishing and collection of jungle produce.	Padi, new tapioca, yams, sweet potatoes, etc. Sale of jungle produce.

From Jin-Bee *Land, People and Economy in Malaya* (Longman) p. 181

Extract 1

AN ACCOUNT OF THE CLIMATE OF MALAYA

Largely because of its position between two oceans Malaya is a wet country. Only in the highest parts of Britain is there as much rainfall as in the driest parts of Malaya. Twice a year the wind system which controls the weather of south and east Asia sweeps back and forth in rhythm across the Malayan peninsula. From October to March north-east winds blow from the South China Sea. These bring heavy rain to the eastern side of Malaya (Map 6). From June to September the south-westerly winds dominate, but because Sumatra shelters southern Malaya, the hot summer months are often moderately dry (Map 7). The months of April–May and October–November are periods of changeover and often have disturbed weather with much heavy rain. Each month in Malaya has some rain, and some have more than 635mm (25″). The wettest parts of Malaya are high up in the mountains. Rain falls heavily in Malaya, but only rarely does it last for days on end. Often a storm (usually in the afternoon as a result of convection) blows over in a few hours and the hot sun makes the air steamy afterwards (extract 2).

Malaya is only just north of the equator and thus it has very warm and even temperatures. It is almost always more than 24°C (75°F), the temperature of warm summer days in England. Often the nights are a little cooler than the days, but there is not much variation between seasons. The coolest places are the highest.

Extract 2

Then, away at the eastern end of the valley the clouds banked together and became dark and swollen. They moved slowly and heavily in the sky and in the jungle there was no movement. Only the heat and the stillness and the silence of the midday. And the bank of clouds came surging up the valley, blanketing the hilltops, and from afar came the grumbling of thunder and the noise of the rain in the trees like soldiers marching. Suddenly a soft wind came, gently, moving the tall grasses, whispering through the tops of the high trees. The aborigines called out, 'It will rain, Tuan. It will rain.' Hari Singh stirred, rolled over and looked up at the sky. I breathed the wind in through my mouth, making my lungs go big with it; pulled open the front of my shirt, feeling it cool on my bare chest. The soft wind became stronger and less gentle and the leaves moved and then the branches and then the trees themselves swayed in the strong, sudden wind. I sat waiting for the rain, thankful for the wind, listening to its music high in the trees.

The noise of the rain came first, moving swiftly along the valley, and then big drops of rain spattered into the dust making a speckled pattern on the dried earth of the track across the clearing. It hissed on the bare rocks and then the clouds were upon us and the rain was coming from above, forcefully, pounding down into the parched earth; running in little rivers between the cracks in the boulders, splashing in puddles, seeping down deep into the dried grass; cascading in tiny waterfalls from the ends of branches; spouting from lengths of creeper; dripping in crystals from the tips of the leaves; bubbling and gurgling as it rushed in small torrents through the roots of the trees. The air became brighter and the sultriness of the day vanished. The Temiar moved out from under the trees and stood in the wet, their faces upturned to the sky. I stood up and took off my shirt, feeling the sharp stinging of the rain on my back and chest, feeling the water trickling down the small of my back and down my thighs. We stood in the open, feeling the rain and enjoying it.

The rain poured heavily and the trees all along the valley were bent under the force of it. Sheets of water were dashing against the earth, cascading swiftly into the streams, and the wind caught the rain and tossed it back against the mountains. The mountains roared, the swollen river sang with the noise. We laughed together and shouted to make ourselves heard above the noise of the drenching rain.

After the rain stopped we continued our march. The climbing became more difficult and the track slippery. The afternoon sun shone into the valley. Swirls of mist were hanging on the hillsides and white scarves of low cloud draped the ridges. It was steamily hot.

Abus now walked behind barefooted—his proud shoes hanging by the laces across his neck. Chabok climbed, just ahead of me—his feet digging into the ground as mud squirmed between his splayed toes like red-brown toothpaste. Hari Singh, at the back with the porters, was suffering from cramp a great deal. We were all moving slowly. It was at this stage that I found I had forgotten to bring any salt tablets with me—a fact that I was to regret bitterly during the next few days. From the crest of another ridge we looked back the way we had come and the rain-washed valley, shafted with sun and mist, looked desolately beautiful.

Source: Slimming, *Temiar Jungle: a Malayan Journey* (John Murray, 1958).

Extract 3

Awang is a young man of the Temiar, one of the aboriginal groups who inhabit the uplands of Malaya. With his wife, Along, and about thirty other people he lives in the mountains of south-west Kelantan. This particular group of Temiar live near the headwaters of the Sungei Ber. You can find it on Maps 8 and 9. The river flows east for about twenty miles until it joins the larger Sungei Nenggiri, as the upper Sungei Kelantan is called. Some of the highest mountain peaks of Malaya lie in this area. Range after range of jungle separates it from the vastly different coastal lowlands.

(Source of Extracts 3, 4, 5, 6, 8, 9 and 10: Ward, *Malaya and Singapore,* Educational Supply Association, 1963.)

Extract 4

The group of Temiar to which Awang belongs have always lived in this area. It is their *saka*, the land belonging to their fathers. Similar groups occupy many other remote river valleys, but the total number of people is small. Occasionally people from neighbouring valleys meet but generally they have few visitors. There is little contact with Malays, Chinese or Europeans from the outside world.

Extract 5

The Temiar, like many other primitive jungle peoples, live together in community houses called 'longhouses'. You can see a plan of Awang's longhouse in Figure B. It is very simple to build such a house. First the men of the group fell trees and clear the ground in the chosen place, leaving one or two stumps to help support the house. They collect sturdy bamboos from the jungle and use them and a few sapling trunks to support the structure and form corner posts, roof supports and rafters. More bamboos are laid horizontally to make the floor, and a few are used to form the walls. The floor is four or five feet above the ground, and a ramp of bamboos, or a notched tree trunk, forms a ladder up to the door. The roof and part of the walls are covered with a thatch of palm leaves.

Inside the house there are definite positions for each family. These consist of a hearth made of earth placed inside a wooden square. Two or three logs smoulder continually in the hearths and there is always a pile of firewood drying nearby. Smoke filters out through the roof. The sleeping area for each family is near its hearth. On the walls hang tools, fishing nets and lines, and the rafters are a storage place for spare weapons, traps, bamboo lengths, mats and other objects.

Extract 6

The Temiar, like all the aborigines in Malaya, know a great deal about the jungle. They know the uses to which every plant can be put as food or shelter, or to make utensils or tools, or as medicine. They understand the lives of animals, and the growing cycles of plants, especially when the end result is edible. For example, one of the native fruits of Malaya is the *durian*. It grows on big trees which bear fruit in July and August and sometimes again about December. The fruit has a rough green spiny coat but inside this each seed is surrounded by a custard-like yellow flesh, which is very pleasant to eat, although the fruit has a very strong unpleasant odour. When the *durian* season arrives Awang's people move to a temporary camp near a *durian* grove on the banks of the Sungei Ber, and stay there feasting on *durian* for several days.

Probably the most important single plant to the Temiar is the bamboo. There are many different sorts of bamboo. Some grow 60 feet high and have stems several inches across. Others are thin and slender. Some have spines on their stems and all grow quickly and densely. The big ones are used for building houses, bridging rivers and making rafts. The bamboo stems are hollow but are stiffened at intervals by solid cross-walls called nodes. Bamboo is, in fact, a giant grass. Short sections of wide diameter stems are used as containers. The quivers for blowpipe darts are made in this way. It is always necessary to have containers for water, and the women carry and store it in bamboo lengths about four or five feet long with a node at the bottom end. The making of blowpipes requires thin bamboo with clear stems up to eight or nine feet long. Such bamboo grows only on high mountains in Malaya and the Temiar make long journeys specially to get it.

Extract 7

The technique of ladang cultivation
A site of 20 acres or more is selected on the basis of the appearance of the ground and an initial area of 2 to 3 acres is felled with axes and parang. A fairly steep hillside is usually chosen so that there will be a good updraught when firing takes place. The tallest trees at the highest point are cut down and on falling drag down the smaller trees in their paths. In this way a great deal of extra labour is saved. The timber is left to dry for three to six weeks and is then set on fire. When the ashes have cooled, the crops—maize, tapioca, hill padi, banana, chillies and sugar cane— are planted. The planting holes are made with pointed digging sticks and a few grains of padi or maize tossed into each hole. Tapioca, banana and sweet potato are planted by cuttings. The work may be done communally or by family groups. House building, however, is always a communal effort, with the men doing the heavy work such as cutting the poles, while the women make the thatch for the roofs.

After the houses have been built the main *ladang* is cleared by communal effort and the timber burnt when dry. The burning must be carefully controlled in order that the houses are not set alight or the existing crops destroyed. Planting takes place as soon as the *ladang* has cooled.

Source: Jin-Bee, *Land, People and Economy of Malaya*, Longman, 1963.

Extract 8

Most of the daytime of the Temiar is taken up in the production of food. The main sources of supply are the *ladangs*. Although every year new clearings are prepared there is little difference in the sequence of work. Awang's group have several *ladangs* in use. The largest is about six acres and there are three others of about three acres each. At the end of each wet season the sites for the new clearings are chosen by Bongsu and the other men of the group. (Kelantan faces the South China Sea and winds from the north-east bring rain from November to March.) All the group then move to the site of one of the new *ladangs*, on the valley slopes, and live in temporary shelters for some weeks. The men start felling the forest with axes and *parangs* or jungle knives.

A clearing is used only for two years, as by the end of that time the soil has become less fertile. The land requires a rest period of many years so that forest vegetation can cover it and refertilise it through the rotting of dead leaves and branches. If the full forest does not have time to develop before an area is reburnt and recultivated a dense growth of shrubs (called *belukar* in Malaya) and frequently a tough grass (called *lalang*) appear. *Lalang* is very hard to remove, and such areas are not useful either for aborigine gardens or for growing forest trees. The Temiar understand this, and under normal conditions they clear some acres of new forest each year. They leave their old *ladangs* to return to forest.

Extract 9

About once a year the Temiar make a journey down the valley to Bertam. They make rafts of lashed bamboo lengths on the edge of the river. Each carries three men, while the cargo is lashed to the raft to prevent it floating away when the raft goes below the surface. The journey is very exciting because there are many rapids to shoot. In the afternoon they reach the junction of the Sungei Ber and the Sungei Nenggiri, and Awang's people stay the night in this area with another group of Temiar.

Next day the three men go on down the Nenggiri, which is much broader and smoother than the Sungei Ber. By late afternoon they reach the great bend where the river runs east to Bertam. Here they find a suitable sleeping site, usually on a river terrace about twenty feet above river level. Two of the men go off into the jungle to find palm leaves for a temporary shelter, while the other collects wood, and sets about making a fire, using a flint to ignite it. One of the men brings back a pheasant he has shot with a blowpipe, while the other returns with some wild bananas. These and the cooked tapioca they have brought with them form the evening meal.

The next morning they set out again, to reach Bertam by midday. Here they stay in a rest house built by the Malayan Department of Aborigines. They abandon the bamboo rafts, and take their goods to the store of a Chinese trader. In return for their produce, they take back rock salt, some lamp oil, a length of cloth, a new parang, and some tobacco. On other occasions they might take back rice grown on the plains round Kota Bharu.

The journey back takes much longer as it is made on foot, but the Temiar men are lucky to get a lift back up to the junction of the Sungei Betis in a government boat belonging to the Department of Aborigines, as one of its staff is going upstream to visit a group in the Betis valley.

Extract 10

What the future holds for the Temiar people is difficult to know. They may not be able to go on living their primitive life in the forests. The young men may find that by venturing out they can earn money to buy food and clothing instead of painstakingly searching the forests to provide them. It is possible that groups like the Temiar will merge with the overall Malayan population. They could lose their language, their craft and skills, their identity as Temiar people. But it is almost certain that more and more European medicines and foods will penetrate to such aboriginal groups. This may strengthen them by improving their health, their birth rate could rise and their death rate fall. This could put much pressure on their forest environment. On the other hand, diseases they were not accustomed to could wipe them out. It may be that through the care of the Malayan Department of Aborigines, groups such as the Temiar will move out of their jungle fastnesses, and perhaps settle on its fringes, supporting themselves by small craft industries such as basket making and wood carving. They might well become submerged by more numerous and more sophisticated peoples, as has happened in other parts of the world.

A. *To establish the location of Malaya in its 'world region'*

1. With the help of your atlas, fill Table 1, comparing the latitude and longitude and size of the Malayan peninsula with Britain. Approximately how long would it take to reach Malaya (a) by ship (b) by aeroplane?

Table 1

	Malayan Peninsula	Britain
Latitude	....	....
Longitude	....	....
Greatest length	....	....
Greatest width	....	....
Time distance (sea)	BRITAIN – MALAYA:	
Time distance (air)	BRITAIN – MALAYA:	

2. With the help of your atlas, mark and name on Map 1
   (a) The countries of Malaysia (Malaya, Sarawak and Sabah (British North Borneo));
   (b) Colour these in, and then in a different colour shade in the islands making up *Indonesia* (not all of which are shown on this map) (Java, Sumatra, Bali, Lombok, Kalimantan (Borneo) and Sulawesi (Celebes));
   (c) Other main islands and mainland countries, indicating approximate boundaries;
   (d) The main rivers shown;
   (e) The main towns shown;
   (f) The Equator and longitude 100° E.

B. *To establish the location of the Temiar people in the Malayan peninsula and the nature of the environment in which they live*

1. Refer to Maps 2 and 9 and Extract 3. The location of the Temiar people on Map 2 is in the vicinity of

   A
   B
   C
   D
   E.

2. Which of the following most characterise(s) the environment in which the Temiar people live?

   1. upland
   2. lowland
   3. forest
   4. marsh. (NB Coding as for MS4 items page 201.)

3. Refer to Maps 5–7; Fig. A, Table A and Extract 1. Answer the following questions on the climate of Malaya.

   (a) In general the climate is .... (temperature) and .... (rainfall), with an annual rainfall of over ...., and a very small .... of temperature, of................

   (b) The position varies, however, between different parts of Malaya. Rainfall amounts in summer tend to be less in .... Malaya, which is sheltered by the island of .... On the other hand, heavy rain is received on the east coast, brought by winds crossing the .... The wettest and coolest places in Malaya are ....

   (c) The climate of Malaya is of the equatorial monsoon type. From other sources find out the meaning of the word *monsoon*.

   (d) Draw a labelled sketch map to show how the monsoon process affects the Malayan peninsula.

   (e) In Extract 1 it is stated that heavy rainstorms occur daily as a result of *convection*.
   - (i) How does this relate to the graph of daily rainfall (Fig. A)?
   - (ii) Find out what is meant by convection, drawing a labelled diagram to illustrate.

   (f) (i) Draw a temperature and rainfall graph to illustrate the figures for Penang (Table A).
   - (ii) What does the graph show, in relation to the description given in Extract 1?
   - (iii) State *four ways* in which the climate differs from that of your home area in Britain.

   (g) Refer to Extract 2.
   - (i) Describe in your own words the weather changes during the day, referring especially to the relationship between temperature, wind and rainfall.
   - (ii) Indicate briefly how the coming of the rain affected the feelings of the people in the group. Why should this be the case?
   - (iii) What are the effects of the rainfall likely to be on (A) the jungle landscape; and (B) the patterns of work of the people?

4. (a) Refer to the three photographs, Plates 1–3. Describe in your own words at least *three* of the characteristic features of the Malayan forest.
   (b) How does it compare with (i) temperate deciduous and (ii) coniferous forest? Give at least *three* similarities or differences in each case.

5. (a) Outline ways in which relief and climate affect the natural vegetation of central Malaya.
   (b) Find out from other sources something of the nature of the soils of the area (i) under forest cover; (ii) after the forest cover has been removed.

c. *To demonstrate ways in which the idea of adaptation to environment is exemplified by the case of the Temiar group*

1. The type of agriculture practised by the Temiar is *shifting cultivation*.
   (a) State briefly what this means.
   (b) Show how it differs from
      (i) padi farming on the Malayan lowlands,
      (ii) food collection,
      (iii) nomadism.

2. Refer to Extracts 7 and 8.
   (a) Shifting cultivation involves the creation of a clearing or ....
   (b) Relate in *four stages* the cycle by which forest eventually returns to forest under this system.
   (c) The main reason why the clearing is abandoned after two years or so is the fact that
      A the forest has invaded the farmland
      B the settlement is regularly invaded by hostile tribes
      C the soil has become less productive as a result of tropical downpours washing away fertility
      D the people like a change of environment at regular intervals.
      E wild animals, insects and tropical diseases drive the people to safer or healthier locations.
      (Tick the correct answer.)
   (d) With the help of Table B, Extracts 5, 6, 7 and 9, and Plate 1, show how the Temiar use the forest environment for purposes other than the production of food.

(e) Refer to Fig. B, Extract 5 and Plate 1.
  (i) Describe the living quarters of the Temiar people and of the group illustrated in the photograph.
  (ii) How do the two compare? Try to explain any differences you note.

3. (a) The shifting cultivation system helps to *conserve* the forest. Give a reason why this is so.
   (b) What would happen, however, if this system were practised in a densely populated forest area?

4. (a) The economy practised by the Temiar is mainly of a *subsistence* type, meaning that the products are collected or produced entirely or very largely for their own use. Which of the following reasons help(s) to explain this
      1 The remoteness of the forest restricts trading opportunities
      2 The Temiar are so isolated that they do not realise there are other people to trade with
      3 There is little surplus of food and other products available to trade with
      4 The Temiar do not like using other people's products.
      (NB Coding as for MS4 type, page 201.)
   (b) Table B suggests that some of the aboriginal tribes do some trading, however. This takes the form of exchange of .... for ....

D. *To demonstrate the impact of the external world on the Temiar and other aboriginal people of Malaya*

Over time, contacts with the outside world have been established by trading; missionary effort; government agencies; international agencies; and, in the case of Malaya, major conflicts over the last thirty years or so, including the Japanese invasion of World War II; internal strife between the British and Communist guerrillas after World War II (Plate 2) and troubles between Indonesia and Malaysia (which resulted in jungle warfare training of the type shown in Plate 3).

1. (a) Show how Plate 2 illustrates the idea of *technological change*, through the feature shown above the forest canopy, and from what you know about what is going on below the forest canopy.
   (b) In what way could the form of contact shown be (i) helpful (ii) damaging to the local people?

2. (a) Refer to Extracts 3, 4 and 9. State *three* difficulties in establishing contacts between the Temiar and other people.
   (b) Refer to Extract 10. State two possible advantages for the Temiar arising from the establishment of contact with the outside world.
   (c) This extract also suggests that the people might lose their *identity*. Explain the meaning of this statement.

E. *To draw attention to the idea of different environmental perceptions*

1. *A hostile environment*
   (a) Refer to Plate 3. Give *three* reasons why the soldier shown on the picture might regard the natural environment in which he is placed as 'hostile'.
   (b) Suggest ways in which the Temiar people might take a different point of view.
   (c) Assume you are a Temiar youth who has never set eyes on a white man before. Discuss possible interpretations you might put on his presence, and speculate on the world from which he might have come.
   (d) What sort of information would you need to support or correct your speculation?

2. *A 'primitive' way of life*
   Imagine you are a soldier serving in the Malayan jungle during World War II.
   (a) Write a letter home to your family trying to establish that the local people are 'primitive'.
   (b) Supposing you know the native language well enough to communicate, indicate (i) how you would try to convince a Temiar that he lived a 'primitive' way of life; (ii) how he might reply.
   (c) Write down a list of ways in which the Temiar way of life and skills (i) differ from (ii) are similar to your own.

F. *To demonstrate that the problems facing the Temiar are similar to those facing other aboriginal groups in the world*

1. (a) With the help of a dictionary, define the term 'aboriginal'.
   (b) Give four examples of aboriginal groups, stating the part of the world in which each is found, and giving very brief details of the

nature of the environment (equatorial forest, desert, etc). Name a 'competing' group of people, past or present, for each example.

Group	Area	Environment	Competitor
(i)..................	....	....	....
(ii)..................	....	....	....
(iii)..................	....	....	....
(iv)..................	....	....	....

(c) Locate these groups on an outline map of the world. Show on this map the general distribution of different aboriginal peoples, equatorial forest and desert environments.

(d) What do the equatorial forest and desert environments that have 'attracted' aboriginal peoples have in common?

2. *Project—The clash of cultures*

   (a) Different class groups (or individuals) should choose examples of cases in which, in the past or today, an aboriginal culture has suffered from contact with a more advanced culture. Information can be collected from encyclopaedias, the *Geographical Magazine* and other similar sources, newspaper accounts, history and geography texts, travel books, documentary films on television, etc.

   (b) In each case the group should, for their choice, (i) describe the nature of the environment and the aboriginal group's adaptation to it, in words, maps, drawings and models; (ii) show differences between the aboriginal and the competing culture, identifying the nature of the problem; (iii) suggest ways in which the problem can be overcome; (iv) report back to the class as a whole, using this background as a basis for informed debate of the issues.

Second Curriculum Unit

The Changing Accessibility of Southport

Placing in curriculum scheme (see p. 260)

    Integrating theme: **Movements and Networks**
    Sub-section: Journeys to work and for pleasure
    Timing: Unit in final term of third year, taking not less than three weeks.

Aims

As with the previous unit, there are broad cognitive and social aims which are common in all cases. Here it is also appropriate to think of stimulating interest in the local area and, very important in urban and transport studies, to integrate historical with spatial perspectives. A spatial approach is aimed at, as appropriate to this topic.

Objectives

These are deliberately not specified here, for reasons which will become apparent when the 'questions' section is reached (page 304).

Materials: resources for learning

In this case, the information sections *are* included with the 'worksheets'. The range of materials utilised includes maps, photographs and descriptive extracts, and also, in this case more particularly, a series of matrices, tables and different sorts of graphs.

The worksheets

1. Introduction: change through time—population

The resort and dormitory town of Southport grew largely in the nineteenth century, as the figures in Table 1 show:

Table 1

Dates	Population
1801	2 500
1821	3 000
1841	8 500
1861	16 000
1883	42 000
1901	64 000
Today	84 000

As good communications are essential to such a town, to promote access for holiday makers and commuters, it could not prosper until adequate transport facilities were developed. Before 1792 Southport did not exist, and the original village of the area, named North Meols, was isolated to the east by a belt of low lying mossland, water-logged in winter (Map 1).

Dates of opening of Leeds and Liverpool Canal and railways

Leeds and Liverpool Canal (+ Bridgewater Canal extension to Wigan) —before 1800.
Southport–Liverpool Railway—1850
Southport–Manchester Railway (via Wigan)—1855
Southport–Preston Railway—1882

Extract 1 Canal

To such as are more disposed to economise money than time, the canal packets offer a cheap conveyance from Liverpool and Manchester as well as on the whole line of intermediate country to Scarisbrick Bridge,*

---

* Scarisbrick Bridge is shown on Map 1. Some of the early travellers were miners from the Wigan area who walked the remaining six miles to Southport. Others came from Manchester and Liverpool—before the railway era the only reasonable road was via Ormskirk (Map 6)—and, if they could afford it, hired coaches which took them from Scarisbrick Bridge to Southport.

where a number of hansom carriages are stationed to convey passengers to this place of fashionable resort.

Source: E. Baines *History, Directory, and Gazetteer of the County Palatine of Lancaster* Vol. 2 (1825) (David & Charles reprint, 1968), p. 552.

Extract 2   Rail

The week which ended Saturday, June 2nd, was a memorable one for Southport. Never before within memory has the town witnessed so bustling a scene as its streets presented during Whit-week. The railways from the manufacturing districts poured in their thousands daily, who flowed through the streets in one vast long stream, and swarmed on the vast expanse of shore like a newly disturbed ant-hill.

Source: *The Southport Visiter* (sic) June 7th 1855 (on opening of railway from Manchester).

Extract 3   Rail

That if the proposed line of railway were opened, so that persons engaged in business in Liverpool could go to and fro at little expense of time and money, great numbers of them would reside at Southport during the summer, and many would make it their permanent place of abode.

Source: Local petition to the House of Lords, 1847. Quoted in F. E. Bailey, *A History of Southport* (1955).

(a) Refer to Table 1 and draw a line graph to illustrate the growth of population of Southport, with population forming the vertical axis and dates the horizontal axis.
(b) Refer also to Extract 2, and mark on the graph an arrow to indicate the period at which railways first reached Southport. Is there a connection with (a)?

2. *The effect of physical features on lines of communication*

(a) Refer to Map 1 and either a ¼" or 1 : 50 000 OS map of this area. Give reasons for the detours in the routes at points A, B and C on Map 1.
(b) Write a brief explanatory account of how physical features have affected, if at all, (i) canal, (ii) rail and (iii) road communications west of Wigan.

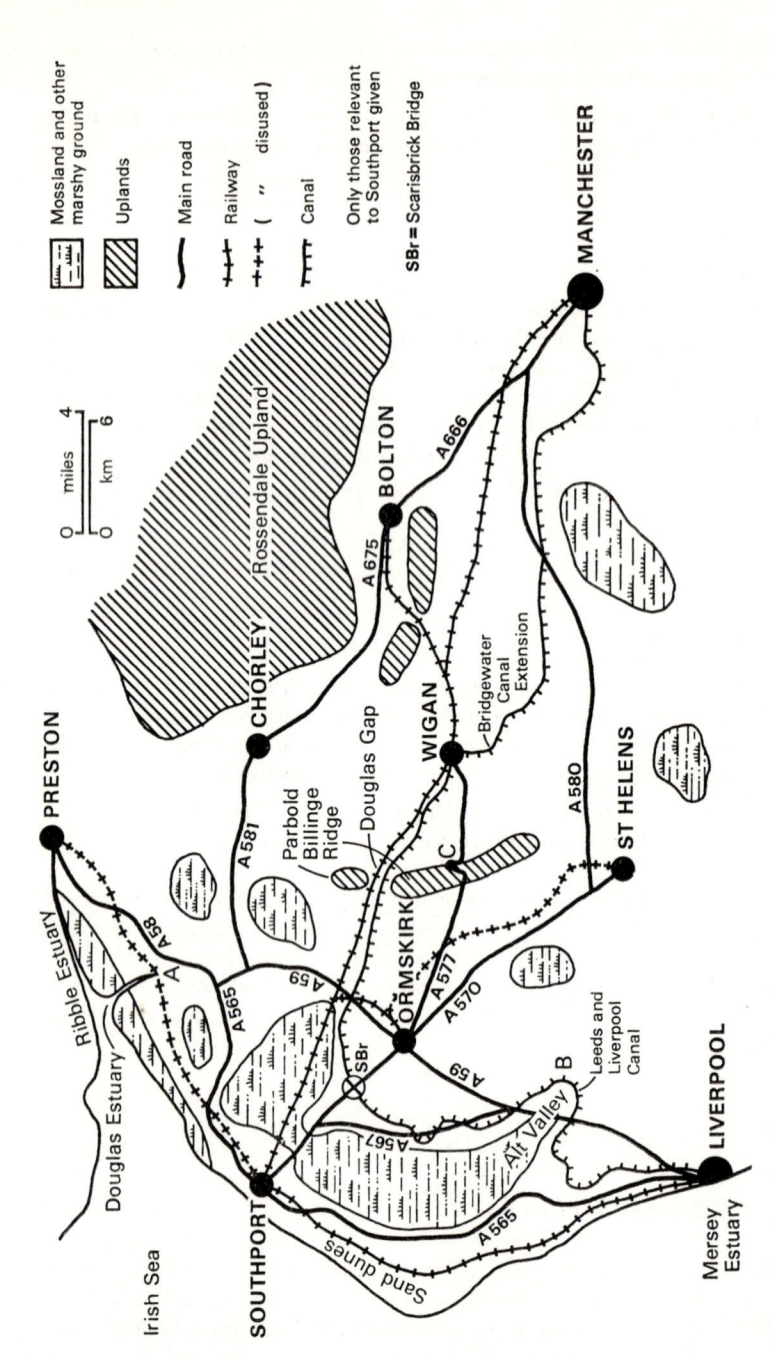

Map 1 Southport's communications links

3. *Access.* To illustrate the concept of access in terms of ground distance

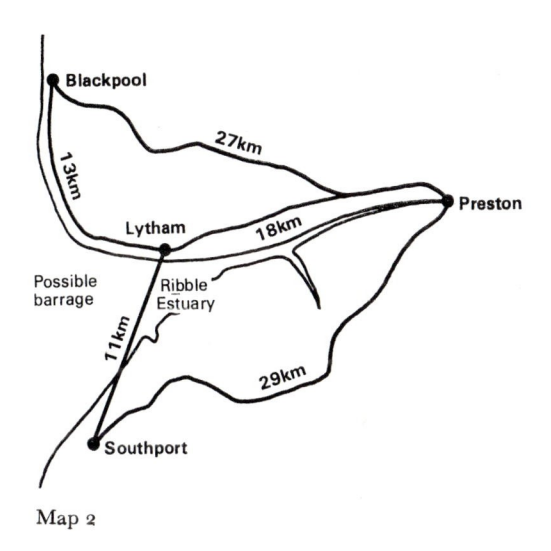

Map 2

Present road distance

	B	L	P	S
B	//			
L		//		
P			//	
S				//

Matrix 1 Pre-barrage road-distance

New road distance

	B	L	P	S
B	//			
L		//		
P			//	
S				//

Matrix 2 Post-barrage road-distance

(a) Complete the matrices, using information on Map 2.
(b) Which town is most centrally placed (has shortest total road distance to all the others).
(c) Work out the straight line distance between the towns (ie construct new matrix).
(d) Calculate *detour index* for each town (divide sum of its road distance column by straight line distance and multiply by 100). By comparing pre- and post-barrage figures examine its impact on the four towns.

(Based on Briggs, *Introducing Transportation Networks* (University of London Press, 1972), p. 42.)

Table 2 Distances between Southport and important towns in south Lancashire

	Kilometres		
Southport to	Straight Distance	Actual Road Distance	Detour Index
Preston	25	29	
Bolton	40	50	
Wigan	27	33	
Manchester	54	64	
St Helens	29	31	
Liverpool	25	33	

(e) Complete the missing detour indices in Table 2. These give a measure of the directness of access between places.

(f) Work out the detour indices (see Map 1) for the railway lines between Southport and Manchester (via Wigan) ...., St Helens .... Liverpool ...., Preston ....

(g) Which two towns in each case are (i) most directly ...., ... (ii) least directly ...., ... linked by road to Southport?
(iii) Complete Map 3 in the manner shown for Preston, using information from Table 2.

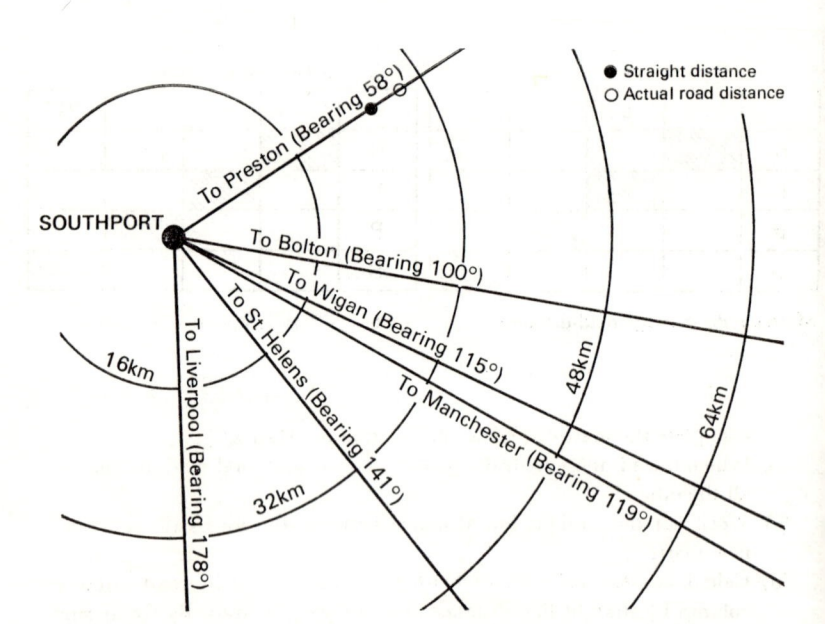

Map 3 Road distance map (Based on Everson & Fitzgerald, *Settlement Patterns*. Longman, 1969), pp. 125–6.

(h) Briefly outline your judgement of the effectiveness of the different methods of presentation of information in Table 2 and Map 3.
(i) Have these methods shed any new light for you on the idea of 'access'? If so, show how.

4. *To illustrate the concept of time distance*

Table 3 The changing accessibility of Southport over the years in respect of *time distance**

Southport to	Travelling Times (to nearest 5 minutes)					
	Foot (A)	Stage-coach (A)	Canal Stage-coach (A)	Rail (B)	Bus (B)	Car (A)
Preston	4h 30m	2h 15m	(NA)	30m (SC)	55m (E)	30m
Bolton	7h 45m	3h 30m†	(NA)	50m**	2h†	1h†
Wigan	5h	2h 30m	4h 45m	25m	1h 30m	45m
Manchester	10h	5h†	8h 30m	50m**	2h 30m	1h 30m§
St Helens	4h 45m	2h 25m‡	(NA)	1h 15m (S) (SC)‡	1h 15m‡	45m‡
Liverpool	5h	2h 45m‡	5h 30m	40m(S)	55m(E)	45m
Approx Dates	Pre-1800	1800–1850		1850 onwards 1900 onwards		

KEY (A) The following average speeds are assumed—
  Foot and Canal boat   4 mph
  Stagecoach   8 mph
  Car   30 mph
 (B) For rail and bus journeys, timetable times are given
 (S) Stopping trains (express services not significant)
 (E) Limited stop buses (giving faster times than normal services)
 (SC) Rail service now closed   (NA) Not applicable

{ † via Chorley;   ‡ via Ormskirk;   } See
{ ** via Wigan;   § via A580 (East   } Map 1.
{   Lancashire Road)   }

* This table and key are complicated, and it is essential that you should read them carefully. It is useful to go through them with the rest of the class, so that your teacher can clarify any difficulties.
  As this is an exercise going back in time, mileage distances will be used rather than kilometres. But bear in mind that you were previously working in kilometres.

(a) Refer to information given in Table 3 (page 295). (i) Complete the bar graph (Fig. 1) in the way the first section has been done.
(ii) Write down the different forms of transport in order of speed from fastest to slowest.

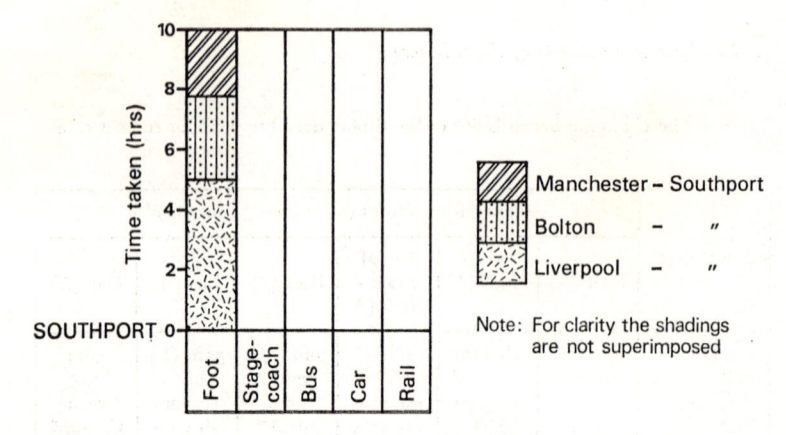

Fig. 1

(b) Refer again to Table 3. (i) Indicate a route for which the order on Fig. 1 is not strictly accurate. (ii) Refer to Map 1, and give a possible reason.
(c) Refer to Table 1 and to Table 3. (i) Which form of transport led to the most marked improvement in the accessibility of Southport measured in terms of time distance?.......... (ii) At what period was this form of transport introduced?.......... (iii) At what period did Southport's population increase most rapidly?.......... (iv) Comment briefly on the significance of the answers to (ii) and (iii).
(d) Refer, if available, to the new 1:50 000 maps of South Lancashire, or an up-to-date road map. Assuming speeds of 50 kph on ordinary roads and 100 kph on motorways, work out approximately the present time distance between (i) Southport and Manchester (using A567, then M57 and M62).......... (ii) Liverpool and Manchester (using M62)..........

5. *To illustrate the concept of cost distance*

Today, the most rapid form of transport to Southport, as shown on Map 4 opposite, is not necessarily the most used. One possible reason for this may be because of the question of *comparative costs*.

Plate 1 An aboriginal ladang in the Malayan highlands (The village shown here is not a Temiar village.) *Camera Press*

Plate 2 An airdrop over the Malayan forests *Camera Press*

Plate 3 A close-up of the Malayan jungle *Camera Press*

Plate 4 Steam train on Cheshire Lines Railway running through sandhills near Southport (Lord Street) in the late 1940s or early 1950s

Plate 5 Electric train *from* Liverpool to Southport at Freshfield Station (see Map 7), 1964

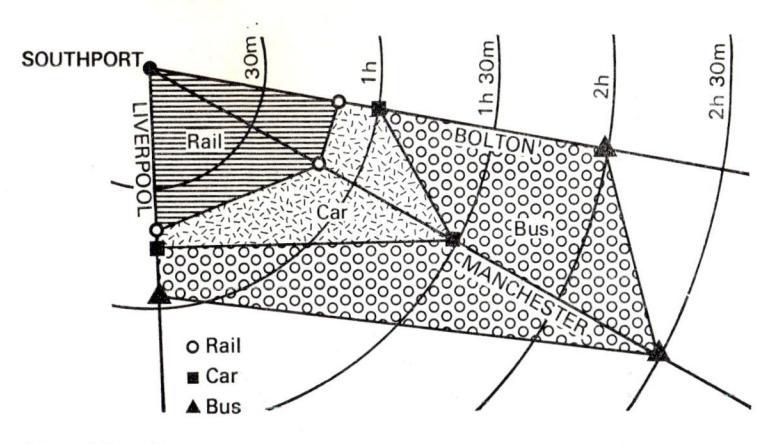

Map 4 Time distance map

Map 4 is a time distance map for connections between Southport and Bolton, Manchester and Liverpool.

(a) On which route is it most advantageous and on which least advantageous to use rail transport in terms of time distance?
   Most advantageous..........
   Least advantageous..........

(b) On which route is it least disadvantageous and on which most disadvantageous to use bus transport in terms of time distance?
   Least disadvantageous..........
   Most disadvantageous..........

Table 4 Cost of travel from Southport to Bolton, Manchester and Liverpool (in 1974)

Southport to	Train*	Bus†	Car‡
Bolton	£1.12	£1.30	£3.10
Manchester	£1.49	£1.47	£4
Liverpool	76p	62p	£2

* Day return fare (starting before 9.30 am)
† Return fare
‡ Assessed at 5p per mile (hence 80 miles return journey Southport–Manchester would be £4, which approximately covers the average cost of petrol, depreciation, etc, at 1974 prices).

(c) Complete *cost distance* Map 5 (page 298), using similar methods to those on Map 3, and information given in Tables 2 and 4.

297

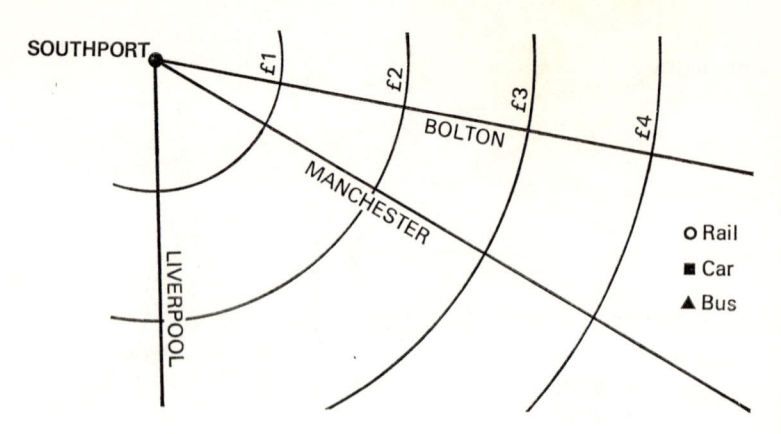

Map 5 Cost distance map

(d) Write a brief account to bring out differences between Maps 4 and 5.
(e) Using information given in previous maps and tables (a) describe differences in routes available, and time taken in travelling between Manchester and Southport (i) today, (ii) about 1830; (b) explain the various considerations you would take into account in deciding on a particular means of travelling at these two dates. (Do not necessarily confine your reasons to information given above; other factors can operate also.)

6. *To illustrate the concept of economic competition in a geographical setting*

Competition between routes (Southport – Liverpool)
Information
Before 1850 a traveller from Liverpool to Southport could take three main routes, as Table 3 and Map 6 show.

In 1884, an alternative rail route, known as the Cheshire Lines Extension railway (see Plate 4) was built between Liverpool (Central Station) and Southport (Lord Street Station)—connecting near Gateacre Station with a line from Manchester Central—in direct competition with the coastal line between Liverpool Exchange and Southport Chapel Street stations (see Plate 5). Information about this is given on Map 7 (page 300) and in Table 5. The Cheshire Lines railway to Southport closed in 1953. In 1904, the Exchange–Chapel Street line was electrified, allowing a considerable gain in time distance (see Table 5), as electric trains did not need to 'get up steam' on leaving each of the many stations on this commuter line.

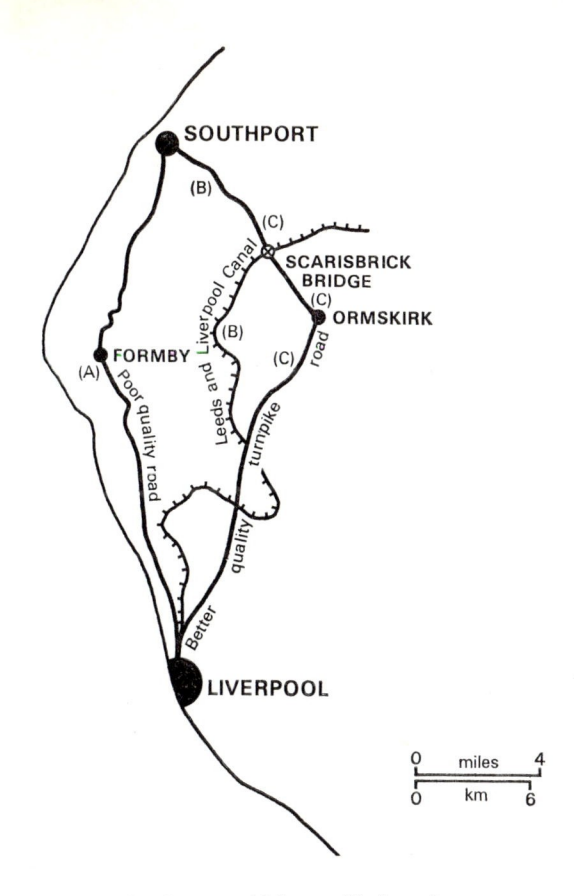

Map 6 Routes between Southport and Liverpool before 1850

Table 5

		Southport – Liverpool	Journey Times	Trains per Day
1952		Chapel St – Exchange	40 mins (S)	71
		Lord St – Central	1 hr 20 mins (S)	3
1887		Lord St – Central	1 hr 20 mins (S) 48 mins (E)	13
		Chapel St – Exchange	57 mins (S) 35 mins (E)	19

(S) Stopping Train
(E) Express

(a) (i) Refer to Map 6, and calculate the detour indices for routes (A) (foot) .... (B) (canal/stagecoach) .... and (C) (stagecoach) ....

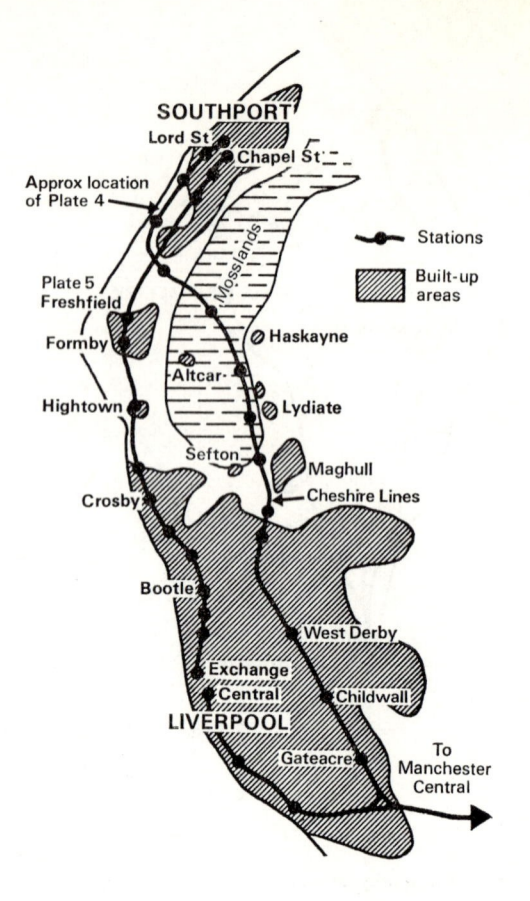

Map 7 Routes between Southport and Liverpool 1884–1953

(ii) Which is the longest route from Liverpool to Southport in terms of distance 'on the ground' ....; time distance ....?
(iii) State in each case one reason for using each of the routes (A) ....; and (B) .... (C) ....
(b) Refer to Map 7, and calculate the detour indices of the two railway routes: (i) Chapel St – Exchange..........; (ii) Lord St – Central ....
(c) Refer to Table 5 (on page 299) and compare the rail services available between Liverpool and Southport in 1887 and in 1952.
(d) Give as many reasons as you can to suggest why the Lord St – Central railway route (Cheshire Lines) was not competitive with the Chapel St – Exchange route, on the basis of evidence from the maps and photographs.

7. *To investigate the growth and decline over time of a rail network**

This involves a look at the science of *topology*, a branch of geometry, which is concerned with the *relationships* between points, lines and areas, all of great importance in geography, but NOT with actual distances, straightness of lines, or size of areas (pages 64–5). The following terms are used. (See also Fig. 2.)

Node—point
Arc—line (edges)
Region—area
Network or Graph—combination of nodes and arcs

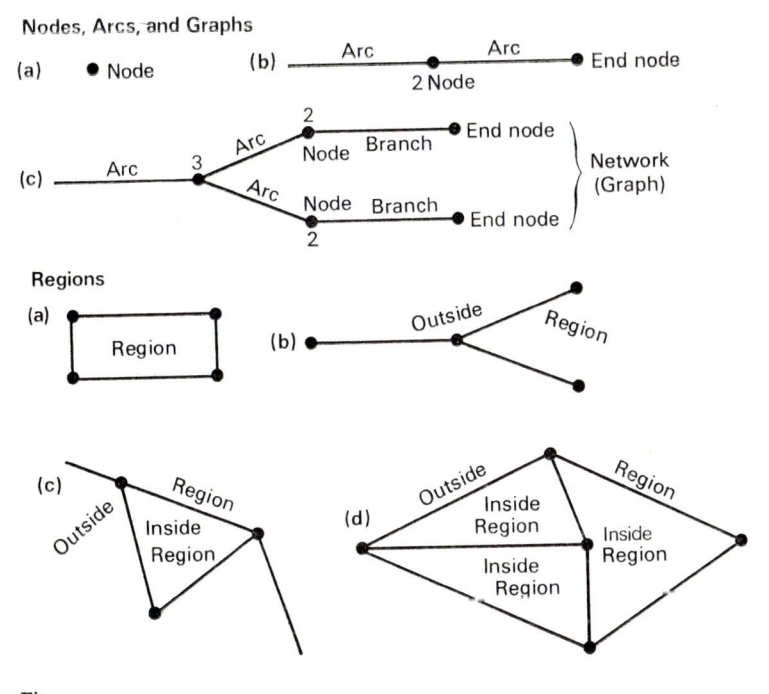

Fig. 2

---

* Reference should be made to Briggs, *Introducing Transportation Networks* (University of London Press, 1972) for fuller details of this method and its rationale.

Connectivity—This refers to the completeness of links between nodes. A high degree of connectivity implies a high density of transport network and an area of economic prosperity. A low degree of connectivity suggests either the opposite, or perhaps an area in an early stage of economic development. Indices used to measure connectivity (including region-branch ratio and cyclomatic number) are a useful means of comparing the transport networks of different areas. The existence of a large number of branches and end nodes in a network indicates a low degree of connectivity. The existence of regions in a network suggests a high degree of connectivity.

Region-branch ratio explains itself.

Cyclomatic Number—number of arcs − number of nodes + 1. (Based on Briggs: pp 14–15.) See Fig. 3 for examples.

Region – Branch Ratio = 1:4

Cyclomatic Number = 6 − 7 + 1 = 0

B = Branch
IR = Inside Region

Region – Branch Ratio = 4:0

Cyclomatic Number = 9 − 7 + 1 = 3

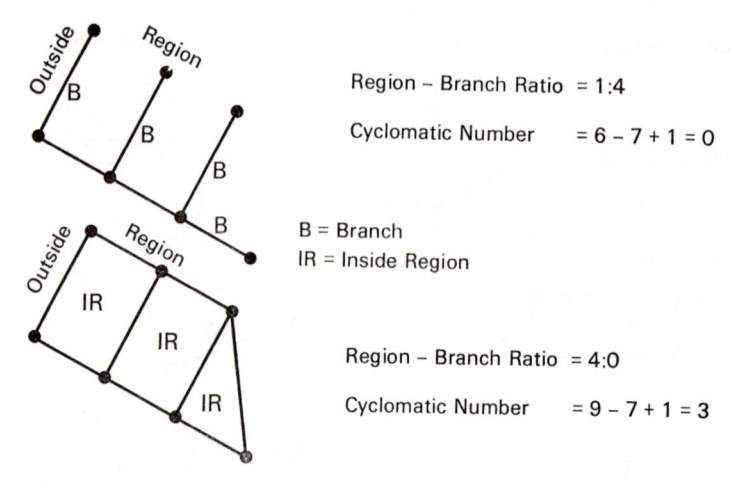

Fig. 3

(a) Work out the region branch ratios and cyclomatic numbers in the examples given in Fig. 4.
(b) Describe the changes which have taken place in the system over the last 125 years, placing them in the most appropriate of the following three periods: (i) 1850–75; (ii) 1875–1950; (iii) 1950 to date.
(c) What is the main advantage of using the method of analysis given above?
(d) From other sources, find out the various reasons which brought about the growth and decline of the railway system in south-west Lancashire. Refer back also to pages 290–1.

(i) 1850 region-branch ratio..........
Cyclomatic number..........

(ii) 1875 region-branch ratio..........
Cyclomatic number..........

(iii) 1900–50 region-branch ratio..........
Cyclomatic number..........

(iv) 1975 region-branch ratio..........
Cyclomatic number..........

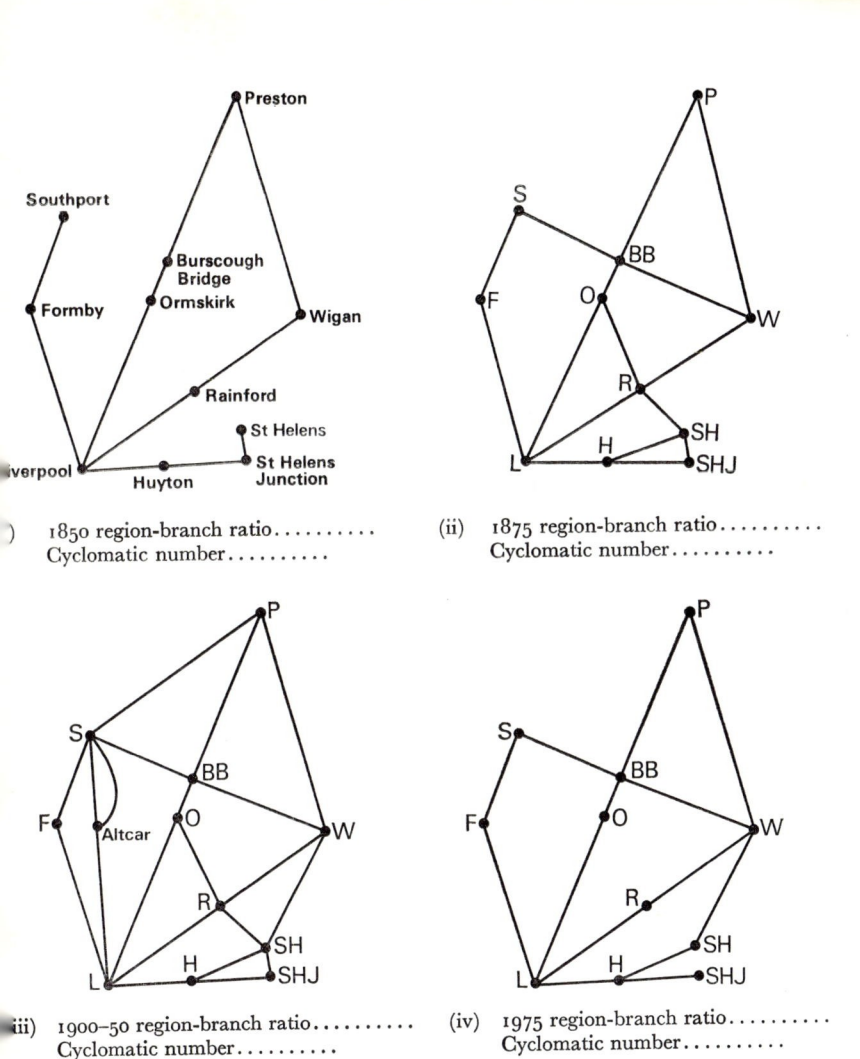

Fig. 4 The railway networks of south-west Lancashire

Priority readings

1. CRAVES, N. J. *Geography in Secondary Education* (Geographical Association), Chapter 5, pages, 11–53.
2. LONG, M. & ROBERSON B. S. *Teaching Geography* (Heinemann). See, for example, Chapters 3–13.
3. WALFORD, R. (ed.) *New Directions in Geography Teaching* (Longman). See Part I, pp. 9–66.

4. See *Classroom Geographer* (obtainable from N. E. Sealey, 3, Wensleydale, Luton, Beds.) for many examples of ideas for planning lesson units.

Questions for investigation and discussion

1. Identify the abilities which are being assessed in each of the questions in the Malayan curriculum unit.
2. On the lines suggested in the Malayan curriculum unit, specify a series of objectives appropriate to the material in the 'Changing accessibility' curriculum unit.
3. Identify a topic you wish to provide for a particular secondary school age group. Use the matrix entitled Area of Study (see also pages 209–10), which you should enlarge for use, to specify the detailed concepts and exemplars which will concern you.* In the 'boxes' under 'Principles' provide a code number relating to a separate sheet which will be needed to provide space for writing out the principles.

Area of Study   Content Levels

Abilities	Exemplars (incl. materials)	Concrete Concepts		Abstract Concepts		Principles
		Vern.	Tech.	Vern.	Tech.	
Recall Skills						
Comprehension Skills						
Problem-solving Skills						
Creative Skills						

* It is not, of course, appropriate to fill in all the boxes (conversely some of the concepts will presumably appear at more than one ability level).

16 Conclusion

Attention was drawn in the introductory chapter to the broad interpretation placed upon the term 'evaluation' in this book. It has been argued that the teacher's work inputs should be as closely scrutinised as the pupil's, and the two seen as integral parts of one curriculum process. A linked aim has been to erode the credibility gap between theory and practice. In attempting this, theory has been related both to the classroom context in general and to a subject area in particular. In these final chapters, theory has been explicitly translated into practical schemes of work.

There are obviously many effective teaching schemes in operation which do not seem to have this kind of backing of theory. This usually means that they go back to earlier, perhaps in some cases satisfactory, models. Reliance purely on practical experience can, however, easily result in stagnation and even complacency. Conventional wisdom is not appropriate to a changing situation—the one in which the contemporary teacher finds himself—which requires the adaptability, open-mindedness and autonomy of the 'extended professional'.[1]

There are those who are resistant to the infusion of educational theory yet would claim to be innovators in their own field. Here the danger is that change may be of an exclusive, subject-orientated variety, in which little attention is paid to extra-subject variables. A new type of orthodoxy replaces an earlier one. Conversely, change from outside the disciplines can also be blinkered, equally concentrated upon a single variable, reflecting, maybe, a commitment to a child-centred ideology. Thus the disciplinary contribution comes to be seen as expendable, and the balance of the curriculum process is again distorted.

It is insisted that there are differences between a course consciously underpinned by theory, and one which is not. These might briefly be illustrated by the Malayan course unit (pages 267–8). In, for example, an 'enlightened traditional' (page 74) approach, the in-depth case study element would probably be present, but there might well be a tendency to devote over-much attention to the 'folksy' content about the aboriginal group, with each element in the wealth of interesting material in the Marion Ward case study treated as of equivalent weight. No criteria for selective emphasis would be present. Important concepts and principles would not *as of necessity* be highlighted as central objectives of learning. They would remain implicit. Comparisons between 'primitive' and 'advanced' societies would tend to be of the 'them and us', 'contrasted ways of life' variety. The notion of treating the materials openly as a contribution to social education would not be envisaged, at least not in any calculated way.

Having said all this, it has to be accepted that the innate quality of the teacher *does* ultimately over-ride in importance theoretically-based learning frameworks, however cogent these may be. In themselves, such bases can make only preliminary contributions. To be effective, they need to be internalised by those who have to put them into operation. All teaching schemes will benefit from a sound theoretical underpinning. But this is different from saying that such an underpinning is a guarantee of good practice.

An historical perspective has been presented to throw light on the slow accretion of progress in geographical education through, for example, the introduction of new and gradually accepted models: in this century the Herbertson model, the case-studies model and now explicitly conceptual models. There have been others which have not gained acceptance. Is it too optimistic to believe that this slow progress has led to a healthier state in geography education today than thirty years ago, and healthier then than thirty years before? Even if this is the case, there have at *all* stages been good and bad geography teaching, forces of progress and reaction. Advantages today are that developments in both curriculum theory and the academic world of geography are running on converging tracks; there is a broader appreciation of the need for practitioners and theoreticians to co-operate in structured curriculum planning; the examination boards are at last becoming seriously involved in curriculum change. If the need for in-service provision to cope with the increasingly burdensome demands on teachers is met, there is just a chance that history may prove to be a less than accurate predictor, and fairly rapid improvement may take place.

'If well taught' is, however, one of the biggest provisos there is. It means more than having practical skill, though technical prowess is essential. If, as applied to geography, it does not mean trying to infuse meaning and refine thinking, and to seek a major role for the subject in social and environmental education, then, like

E. G. Ravenstein in 1885, 'I am quite willing to admit that the hours spent upon geographical instruction might be employed to better purpose.'[2]

References

1. See HOYLE, E. (1974) 'Professionality, professionalism and control in teaching,' *London Educational Review*, **3**, 13–19.
2. RAVENSTEIN, E. G. (1885) 'The aims and methods of geographical education' in *Report of the Proceedings of the Royal Geographical Society in Reference to the Improvement in Geographical Education* (1886) (Murray, London), 163.

Index

Affective Domain (Kratwohl-Bloom), 28, 34–6, 80, 131, 247, 249
Aims in education, 4–6, 9–11, 14–18, 20, 22, 34, 42, 48, 73, 131, 169, 171, 208, 261, 265, 267, 289
Ambrose, P. J., 67, 93
American High School Geography Project, 96–7
Analysis (Bloom category), 29–30, 33, 37, 91, 113, 149, 213, 235
Application (Bloom category), 29–31, 33, 37, 91, 149, 179, 211–13, 232
Area-based studies, 116, 120–21
Assessment, 3, 5–7, 26, 30, 35, 37, 109, 143, 171–2, 210–11
  Formative (internal), 155, 158, 165–167, 171, 192, 240–41, 266, 269
  Summative (*see also* external examinations), 165–8, 171
Attitudes, 16, 34–7, 42, 49, 67, 131, 141, 148, 157, 197–8
  Assessment of, 7, 35, 172, 246–52
Ausubel, D. P., 1, 32–3, 37, 49, 93, 131, 155
Autonomy (as an aim), 9–11, 19, 34, 48, 131, 265, 305

Bailey, P. J. M., 151
Beliefs, 34, 51, 69
Bennetts, T., 44
Bernstein, B., 73, 111, 121, 126, 129
Berry, B. J. L., 69
Blaut, J. M., 132–4
Bloom, B. S., 28–35, 37, 44, 91, 148, 155, 212–13, 233, 251
Briggs, K., 293, 301
Bruner, J. S., 49, 93, 120–22, 134, 143, 261
Bulletin of Environmental Education (BEE) 92

'Capes and Bays', 17, 73, 75, 78, 208
Carswell, P. J. B., 34, 247–9
Case (sample) studies, 59, 74, 85–6, 89, 158, 243, 255–7, 261, 305

Centre for Educational Research and Innovation (CERI), 5
Certificate of Secondary Education (CSE), 84, 150, 152, 171, 239–42
Child-centred education, 106–7
Classification (Bernstein), 74, 111, 252
Cognitive Domain (Bloom), 28–30, 35–6
Cole, J. P., 64, 92, 244
Combined (Related) Studies, 105, 108, 127
Component skills (of teaching), 146–8, 150
Comprehension (Bloom category), 29, 32–3, 37, 149–50, 209, 211–13, 216
Concentric approaches, 15, 85–6, 121, 158, 255–8, 261
Concept(s), 6, 10, 26–7, 32–3, 37–9, 40–4, 49–52, 54, 91, 93–6, 110, 118–19, 122–5, 134, 136–40, 148, 150, 158, 194, 206, 212–13, 228, 233, 255, 257–8, 268, 306
  Abstract, 39–40, 93, 97, 100
  Concrete, 39, 41–2, 136
  Derived, 50–3
  Enrichment of, 137, 157–8
  Indigenous (discrete, peculiar, unique), 49–55, 109
  Key, 40, 113, 121
  Technical, 39–41, 50, 93, 97, 100, 117, 159, 268
  Trans-disciplinary, 41, 50, 114, 121, 123, 125
  Vernacular (common-sense), 39–41, 50, 52, 100, 117, 121, 136, 159, 267
Concept-based learning, 86–7, 120–21
Conceptual frameworks (structures), 42–3, 48, 51, 54, 93–6, 255–7, 262–263, 306
Conceptualisation, Levels of, 132, 136–140, 159
Course work, Assessment of, 7, 172, 239–42, 245–6
Creativity, 11, 33, 37, 108, 149, 171, 179, 211–12, 229, 239, 245

308

Criteria
  choice of curriculum content. 28, 38–39, 41–2, 99, 154, 306
  of truth (Hirst), 27, 32, 48–54, 117
Criterion-referenced tests, 165, 216
Cultural Heritage, 17, 42
Culture bias, 182–3
Curriculum
  Collection-type, 111
  Common core, 105
  Frameworks, 7
  Integration, 6, 105–9, 111–12, 115, 120, 125–6, 255, 266
  Models of, 4–5, 8, 256–61, 305–6
  Planning, 3, 9, 11, 22, 27, 30, 38, 47–48, 73–4
  Process, 3–5, 7, 305
  Theory, 1–2, 87, 306
  Units, 7, 22, 44, 53, 100, 125, 258, 266, 303

Data response questions, 185, 229
David, T., 57–8, 70
Davis, W. M., 82–3, 86
Decentration, 134–5
Determinism, 58, 60, 65, 73, 78–9, 91, 156, 202, 205, 213
Dickinson, R. E., 93
Discrimination index, 192, 216
Distractors (multiple choice items), 190, 206–7, 213, 216
Domicentricity, 134
Drives (*see also* pupil motivation)
  Achievement, 10, 143, 145
  Affiliation, 10, 143–5
  Cognitive, 10, 143, 145, 156

Ebel, R. L., 177, 182, 196
Ecosystem(s), 62, 69, 89–90, 258
Educational Testing Service (ETS), 215
Educational Theory and Practice, 1–3, 7, 265, 305–6
Empathy, 10–11, 18, 251, 267
Environment
  Behavioural/Phenomenal, 61, 66, 87
Environmental
  Education, 10, 14, 116, 266, 306
  Preferences, 67
Environmentalism, 58, 81
Essay(s), 7, 26, 172, 175–85
  Marking, 156, 176, 184, 189
European Studies, 121, 124
Evaluation, 3–5, 211, 213, 305
  (Bloom category), 30, 33, 37, 91
Everson, J., 244, 294

Exemplars, 3, 33, 37, 42, 44, 73, 137, 139, 194, 212
External Examinations, 35, 73–5, 84, 145, 151, 165–9, 175, 195, 199
  Backwash effect on schools, 195, 209
  in Curriculum Innovation, 170–1, 306
Extrapolation (Bloom category), 30, 37
Eyre, S. J., 78, 89

Facility Index, 192, 216
Fairgrieve, J., 13, 15–16, 77, 86
Feedback, 5, 28, 150, 156–7, 159, 166–7, 184–5, 192–3, 215–16, 229, 240, 247, 266, 269
Field work, 74, 81–4, 151, 171, 239–45
Fitzgerald, B. P., 76, 88, 294
Framing (Bernstein), 74, 111, 252

Gagné, R. M., 27, 32–3, 37, 49, 93, 157
Geikie, A., 17, 77
General Certificate of Education (GCE), 165, 179, 182, 238–40
Geographical Association (GA), 184
Geographical
  Factors, 60, 73, 79, 201, 208, 213
  Games, 90–1, 183
Geography
  Behavioural, 61, 65–9, 92, 183
  Mathematical, 64–5, 88
  Models in, 63–4, 69, 77, 86–7, 89, 132
  'New', 58–9, 63, 67, 76–7, 86–8, 100, 172, 265
  Quantitative, 58–9, 64–5, 69, 87–8
  Reality in, 81–6, 158
  Regional, 37, 53, 57, 59, 62–3, 70, 77–9, 86–9, 93, 248
  Scientific, 88, 183, 244–5
  Social Justice and, 68, 70, 248
  Traditions of (Pattison), 37, 54, 57–8, 73, 99, 261, 265; Area studies, 57, 59, 69, 73–4, 78, 99; Earth science, 58, 99, 115, 118, 258; Man-Land/Environment, 50, 53–4, 57, 61–2, 69, 78, 99, 258, 267–8; Spatial, 53, 57, 59, 62, 69, 94–6, 99, 289
Geography, 92, 216
Geography for the Young School Leaver, Project (Avery Hill College), 104
Geography 14–18, Project (Bristol), 92, 170
Geography in an Urban Age (AHSGP), 97
Goldsmith, Rev. J., 14, 75, 79
Gould, P. R., 92, 100, 124, 135

Graphicacy (Balchin), 69, 80, 133, 141, 183
Graves, N. J., 52-3, 119
Guesswork, 196-8, 200

Haddon, J., 16, 20
Haggett, P., 62-3, 95
Harris, A., 9-11, 18
Harvey, D., 53, 60, 68, 87
Heimatskunde, 81-2
Herbertson, A. J., 77-9, 86, 306
Hirst, P. H., 18, 27, 30, 32, 48-53, 55, 57, 70, 93, 112-13, 125
Historical perspective, 3, 73-4, 167-9, 306
History, Geography and Social Science 8–13 Project (Liverpool), 36, 40
Home-school relations, 156-7
Hudson, B., 172, 189, 239
Humanities, 27, 105, 109, 112-13, 115, 117-19, 122
Hypothetico-deductive reasoning, 134, 136, 139-40

Idiographic, 59, 100, 117
Incorporated Association of Assistant Masters (IAAM), 242
Indoctrination, 10, 93
In-service provision, 6, 111, 127, 198, 306
Inspectorate (HMIs), 75, 82, 85
Instrumental (aims), 12-14, 24, 143, 171
Inter-disciplinary Enquiry (IDE), 62, 69, 109-10, 112, 118-19, 121, 123-124, 127, 151, 265-6
Interest (enquiry) based approaches, 76-7, 106-8, 123, 154
Interpretation (Bloom category), 29, 37, 211

Jargon, 7-8, 89
Jay, L. J., 77-8, 80
Joint Matriculation Board (JMB), 246
Journal of School Geography, 15

Kelly, P. S., 170
Keltie, J. Scott, 75
Kerr, J. F., 4, 8
Kirk, W., 66
Knowledge (Bloom category), 28-32, 212-13
  (Harris, Hirst, etc.), 4, 10, 25-8, 32, 48-9, 148-9
  Common-sense, 47, 52
  Fields of (Hirst), 49-52, 70, 113
  Forms of (Hirst), 27, 49-53, 113
  Sociology of, 47-8
  Structure of, 27-8, 38, 47-50, 107-9, 112, 118, 265
  Unity of, 107-8
Kratwohl, D. R., 27, 34, 247, 249

Learning
  Concept, 33, 37
  Developmental, 32, 132-40
  Individualisation of (independent), 28, 145, 151, 156-8, 269
  Mastery (Bloom), 142, 155
  Meaningful, 18, 32, 37, 86, 131-2, 136-7, 143, 195, 265
  Principle (proposition), 33, 37, 140
  Rote, 17, 32-3, 37, 73, 75, 78-80, 85-86, 195, 209
  Time as a factor in (Carroll), 142
Liberal education, 48, 50, 52
Literacy, 11, 69, 80, 141
Local studies, 120-21, 154, 257
Locational Analysis in Human Geography (Haggett), 95
Long, M., 85-6, 247
Lowenthal, D., 65, 67

Macintosh, H. G., 170, 172, 189, 215, 239, 242
Mackinder, H. J., 77, 80, 86
Macro-environment, 132-4
Mager, R. F., 23-4, 28, 30, 35
Man: A Course of Study (Bruner), 122
Map(s) (as tools, etc.), 57, 63-4, 80, 88
  Cognitive/Mental, 67, 69, 91-2, 132-133
  Reading/interpretation, 79-80, 120, 136
Mappability (Simons), 53
Masterton, T., 121, 189
Micro-teaching, 150, 152-3
Mixed-ability teaching, 127, 141, 151, 154, 157
Moderation, 240-42
Moral Education/Judgement, 10-11, 18, 52, 112, 115
Multiple Choice and Structured Questions in Geography (Marsden), 216
Multiple Choice Item(s), 7, 172, 190-224
  Analysis, 215-23
  Banking, 215, 223-4
  Reviewing, 215, 223
  Types, 196, 199-202
Multiple marking (of essays), 176

National Foundation for Educational Research (NFER), 215
National Society for the Study of Education, 23
Nomothetic, 59, 100, 117
Non-verbal communication, 147, 249
Norm-referenced tests, 165
Note taking (Howe), 74, 150–1
Numeracy, 11, 69, 80, 141, 183
Nuttall, D. L., 182, 239
Nystuen, J. D., 94–5

Object lessons, 84–5
Objective questions/tests, 172, 177, 185, 189–90, 228
Objectives, 4–6, 9, 17–18, 22, 28–9, 32, 34, 37–8, 43, 49, 52, 117, 122, 169, 179, 206, 209, 211, 235, 265, 267–8
  Behavioural (operational), 22–6, 30–31, 44
  Levels of generality of, 25–7, 37–8, 40, 42, 121, 265
  Pre-specification of, 23, 25–8
  Triviality of, 25–6, 28, 39, 76, 198
  Worthwhileness of, 28, 32, 39, 41, 99
Options (multiple choice tests), 190, 206–7
Organisation for Economic Cooperation and Development (OECD), 5–6, 8
Outdoor Pursuits, 116

Participant observation, 248–50
Pattison, W. D., 57–8, 61, 70
Payment by results, 22–5
Pedagogic control (Holly), 145
Peel, E. A., 139
Perception(s), 61, 67, 69, 92, 114, 135
Percepts, 137
Perceptual problems, 132–5, 141, 158
Peters, R. S., 18, 38, 112, 125
Philosophy of Education, 3, 48
Physiography (Huxley), 85
Piaget, J., 2, 39, 133–4, 140
Pickles, T., 77–8
Pre-disciplinary, 106–8
Pre-testing (multiple choice items), 192–3, 198, 215–16, 223
Principles (propositions), 10, 26–7, 32–33, 37–9, 40, 42, 44, 49, 77, 91, 97–100, 110, 119, 122–3, 125, 148, 268–9, 306
Pring, R., 1, 32, 48, 107, 109
Problem issues, 10, 16, 18, 35, 41, 68, 87, 93, 110, 122, 247–8, 267
Problem-solving (posing), 33, 37, 41, 86, 92, 109, 140, 149, 179, 211–13, 244–5
Professionalism, 127, 241–2, 305
Progressivism, 107–8, 126–7, 144
Psychology of Education, 2–3, 49, 131
Psychomotor Domain (Bloom), 28, 108
Pupil
  Alienation, 144–5, 154–5
  Interests, 5, 10, 17, 36, 74, 76–7
  Motivation, 49, 73, 91, 108, 142–3, 145, 155–6, 159, 167, 171, 246
  Profiles, 143, 171, 239

Questioning skills, 147, 150
Questionnaires, 88, 92, 250–51

'Realms of Meaning' (Phenix), 49
Recall (factual), 28–9, 31–2, 37, 73, 149–50, 171, 180, 190, 198–9, 208–212, 216, 228, 232–3, 235, 247
Reinforcement, 91, 147, 154–9, 169
Reliability (test), 175–6, 191, 229
Resources, 15, 42, 127, 145, 151
Response levels (Peel/Rhys), 139–40
Rhys, W., 139
Roberson, B. S., 77, 85–6
Robinson, F. G., 131, 155
Role-playing, 90–1, 100, 251–2
Royal Geographical Society, 75–6

Schools Council, 36, 40, 92, 126, 170, 239, 242
Science in Geography (Fitzgerald), 76
Scientific enquiry, 10, 52–3, 59–60, 82–83, 87
Self-fulfilling prophecy, 144–5, 251
Senior Geography (Herbertson), 77
Shipman, M. D., 126
Simons, M., 52–3, 70
Simulation, 63, 86, 90–91, 100, 110, 183
Skilbeck, M., 28
Slater, F., 89, 140
Smith, D. M., 68–9
Social Education, 10, 18, 41, 117, 119, 266, 306
Social Justice and the City (Harvey), 68
Social Sciences, 27, 41, 50–3, 57, 60, 69–70, 87, 109, 112–9, 122–3
Social Studies, 116, 135
Sociology of Education, 3, 47
Sockett, H., 25, 32
South-western Examinations Board (CSE), 242–3
Spiral curriculum (Bruner), 120, 257, 261–3
Stea, D., 67, 132–4

Stem (multiple choice items), 190, 204–206
Stereotypes, 13–17, 20, 78–9, 92, 100, 107, 144, 150, 209
Stimulus material, 137, 139, 203–4, 206, 213, 229–30, 260–61, 267–9, 289
Stoddart, D. R., 62, 89
Streaming, 154, 169
Structured questions, 7, 172, 185, 228–237
Structuring factors (in course planning)
　Balance, 48, 99, 118–19
　Focus, 55, 120–25
　Sequence, 119–20, 257
Subject-centred approaches, 41, 50, 74, 99, 107, 111, 120, 127, 305
Subject status, 47, 76, 169
Synthesis (Bloom category), 30, 33, 37, 113–14, 151, 211, 229
Systems thinking, 61–2, 68, 70, 79, 89

Taxonomy of Educational Objectives (Bloom et al), 28
Teacher
　accountability, 23, 28, 43, 167
　as communicator, 145–52
　as entrepreneur/manager, 151–4, 159, 242
　expectation, 77, 144–5, 241
Test specification, 26, 209–11, 229–30
Text books, 17, 19, 24–5, 77, 80, 82, 84, 100, 261
Thinking (cognitive, intellectual) skills, 10, 18, 26–9, 36–8, 48–9, 80, 82, 108, 131, 141, 154, 158, 171, 185, 191, 265

Convergent/divergent thinking, 142, 192, 239
Deductive/inductive thinking, 17. 60, 87
Topic-based approaches, 118, 121, 255
Topology, 64–5, 88, 134
Traditionalism
　'enlightened', 74, 100
　'hard-core', 73–5, 100
Transfer of training, 49, 166
Translation (Bloom category), 29, 37, 235, 244
Tyler, R. W., 26–7

University of London School Examinations Council, 179

Validity, 229
　Concurrent, 178
　Construct, 178–9, 181–3, 192
　Content, 178–9, 191, 238
　Predictive, 166, 178, 248
Value judgements, 9–11, 18, 30, 92, 149, 247–8
Values, 5, 9, 34–7, 42, 50, 67, 73–4, 93, 110
Vaughan, J., 14, 79
Vernon, P. E., 189, 196
Vygotsky, L. S., 39, 140

Walford, R., 91–2
Wall, W. D., 154–5
Warwick, D., 105–6, 108
Wheeler, D. K., 4, 8
White, R., 92, 100, 135
Worksheets, 156–8, 269, 289
World Coverage, 17, 73–4, 77–8, 85–6, 159

The author and publishers regret that owing to lack of space, they have been unable to include in the index the names of all the writers whose works have been referred to in the text